THE IMPACT OF
THE UK HUMAN RIGHTS ACT
ON PRIVATE LAW

The Human Rights Act 1998 has had a profound effect in numerous private law decisions and has been the subject of extensive academic debate, in particular, on the issue of the extent to which it has horizontal effect and its application in disputes between individuals.

With contributions from a variety of academics and practitioners, this volume covers and contributes to the academic debate on horizontal effect and considers how theory matches up with case law; the limits of the Act for private law; and its impact on key areas including privacy, defamation, negligence, nuisance, property, commercial law and employment. Together, the book provides a practical critique of the areas discussed, which will be of academic interest to theorists and of practical benefit to lawyers and judges who wish to understand how the academic debates can be brought to bear in particular cases.

DAVID HOFFMAN is a practising barrister in the fields of chancery and commercial law. He is a co-author of the student textbook *Human Rights in the UK* and was formerly a law lecturer at Somerville College, Oxford.

THE IMPACT OF THE UK HUMAN RIGHTS ACT ON PRIVATE LAW

Edited by

DAVID HOFFMAN

CAMBRIDGE UNIVERSITY PRESS
Cambridge, New York, Melbourne, Madrid, Cape Town,
Singapore, São Paulo, Delhi, Tokyo, Mexico City

Cambridge University Press
The Edinburgh Building, Cambridge CB2 8RU, UK

Published in the United States of America by Cambridge University Press, New York

www.cambridge.org
Information on this title: www.cambridge.org/9781107009325

© Cambridge University Press 2011

First published 2011

Printed in the United Kingdom at the University Press, Cambridge

A catalogue record for this publication is available from the British Library

Library of Congress Cataloguing in Publication data
The impact of the UK Human Rights Act on private law / edited by David Hoffman.
    p.   cm.
Includes index.
ISBN 978-1-107-00932-5 (hardback)
1. Human rights – England.   2. Civil law – England.   3. Great Britain.
Human Rights Act 1998.   I. Hoffman, David, 1971–   II. Title: Impact of the
United Kingdom Human Rights Act on private law.
        KD4080.I485   2011
    342.4208′5 – dc23   2011026516

ISBN 978-1-107-00932-5 Hardback

CONTENTS

RODERICK BAGSHAW is Tutor and Fellow in Law at Magdalen College, University of Oxford, and has been teaching tort and administrative law in Oxford for the last sixteen years. He is the co-author (with Nicholas McBride) of a textbook on tort law, *Longman Law Series* (3rd edn., 2008).

AMY GOYMOUR is the Hopkins-Parry Fellow in Law at Downing College, University of Cambridge, where she teaches land law, Roman law and restitution. Her research interests lie in the fields of real and personal property, restitution and the intersection of private law with human rights. Publications include 'Proprietary Claims and Human Rights: A "Reservoir of Entitlement"' [2006] CLJ 696 and 'Conversion of Contractual Rights' [2011] LMCLQ 67.

DAVID HOFFMAN is a chancery/commercial barrister at 18 St John Street Chambers, Manchester, former lecturer at Somerville College Oxford and co-author with John Rowe QC of a popular textbook on the Human Rights Act 1998, *Human Rights in the UK* (3rd edn., 2009), as well as author of several *Current Law* statute annotations on terrorism law.

CHRISTOPHER MCNALL is a chancery barrister and mediator at 18 St John Street Chambers, Manchester, before which he taught law at the universities of Warsaw, Oxford and Cardiff. He is a member of the Attorney-General's Provincial Panel of Counsel and a contributor to the *Oxford Encyclopaedia of Legal History*.

DONAL NOLAN is the Porjes Foundation Fellow and Tutor in Law at Worcester College, Oxford and a CUF Lecturer in Law in the University of Oxford. Subjects he has taught include tort, contract, international trade law, restitution and commercial law. His research interests lie in tort and contract law, and he has published on a range of subjects within those fields, including nuisance and *Rylands* v. *Fletcher*, product liability,

liability for psychiatric injury, the liability of public authorities and equitable estoppel. His recent publications include 'Offer and Acceptance in the Electronic Age' in Andrew Burrows and Edwin Peel (eds.), *Contract Formation and Parties* (2010) and (with Stephen Bailey) *The Page* v. *Smith Saga: A Tale of Inauspicious Origins and Unintended Consequences* (2010).

KEN OLIPHANT is Director of the Institute for European Tort Law, Austrian Academy of Sciences and Professor of Tort Law, University of Bristol. He previously held faculty positions at King's College London (1988–99) and Cardiff University (1999–2006). He has written extensively in the fields of English and European tort law. Publications include: *Tort Law: Text & Materials* (4th edn., 2010) (with Mark Lunney); *Tort Law*, Common Law Series (2nd edn., 2007) (general editor); *Aggregation and Divisibility of Damage* (2009); *Tort and Insurance Law*, Vol. 26 (editor). He has recently finished the revision and updating of the title on 'Tort' for *Halsbury's Laws of England* (5th edn., 2010). He is founding General Editor of the *Journal of European Tort Law*, UK correspondent of the *Torts Law Journal* and a member of the editorial advisory board of the *Journal of Professional Negligence*, the *Journal of Law and Society* and the *Victoria University of Wellington Law Review*. He is a member of the European Group on Tort Law, and in 2009 was elected to membership of the American Law Institute, becoming its only member in Austria.

HAZEL OLIVER is a practice development lawyer at Lewis Silkin LLP specialising in employment and discrimination law, and a part-time Employment Tribunal judge. She has lectured in discrimination law at the London School of Economics, and holds an MA and BCL from the University of Oxford, as well as a Masters on electronic surveillance in the workplace from the University of Toronto. She has published on a range of subjects in employment law, including on both sexual orientation discrimination and privacy rights in the *Industrial Law Journal*, and surveillance and privacy at work for the Institute of Employment Rights.

GAVIN PHILLIPSON is a Professor at Durham University Law School, and formerly a Senior Lecturer at King's College, London. He is author of several recent leading articles on civil liberties and the Human Rights Act, co-author (with Professor Helen Fenwick) of *Media Freedom under the Human Rights Act* (2006), and co-editor (with Professor Fenwick and Roger Masterman) of *Judicial Reasoning Under the Human Rights Act* (Cambridge University Press, 2007). His most important contribution has been in the area of horizontal effect and the development of a common law right to privacy, on which he has published several influential articles in the *Modern Law Review*, as well as chapters in the above books. These have been cited with approval by the House of Lords in *Campbell* v. *MGN Ltd* (2004) and by the Court of Appeal in *McKennitt* v. *Ash* (2006) and in *Douglas* v. *Hello! Ltd (No. 3)* (2005). He has taught Masters courses on comparative privacy law at the universities of Melbourne, King's College London and City University.

FRANCIS ROSE is a Professor of Commercial Law at the University of Bristol, as well as a barrister and associate of chambers at Quadrant Chambers, former Professor of Commercial and Common Law at the University of Buckingham, and, before that, a Fellow of St John's College, Cambridge. He was the Director of the Norton Rose Centre of Commercial Law within the Bristol Law Faculty from 2000 to 2005. Francis is General Editor of *Lloyd's Maritime and Commercial Law Quarterly*. He is also General Editor of the *Restitution Law Review* and was Editor-in-Chief of the *Company, Financial and Insolvency Law Review* and has published widely in the areas of commercial law (particularly maritime law and international trade law), restitution and contract. He is the author of a number of major works in the area of maritime law: *Marine Insurance: Law and Practice* (2004); *General Average: Law and Practice* (2nd edn., 2005); and *Kennedy and Rose: The Law of Salvage* (7th edn., 2009). His work, *Marine Insurance: Law and Practice*, was awarded the 2005 British Insurance Law Association Book Prize.

JOHN SORABJI is a barrister and is currently the Legal Secretary to the Master of the Rolls and Head of Civil Justice. He is an Assistant Editor of the *Civil Justice Quarterly*, for which he is a regular contributor of editorial notes and articles. He has also published in the *European Business Law Review*. In 2008 he was the senior editor and senior contributing author of the Civil Justice Council's advice to government, *Improving Access to Justice through Collective Actions: Developing a More Efficient and Effective Procedure for Collective Actions*. He has lectured at the universities of Oxford, Cambridge and University College London on civil justice, as well as contributing to conferences both in the United Kingdom and abroad on collective action reform. He has a doctorate from Oxford University.

JAN VAN ZYL SMIT is a Lecturer in Law at Oxford Brookes University, where he teaches constitutional and administrative law. He completed a DPhil at Magdalen College, Oxford in 2009 on the interpretation of statutes under the Human Rights Act. His research on this topic has been published in the *Modern Law Review*, 'The New Purposive Interpretation of Statutes: HRA section 3 after *Ghaidan* v. *Godin-Mendoza*' (2007). He has served as a Law Clerk at the Constitutional Court of South Africa. His current research interests include the use of proportionality standards in human rights review, and linguistic accounts of statutory interpretation.

JASON N. E. VARUHAS is a Junior Research Fellow at Christ's College, Cambridge. In 2011 he completed his PhD at the University of Cambridge on damages for breaches of human rights. He has previously taught law at Victoria University of Wellington and Downing College, Cambridge. He has served as a Judge's Clerk at the New Zealand Court of Appeal and is qualified as a barrister in New Zealand. His research interests include public law, the law of torts and remedies, and he has recently published on a range of subjects within those fields, including human rights damages, judicial review of governmental rejections of Ombudsman findings, and the respective roles of the courts and Parliament in the determination of human rights issues.

ALEXANDER WILLIAMS is a Lecturer in Law and Deputy Director of the Human Rights Centre at the University of Durham. He is a graduate of the universities of Cambridge and Durham and was a Graduate Teaching Assistant at Durham from 2008 to 2010. He researches and teaches in the field of public law and human rights.

ALISON L. YOUNG is a Tutor and Fellow in Law at Hertford College and Lecturer at the University of Oxford. She has been teaching constitutional law and administrative law in Oxford for the past twelve years, and also teaches European Community law, comparative public law and constitutional theory. She has published in the areas of public law and is the author of *Parliamentary Sovereignty and the Human Rights Act* (2009).

FOREWORD

This is both a timely and an important book. It is timely because its publication comes as both the nature of rights and the extent to which they should be protected are very much a matter of debate. There are also ongoing discussions as to what rights should be protected and to what extent they should be balanced by concomitant responsibilities. There is a further debate as to whether they should be protected by the Human Rights Act 1998 ('the HRA') and the European Convention on Human Rights ('the Convention') or by some entrenched British Bill of Rights. This book, and the arguments which it develops through its analysis of the effect that the HRA has had on private law disputes, ought to play a significant role in that debate. And it should play an important role in the development of the UK's commitment to the protection of human rights and responsibilities.

This book is a timely and important book for another reason. Its publication comes as we enter the first years of the HRA's second decade. The HRA came into force on 2 October 2000. We have had just over ten years to grapple with changes it has brought – with the rights which, in the famous phrase, it brought back home. In those ten years it has had a profound effect on the development of our law; an effect which was anticipated at the time. As the then Lord Chancellor, Lord Irvine, said in 2001:

> What we *can* expect more of, however, is radical interpretation of legislation by the courts. This will sometimes be necessary in order to achieve compatibility with the Convention and will, in some cases, require practices and procedures to change to bring them into line with legislation interpreted in this way.

A 'radical interpretation of legislation' was not the HRA's only product. By requiring the courts, as public authorities, to act consistently with the rights guaranteed in the Convention, the HRA provides the basis for the development – and I would suggest that it is a radical development – of

xi

the common law. The development of the right to respect for privacy, set out in Article 8 of the Convention, as Gavin Phillipson discusses in his detailed examination of the post-HRA evolution of breach of confidence, is currently one of the most striking examples of this effect. That effect was also anticipated when the Human Rights Bill was before Parliament. That point was made most succinctly by Lord Phillips MR in *Douglas* v. *Hello! Ltd (No. 3)*, when he observed how

> The enactment of the Human Rights Act 1998 provoked a lively discussion of the impact that it would have on the development of a law protecting privacy. The Government has made it clear that it does not intend to introduce legislation in relation to this area of the law, but anticipates that the judges will develop the law appropriately, having regard to the requirements of the Convention for the Protection of Human Rights and Fundamental Freedoms: see the comment of Lord Irvine of Lairg LC in the course of the debate on the Human Rights Bill (*Hansard*, HL Debs., col. 771, 24 November 1997) and the submissions of the United Kingdom in *Spencer (Earl)* v. *United Kingdom* (1998) 25 EHRR CD 105.

Lord Irvine's comment was that, while the government did not intend to introduce a statutory right of privacy, it expected, once the Human Rights Bill was enacted, that 'the judges would develop the law appropriately having regard to the requirements of the Convention'. It is perhaps easy to forget that it was Parliament's intention that the common law, including private law, would develop after the HRA came into force consistently with the rights guaranteed by the Convention. As Lord Irvine explained the position,

> it is right as a matter of principle for the courts to have the duty to act compatibly with the Convention not only in cases involving other public authorities but also in developing the common law in deciding cases between individuals.
>
> (HL Debs. col. 783, 24 November 1997)

With that in mind, it is strange to think that the extent to which the HRA was intended to have an impact on the development of private law remains today, as it did for Lord Nicholls in *Kay* v. *Lambeth LBC*, a question which 'still awaits authoritative decision' in our courts. But while it is one thing to make the point that the HRA would require the courts to develop the common law consistently with the Convention, it is another to say how and to what extent it would do so.

In the HRA's second decade it is reasonable to expect that the answer to the question which Lord Nicholls identified will come. One possible answer is that the court, as a branch of the state, subject to the duty not to act in a way which is incompatible with rights guaranteed by the Convention, is required to give direct horizontal effect to those rights as between individuals. By increments, the court may give birth to a new branch of the law of torts: the action for breach of human rights. It has to be said that as possibilities go, this is less likely than many, but it is a possible answer. On the other hand, the development of the tort (if it is a tort) of breach of confidence, as Alison Young in her illuminating chapter suggests, provides an instance of an alternative possible answer: indirect horizontal effect. Sufficient instances of such developments in relation to a number of torts may provide the basis for the courts to identify a grand unifying theory from which a freestanding action for breach of human rights could then be identified. Indirect horizontal effect might then give birth to direct horizontal effect. That would be a further possible answer. The most likely possibility of the three, at least viewed from the perspective of the present time, is the second. It is particularly difficult to see any real support for the first possibility, despite the strong academic support for the idea, which Alison Young identifies. Nor is there, at least looking at the current jurisprudence, any real basis for discerning any general trend from which a grand unifying theory could be identified. However, as the past ten years have shown, it is not possible to predict with any confidence the way in which the law will develop in this important and topical field.

However, the fact that such questions remain open for authoritative decision serves to underline the real importance of this book. It ranges very widely, but also very deeply, over all the significant issues arising from the effect which the HRA has so far had on private law and it does so with a perspicacity, and analytical acuity, which are truly impressive. It should prove to be a fertile source of discussion for academics, a valuable source of argument for practitioners and a fruitful source of information for the courts. It will serve these very valuable purposes because the law is never in a state of near-perfection, let alone perfection, despite what the prejudices of each generation may suggest (and, as Amy Goymour notes, the 1829 Real Property Commissioners asserted in respect of the law of real property). That is as true of all aspects of our private law, as it is true of our attempts to give effect to the rights guaranteed by the Convention. A critical and perceptive eye and an original and informed mind are always called for, and this book provides both.

Lord Neuberger of Abbotsbury, MR

PREFACE

This book, as the title suggests, explores the impact of the Human Rights Act 1998 ('the HRA') on the private law of England and Wales. The HRA applies throughout the United Kingdom, and so it is hoped that the discussion here will assist those practising in the UK's other jurisdictions, most obviously Scotland and Northern Ireland, but no attempt has been made to address the detail of the law in those areas, and where Welsh law has been modified by the Welsh Assembly, the discussion should be taken to apply to English law.

The scheme of the book and the inquiry being undertaken by it is more fully explained in the Introduction (Chapter 1). The purpose of this Preface is to point up a particular feature of this book in light of its multiple authors. Often such works are simply a set of essays on a common subject, and can be read individually with no loss of understanding. This book is intended not to be quite as severable as that. There is a common project being undertaken, which does mean that the reader will get the best out of it by considering various chapters together.

In particular, the discussion of the substantive areas of law which are covered will all assume that the reader has looked at the Introduction, which discusses the common field of inquiry and some of the reasoning structure which we think applies regardless of the substantive area, and the chapter on mapping horizontality (Chapter 2), which sets out the terminology which is being used for this key concept. Where relevant, individual chapters will also assume knowledge of the way the HRA affects statutory interpretation (Chapter 3); the approach to public authorities (Chapter 4); precedent and the effect of section 2 (Chapter 5); remedies available under the HRA itself (Chapter 11), etc.

Thus, the structure of the book is more akin to a monograph. The various authors do not all agree in their views on the topics under consideration, but what is common to the book is the structure of the inquiry and the questions being considered. It is hoped that having multiple authors will bring out the range of views on the areas we consider, without detracting from the use of the book as a coherent whole to provide an overview of the subject. Also, we do not aspire to cover every area of private law, but we hope that we have covered many of the most significant areas of contract, tort and property law.

The law discussed is as at 10 November 2010 (with occasional references to later material).

ACKNOWLEDGEMENTS

This is an appropriate opportunity for the contributors generally, and the editor in particular, to express some thanks. This genesis of this book was in papers delivered at two seminars organised by the editor and held in Oxford in 2007 and 2008, and the contribution of those who attended and enthusiastically entered into the discussion, whether or not they presented a paper and whether or not they have written for this book, has been a valuable one. Thus, our thanks to attendees who, in addition to various of the contributors, included Jamie Edelman, Steven Hedley, Tom Hickman, Angus Johnston, Jonathan Morgan, Nicole Moreham, Robert Stevens, Rachel Taylor and Jane Wright. Thanks also to Richard Hart for sponsoring the first seminar and Roderick Bagshaw for arranging its hosting; and to Alison Young for arranging the hosting of later discussions.

We would also like to thank those who have kindly reviewed parts of this book in manuscript, including Angus Johnston and various anonymous reviewers. Some authors have noted further assistance in individual chapters. All assistance has been very much appreciated; any errors which remain are, of course, the responsibility of the contributors.

Our thanks also to all those at Cambridge University Press who have worked on the publication process, and in particular Finola O'Sullivan, for her support and hard work in steering this book towards publication.

TABLE OF CASES

TABLE OF STATUTES

References to the Human Rights Act 1998 and to the Articles of the European Convention on Human Rights 1950 have been omitted since both are discussed *passim*.

TABLE OF STATUTORY INSTRUMENTS

TABLE OF EUROPEAN UNION LEGISLATION

ABBREVIATIONS

The following will be used throughout:

the HRA	The Human Rights Act 1998; sections not otherwise identified refer to the HRA.
the Convention	The European Convention on Human Rights.
the Convention rights	The rights which are protected by the Convention in Schedule 1 to the HRA. Article and Protocol, where not otherwise identified, refer to the Convention. 'P1-1' is used for Protocol 1, Article 1.
the Strasbourg court	The European Court of Human Rights (sited in Strasbourg).
the Commission	The European Commission on Human Rights (which was a first level of decision under the Convention until abolished in 1998).

References to chapters refer to this book unless stated otherwise. Within each chapter, references to cases and articles are abbreviated after their first mention, so any such reference will be to an earlier footnote in the same chapter. Square brackets are used for paragraph citations within cases.

Introduction

DAVID HOFFMAN, GAVIN PHILLIPSON
AND ALISON L. YOUNG

> The court's own practice and procedures must be Convention compliant. Whether, and in what circumstances, the court's section 6 obligation extends more widely than this, and affects the substantive law to be applied by the court when adjudicating upon disputes between private parties, still awaits authoritative decision.
>
> Lord Nicholls of Birkenhead, *Kay* v. *Lambeth LBC* (2006)[1]

1.1 The Human Rights Act 1998

The scope of inquiry of this volume is the impact of the Human Rights Act 1998 ('the HRA') on the private law of England and Wales. The HRA gave effect in UK domestic law to the rights guaranteed by the European Convention on Human Rights 1950 ('the Convention', 'Convention rights'), to which the United Kingdom has been a party since its inception. Prior to the HRA, the Convention had only a limited role to play in English law through the principles of English law which influenced its drafting;[2] through the duty on the courts to interpret the law in accordance with the Crown's international treaty obligations where possible;[3] and through the possibility of a case before the European Court of Human Rights in Strasbourg ('the Strasbourg court'), albeit that these have in practice been complied with by the UK Government although on occasions with significant delay. One further indirect influence was through membership

---

1 [2006] 2 WLR 570 at para. 61.
2 Indeed, the Civil Service played a key role in its drafting and creation: see A. W. B. Simpson, *Human Rights and the End of Empire: Britain and the Genesis of the European Convention* (Oxford University Press, 2004).
3 *Attorney-General* v. *Guardian Newspapers Ltd (No. 2)* [1990] 1 AC 109 at 283 *per* Lord Goff.

of the European Communities and Union since the Court of Justice of
the European Union has accepted that general principles of European
Community law include protection of fundamental rights derived from
the common traditions of the laws of Member States.[4]

The HRA brought four key changes into our law:

(1) it required all public authorities (including the courts) to act in a way
that is compatible with Convention rights (section 6);
(2) it required legislation to be read in a manner compatible with Convention rights as far as possible (section 3, but retaining parliamentary
sovereignty in that the courts must give effect to the legislation if
such an interpretation is not possible, and because section 3 is not
entrenched);
(3) it required courts deciding questions about Convention rights to take
into account the decisions of the Strasbourg court, thus bringing an
additional body of case law into the reasoning of the courts in all
relevant cases (section 2); and
(4) it provided for a cause of action for breach of Convention rights by a
public authority (section 7) and empowered courts to award damages
for such breach (section 8).

In the ten years since the HRA came into force, it has led to a number of
changes in the law, some highly controversial.

One of the most important areas of controversy from the outset was
the extent to which the courts, as a public authority, had to give effect
to Convention rights in disputes between individuals (and other private
persons such as companies). The essential issue is as follows. The HRA
requires courts to act compatibly with the Convention, since courts are a
public authority (section 6(3)). That adds little to the court's role where
an action involves a public authority, such as a claim for breach of the
HRA or judicial review, although it clarifies that the courts' own practices
and procedures must be Convention-compliant. But this leaves open the
key question at the heart of this work: whether and how far the HRA
has horizontal effect: that is, an impact on private law disputes, by which
is meant those disputes which do not involve the government or state
institutions, but dealings between individuals, whether arising out of
property, contract, wrongs or otherwise.

4 See now Charter of Fundamental Rights of the European Union (2007/C 303/01) and
Treaty on European Union as amended by the Lisbon Treaty (2007/C 306/01) Article 6
and Protocol 8 under which it is proposed that the EU will directly accede to the European
Convention.

Our aim is not just to review the case law over the spread of private law. There are more general and fundamental principles and issues to consider:

(1) What do we mean by horizontal effect: what are the possible meanings and on what basis should we (or the courts) decide between these possibilities?

(2) What principles should govern consideration of whether private law is or should be affected by the HRA – and is a private law cause of action always a necessary or appropriate way of giving effect to a Convention right?

(3) To what extent has the HRA in fact been applied directly or indirectly to disputes between private individuals: has the HRA been given horizontal effect, and if so how, where and to what extent?

(4) Has the HRA been applied consistently over different areas of the law? Are there reasons for any differences and what principles should the courts be considering to ensure that such differences are properly justified?

The heart of these questions is a constitutional one: given the courts' role as a core state institution, but one which is (in our legal system) subsidiary to Parliament, how far should the courts give effect to the HRA against the background of the general law? How far does and should it matter whether the cause of action in question is based on statute or common law? These are questions which apply across the whole spectrum of areas affected by the HRA: in this work, they will be considered only as they apply to private law.

1.2 What is private law?

Private law governs the relationships between individual parties, rather than between individuals and the state – so does not include the law which is applied in the public interest even when it concerns dealings between individuals, such as criminal law. It can be subdivided in a number of ways. The classic Roman law model delineates between property, obligations and status. This is a useful starting point, as long as it is borne in mind that these are by no means mutually exclusive categories. By way of example, a contract is a relationship between persons which creates legally binding obligations and the starting point is to determine when such a relationship has come into being and the consequences for the parties. It may relate at least in part to specific property, or at least involve the transfer of property (payment if nothing else). Moreover, certain persons have more limited rights to enter into contracts or have more legal protection from the consequences of doing so. Thus, discussion of the 'law of contract' primarily involves the parties' obligations, but also impacts on property and status.

Thus, the following, among others, could be said to be core principles of the private law of obligations,[5] or at least principles which underlie at least part of the areas referred to: that serious promises should be enforced (*pacta sunt servanda*) – contracts; that compensation should be paid for wrongs suffered to protected individual interests such as personal integrity, property and reputation – torts; that unjustified enrichments should be reversed; that persons should be protected from unconscionable or exploitative conduct. The law of property requires there to be clear and cohesive rules about what counts as property, how property is transferred, how it is registered (in some cases) and who owns it, or can claim it, in situations of dispute. The laws of personal status require rules about parentage, capacity, succession, marriage, rights in respect of one's family and so on.

The principles underlying private law are not principles which are typically found in a list of human rights such as the Convention (with some notable exceptions). The main reason for this is that a key aspect of *human* rights is that they set out an individual's basic rights against, or entitlements from, the state. Thus, where the state has no role to play in the creation or governance of private rights, other than providing a state-sanction mechanism for resolving disputes about such rights, the principles which underlie those rights may not be listed as, or find reflection in, 'human' rights. However, *human* rights also claim higher importance: they reflect what we value most about ourselves, and protect basic autonomy, dignity and equality.[6] In this sense, basic principles of private law are often just as fundamental. It is arguably a basic entitlement that individuals can order their lives by reaching binding agreements; that they can own property and have a measure of freedom over its transfer and possession; that they can seek redress when their basic interests are interfered with without justification; that they can enter into arrangements

---

5 Leaving to one side the moral or other justification for these principles, but simply as statements of basic principles which are generally recognised to form some part of English law.

6 There is, of course, an extensive literature on the underlying basis for what is meant by human rights; for a fuller discussion by one of the present authors see D. Hoffman and J. Rowe, *Human Rights in the UK*, 3rd edn. (London: Pearson, 2009), ch. 2.

which govern their family life, such as marriage, joint ownership of property, arrangements for succession of property and so on.

Thus, as with many lists of basic rights, these private law rules and underlying principles do not in and of themselves feature in the European Convention. On the other hand, the Convention rights do frequently assume that such rules exist, precisely because they are so fundamental. Otherwise the rights to, or in respect of, for example, home (Article 8), property (Article 1 Protocol 1) or marriage (Article 12) would have no meaning. Likewise, that there are laws governing the resolution of disputes between citizens is assumed, in part, by the right to a fair trial (Article 6) which refers expressly to the legal determination of 'civil rights and obligations'.

Yet, in our law, the HRA makes core human rights applicable throughout the legal system and not just in extreme cases. The more obvious cases are where these rights act as brakes on the power of the state. Their proper application in private law cases, disputes between individuals, is less obvious, and raises difficult questions. The state tends to take a more restrained view, policing such disputes to enforce their resolution or avoid criminal side-effects. That is, of course, unless some emanation of the state is involved in that dispute as a party, in the capacity, for example, of being a property owner or contractual party, in which case there is a live question as to how that body's capacity as an actor subject to the regular private law interacts with its obligations under the HRA.

The courts are already grappling with the underlying question about the extent to which the principles which underpin private law (whether those suggested above or others) interact with the more state-focused principles which underpin human rights. How do these find an expression in the way cases are or should be decided? What weight should be given to them as against listed human rights? It is not at all clear that, so far, a coherent methodology or consistent underlying theory is being applied by the courts. Indeed, it is not always clear what the questions *are* on which the court should be addressed for it to form a cogent and principled view. These two approaches to private law disputes – on the one hand, the basic principles of our private law, and, on the other, the need to ensure that fundamental rights are protected – have already caused tensions which can be seen in the cases. For example, is a body discharging functions which might otherwise be discharged by the state, such as managing a parish church, or providing residential care for the elderly, enforcing its property rights in the usual way or acting primarily under the contract which governs its relations with the party who is being provided with a service, and so is a private actor, or is it to be treated as properly subject to the obligations of the state to protect fundamental rights?[7] Or, indeed, does it, or should it, make a difference how we answer that question?

1.3 The scope of the HRA to affect private law

> The general question of horizontality has not yet been resolved by a court. Indeed, it may never be resolved judicially at the same high level of abstraction on which the debate has been conducted for the most part in the law books and legal periodicals.
>
> (Mummery LJ, *X* v. *Y* (2004))[8]

The issue with section 6 of the HRA is the extent to which it has a horizontal effect and obliges the courts to apply Convention rights in disputes between private individuals. The first question is definitional: what do we mean by horizontal effect? This is a deceptive question: not only do different writers use the phrase in distinct ways, or have in mind different techniques, but also there are a variety of ways in which the HRA does or could impact on disputes between private individuals.

Chapter 2 therefore considers this question: Alison Young maps out different ways in which the HRA has an effect on disputes between private individuals. This chapter sets out a terminology which will be used throughout this book, differentiating between different views of what is meant by horizontal effect. It is important to distinguish between ways in which the HRA impacts on different situations: in particular, distinguishing between where it applies directly, such as where it is the basis of a claim under section 6, or an interpretation of a statute under section 3,[9] or where the court has to apply it in respect of the court's own procedures; or indirectly, such as where the HRA is being used to argue that a cause of action should be extended to give effect to a Convention right. Whether the HRA should apply directly between private individuals or, if indirectly, what that means for the common law, has been the subject of lively academic debate, which Young summarises.

Of course, in order to determine where the HRA has an application in private law, it is useful to be aware of where it applies directly, which

---

7 These examples are, of course, taken from *Aston Cantlow Parochial Church Council* v. *Wallbank* [2003] UKHL 37, [2004] 1 AC 546 and *YL* v. *Birmingham City Council* [2007] UKHL 27, [2008] 1 AC 95 which are discussed in Chapter 4.

8 [2004] ICR 1634 at [45].

9 Though this may be more properly considered a form of indirect effect if it applies as between private individuals, discussed at p. 37.

is to say where one party is a public authority within the meaning of section 6 such that there can be a direct claim under the HRA. The particular focus is the effect of section 6(3)(b), which introduces the notion of a 'hybrid' or functional public authority, such that a 'public authority' under the HRA includes 'any person *certain* of whose functions are functions of a public nature' (emphasis added). This is considered by Alexander Williams (Chapter 3), in particular following the key case of *YL*. This is the direct application of the HRA, vindicated by a private action, but not, as such, private law – yet at the same time, one cannot consider what private law is in this context without being aware of its boundaries. This is not least because the private law rights of the body in issue would appear to have distorted the court's approach to what is a public authority for the purposes of liability under the HRA – the concern is not to disadvantage a body which might sometimes be caught by the HRA by removing its own rights. If this is indeed something of a red herring, as Williams argues, then the courts have limited the protection provided by the HRA unnecessarily, and he suggests that, for hybrid public authorities, that is, bodies performing a public function some of the time, it is not necessary to treat them as without their own rights for all purposes. Arguably, this is an area where private law has impacted on the HRA, rather than the other way round.

1.4 Techniques which apply to the HRA

The second question is about one aspect of the proper scope of the HRA. When a court encounters the HRA in a private law case, how should the court approach its analysis? What factors govern the question as to whether a private law cause of action is always a necessary or appropriate way of giving effect to a Convention right? The HRA itself, notoriously, makes no explicit provision for its application against anything other than 'public authorities' against which actions for breach of the Convention rights can be brought directly. As has been observed elsewhere, the HRA also 'compounds this silence on horizontal effect by a complete absence of reference to the common law'.[10] It is from this basic omission that much of the difficulty with the horizontal effect debate flows. But this also means that the *statutory* aspect of horizontal effect – the application of section 3 to statutes governing relations between private parties – has

---

10 G. Phillipson, 'The Human Rights Act, "Horizontal Effect" and the Common Law: a Bang or a Whimper', *Modern Law Review*, 62(6) (1999), 824 at 825.

caused much less difficulty, since in this context the HRA has a necessary application if the Convention rights are relevant to the dispute before the court. Indeed, this type of horizontal effect has been accepted without any controversy by the courts. The much more difficult issue arises where the HRA is being referred to in the context of the common law, where the question turns on the court's position as a public authority under the HRA.

There are, or should be, two distinct levels to this analysis: first, the scope of the Convention right under consideration and its compatibility with existing domestic law; and, second, the effect that can or should be given to the Convention right through the techniques provided by the HRA.[11]

The first level involves consideration of more than one distinct question:

(a) What is the meaning or scope of the right under discussion: for example, is Article 8 *prima facie* engaged by the unwanted taking of photographs of a person in a public place?

If the Convention right contains possible justifications for interfering with it, do any of these apply? For example, is the taking of photographs justified by national security under Article 8(2), or by the rights of others (for example, their Article 10 right to freedom of expression)?

(b) Does the Convention right, properly understood, apply only to the state itself or does it impose an obligation on the state to intervene as between private individuals: that is, does it have 'horizontal applicability'? For example, does Article 8 oblige a state to act to protect persons from having their privacy infringed by the publication of press photographs?

Answering this first stage as to the applicability of the Convention requires the courts to have regard to the Strasbourg jurisprudence in accordance with section 2, although there is a live issue as to the extent to which the domestic courts are limited by the decisions of the Strasbourg court, and the extent to which the courts are free to develop their own interpretations of Convention rights beyond the definitions provided by the Strasbourg court. This is a topic considered by Alison Young in

---

11 The analysis set out here has built on G. Phillipson, 'Clarity Postponed: Horizontal Effect after *Campbell*', in H. Fenwick, G. Phillipson and R. Masterman (eds.), *Judicial Reasoning under the UK Human Rights Act* (Cambridge University Press, 2007), pp. 143, 149.

Chapter 5. The need to take the Strasbourg jurisprudence into account when determining the meaning of Convention rights interacts with the English doctrine of precedent, which is also discussed: what happens where a Strasbourg court decision contradicts binding English precedent – something that has proven to be a practical issue in a number of areas, most notably in the area of housing law?[12]

Having determined the scope of the Convention right, if the court then considers that current law is either incompatible with what the Convention right requires, or that there is no law which properly gives effect to what the right requires, then it moves to the second level of the analysis. Here the focus shifts from the meaning and scope of the Convention rights to the particular instrument giving them domestic effect – the HRA itself: should the positive obligations on the state to intervene as between private individuals arising from the right be given effect in domestic law by the courts and if so, how (that is, is this a case of 'horizontal effect')?

The second level of analysis will have a different structure depending upon whether the law being considered is based on statute or common law.

If there is a *statute*, the state has already intervened in the situation, creating the law which is to be applied in an instrument to which the HRA applies. The question then is whether or not this state intervention is compatible with the Convention right (as determined at level one). That is, does the statute require or permit a breach of the Convention: can the court use section 3 to interpret the statute to be compliant with the Convention, or must it use section 4 to declare that the statute is incompatible with the Convention right?

In Chapter 4, Jan van Zyl Smit looks at the way in which the HRA has been used to interpret statutes and give effect to Convention rights 'so far as it is possible to do so', taking as its cornerstone the leading case on statutory interpretation of *Ghaidan* v. *Godin-Mendoza*,[13] which is itself a private law case. Here the interpretation of housing law was effectively revised to avoid discrimination, giving a tenant rights in respect of tenancy succession. Statute law now pervades our legal system, so the scope for the HRA to affect private law claims in this respect is significant. There is also a discussion of the scope of declarations of incompatibility, again

---

12 Most recently in *Manchester City Council* v. *Pinnock* [2010] UKSC 45 [2010] 3 WLR 1441 and *Hounslow LBC* v. *Powell* [2011] UKSC 8, discussed in Chapter 12.
13 [2004] UKHL 30, [2004] 2 AC 557.

available equally in a private law case, and the extent to which they can be said to provide a remedy for a breach of the HRA. Both mechanisms raise questions of judicial technique, including the extent to which legal certainty can be maintained while judicially enforcing, or prompting Parliament to enforce, Convention rights.

If the law in question is *common law*, then, as discussed above, we are into the heart of the debate on horizontal effect. Does the HRA have any application in relation to substantive law here, as opposed to remedies and procedures? If so, what kind of application does it have, and with what degree of force?

There is an underlying issue of institutional or constitutional competence and separation of powers here, which rightly influences the debate around the use of the HRA to create horizontal effect, found in both case law and statute law: namely, the distinct roles of the courts and Parliament in relation to the HRA. This is considered in Young's discussion of precedent: the scope for section 2 to act as a limit on the way in which the Convention rights are developed appears to be more flexible in the private law context than the public law (or private statutory) context, where the courts appear to be less likely to regard decisions of the Strasbourg court as providing a ceiling to the definition of Convention rights. This is explained in part by the different constitutional role of the courts when determining and developing the common law in the absence of statutory provisions.

The other side of that argument in the common law context is whether a particular development, which may be open to the courts to give better protection for a Convention right, is a step which the judges should take: should they instead leave the matter for Parliament to deal with, given its role as the primary law-maker in the UK constitution? In the common law context, the courts do not have the option of a declaration of incompatibility under section 4, which signals both the inability of the courts properly to remedy the matter and an invitation to Parliament to consider doing so through legislation; nevertheless, the underlying issue of the constitutional and institutional limits on the law-making role of the courts applies in both the statutory and common law situation.

This issue – the extent to which it is appropriate for the courts to implement the Convention rights through the mechanism of judge-made law – is considered in Chapter 6 by Roderick Bagshaw. The discussion is in terms of the law of torts, since remedies for wrongs is the area where the courts have been or may be most tempted to apply the HRA directly through the mechanism of common law, or through a new cause of action to give direct protection to the interest underlying a Convention right which is deemed to be insufficiently protected by the common law. The principles discussed pervade private law, being concerned with any situation where a wrong is being considered. An especially difficult case is where a public authority is sued for a private cause of action which potentially involves one or more Convention rights: should the (private) law of tort be relied upon, or is it better to simply rely upon the public authority's duty under the HRA?

1.5 The HRA'S impact across private law

Even now that the equivalent of article 8 has been enacted as part of English law, it is not directly concerned with the protection of privacy against private persons or corporations. It is, by virtue of section 6 of the 1998 Act, a guarantee of privacy only against public authorities.

(Lord Hoffmann, *Campbell* v. *MGN Ltd* (2004))[14]

The foundation of the jurisdiction to restrain publicity in a case such as the present [involving no public authorities] is now derived from Convention rights under the [European Convention]. This is the simple and direct way to approach such cases.

(Lord Steyn, *Re S* (2005))[15]

In order to find the rules of the English law of breach of confidence we now have to look in the jurisprudence of Articles 8 and 10. Those articles are now not merely of persuasive or parallel effect but . . . are the very content of the domestic tort that the English court has to enforce.

(Buxton LJ, *McKennitt* v. *Ash* (2007))[16]

All of these issues within the analysis of the application of the HRA will be affected by the view that is taken about the aim and purpose of the HRA, and the constitutional propriety of the different options open to a court. This will then feed back into all the stages of analysis discussed above: the breadth of rights and the scope of the HRA and the Convention Articles; how the courts should interpret the Strasbourg case law; whether the courts should use section 3 or section 4 in statute law cases; how far the courts should develop the common law. Those who take a broader view of the effect of the HRA, those advocating some form of direct horizontality, will maintain that courts *must* always give effect to Convention obligations

14 [2004] 2 AC 457 at [49].   15 [2005] 1 AC 593 at [23].
16 [2006] EWCA Civ. 1714, [2008] QB 73 at [11].

in private law, if necessary by inventing new causes of action. Those who take a narrower view will disagree.

Then our third question is: how has the HRA been given horizontal effect in practice? How much has this varied in different areas of law? Has the impact of the HRA brought about actual changes in the law? These questions are addressed in the remaining chapters of this book.

The area in which a private law cause of action has been most obviously and controversially reshaped by the HRA is breach of confidence, as it can be applied to protect personal privacy. Gavin Phillipson in Chapter 7 provides a detailed consideration of this issue. It is arguable that the old breach of confidence action has been remodelled – some would say, out of all recognition – as a vehicle for the implementation of the Article 8 right to respect for a private life and its associated Strasbourg case law. As can be seen from the quotations above, because this is unarguably the area of common law in which the influence of the Convention has been strongest, it also provides the most extensive set of examples of different models of horizontal effect being manifested in practice; it highlights also how different theoretical vantage points mandate different critiques of the judicial engagement with the issue. Phillipson teases out the different strands of reasoning on horizontality in the case law, seeking to refute the claim that recent decisions and the arguable creation of a new tort of 'misuse of private information' show clear judicial acceptance of 'full' or 'direct' horizontal effect. He also seeks to answer the question, *why* it is in this area of law that the strongest degree of horizontal effect has arisen, and considers whether the jurisprudence in this area may be taken as a kind of showcase for the views of the judiciary on the way(s) in which the HRA can have horizontal effect in general. He argues that particular factors surrounding breach of confidence and privacy mean that the clear judicial receptiveness to Convention-driven development of the common law apparent in this area should not necessarily be expected elsewhere: in short, that the jurisprudence in this area is best considered as something of a special case, as opposed to providing a judicial answer to the *general* question of common law horizontality.

But, of course, breach of confidence is not the only area where the Convention rights have affected private law causes of action. In discussing the law of nuisance, Donal Nolan (Chapter 8) considers how the HRA has already interacted with the existing law, and the scope for future movement, especially on the issue of whether it affects the rights of non-householders to a remedy. Nuisance is a good example of an area where there may well be parallel claims against a public body under the

Act and at common law. Thus, the scope for actions which protect the same interests as nuisance but are brought directly under the HRA merits consideration, because there is scope for these to affect the remedies which the courts provide at common law – raising precisely the issue of whether the common law should expand to provide a remedy under the HRA or whether it is better to have distinct remedies, which may lead to different results depending upon whether the defendant is a public authority.

We turn to defamation: in Chapter 9, Ken Oliphant considers where the HRA has been used to challenge established principles of the law of defamation, or otherwise develop defamation law, given the obvious interaction between that area and the rights to, and limitations on, the Article 10 right to freedom of expression. It is notable that the HRA has had little impact, though with some exceptions which are discussed, perhaps because the courts had already been alert in this area to the need to protect freedom of expression.

Discrimination is a fast-developing area, and another area where the wrongs for which a claim can be brought directly vindicate a basic right. The limit on the scope of the Convention here is that Article 14 applies in conjunction with another Convention right, and is not free-standing. In her discussion (Chapter 10), Hazel Oliver considers how this interacts with the existing law on discrimination, and to what extent Article 14 has the scope to assist in the development of the law.

The law of wrongs comprises both substantive law and remedial law, and the issue of interaction between the HRA and the law of damages, what might be termed remedial direct effect, is considered by Jason Varuhas (Chapter 11). The key issue here is the comparison between the general law of damages and the measure of remedies under the HRA itself. Have awards under the HRA had an impact on the wider law; has the wider law influenced awards under the HRA; and, in either case, how should they interact? In particular, the courts have resisted using the general law of damages to determine the level of compensation awarded under the HRA. Is this justified? Would it be more consistent or principled to apply the same principles to damages in both areas? This is especially so considering those torts which vindicate interests protected under the Convention such as personal security and liberty.

We then move to areas of property law. Amy Goymour (Chapter 12) provides a comprehensive survey of the law of property and housing as affected by the right to property in Article 1 of the First Protocol to the ECHR ('P1–1') and the Article 8 right to a home, reviewing both the areas where these rights have been considered as having some application, and considering whether our property law is compatible with them. The P1–1 right to property does not constitute property rights, but it does apply when they are affected by statutory intervention, or otherwise varied or transferred by law, and Article 8 can then kick in when the intervention of the court impacts on the home, especially a family home.

This area has also seen a lively interplay between the domestic and Strasbourg courts, especially in two areas: limitation in the form of adverse possession as a state-imposed restriction on property rights; and the interplay between the Article 8 right to respect for home with the law of property's approach to recovering possession of rented property in the event of breach or termination. This has caused a real debate between the House of Lords/Supreme Court and the Strasbourg court on how to balance the need for the efficient resolution of possession proceedings, which pass through the courts in their thousands, with the need to ensure that tenants of public authorities have some opportunity to raise issues of Convention compliance, most recently in the leading case of *Pinnock*.[17] The public nature of the landlord in such cases does not reduce the possible impact upon the general law.

In the same vein, while the law as to how personal property and choses in action, such as rights under contracts, are constituted is not impinged upon by the Convention, the way in which these are enforced by the courts can be. This is especially so in areas where there is a statutory overlay, but also in areas which impact on other interests of individuals. Thus, rights under contracts which are regulated to protect consumers, or which engage general public interest, are considered in the discussion on commercial law by Francis Rose (Chapter 13), who also considers the impact of the Act on other aspects of commercial law, such as the personality of other commercial actors, such as companies, and the impact upon commercial dispute resolution procedures, such as arbitration. In a similar vein, the scope of the HRA to bear on claims for unjust enrichment is considered by David Hoffman (Chapter 14). These are not areas where the impact of consideration of basic rights is especially great, but there is an overlap, especially where the state has intervened to regulate commercial activity or remedies for breaches of obligations, and therefore they bear consideration in the present context.

Another area where contracts are heavily regulated is the area of employment law. Again, this is an area which is so fundamental to the employee's personal life that it cannot but engage with basic rights.

17 *Pinnock* [2010] UKSC 45, [2010] 3 WLR 1441.

Employment law seeks to support the employee against the superior power (in that context) of the employer. Hazel Oliver (Chapter 16) discusses how the HRA interfaces with this in a number of areas where the actions of employers affect the employee's basic well-being: privacy and private life; correspondence; religion; self-expression; right of association in trade unions.

Another area which cuts across contract and property and which is governed by statute, and therefore represents state intervention, is the law of insolvency. The institution of bankruptcy exists to protect debtors; in as far as it avoids imprisonment for debt, that itself supports a right which is often recognised as a human right.[18] But balance is needed to ensure that the property and contractual rights of creditors are not left unduly unprotected. As Christopher McNall (Chapter 15) explores in his discussion, this is especially so where a balance has to be struck between the commercial interests of creditors (their property rights) and the interests of the bankrupt's family in their home.

Finally, we consider the issue of how the HRA applies to the courts' own procedure in private law disputes, which is to say the law of civil procedure. This is considered by John Sorabji (Chapter 17), who discusses the extent to which Article 6 adds anything by way of procedural direct effect. We then offer some concluding remarks to complete the discussion (Chapter 18).

This is inevitably not a complete survey of the whole of private law, but we hope to have touched on many of the most important areas to have been affected by the HRA sufficiently to elucidate the consequences for private law of this important piece of legislation.

---

18 Article 11 of the United Nations International Covenant on Civil and Political Rights is the right not to be imprisoned for debt; and Art. 1 of the Fourth Protocol to the European Convention is in equivalent terms.

2

Mapping horizontal effect

ALISON L. YOUNG

There is a wide variety of possible models of horizontal effect of Convention rights following the enactment of the HRA. This diversity stems, in part, from a lack of clear legislative guidance. The primary, although by no means the sole, source of horizontal effect is found in sections 6(1) and 6(3)(a) of the HRA. Section 6(1) provides that: 'It is unlawful for a public authority to act in a way which is incompatible with a Convention right'. Section 6(3)(a) states: 'In this section public authority includes a court or tribunal'.

These two sections render it unlawful for courts and tribunals to act in a way that is incompatible with Convention rights. This would appear to include situations when courts perform their adjudicative function, in both public and private law. As such, it is unlawful for courts to act contrary to Convention rights when deciding cases between two private individuals.[1] The creation of horizontal effect in this manner is also supported by statements from the Lord Chancellor and from Jack Straw MP when discussing the Human Rights Bill during its progress through both Houses of Parliament.[2]

---

1 This consensus was drawn in the earlier literature discussing the horizontal effect of Convention rights under the HRA. See, in particular, K. Ewing, 'The Human Rights Act and Parliamentary Democracy', *Modern Law Review*, 62 (1999), 79, 89; M. Hunt, 'The Horizontal Effect of the Human Rights Act', *Public Law* (1998), 423, 438; G. Phillipson, 'The Human Rights Act, "Horizontal Effect" and the Common Law: a Bang or a Whimper?', *Modern Law Review*, 62 (1999), 824, 824, 827; B. Markesenis, 'Privacy, Freedom of Expression and the Horizontal Effect of the Human Rights Bill: Lessons from Germany', *Law Quarterly Review*, 115 (1999), 47, 73; R. Singh, 'Privacy and the Media after the Human Rights Act', *European Human Rights Law Review* (1998), 722, 722, 724–6; and Sir William Wade, 'The United Kingdom's Bill of Rights', in J. Beatson, C. F. Forsyth and I. Hare (eds.), *Constitutional Reform in the United Kingdom: Practice and Principles* (Oxford: Hart, 1998), pp. 62–4.

2 See, e.g., HL Deb., vol. 582, col. 1232, 3 November 1997; HL Deb., vol. 583, cols. 771 and 783, 24 November 1997 and of Jack Straw MP in the House of Commons, HC Deb., vol. 314, col. 406, 17 June 1998.

Although it is clear that these sections require the creation of horizontal effect of Convention rights, what is less clear is the form that such horizontal effect should, or does currently, take. Section 6(1) does not delineate the manner in which the court is required to decide cases in order to ensure that it does not act contrary to Convention rights. This gives rise to confusion surrounding the extent to which English law has accepted a form of horizontal effect following the enactment of the HRA.

This problem is exacerbated by a plethora of contradictory judicial statements concerning the scope of horizontal effect, combined with an apparent reluctance on the part of the judiciary to discuss the specific model of horizontal effect created by the HRA.[3] In addition, there is disagreement surrounding the purpose of the HRA: is it a means of ensuring that the United Kingdom complies with its international obligation found in the Convention, or a mechanism for providing a domestic protection of human rights, enabling courts to provide a stronger protection of rights than that found in the Convention?[4] The former interpretation may give rise to a narrower scope of horizontal effect, specifically given that the Convention is a document in international law, binding upon states, not upon individuals.[5] The latter interpretation may provide for a broader definition of horizontal effect.[6]

This chapter aims to provide a framework within which to assess the horizontal effect of Convention rights in English law. First, it will explain the meaning of horizontal effect, before providing an account of different models of horizontal effect. The aim is not to advocate a particular model, but to delineate between different permutations of horizontal effect, in

---

3 See G. Phillipson, 'Clarity Postponed: Horizontal Effect after *Campbell*', in H. Fenwick, R. Masterman and G. Phillipson (eds.), *Judicial Reasoning under the UK Human Rights Act* (Cambridge University Press, 2007), p. 143.

4 This disparity is referred to as a dispute between the Convention as a ceiling (i.e., the court need merely ensure that Convention rights are adhered to) or a floor (i.e., that Convention rights provide an example of a minimum protection that courts need to ensure are protected, but they are encouraged to provide a stronger protection of rights than that found in the Convention when appropriate).

5 Although certain articles of the Convention have been interpreted so as to include positive obligations for states and some commentators argue that many, if not all, of the articles of the Convention have horizontal applicability: see D. Beyleveld and S. Pattinson, 'Horizontal Applicability and Horizontal Effect', *Law Quarterly Review*, 118 (2002), 623.

6 This dispute may explain, in part, the difference of opinion surrounding the scope of the definition of public authorities in *YL* v. *Birmingham City Council* [2007] UKHL 27 ('*YL*'), in particular, the contrasting approaches of Lord Bingham [4] and Baroness Hale [54]–[55], [61] in the minority, to Lord Mance [87]–[88], [102] in the majority.

order to establish a common terminology that will be used both to clarify the legal position and also to facilitate further debate.

2.1 Defining horizontal effect

Horizontal effect appears to be simple to define. It occurs when an individual is subject to an obligation to respect the human rights of another. However, appearances can be deceptive. Evidence of the difficulty surrounding the definition of horizontal effect can be found in the first academic commentaries delineating the possible horizontal effect of the HRA and its impact upon private law. Ian Leigh provided the widest range of terminology, distinguishing between six different types of horizontal effect:

(i) direct statutory horizontality;
(ii) public liability horizontality;
(iii) intermediate horizontality;
(iv) remedial or procedural horizontality;
(v) indirect horizontality;
(vi) full, or direct horizontality.[7]

Direct statutory horizontality stems from section 3(1) of the HRA which requires, 'so far as it is possible to do so', that primary and subordinate legislation be 'read and given effect in a way which is compatible with Convention rights'. The obligation placed upon the courts to read and give effect to legislation in this manner is not confined to cases where a Convention-compatible reading would require the imposition of an obligation to uphold Convention rights on public bodies. It also applies to cases where two private individuals are before the court, even where this creates an obligation for a private individual to uphold Convention rights. This is illustrated by the seminal House of Lords decision in *Ghaidan* v. *Godin-Mendoza*,[8] where a Convention-compatible reading of paragraph 2 of Schedule 1 to the Rent Act 1977 created an obligation on a private landlord to treat the surviving homosexual partner of a statutory tenant as a 'spouse' and, therefore, a statutory tenant. As such, the landlord was not able to obtain an order for possession of the flat, thereby protecting the Article 8 right to the family home of Mr Godin-Mendoza.[9]

---

7 I. Leigh, 'Horizontal Rights, the Human Rights Act and Privacy: Lessons from the Commonwealth?', *International and Comparative Law Quarterly*, 48 (1999), 57, 74–85.
8 [2004] UKHL 30, [2004] 2 AC 557.   9 See Chapter 4.

Public liability horizontality stems from section 6(3)(b) of the HRA, which includes 'any person certain of whose functions are functions of a public nature' within the definition of a 'public authority', albeit only with regard to their actions when performing this public function.[10] Public liability horizontality occurs as the definition of a public authority examines functions and not merely the composition of an institution, or its connection to the state.[11] Consequently, it is possible that a private company will be required to uphold Convention rights when performing a public function.[12] Intermediate horizontality derives from section 6(1), but is not dependent upon the classification of the courts as public authorities under section 6(3)(a) of the HRA. It occurs where an individual is able to bring an action against a public body for failing to protect Convention rights, when this failure stemmed from the actions of a private individual. The success of the action may have the indirect consequence of imposing an obligation to uphold Convention rights upon a private individual.

Leigh's final three examples of horizontality all stem from an interpretation of the duty of the courts, as a public authority, to refrain from acting in a manner that is incompatible with Convention rights. Remedial or procedural horizontality focuses on the discretionary powers of the court to issue court orders or to grant remedies in private law actions. Ensuring that court orders and remedies are not contrary to Convention rights could indirectly impose an obligation to respect Convention rights on private parties: for example, if the court were to grant an injunction preventing an individual from acting in a manner that would breach the Convention rights of others.[13] In addition, remedial horizontality may occur through the application of section 12, which requires the court to pay special attention to the protection of freedom

---

10 Section 6(5).
11 Despite the functional focus of s. 6(3)(b) itself, concerns as to the composition of a body performing a public function, and of its enmeshment with the state, have also been deemed relevant to the determination of whether a body is a 'public authority' for the purposes of the HRA. See *Poplar Housing and Regeneration Community Association Limited* v. *Donoghue* [2002] QB 48; *R (Heather)* v. *Leonard Cheshire Foundation* [2002] EWCA Civ. 366, [2002] 2 All ER 936; *YL*.
12 Discussed in more detail in Chapter 3.
13 *Re S (A Child) (Identification: Restriction of Publication)* [2004] UKHL 47, [2005] 1 AC 593 could be categorised as an example of remedial horizontality deriving from s. 6(1) and (3)(a), concerning the discretion of the court to issue an injunction restraining the publication of the identity of a child whose mother was accused of murder.

of expression found in Article 10 when granting injunctions restricting publication.[14]

Indirect horizontality refers to the way in which Convention rights may inform the common law, giving rise to potential modification of the common law, creating obligations on private individuals to uphold Convention rights. Direct or full horizontality occurs when courts are 'required to create appropriate rights and remedies by revising the common law to protect Convention rights subject only to the limitation that a clear statute must prevail'.[15]

Raphael draws a different threefold classification of possible forms of horizontal effect:

(i) developmental obligation;
(ii) remedial horizontal effect; and
(iii) developmental influence.[16]

Raphael's developmental obligation is equivalent to Leigh's indirect horizontality, referring to the way in which the court may be required to develop the common law, to ensure that courts do not act contrary to Convention rights. Remedial horizontal effect is equivalent to, and shares the same terminology as, Leigh's remedial or procedural horizontality. Developmental influence refers to a form of horizontal effect that is not classified by Leigh. It does not stem from any specific statutory provision of the HRA, but from the existence of the Act in and of itself. The existence of the HRA would be taken into account by the court when developing the common law, in the same way that other statutes may influence the development of the common law.

This analysis does not merely reflect the initial difficulties in devising terminology to describe new legal phenomena. It reflects three deeper issues that make it difficult to provide a clear and succinct definition of horizontal effect in English law:

(i) the plethora of sources of horizontal effect;
(ii) the difficulty of distinguishing between 'public' and 'private'; and
(iii) the different ways in which we can analyse the imposition of an 'obligation' on an individual.

---

14 *Douglas* v. *Hello! Ltd* [2001] QB 967 and *Cream Holdings Ltd* v. *Banerjee* [2004] UKHL 44, [2005] 1 AC 253 are examples of the court applying s. 12 of the HRA so as to ensure an adequate protection of the Convention right to freedom of expression.
15 Leigh, 'Horizontal Rights', p. 86.
16 T. Raphael, 'The Problem of Horizontal Effect', *European Human Rights Law Review* (2000), 493, 494–5.

2.1.1 Sources of horizontal effect

There are six different sources of the horizontal effect of Convention rights created by the HRA.

(1) Section 3(1)

Section 3(1) is the source of *statutory horizontality*. It occurs as courts are obliged to read and give effect to primary and secondary legislation so as to ensure its compatibility with Convention rights, even when Convention-compatible readings require the imposition of obligations on private parties to respect the rights of others.

(2) Section 12

Section 12 creates a restricted form of *remedial horizontality*. It requires courts to pay particular attention to the Convention right of freedom of expression when deciding whether to grant injunctions restraining publication.

(3) Section 6(1)

Section 6(1) renders it unlawful for a public authority to act in a manner which is incompatible with Convention rights. The section, in and of itself, applies to core public authorities: that is, institutions of the state.[17] It gives rise to *intermediate horizontality*, where an individual is able to bring an action against a public authority, which has the result of creating an obligation on a private individual to act in a manner that respects the Convention rights of another.

(4) Sections 6(1) and 6(3)(b)

Section 6(3)(b) provides a broad definition of public authorities, giving rise to *public liability horizontality*. This occurs when private individuals that are not institutionally connected to the state perform a public function. Section 6(1) requires such bodies to act in a manner compatible with Convention rights when performing this public function.

(5) The Act itself

The HRA in and of itself is the source of Raphael's developmental influence. It will be referred to here as *background horizontality*. This can occur

---

17 See *Aston Cantlow Parochial Church Council* v. *Wallbank* [2003] UKHL 37, [2004] 1 AC 546.

when the existence of the HRA provides the impetus to develop the common law to ensure that its provisions reflect Convention rights. There is no obligation on the court to develop the law in this way, and horizontality that occurs in this fashion is similar to situations where international law, or cases from other jurisdictions, are used as a justification for developing the common law so as to reflect human rights, giving rise to a duty on private individuals through the provisions of the common law to uphold the Convention rights of another.

(6) Section 6(1) and 6(3)(a)

As discussed above, section 6(3)(a) expressly includes courts in the definition of a public authority. This is the source of *direct* and *indirect horizontality*, as well as *procedural* and *remedial horizontality*. Although Leigh does not draw a distinction between procedural and remedial horizontality, they are best understood as referring to different forms of horizontal effect. *Procedural horizontality* occurs when the court, as a public authority, exercises its inherent or statutory powers to regulate its own procedures by managing cases or granting court orders, which create obligations on private individuals bound by such court orders. When issuing such orders, the court cannot act in a manner that is contrary to Convention rights. *Remedial horizontality* occurs when courts exercise their discretionary powers to grant remedies, where again they must ensure that the remedy in question is not contrary to Convention rights. A discretionary remedy may include an injunction to prevent a private individual from acting in a manner incompatible with Convention rights.

2.1.2 Public and private

English law provides for three possible delineations between 'public' and 'private'. First, it can refer to the nature of the institution. 'Public' bodies are those that are connected to, and form part of, the institutions of the state. Oxford City Council is a public body in the way that the Oxford Taxi Co. is not, because the former is part of the institutions of the state. When analysing the distinction between 'public' and 'private' in this manner, public authority horizontality is a form of horizontal effect. When a private institution is classified as a 'public authority' because it provides public services, then the private institution finds that it acts unlawfully if it acts contrary to Convention rights when providing this public service. As such, a private institution is required to uphold the Convention rights of other private individuals.

Second, the distinction between 'public' and 'private' can refer to the classification of the law applied to a particular legal dispute. Although English law does not have a strict divide between 'public' and 'private' law, there are nevertheless substantive provisions of the law that do not normally apply to private individuals: in particular, the obligations in respect of decision-making which are the basis of judicial review. Section 6(1) has been interpreted as creating a new form of illegality, one of the heads of judicial review. When analysed in this way, 'public liability horizontality' is not a form of horizontal effect. It is merely an example of a broader definition of the 'state', which expands the scope of public law to apply to bodies that, although not institutionally connected to the state, are nevertheless performing public functions and so are to be treated as part of the state. Consequently, they are subject to upholding Convention rights – an aspect of public law – in the same way as institutions of the state.[18]

A similar argument can be made with regard to intermediate, remedial and procedural horizontality. The primary obligation in remedial, procedural and intermediate horizontality is placed upon an institution of the state. In intermediate horizontality, an action is brought against a public body in order to require that public body to act to prevent a private body from infringing human rights. For example, an action may be brought against the police to protect the Convention rights of one group of demonstrators from infringement by the actions of counter-demonstrators. Although this may require the counter-demonstrators to act differently, in order to respect the human rights of the first group of demonstrators, the legal action is not brought directly against a private party, but against a public body: the police. An individual will bring a judicial review action against the state in order to require it to protect his or her Convention rights from infringement by the actions of other individuals.

Remedial and procedural horizontality operate in a similar manner. They both impose an obligation upon the court to uphold Convention rights when exercising its discretionary powers to issue remedies or grant court orders. Although the remedy or court order may impose an obligation upon a private party, it is the court – a public body – that is

---

18 There is disagreement concerning whether those bodies that would be classified as public bodies for the purpose of the HRA would also be classified as public bodies for the purposes of other forms of judicial review. All that is claimed here is that liability under s. 6(1) is a public as opposed to a private obligation.

legally required to act in a manner that upholds the Convention rights of others.[19]

Third, a distinction can be drawn between public and private regarding the nature of the judicial procedures required, or the nature of the remedies that can be granted by the court. This analysis would also not classify public liability horizontality and intermediate horizontality as examples of horizontal effect. Both of these forms of horizontality would be based either in an action for judicial review, or through the provisions of section 7 of the HRA, with remedies as set out in section 8 of the HRA. As such, they would be examples of public law as opposed to private law, utilising public law procedures and obtaining public law remedies.

The scope of horizontal effect, therefore, may well depend upon the approach taken to the definition of a 'private' body. This chapter does not adopt a specific approach to the distinction between 'public' and 'private', but rather considers the broadest range of possible horizontal effects, explaining how some of these effects might fail to be classified as examples of horizontal effect if different analyses were provided. This is for two reasons. First, the aim of the chapter is to clarify terminology in order to enable a uniform approach and to facilitate debate. As such, a broader definition is required in order to ensure that all possible forms of horizontal effect are included, with the ability for further discussion as to the merits of including particular examples as core as opposed to peripheral examples of horizontal effect. Second, as will be discussed later, the scope of horizontal effect raises two different conceptual issues: (i) the desirability, or otherwise, of imposing obligations to uphold human rights on private individuals who enjoy human rights in their own capacity;[20] and (ii) the desirability, or otherwise, of integrating human rights obligations into the existing provisions of private law. Both of these issues are relevant to an assessment of the impact of the HRA upon private law. A broad definition of horizontal effect ensures that both of these issues can be discussed.

2.1.3 The nature of the obligation

It was argued above that intermediate, remedial and procedural horizontality could be classified as peripheral examples of horizontal effect, as they

---

19 The classification of these types of horizontality will be discussed in more detail when examining the nature of the 'obligation' imposed upon private bodies by horizontal effect.

20 For the view that this is not as much of a problem as sometimes thought, see Chapter 3.

take a different form from direct or indirect horizontality. An alternative explanation of these forms of horizontality derives from the distinction between primary and secondary obligations. Intermediate, remedial and procedural horizontal effect do not impose primary legal obligations upon a private individual. Rather, the primary legal obligation rests with a public body. However, this legal obligation creates further secondary obligations for private individuals. This distinction can be explained further by analysing examples of indirect horizontality and intermediate horizontality in more detail.

Indirect horizontal effect occurs when existing provisions of the common law are interpreted in a manner which protects Convention rights, or the values inherent to or underpinning Convention rights. The law then imposes an obligation upon a private body to act in such a manner as prevents them from infringing the Convention rights of another individual. *Campbell* v. *MGN Ltd*[21] is a clear example of indirect horizontal effect. The *Mirror* published articles describing Naomi Campbell's battle to overcome drug addiction, which included photographs of Ms Campbell on a public street, leaving a meeting of Narcotics Anonymous. In publishing this information, the newspaper had breached a duty of confidence, publishing information that a reasonable person of ordinary sensibilities would have considered to be private. The tort of breach of confidence was interpreted so as to include the protection of Naomi Campbell's right to privacy, as found in Article 8 of the Convention. The newspaper was placed under an obligation not to publish information in contravention of the tort of breach of confidential information. This, in turn, placed the newspaper under a legal obligation not to publish information that would breach Naomi Campbell's Convention right to privacy.

A contrast can be drawn between *Campbell* and examples of intermediate horizontal effect. Leigh's examples of intermediate horizontal effect stem from positive obligations to uphold Convention rights that may be placed upon the state. In turn, these positive obligations may require the state to act to prevent private individuals from breaching the Convention rights of others. Were the state to refuse to act, another individual could bring an action against the state to require the state to act so as to protect their Convention rights. For example, section 1(1) of the Interception of Communications Act 1985 prohibits private individuals from intentionally intercepting 'a communication in the course of its transmission by

---

21 [2004] UKHL 22, [2004] 2 AC 457.

post or by means of a public telecommunication system'.[22] However, an individual cannot be prosecuted for an offence under this section without the consent of the Director of Public Prosecutions (DPP).[23] If the *Mirror* had obtained information about Naomi Campbell's drug addiction by tapping Ms Campbell's phone and intercepting a phone call between Ms Campbell and her drug addiction counsellor, they would have breached section 1(1) of the 1985 Act. However, Ms Campbell's right to privacy would not be effectively protected unless the DPP consented to bringing a prosecution under the Act against the *Mirror*. If the DPP were to refuse to give consent to such an action, then Ms Campbell could bring an action against the DPP under section 7 of the HRA, claiming that the DPP had acted unlawfully by failing to give consent to the prosecution, as to do so was to fail to act in a manner compatible with Ms Campbell's Convention right to privacy. The primary obligation to uphold Convention rights rests with the state – the DPP who, through section 6(1) of the HRA, is required to act in a manner compatible with Convention rights. But this may indirectly place an obligation in criminal law upon a private individual – the *Mirror* – to act in a manner that upholds Ms Campbell's Convention right to privacy.

Another possible example of intermediate horizontality can be found in developments in European Union law, which has developed a broad interpretation of direct effect, including the creation of exclusionary effect. Of particular relevance are 'triangulation' cases, for example, *Wells* v. *Secretary of State for Transport, Local Government and the Regions.*[24] The Secretary of State had granted planning permission to the owners of Conygar Quarry which enabled them to carry out quarrying activities. Mrs Wells lived adjacent to the quarry and objected to the quarrying activities carried on at the site. Directive 85/337 placed the state under an obligation to carry out an environmental impact assessment as part of the process of granting planning permission for the quarry. This environmental impact assessment was not carried out. Consequently, the planning permission for the quarry was deemed unlawful. The owners of Conygar Quarry were prevented from continuing their quarrying operations until further planning permission could be granted following an environmental impact assessment.

22 Leigh uses the example of s. 1 of the Interception of Communications Act 1985 when explaining possible ways in which intermediate horizontality may be used to protect privacy. See Leigh, 'Horizontal Rights', p. 78.
23 Interception of Communications Act 1985, s. 1(4)(a).
24 C-201/02, [2004] ECR I-723.

The case is an example of 'triangulation' because of the way in which the legal action was brought. Mrs Wells did not initiate legal proceedings against the owners of the quarry, but against the state. The obligation to carry out an environmental impact assessment was placed by the directive upon the state, not upon the private owners of the quarry. Mrs Wells brought an action to overturn the decision to grant planning permission to the quarry. As a consequence, the quarry was required to cease quarrying at the site. In doing so, it was faced, in practice, with the obligation of acting in a manner that did not contravene Mrs Wells' environmental rights. A similar method could be used to protect Mrs Wells' Convention rights under the HRA.[25]

In both Leigh's example and the triangulation example of intermediate horizontality, the primary obligation to uphold Convention rights is placed upon the state. However, an action brought against the state for failure to uphold its positive obligations under the Convention results in the indirect imposition of an obligation upon a private individual to respect the Convention rights of others. These examples demonstrate two distinctions between intermediate horizontality and indirect horizontality. First, as discussed above, there is a difference between whether a private party faces a primary or a secondary legal obligation to act in a manner to uphold Convention rights. In intermediate horizontality, the primary legal obligation rests with the state. Private individuals face only a secondary legal obligation. A legal action cannot be brought against them to require them to comply with Convention rights. However, a successful legal action against the state results in a legal decision that changes the position of the private individual, requiring them to act differently and, in turn, to protect the Convention rights of others.

Second, the nature of the obligation imposed upon the private individual is different. In *Campbell* v. *MGN Ltd* the newspaper had a duty not to act in a manner that contravened Ms Campbell's right to privacy, stemming from an interpretation of the common law tort of breach of confidence. In our discussion of Leigh's example, based on section 1 of the Interception of Communications Act 1985, the newspaper had an obligation not to intercept Ms Campbell's phone conversations, thus preserving an aspect of Ms Campbell's right to privacy, imposed by the

---

25 See, e.g., *López-Ostra* v. *Spain* (1995) 20 EHRR 277 and, more recently, *Hatton* v. *United Kingdom* (2003) 37 EHRR 611, for a discussion of the extent to which Art. 8 imposes positive obligations upon the state to protect environmental rights; this area is discussed further in Chapter 8.

criminal law. In our triangulation example, the quarry company has an obligation not to quarry until granted permission to do so under planning regulations, which may indirectly protect the Convention rights of neighbouring householders.

Campbell is best understood as creating a Hohfeldian claim right.[26] Campbell has a *claim right* to privacy. The newspaper has a *correlative duty* to refrain from publishing information that breaches Campbell's right to privacy. The same analysis does not apply to Leigh's example of intermediate horizontality. This situation is best analysed as a *power* in the hands of the DPP to prosecute the newspaper, giving rise to a corresponding *liability* to prosecution faced by the newspaper. The criminal law, in turn, provides what Harris refers to as a *fencing duty*, protecting the *domain right* of privacy of Campbell by subjecting the newspaper to a *liability* if it prints information obtained in breach of laws designed to protect Campbell's right to privacy.[27]

In our triangulation example, Wells has an *immunity* from quarrying that does not comply with her right to enjoy her home free from a damaging impact upon its environment and the quarry owners have a corresponding *disability* from quarrying without the required planning permissions that respect environmental rights. The state has a *power* to issue planning permission to quarries. When it does so, it has a *duty* to ensure that it respects environmental rights. Once the state exercises its *power* to grant planning permission to the quarry, the quarry possesses a *privilege* or *liberty* to quarry and Mrs Wells has *no right* to stop the quarrying.

Procedural and remedial horizontality may create obligations for private individuals to respect the Convention rights of others in a manner similar to our triangulation example of intermediate horizontal effect. *Re S*[28] is an example of remedial horizontality. The court enjoyed a power to issue a court order, preventing the publication of information that would lead to the identification of CS, an eight-year-old boy, whose mother was accused of murdering her elder son, CS's brother. The *power* of the court is matched with the potential *liability* of media institutions and others to ensure that they act compatibly with the court order. When exercising its powers, the court has a *duty* under section 6(3)(a) of the HRA to ensure

---

26 W. N. Hohfeld, 'Some Fundamental Legal Conceptions as Applied in Judicial Reasoning', *Yale Law Journal*, 23 (1913), 16.

27 J. W. Harris, 'Human Rights and Mythical Beasts', *Law Quarterly Review*, 120 (2004), 428, 434–5.

28 *In re S (A Child)(Identification: Restrictions on Publication)* [2004] UKHL 47, [2005] 1 AC 593.

that it upholds CS's Convention right to privacy, as well as the Convention right to freedom of expression of the media institutions. The issuing of the injunction creates *fencing duties* on media institutions, protecting the *domain right* to privacy of CS.

As with the analysis of the public–private divide, a broad interpretation of 'obligation' will be adopted, for the same purposes of inclusiveness. Our analysis of the public–private divide and the definition of obligations, gives rise to the following inclusive definition of horizontal effect:

> Horizontal effect occurs when an obligation to respect the Convention rights of another is imposed upon a private individual.
>
> (i) A 'private individual' refers to an individual who is not part of the institutions of the State, even where that individual is performing a public function.[29]
>
> (ii) An 'obligation' extends beyond a duty to uphold the correlative Convention right of another and includes fencing duties, liabilities and disabilities.[30]

2.2 Differentiating horizontal effect

The horizontal effect of Convention rights deriving from the HRA also needs to be distinguished from three further phenomena:

(i) horizontal applicability;

(ii) the scope of the section 6(1) obligation of a court, as a public authority, to ensure that it does not act in a manner incompatible with Convention rights; and

(iii) the impact of Convention rights upon private law.

Horizontal applicability is a necessary prerequisite for horizontal effect. Both the scope of the court's obligation under section 6(1) and the impact of Convention rights upon private law overlap with, but are nevertheless conceptually distinct from, horizontal effect. Horizontal effect may derive from the court's duty to act in a manner compatible with Convention rights, but may also stem from other sources. Moreover, the court may face other obligations to act in a manner compatible with Convention rights that do not give rise to the imposition of an obligation on private individuals to respect the Convention rights of another individual. In the

---

29 Thus, it includes public liability horizontality through the predominantly functional definition of a 'public authority' found in s. 6(3)(b) of the HRA.

30 This definition, therefore, includes intermediate and remedial horizontality.

same manner, Convention rights may modify areas of the private law that do not require the creation of obligations for private individuals to respect Convention rights.

2.2.1 Horizontal effect and horizontal applicability

In order to give rise to horizontal effect, Convention rights must have horizontal applicability – the nature of the Convention right must be such that it is capable of creating obligations for private parties to respect the right in question.[31] Horizontal applicability refers to our conception of the underlying right. Horizontal effect refers to the means through which horizontal applicability is achieved. Horizontal applicability applies at the first level of analysis, when courts define Convention rights. Horizontal effect applies at the second level of analysis, determining the way in which the horizontal application of Convention rights is achieved in English law.[32]

Whether rights should have horizontal applicability depends on arguments of political theory, as well as upon an analysis of the particular right in question. Human rights were historically regarded as imposing obligations upon the state, not upon private individuals. States were regarded as possessing more power than private individuals, giving rise to a greater ability to harm human rights Such analyses were often coupled with a narrow definition of 'human rights', focusing in particular upon traditional conceptions of civil liberties. Moreover, to impose an obligation to uphold human rights upon private individuals could create conflicts between human rights that do not arise when human rights obligations are imposed upon the state. The state does not possess human rights. As such, it only retains the obligation to ensure that its actions do not restrict the human rights of others. Private individuals do possess human rights. An obligation to uphold the human rights of another may contravene their own rights, damaging personal autonomy.

These reasons are prevalent in theories of individual liberalism and lead to a narrow scope of horizontal applicability and horizontal effect for human rights provisions. Arguments from social democracy reject these premises, arguing for a broader horizontal application, and thus horizontal effect, of rights. Such theories focus on the power of private

---

31 For a discussion of the distinction between horizontal effect and horizontal applicability, see Beyleveld and Pattinson, 'Horizontal Applicability and Horizontal Effect', pp. 627–8.

32 See Introduction, pp. 8–10.

individuals to restrict rights. This is often coupled with a more wide-ranging interpretation of human rights, focusing especially upon the inclusion of social and welfare rights. Private employers, in particular, are in a position to harm the social and welfare rights of others, as are private bodies to which the provision of social welfare has been delegated. Although such private bodies also enjoy human rights, such conflicts are regarded as capable of resolution through the definition of the rights in question, rather than as providing a justification for denying the horizontal effect of human rights provisions.[33] By defining human rights in this way, the rights of an employee, for example, may not be violated by the legitimate actions of the employer which promote or protect his or her own human rights.

Although arguments for horizontal applicability may influence the *extent* to which human rights are given legal effect, they have little bearing on the *means* through which horizontal effect is achieved. Models of horizontal effect are influenced by institutional, legal and constitutional factors. First, court structure may influence the model of horizontal effect that is adopted. It is easier for horizontal effect to be achieved through private law when there is no strict division between public and private law courts and where courts decide both constitutional and other legal issues. Second, models of horizontal effect are influenced by the legal provisions governing the application of human rights in that legal system – in English law the HRA. Third, constitutional features are also relevant, particularly concerning the relative powers of the legislature and the court.[34]

2.2.2 Section 6(1) obligation of the court

Sections 6(1) and 6(3)(a) of the HRA provide the main source of horizontal effect of Convention rights, by regulating the way in which courts perform their adjudicative function. In addition, section 6(1) may also require the court to act in a manner so as to uphold Convention rights when performing its other functions. Horizontal effect may arise when the court performs other functions, as was demonstrated by procedural and remedial horizontality. However, it is also possible that no horizontal

---

33 For further discussion of how these different theories influence both horizontal applicability and horizontal effect, see M. Tushnet, 'The Issue of State Action/Horizontal Effect in Comparative Constitutional Law', *International Journal of Constitutional Law*, 1 (2003), 79.

34 See Tushnet, 'The Issue of State Action'.

effect is created by the obligation of the court to act in a manner that is compatible with Convention rights. As such, it is important to differentiate horizontal effect from the duty of the court under section 6(1). The two are not coterminous.

Re S provides an example of how section 6(1) of the HRA may create jurisdiction for the High Court to issue court orders restraining publication of the names of those whose Convention right to privacy may be harmed following a criminal trial, even where those involved are not witnesses to the criminal trial.[35] The issue of a court order in this instance created horizontal effect, giving rise to a liability on the part of media institutions not to publish information that would harm the Convention rights of the child in question. However, the exercise of the inherent jurisdiction of the court to issue court orders may also require the court to act in a manner compatible with Convention rights in situations that do not create horizontal effect. For example, in *Sunderland* v. *PS*,[36] when determining whether to issue a court order authorising the detention of a vulnerable adult, section 6(1) required that the court's inherent jurisdiction be 'moulded and adapted' to ensure that it complied with Convention rights.[37] Such a court order, in and of itself, does not give rise to horizontal effect, as it does not impose an obligation to respect Convention rights upon private individuals.

In a similar manner, the court is required to exercise its discretionary statutory powers in a manner that is compatible with Convention rights. Not every exercise of such powers will create horizontal effect. For example, in *Smith (on behalf of the Gipsy Council)* v. *Evans*,[38] the court possessed a discretionary power under section 4(1) of the Caravan Sites Act 1968 to suspend, for up to twelve months, the enforcement of an order for possession brought by a local authority to evict a licensee from a caravan site 'as the court thinks reasonable'. The Court of Appeal held that section 6(1) of the HRA required courts to exercise this power in a manner compatible with Convention rights. No horizontal effect arose here as the suspension of the order of possession in these circumstances would impose an obligation to respect the Article 8 rights of the licensee upon the local authority. Although such obligations may give rise to intermediate horizontality, no intermediate horizontal effect is created in this case as

---

35 This inherent jurisdiction was found not to extend to the Crown Court in *Re Trinity Mirror Plc (A and another (Minors acting by the Official Solicitor) intervening)* [2008] EWCA Crim. 50, [2008] 2 All ER 1159.

36 [2007] EWHC 623 (Fam), [2007] 2 FLR 1083.   37 *Ibid.* at [22] *per* Munby J.

38 [2007] EWCA Civ. 1318, [2008] 1 WLR 661.

the action was brought by an individual against the local authority to protect her Convention rights. Nevertheless, the case provides an example of the duty of the court under section 6(1) to exercise its discretionary powers in a manner compatible with Convention rights.

In addition, section 6(1) also requires the court to act in a manner compatible with Convention rights when adjudicating disputes between a private individual and institutions of the state. In *R (A)* v. *Secretary of State for the Home Department*,[39] Keene LJ argued that section 6(1) required that courts, when reviewing a detention order, should decide for themselves whether the detention order was compatible with Article 5, as only then could the court be assured that it was acting lawfully by ensuring that its decision did not contravene Convention rights.[40] The court's duty under section 6(1), therefore, may require it to adopt more stringent forms of judicial review. This duty does not normally give rise to horizontal effect, as its outcome determines the extent to which public authorities are required to act so as to uphold Convention rights.[41]

2.2.3 Impact of the Human Rights Act upon private law

Horizontal effect is only one of the ways in which the HRA may have an impact upon private law. This is because of the divergent nature of the distinction between 'public' and 'private' in English law. Where a 'public' body is a party to a 'private' law cause of action, the HRA may affect the court's decision and result in a modification of private law as it applies to public authorities, with a potential knock-on effect for how it applies as between private individuals. The existence of the HRA, particularly the possibility of obtaining damages for a breach of Convention rights under section 8, may be used as a justification either for developing the common law to ensure that it mirrors Convention rights or to prevent this development. This tension is apparent in *Chief Constable of the Hertfordshire Police* v. *Van Colle*.[42] The case concerned whether, when an individual has alerted the police to evidence that another has threatened to kill or

---

39 [2007] EWCA Civ. 804, [2007] 4 All ER (D) 467.
40 *Ibid.* at [73]–[75]. Keene LJ also argued that s. 6(1) motivated the conclusion of the House of Lords in *Huang* v. *Secretary of State for the Home Department* [2007] UKHL 11, [2007] 2 WLR 581, which concluded that, when carrying out a statutory appeal, the special immigration authorities were to decide for themselves as to whether a particular immigration decision was compatible with Convention rights, as opposed to carrying out a function of secondary review.
41 Although public liability horizontality may arise here.
42 [2008] UKHL 50, [2009] AC 225.

inflict violence against that person, that individual, or his or her relatives, should be able to recover damages should the negligent actions of the police lead to the death of, or harm to, the individual in question. As well as the possible claim in tort law, there could, in certain circumstances, also be a claim under the HRA that the police had failed to uphold the positive duty of the state with regard to the right to life found in Article 2 of the Convention. Lord Bingham recognised that the existence of liability under the HRA could not be used to ground the development of a new tort mirroring the Convention right, but that in some instances the common law 'had evolved in a direction signalled by the Convention'.[43] Lord Brown reached the opposite conclusion, arguing that the existence of liability under the HRA rendered the development of the common law redundant. Common law liability and liability under the HRA served different purposes and, therefore, should be kept separate; see Figure 2.1 for an illustration.[44]

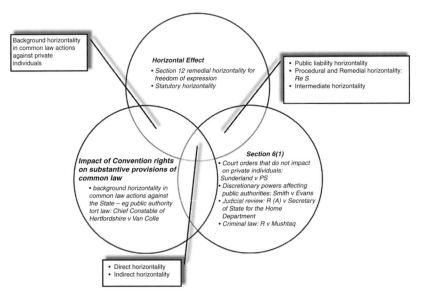

Figure 2.1 Inter-relationship between horizontality, the impact of the HRA on private law and the role of section 6

---

43 *Chief Constable of the Hertfordshire Police* v. *Van Colle* [2008] UKHL 50, [2009] AC 225 at [58] ('*Van Colle*'). Lord Bingham referred in particular to the Court of Appeal decision in *D* v. *East Berkshire Community Trust* [2003] EWCA Civ. 1151, [2004] QB 558 at [55]–[88].
44 *Van Colle* at [136]–[139].

2.3 Delineating horizontal effect

Our definition of horizontal effect relied upon Leigh's and Raphael's list of different forms of horizontal effect. As such, we have already outlined the following different forms of horizontal effect:

  (i) public liability horizontality;
 (ii) intermediate horizontality;
(iii) statutory horizontality;
(iv) background horizontality;
 (v) remedial horizontality; and
(vi) procedural horizontality.

This section seeks to provide further explanation of direct and indirect horizontal effect. It will first explain the difference between the two, before distinguishing further between different forms of indirect horizontal effect.

2.3.1 The distinction between direct and indirect horizontal effect

The distinction between direct and indirect effect depends on the *means* by which human rights are pleaded before the court, rather than the *extent* to which a particular legal system accepts horizontal effect – so it does not follow that direct horizontality provides for a greater protection of rights than indirect horizontality. *Direct horizontal effect occurs when an individual pleads a breach of a Convention right in and of itself before the court*, obtaining redress against *another* individual. *Indirect horizontal effect* occurs when *the applicant pleads other legal provisions, which are in turn interpreted so as to contain or reflect* the Convention right in question. It is the alternative legal provision itself that imposes the obligation. This obligation reflects or mirrors the obligation found in a Convention right.[45] *Campbell* v. *MGN Ltd* was referred to above as an example of indirect horizontal effect, as the obligation to uphold Convention rights arose from reading the tort of breach of confidence so that it reflected, if not mirrored, Article 8. *Campbell* would have provided an example of direct horizontal effect if Ms Campbell had been able to bring

---

45 Phillipson, 'The Human Rights Act, "Horizontal Effect" and the Common Law: a Bang or a Whimper?', p. 826 and Hunt, 'The "Horizontal Effect" of the Human Rights Act', pp. 428–34.

a specific cause of action against the newspaper for breaching Article 8, without using the basis of the existing common law tort of breach of confidence.[46]

An alternative method of drawing the distinction between direct and indirect horizontal effect analyses the distinction from the perspective of the individual who is made subject to an obligation to uphold Convention rights. *Direct horizontal effect* occurs when an *individual* is made subject to Convention rights. Private individuals are required to act so as to respect the Convention rights of others. *Indirect horizontal effect* occurs when the *law* is made subject to Convention rights. Individuals may then face an obligation to uphold Convention rights through a modification of the law required to ensure that it complies with Convention rights.[47]

This analysis of the nature of the distinction between direct and indirect horizontal effect emphasises a specific consequence of the distinction in legal systems that differentiate between constitutional law and other law, such that constitutional law overrides legislation that contravenes its provisions. If rights enjoy direct horizontal effect, then they do so because the rights in question are classified as constitutional. Direct horizontal effect requires individuals to act to uphold these constitutional rights. As such, these rights cannot be modified by the legislature. The same is not true of rights that enjoy indirect horizontal effect. Indirect horizontal effect occurs because laws are modified to ensure that they comply with the Constitution. The human right that an individual must ensure he or she upholds is part of the common law. It would be possible for the legislature to legislate contrary to this provision of the common law, modifying the common law so as to remove the horizontal effect (provided that to do so did not breach the Constitution).

Although this distinction has little resonance in English law, where it is possible for Parliament to enact legislation that is contrary to Convention rights and to overturn the HRA,[48] it does illustrate a further consequence

---

46 This is the position in Ireland, where an action can be brought directly against a private individual for a breach of a constitutional right. See Hunt, 'The "Horizontal Effect" of the Human Rights Act', pp. 428–9.

47 S. Gardbaum, 'Where the (State) Action Is', 4 *International Journal of Constitutional Law*, 4 (2006), 760 and G. Taylor, 'The Horizontal Effect of Human Rights Provisions: the German Model and its Applicability to Common-Law Jurisdictions', *King's College Law Journal*, 13 (2002), 187, 190–5.

48 The Scottish Parliament, Welsh Assembly and the Northern Ireland Parliament are required to ensure that their primary legislation is compatible with Convention rights, and cannot overturn this. See Scotland Act 1998, s. 29(2)(d), Government of Wales Act 2006, s. 94(6)(c) and Northern Ireland Act 1998, s. 6(2)(c).

of horizontal effect in English law. If Convention rights were to have direct horizontal effect, then the horizontal effect in question would derive from the HRA. As such, if the HRA were to be repealed, the horizontal effect of Convention rights would also lapse.[49] The same is not true of indirect horizontal effect. Indirect horizontal effect works through the modification of provisions of the common law. Although overturning the HRA would remove the obligation of the court to ensure that the common law mirrored or reflected Convention rights, the common law that had been altered so as to impose an obligation to uphold Convention rights would remain.[50]

All of the forms of horizontality discussed by Raphael and Leigh, other than the obvious exception of their account of full or direct horizontality, are best understood as models of indirect horizontal effect. This is also true of statutory horizontality, even though Leigh refers to this as 'direct' statutory horizontality. Section 3(1) does not create new rights in English law. Rather, it requires the re-reading of primary and secondary legislation to ensure its compatibility with Convention rights, as far as it is possible to do so. As with other forms of indirect horizontal effect, this obligation would cease to exist were the HRA to be overturned, but the interpretations of legislation given by the courts subject to that obligation would remain, unless and until cases were brought challenging these interpretations of statutory provisions following the repeal of the HRA. For the purposes of the rest of this chapter, indirect horizontal effect will be used solely to refer to the modification of common law occurring through the operation of sections 6(1) and 6(3)(a).

Direct horizontality, as the appropriate interpretation of the obligation of the court under section 6(1), is advocated by Wade,[51] Morgan,[52] and Beyleveld and Pattinson.[53] However, it has not been accepted by the judiciary. Judicial statements can, however, be found in support of indirect effect. In order to understand the case law discussing horizontal effect

---

49 Of course, it is possible that further developments of the common law would occur, so as to maintain an obligation for private individuals to uphold Convention obligations. However, this would not be a form of direct horizontal effect.

50 Leaving open the question of whether, in such a situation, these precedents which expanded the common law should be distinguished because of the repeal of the HRA.

51 Wade, 'The United Kingdom's Bill of Rights', pp. 63–4 and 'Horizons of Horizontality', *Law Quarterly Review*, 116 (2000), 217.

52 J. Morgan, 'Privacy, Confidence and Horizontal Effect: "Hello" Trouble', *Cambridge Law Journal*, 62 (2003), 444, 467–8 and 'Privacy in the House of Lords, Again', *Law Quarterly Review*, 120 (2004), 563, 566.

53 Beyleveld and Pattinson, 'Horizontal Applicability and Horizontal Effect', pp. 634–45.

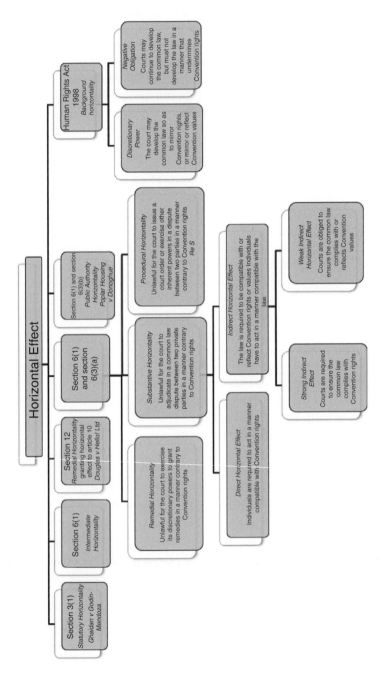

Figure 2.2 Forms of horizontal effect

more clearly we need to delineate further between different models of indirect horizontal effect (see Figure 2.2).

2.3.2 Models of indirect horizontal effect

Two main parameters help to distinguish between different forms of indirect horizontal effect:

(i) *the degree of obligation imposed upon the court* to ensure that private law is modified or extended to take account of Convention rights; and
(ii) whether the common law should be modified to take account of Convention *rights*, or of the *values* underpinning or reflected within Convention rights.

These two parameters combine to provide a range of possible models of indirect horizontal effect. Phillipson draws a distinction between strong and weak versions of indirect effect which will be used here. *Strong* indirect horizontal effect refers to a model of indirect horizontal effect that places an *obligation* upon the court to interpret the common law so as to ensure its compatibility with *Convention rights*. *Weak* indirect horizontal effect refers to the *duty* of the court to ensure that the common law develops in line with the *values incorporated by Convention rights.*[54]

Strong and weak indirect horizontal effect can be distinguished from other models of horizontality that do not place the court under an obligation to develop the law, either according to Convention rights or to reflect values underpinning Convention rights. First, it could be argued that courts do not have a *duty*, but a *discretionary power* to develop the common law so as to reflect the values found in the Convention. This form of indirect horizontal effect is akin to Raphael's 'developmental influence' of the HRA. The values found in the Convention can be used to influence the development of the common law, in the same way that the fact that the United Kingdom was a signatory to the Convention influenced the development of the common law prior to the enactment of the HRA.[55] As such, sections 6(1) and 6(3)(a) have placed no further obligation on the courts, other than to perhaps legitimise the prior practice of the court to harmoniously develop the common law so as to match human rights

---

54 Phillipson, 'The Human Rights Act, "Horizontal Effect" and the Common Law: a Bang or a Whimper?', pp. 829–33.
55 See, e.g., the modification of defamation law in *Derbyshire CC* v. *Times Newspapers Ltd* [1993] AC 534 and *Reynolds* v. *Times Newspapers Ltd* [2001] 2 AC 127.

values reflected in the Convention where the courts deemed it desirable
to do so.

A variation of 'developmental influence' can be found in the 'negative obligation' model of horizontal effect, advocated by Clayton and
Tomlinson.[56] Like the 'developmental influence' model, it does not require
the courts to develop the common law. Rather, it recognises that the HRA
has placed a limit upon the discretionary power to develop the common
law that has always been enjoyed by the court. Following the enactment
of sections 6(1) and 6(3)(a), courts cannot develop the common law in
such a way as to undermine Convention rights. It therefore differs from
the 'developmental influence' model in two respects. First, the source of
indirect horizontal effect rests specifically upon sections 6(1) and 6(3)(a)
of the HRA. The 'developmental influence' model rests upon the influence
of the HRA as a whole. Second, it places a restriction upon the powers of
the court that is not present in the 'developmental influence' model of
indirect horizontality.

2.3.2.1 Models of weak indirect horizontal effect

'Weak indirect horizontal effect' imposes an obligation on courts to
develop the common law so as to reflect the values underpinning
Convention rights. Phillipson's account of models of horizontal effect
provides a further subdivision between models of weak indirect horizontal effect. To understand this variation, we need to examine the distinction
between rules and principles. Rules apply on an 'all or nothing' basis. In
strong indirect horizontal effect Convention rights are applied in this
manner. Courts are required to ensure that the common law develops
so as to mirror Convention rights. Principles are more flexible. Courts
give weight to principles, determining whether to adopt principles or
not. Principles may also compete with other principles. Models of weak
indirect horizontality regard values underpinning the common law as
principles. The values underpinning Convention rights are referred to by
the court and weighed against other competing values.

A distinction can be drawn between regarding the values reflected
in Convention rights as 'fundamental' or as 'ordinary' principles. This
distinction refers to the relative weight accorded to these principles.
'Fundamental' principles are accorded more weight, requiring strong
justifications to overturn such principles. 'Ordinary' principles are not

---

56 R. Clayton and H. Tomlinson, *The Law of Human Rights* (Oxford: Clarendon Press, 2000),
   pp. 234–5, paras. 5.91–5.94.

accorded more weight in this manner. Rather, their importance depends upon the specific context in which they are applied.[57] This distinction between fundamental and ordinary principles reflects two possible models of weak indirect horizontal effect. A stronger version of weak indirect horizontal effect would require the values underpinning Convention rights to be regarded as *fundamental principles*. As such, courts should ensure that the law develops to reflect the values of the Convention, unless there are strong reasons for failing to do so. A weaker model of weak indirect horizontal effect would classify the values underpinning Convention rights as *ordinary principles*. The court should pay regard to these values, but the weight attached to these values would depend upon the context of the right in question.

Judicial statements can be found in support of weak indirect horizontal effect, but there is no indication as to whether the judiciary supports the weaker or stronger version of weak indirect horizontal effect. If anything, judicial pronouncements dictate in favour of flexibility, where the weight to be given to Convention values depends upon the specific context. In *Campbell* v. *MGN Ltd*, Lord Hoffmann appeared to support a model of weak indirect horizontal effect, which would treat the value of privacy as a fundamental value in certain circumstances:

> This House decided in *Wainwright* v. *Home Office* [2003] UKHL 53, [2003] 4 All ER 969, [2003] 3 WLR 1137 that there is no general tort of invasion of privacy. But the right to privacy is in a general sense one of the values, and sometimes the most important value, which underlies a number of more specific causes of action, both at common law and under various statutes. One of these is the equitable action for breach of confidence, which has long been recognised as capable of being used to protect privacy.[58]

Privacy is recognised as 'sometimes the most important value', which would appear to suggest that the value of privacy may, on occasion, be regarded as a fundamental principle. It may also mean that the value of privacy is merely recognised as an ordinary principle that may be the most important principle given the circumstances, even when this is merely allocated ordinary weight.

As well as differences arising from the weight given to the values found in the Convention, there are also differences as to the type of value that courts are meant to be recognising. In the statement of Lord Hoffmann

---

57 Phillipson, 'The Human Rights Act, "Horizontal Effect" and the Common Law: a Bang or a Whimper?', pp. 831–2.
58 [2004] UKHL 22, [2004] 2 AC 457 [43].

quoted above, he refers to the need to give weight to the *values reflected in the Convention*. The court is required to change the common law so as to reflect the value of privacy, reflected in the right to privacy and the family home protected by Article 8 of the Convention. However, judicial statements are also found in favour of the need to develop the common law so as to reflect the *values underpinning Convention rights*. An example is provided in the judgment of Eady J in *Mosley* v. *Newsgroup Newspapers Ltd*,[59] 'Parliament enacted the 1998 statute which requires these values to be acknowledged and enforced by the courts', referring here to the values of the 'citizen's autonomy, dignity and self-esteem' that underpin the right to privacy found in Article 8.[60] Autonomy, dignity and self-esteem are values used to justify granting a right to privacy. As such they underpin the right to privacy. This is contrasted to the value of privacy itself.

Our analysis provides us with four possible permutations of weak indirect horizontal effect:

(a) an obligation on the court to develop the common law, so as to recognise the *values reflected in Convention rights* as *fundamental principles* that must be protected by the common law unless there are strong overriding reasons not to protect these values;

(b) an obligation on the court to develop the common law so as to recognise the *values underpinning Convention rights* as *fundamental principles* that must be protected by the common law unless there are strong overriding reasons not to protect these values;

(c) an obligation on the court to develop the common law so as to recognise the *values reflected in Convention rights* as *ordinary principles* that must be protected by the common law unless, on the balance of reasons, their protection is outweighed by the need to protect other values; and

(d) an obligation on the court to develop the common law so as to recognise the *values underpinning Convention rights* as *ordinary principles* that must be protected by the common law unless, on the balance of reasons, their protection is outweighed by the need to protect other values.

2.3.2.2 Models of strong indirect horizontal effect

Strong indirect horizontal effect occurs when a court is faced with an obligation to develop the common law to ensure its compatibility with

---

59 [2008] EWHC 1777 (QB), [2008] All ER (D) 322.   60 *Ibid.* at [7].

Convention rights themselves. It is advocated most notably by Murray Hunt, who argues that:

> When the Act comes into force, courts will not merely have a power to 'consider' the Convention when interpreting the common law in private disputes, nor will they merely have an obligation to take into account Convention 'values'. Rather they will be under an unequivocal duty to act compatibly with Convention rights. In some cases, this will undoubtedly require them actively to modify or develop the common law in order to achieve such compatibility. Precisely where the line is drawn between legitimate judicial development of the common law and illegitimate judicial 'legislation' is a matter of degree and, ultimately, a matter of legal and political philosophy.[61]

Judicial support for the model of strong indirect horizontal effect can be found in the judgment of Baroness Hale in *Campbell* v. *MGN Ltd*:

> The 1998 Act does not create any new cause of action between private persons. But if there is a relevant cause of action applicable, the court as a public authority must act compatibly with both parties' convention rights.[62]

As recognised in the last sentence of Hunt's analysis, differences can arise in the strength of the duty of the court to develop the common law to reflect Convention rights. There are two main issues that affect the strength of the duty of the court. First, differences arise as to the extent to which the court is required to create new causes of action in order to ensure that the common law mirrors Convention rights. Second, differences can arise as to the extent to which courts can change the common law to reflect Convention rights, when to do so would require the overturning, or distinction, of a pre-HRA decision from higher courts.

2.3.2.2.1 New causes of action   The weakest form of strong indirect horizontal effect would restrict the duty of the courts to develop the common law to mirror Convention rights. This duty would reach its limit when it required the courts to create a new cause of action, essentially creating a free-standing tort that enabled the individual to protect Convention rights from intrusion from private individuals. The statement of Baroness Hale, given above, is an example of this model of strong indirect horizontal effect. Although Baroness Hale advocated the duty of the court to

---

61 Hunt, 'The "Horizontal" Effect of the Human Rights Act', p. 441.
62 [2004] UKHL 22, [2004] 2 AC 457 at [132].

develop the tort of breach of confidence to protect the Convention rights of privacy and freedom of expression, she states explicitly that the court is not required to create a new tort of privacy. Hunt also advocates a model of strong indirect horizontality that does not require the creation of new causes of action.[63]

The strongest form of strong indirect horizontal effect would place no restrictions on the duty of the court. The courts would be required to ensure that the common law mirrored Convention rights, even when to do so would require the creation of a new cause of action. Raphael argues that courts will be required to create new causes of action, arguing that:

> It is well established that the courts have the power to create wholly new causes of action, where no contrary negative precedent exists. If so, refusing to create a new cause of action when you have the power to do so would amount to 'acting incompatibly' just as easily as would refusing to develop the law incrementally when that would be appropriate.[64]

There exists a plausible middle ground between these two extremes, where the court is required to create new causes of action to ensure that the common law mirrors Convention rights, but that this obligation to create new causes of action reaches a limit when courts would be required to develop the common law in more than a merely incremental manner.[65]

2.3.2.2.2 Role of precedent   A further possible limitation on the duty of the court to develop the common law to ensure its compatibility with Convention rights stems from the role of precedent. When developing the common law, either by redefining an existing cause of action or through the creation of a new cause of action, a lower court could be faced with a case from a higher court that defines the cause of action in a manner that is currently incompatible with a Convention right. For example, a lower court faced with the facts of *Campbell* v. *MGN Ltd* may be faced with a prior case of the House of Lords making it clear that the tort of breach of confidence is not concerned with the protection of private information, but with the protection of confidential relationships, meaning that the tort of breach of confidence cannot be extended to cover situations like

---

63 Hunt, 'The "Horizontal" Effect of the Human Rights Act', p. 442.
64 Raphael, 'The Problem of Horizontal Effect', p. 504.
65 This is a possible interpretation of the judgment of Sedley LJ in *Douglas* v. *Hello! Ltd* [2001] QB 967.

the *Campbell* v. *MGN Ltd* case where no relationship of confidentiality existed between Ms Campbell and the photographer.[66]

On one interpretation of strong indirect horizontal effect, the lower court would be bound by the decision of a higher court. As such, sections 6(1) and 6(3)(a) would not require the court to modify the common law so as to ensure its compatibility with Convention rights. On a second interpretation, the court would be required to develop the common law so as to reflect Convention rights. Two justifications can be provided here. First, the decision of the higher court would not be a binding precedent if it were decided prior to the enactment of the HRA. Second, it could be argued that the obligation found in sections 6(1) and 6(3)(a) is strong enough to override the traditional doctrine of precedent.[67]

Our analysis thus provides us with the following seven possible models of strong indirect horizontal effect, as set out in Figure 2.3:

(a) courts have an obligation to develop the common law to ensure its compatibility with Convention rights, even when this requires the court to *create a new cause of action in the face of contrary earlier decisions of a higher court*;

(b) courts have an obligation to develop the common law to ensure its compatibility with Convention rights, even when this requires the court to *create a new cause of action, but this obligation does not require the court to contradict earlier decisions of a higher court*;

(c) courts have an obligation to develop the common law to ensure its compatibility with Convention rights, including creating *a new cause of action provided that this is no more than an incremental development of the common law, even when this would be contrary to earlier decisions of a higher court*;

(d) courts have an obligation to develop the common law to ensure its compatibility with Convention rights, including creating *a new cause of action provided that this is no more than an incremental development of the common law that does not contradict earlier decisions of a higher court*;

(e) courts have an obligation to develop the common law to ensure its compatibility with Convention rights, *but this obligation reaches a*

---

66 The issue of precedent is discussed in more detail in Chapter 5.

67 Beyleveld and Pattinson support this version of strong indirect horizontal effect: see 'Horizontal Applicability and Horizontal Effect', pp. 633–4; as does Raphael, 'The Problem of Horizontal Effect', pp. 501–2.

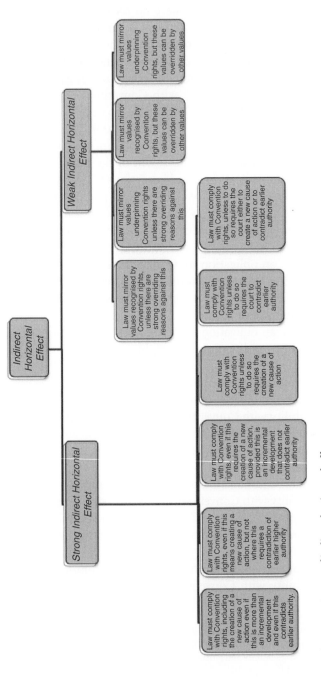

Figure 2.3 Forms of indirect horizontal effect

limit when to do so would require the court to create a new cause of action;

(f) courts have an obligation to develop the common law to ensure its compatibility with Convention rights, *but this obligation reaches a limit when to do so would require the court to contradict an earlier decision of a higher court;* and

(g) courts have an obligation to develop the common law to ensure its compatibility with Convention rights, *but this obligation reaches a limit when to do so would require the court to create a new cause of action or to contradict an earlier decision of a higher court.*

3

Public authorities: what is a hybrid public authority under the HRA?

ALEXANDER WILLIAMS

An analysis of *when* the HRA subjects private bodies to the Convention is highly germane to any discourse concerning the impact of the HRA on private law. The common law horizontal effect mechanism is one route through which to hold private bodies, albeit indirectly, to Convention standards.[1] Another route is through the hybrid public authority scheme – if a private body performs 'functions of a public nature' under section 6(3)(b), it is regarded as a public authority and must respect the Convention during its public activity.[2]

This chapter builds on earlier work which attempts to coax the judges into adopting a wider interpretation of section 6(3)(b).[3] Its central message is that there is no need for the courts to construe that provision as restrictively as they have done since the HRA entered into force. While ostensibly public in nature, hybrid public authorities are institutionally private bodies. The crucial effect of this, coupled with a close analysis of relevant Strasbourg jurisprudence, is that hybrids enjoy Convention rights themselves under the HRA, even during the performance of their public functions. They can therefore assert their own Convention rights as a defence to Convention-based challenges by claimants in court – a powerful method of self-protection which, once properly appreciated, should help ease judicial reluctance to widen the scope of section 6(3)(b).

---

1 See Chapters 1 and 2.
2 Sections 6(1), 6(3)(b) and 6(5). A third route is through the interpretation of statutes under s. 3: see Chapter 4.
3 See A. Williams, 'A Fresh Perspective on Hybrid Public Authorities under the Human Rights Act: Private Contractors, Rights-Stripping and "Chameleonic" Horizontal Effect', *Public Law* (2011), 139.

In substance, then, the hybrid scheme is one of *horizontal* effect – what may be termed 'public liability' horizontality.[4] Section 6(3)(b) may treat private bodies performing public functions as public authorities for the purpose of furnishing claimants with a Convention-based cause of action to bring them to court, but they must be treated by the court as private bodies for the different purpose of allowing them to rely on their own Convention rights. To ensure that the Convention rights of hybrid public authorities are fully protected, the hybrid scheme should be read, it is suggested, as generating 'chameleonic' horizontal effect. Aside from guaranteeing hybrids' Convention rights, the chameleonic model should appeal to the courts for the additional reason that it produces a form of horizontal effect not dissimilar in scope and effect to that which they have already endorsed in the parallel common law context mentioned above.

The chapter begins by introducing the basic problems with the courts' approach to section 6(3)(b) and explains why hybrids should be regarded as capable of relying on their own Convention rights under the HRA. It then considers the importance of the chameleonic model and how the model derives additional support from the courts' case law on common law horizontal effect.

3.1 The hybrid issue

There are two main problems with the courts' approach to the hybrid scheme. The first is that they appear to have taken too narrow an interpretation of the term 'functions of a public nature' under section 6(3)(b). It is clear from the case law that section 6(3)(b) applies to relatively straightforward examples of public activity, such as the exercise by a private organisation of statutory coercive powers.[5] The courts have also held, again not controversially, that section 6(3)(b) will apply to the actions of a private organisation that is created and assisted by a local authority to take over the running of a particular public service.[6] But beyond these contexts claimants have found it notoriously difficult to persuade the courts that a defendant exercises public functions. In particular, the courts have held that the delivery of contracted-out public services by

---

4 See Chapter 2, p. 21.
5 *R (A)* v. *Partnerships in Care Ltd* [2002] EWHC 529 (Admin), [2002] 1 WLR 2610.
6 *Poplar Housing and Regeneration Community Association Ltd* v. *Donoghue* [2001] EWCA Civ. 595, [2002] QB 48; *R (Beer)* v. *Hampshire Farmer's Markets Ltd* [2003] EWCA Civ. 1056, [2004] 1 WLR 233.

a private organisation acting on behalf of central or local government, of itself, is not a public function.[7] This is of especial concern given that contracting-out has now become an accepted and widespread method of delivering such services.[8] In *R (Heather)* v. *Leonard Cheshire Foundation*,[9] the appellants were placed by their local authority in a private care home run by the Leonard Cheshire Foundation (LCF), a charity that delivered the services on the local authority's behalf. LCF later decided to close the home and the appellants claimed that this would amount to a breach by LCF of their right to a home life under Article 8. The Court of Appeal held that LCF was not performing public functions when delivering the residential care services. Giving the judgment of the court, Lord Woolf CJ emphasised that LCF's functions were private, even though the local authority would have been regarded as performing a public function had it delivered the services itself.[10] *Leonard Cheshire* was affirmed in *YL* v. *Birmingham City Council*,[11] in which a bare majority of the House of Lords ruled that a private company in the same position as LCF in *Leonard Cheshire* was not a hybrid public authority. The resulting incongruity and arbitrariness is concerning. Vulnerable service users can plead their Convention rights against the service provider if the local authority decides to deliver the services in-house,[12] but not if it decides – which is completely beyond the service user's control – to contract them out.[13]

---

7 The courts have also held that s. 6(3)(b) does not apply to the delivery of privatised services: *Cameron* v. *Network Rail Infrastructure Ltd* [2006] EWHC 1133 (QB), [2007] 1 WLR 163; *James* v. *London Electricity Plc* [2004] EWHC 3226 (QB).

8 For fuller discussion of the rise in outsourcing and its impact on public law, see M. Hunt, 'Constitutionalism and the Contractualisation of Government' and M. Aronson, 'A Public Lawyer's Responses to Privatisation and Outsourcing', both in M. Taggart (ed.), *The Province of Administrative Law* (Oxford: Hart, 1997), at pp. 21 and 40, respectively.

9 [2002] EWCA Civ. 366, [2002] HRLR 30.

10 *Ibid.* at [15]. It should be stressed that the nature of the function is irrelevant to the *local authority's* Convention liability because the local authority is a core public authority and therefore bound to respect the Convention in everything it does (see below, p. 53).

11 [2007] UKHL 27, [2008] 1 AC 95 ('*YL*').

12 This is because local authorities are core public authorities: see below, p. 51.

13 For criticism of the courts' approach to s. 6(3)(b), see especially P. Craig, 'Contracting Out, the Human Rights Act and the Scope of Judicial Review', *Law Quarterly Review*, 118 (2002), 551; C. Donnelly, '*Leonard Cheshire* Again and Beyond: Private Contractors, Contract and s. 6(3)(b) of the Human Rights Act', *Public Law* (2005), 785; S. Palmer, 'Public Functions and Private Services: A Gap in Human Rights Protection', *International Journal of Constitutional Law*, 6 (2008), 585; A. Williams, '*YL* v. *Birmingham City Council*: Contracting Out and "Functions of a Public Nature"', *European Human Rights Law Review* (2008), 524; Joint Committee on Human Rights, Seventh Report, *The Meaning of Public Authority under the Human Rights Act* (2003–4 HL 39), (2003–4 HC 382); Joint

Parliament has since intervened to reverse the result of *YL* and *Leonard Cheshire*. Under section 145 of the Health and Social Care Act 2008 (HSCA), the delivery of residential care services in these circumstances will amount to a public function under section 6(3)(b) of the HRA. But the reasoning underlying the decisions has been left untouched and remains equally applicable to other contexts in which contracting-out may arise. The reasoning in *YL* and *Leonard Cheshire* is unpalatable because it seems illogical on its face. It is difficult to see how the mere fact of contracting-out a function can change its nature from public to private: if a function is regarded as public when delivered by a local authority in-house, it should equally be regarded as public under the HRA when contracted-out to be performed by a private organisation on the local authority's behalf.[14]

The majority of the House of Lords in *YL* made a number of attempts to explain this argument away, but none were particularly convincing.[15] In particular, their Lordships believed that the performance of functions for commercial gain 'point[ed] against' those functions being public.[16] They seemed to believe the dividing line between 'public' and 'private' under section 6(3)(b), in other words, to mirror the classically liberal distinction between the public-facing state and the self-interested private individual; between bodies created and controlled by law and politics to serve the public interest, on the one hand, and bodies who are entitled to act for their own (lawful) ends, on the other.[17] Though such a divide does appear to run through Strasbourg's jurisprudence on the distinction between governmental and non-governmental organisations under the Convention,[18] it is clear that section 6(3)(b) intends the public–private divide to be drawn in a different place. Excluding commercially motivated

Committee on Human Rights, Ninth Report, *The Meaning of Public Authority under the Human Rights Act* (2006–7 HL 77), (2006–7 HC 410). Cf. D. Oliver, 'Functions of a Public Nature under the Human Rights Act', *Public Law*, (2004), 329.

14 Craig, 'Contracting Out', p. 556.

15 For fuller discussion see Williams, 'A Fresh Perspective on Hybrid Public Authorities', pp. 144–5.

16 *YL* at [116] *per* Lord Mance. Lords Scott and Neuberger agreed.

17 See further *R* v. *Somerset County Council, ex p. Fewings* [1995] 1 All ER 513 (QB) at [524] *per* Laws J; *Leonard Cheshire* [2001] EWHC 429 (Admin) at [72] *per* Stanley Burnton J.

18 See below, pp. 56–7. It also seems to reflect the distinction between core public authorities and private persons under the HRA: D. Oliver, 'The Frontiers of the State: Public Authorities and Public Functions under the Human Rights Act', *Public Law*, (2000), PL 476 at 481–3. See further *Aston Cantlow Parochial Church Council* v. *Wallbank* [2003] UKHL 37, [2004] 1 AC 546 at [14] *per* Lord Nicholls, [62] *per* Lord Hope, [86] *per* Lord Hobhouse and [156] *per* Lord Rodger.

activity from section 6(3)(b) tends to empty it of any real purpose as a provision intended to apply to *private* bodies – bodies who, by their very nature in liberal societies, are entitled to act for their own motivations rather than being bound to serve the public interest.[19] Excluding commercially motivated activity would even seem, as one commentator has observed,[20] to conflict with the uncontroversial ruling of Keith J in *R (A) v. Partnerships in Care Ltd*[21] by excluding the exercise of statutory powers of detention by a private psychiatric hospital from section 6(3)(b). The *YL* reasoning is highly questionable from a doctrinal perspective and the meaning of the term 'functions of a public nature' should therefore still be a live issue for the Supreme Court.

The second problem with the courts' approach to the hybrid scheme is the confusion surrounding the Convention rights of hybrid public authorities themselves. The issue has never been comprehensively addressed in court,[22] but Buxton LJ once curtly stated that when discharging its public functions a hybrid 'has no such rights'.[23] The view that hybrid public authorities are somehow 'stripped' of the ability to rely on the Convention in their public capacities is also held by a surprising number of academic writers, again with little or no supporting analysis.[24]

These issues – the width of section 6(3)(b) and the ability of hybrids to rely on the Convention themselves – are bound to be linked.[25] The more disruptive the impact on private individuals of being subjected to the Convention, the more narrowly one would expect Parliament to have intended section 6(3)(b) to apply. This is an important consideration because the term 'functions of a public nature' is so vague that judges are likely to fall back onto policy and fairness considerations when

---

19 Palmer, 'Public Functions and Private Services', p. 601.

20 J. Landau, 'Functional Public Authorities after *YL*', *Public Law* (2007), 630 at 636.

21 [2002] EWHC 529 (Admin), [2002] 1 WLR 2610.

22 Baroness Hale left the issue 'for another day' in her dissent in *YL* at [74]. Lord Nicholls stated simply that hybrid public authorities should be able to rely on their own Convention rights 'when necessary' in *Aston Cantlow* at [11].

23 *YL* v. *Birmingham City Council* [2007] EWCA Civ. 26, [2008] QB 1 at [75].

24 See, e.g., Oliver, 'The Frontiers of the State', p. 492; H. Fenwick and G. Phillipson, *Media Freedom under the Human Rights Act* (Oxford University Press, 2006), p. 122; H. Quane, 'The Strasbourg Jurisprudence and the Meaning of "Public Authority" under the Human Rights Act', *Public Law* (2006), 106 at 109. Cf. H. Davis, 'Public Authorities as "Victims" under the Human Rights Act', *Cambridge Law Journal*, 64 (2005), 315 at 321. For a fuller discussion see Williams, 'A Fresh Perspective on Hybrid Public Authorities', pp. 145–54.

25 On the link between a public authority's ability to rely on the Convention and the width of the term 'public authority' under s. 6, see Oliver, 'The Frontiers of the State', pp. 490–2.

determining its meaning.[26] If the rights-stripping idea can be convincingly debunked,[27] judges should be less reluctant to extend their interpretation of the public functions term in future.

3.2 Debunking rights-stripping

Aside from courts and hybrid public authorities, which are listed as public authorities by section 6(3)(a) and (b), respectively, the HRA is commonly acknowledged to give rise to a third species of 'core' public authority. The existence of these 'obviously' public bodies is implied by the non-exhaustive wording of section 6(3), which states that public authority 'includes' the public authorities set out in its list. Unlike hybrids, core public authorities must comply with the Convention in everything they do, whether public or private activity. This is because section 6(5) allevi-ates only *hybrids* – and not core public authorities – from the duty to act compatibly with the Convention during their private activity.

It is clear that core public authorities lack Convention rights under the HRA because the HRA affords Convention protection only to 'victims';[28] that is, bodies who qualify as 'non-governmental organisations' under Article 34.[29] The effect of Article 34 is to distinguish between non-governmental organisations, who can file Convention claims in Stras-bourg, and governmental organisations, who cannot. It is difficult to see how core public authorities, inherently part of the fabric of government, could ever claim to be non-governmental organisations under Article 34.[30] It is equally clear that hybrids, by contrast, *do* enjoy Convention rights, at least when they engage in only private activity. This is because hybrids are *private* bodies. Section 6(5) emphasises their institutionally

---

26 In *YL*, Lord Neuberger stated at [128], that the words 'are so imprecise in their mean-ing that one searches for a policy as an aid to interpretation'. Along similar lines, see M. Elliott, '"Public" and "Private": defining the Scope of the Human Rights Act', *Cam-bridge Law Journal*, 66 (2007), 485, 487.

27 In *YL* at [116], Lord Mance stated that SCH, if it were a hybrid public authority, could have relied on its 'ordinary private law freedom to carry on operations under agreed contractual terms' under Article 8(2) as a defence, presumably under the 'rights and freedoms of others' qualification. His Lordship did not refer specifically to SCH's Convention rights, however, and his view that the 'rights of others' extends to a general right to contractual autonomy sits uncomfortably with Strasbourg case law to the effect that Convention qualifications are exhaustive and should be narrowly construed: see *Klass* v. *Germany* (1979–80) 2 EHRR 214 at [42]; *Golder* v. *United Kingdom* (1975) 1 EHRR 524 at [44] ('*Golder*').

28 HRA, s. 7(1).   29 HRA, s. 7(7).

30 *Aston Cantlow* at [8] *per* Lord Nicholls.

private nature by treating them as ordinary private individuals when they act in their private capacities. As private bodies, hybrids will straightforwardly fall within the definition of a non-governmental organisation under Article 34 when engaging in only private activity.

Although the HRA treats hybrids as public authorities for the purpose of generating a Convention-based statutory cause of action against them, it does not follow that the HRA intends to treat them as public authorities for all other purposes, too. Whether or not hybrid public authorities are stripped of their Convention rights when performing public functions depends on Strasbourg's definition of a governmental organisation. Hybrids can be said to lose Convention protection when performing public functions only if Strasbourg would regard them as governmental organisations when performing public functions. It is important not to misinterpret the Strasbourg case law. Domestic courts risk mis-classifying hybrids and wrongly denying them Convention protection if they reach the conclusion that Strasbourg would regard them as governmental organisations too readily. There is an important burden of proof issue here – those who believe that hybrids are rights-stripped must demonstrate convincingly that Strasbourg would regard private bodies as governmental organisations when performing public functions.

A number of judges and academic writers do seem to believe that hybrids become governmental organisations when performing public functions.[31] But this is only a tacit assumption that emerges from their view that the governmental organisation jurisprudence can assist domestic courts in identifying a public function under section 6(3)(b) (that jurisprudence must therefore extend to private bodies performing public functions in their eyes). The flimsiness of this assumption is exposed by a more detailed analysis of the Strasbourg case law with the specific task of determining the rights status of hybrids in mind.

Aside from the definition of a governmental organisation under Article 34, there is another branch of Strasbourg jurisprudence relevant to this task. This jurisprudence relates to the issue of state responsibility. If a body acts in such a way as to affect the enjoyment by a victim of their Convention rights, that body is either an emanation of the state or it is not. If it is an emanation of the state, such as a government minister,[32]

---

31 See Quane, 'The Strasbourg Jurisprudence'; *R (West)* v. *Lloyd's of London* [2004] EWCA Civ. 506, [2004] HRLR 27 at [36]–[39] *per* Brooke LJ; *YL* at [161] *per* Lord Neuberger; *R (Weaver)* v. *London & Quadrant Housing Trust* [2009] EWCA Civ. 587, [2009] HRLR 29 at [35] *per* Elias LJ and [117]–[118] *per* Rix LJ, dissenting.

32 See *Golder*.

the state will be directly responsible for its behaviour in Strasbourg. If the body is a private body rather than an emanation of the state, the state will be responsible for the body's behaviour only indirectly; that is, if the Convention places the state under a positive obligation to regulate the body's behaviour in the circumstances in question. Strasbourg has made it clear that the distinction between emanations of the state and private bodies in this context is identical to the distinction between governmental and non-governmental organisations under Article 34.[33] As a result, the state responsibility jurisprudence also helps identify the meaning of a governmental organisation in Strasbourg. It is not necessary to conduct an extensive analysis of the Strasbourg jurisprudence here,[34] as some examples will suffice to make the point for present purposes that Strasbourg cannot convincingly be said to regard private bodies performing public functions as governmental organisations.

In liberal theory, as discussed above, private bodies and individuals can usually be distinguished from public or 'state' bodies by their motives. Whereas public bodies must serve the public interest, private bodies can act for their own ends within the confines of the law. This basic distinction may be termed the 'selflessness' principle – the lawful selfishness of private bodies contrasts with the necessary selflessness of public ones. To infer with any confidence that Strasbourg regards private bodies performing public functions as governmental organisations, one would need to see a clear example in the case law of a self-serving private organisation, such as a profit-making company, being treated by Strasbourg as a governmental organisation upon the performance of a particular, public, function. No clear examples can be found in the Article 34 context, however. In fact, Strasbourg has recently ruled on two occasions that bodies will *not* be governmental organisations under Article 34 if they possess predominantly self-serving commercial motives.[35] It is true that Strasbourg sometimes uses the term 'public functions' to describe the activities of bodies which it regards as governmental organisations under Article 34. For example, in *Consejo General de Colegios Oficiales de Economistas de España* v.

---

33 *Danderyds Kommun* v. *Sweden* [2001] (App. No. 52559/99), applied in that respect in the Scottish case of *Grampian University Hospitals NHS Trust* v. *Napier* (2004) JC 117; *Hautaniemi* v. *Sweden* (1996) 22 EHRR CD 155; *Novoseletskiy* v. *Ukraine* (2006) 43 EHRR 53 at [82].

34 For fuller discussion see Williams, 'A Fresh Perspective on Hybrid Public Authorities', pp. 145–54.

35 *Islamic Republic of Iran Shipping Lines* v. *Turkey*, 'The Cape Maleas' (2008) 47 EHRR 24 at [73]; *Ukraine-Tyumen* v. *Ukraine* [2010] (App. No. 22603/02) at [27].

Spain,[36] the Commission ruled that the General Council of Official Economists' Associations (GCOEA), a professional regulatory body, was a governmental organisation under Article 34 because it was a 'national authority exercising public functions'. But despite the linguistic similarity of this remark with the term 'functions of a public nature' under section 6(3)(b), domestic lawyers should not assume that the GCOEA was what the HRA would regard as a hybrid public authority. It is by no means clear that the GCOEA, which was created by law to regulate a particular profession, was an institutionally private person entitled to further its own interests, like a profit-making company, over those of the public. Curiously, the Commission also remarked in *Consejo General* that the GCOEA, as a governmental organisation, could *never* file an application in Strasbourg. If Strasbourg really does believe that private bodies become governmental organisations when performing public functions, the Commission is suggesting that these bodies are unable to file applications under Article 34 even in respect of their *private* functions.[37] It is difficult to see why this should be, and no explanation was proffered in *Consejo General* itself. It is far more natural to infer from *Consejo General* that the Commission regarded the GCOEA as a governmental organisation not because it was a private body performing public functions but, instead, because it was a selfless governmental organisation – what the HRA would regard as a *core* public authority – created and controlled to serve the public interest.

Like the Article 34 jurisprudence, the state responsibility jurisprudence can be easily mis-read. In *Costello-Roberts* v. *United Kingdom*,[38] for example, a schoolboy received corporal punishment from the headmaster of his private school and sought to claim a breach of Articles 3 and 8 in Strasbourg. The issue therefore arose as to whether the state could be responsible for the actions of the private school. Despite ruling that there had been no Convention breach on the facts, the Strasbourg court agreed with the applicant that the school engaged the state's responsibility. To support its conclusion, the court made three points.[39] First, states are

---

36 (1995) DR 82-B.
37 Quane, 'The Strasbourg jurisprudence', p. 117. Rather than concluding that the governmental organisation jurisprudence fails to extend to private bodies performing governmental functions, Quane concludes that Strasbourg's 'hybrid' governmental organisation concept is unduly harsh on hybrids and urges Strasbourg to reconsider its remarks in *Consejo General*. In response, see Williams, 'A Fresh Perspective on Hybrid Public Authorities', p. 154.
38 (1995) 19 EHRR 112.   39 *Ibid.* at [27]–[28].

required by Article 2 of the First Protocol 'to secure to children their right to education' and disciplinary functions are not 'merely ancillary to the educational process'. Second, independent schools 'co-exist with a system of public education' in the United Kingdom. Third, 'the State cannot absolve itself from responsibility by delegating its obligations to private bodies or individuals'. It is by no means clear from these rather cryptic remarks that the private school engaged the state's responsibility *as a governmental organisation*,[40] especially given that the court began its analysis of the state responsibility issue by emphasising that the Convention can place states under positive obligations to regulate the behaviour of *private bodies* in specific situations.[41]

It cannot be reliably inferred from either the Article 34 or state responsibility strands of jurisprudence that Strasbourg regards private bodies as governmental organisations when they perform public functions. The better view is that private bodies remain non-governmental organisations through and through. Most obviously this conclusion exposes the irrelevance of the governmental organisation jurisprudence to the meaning of the term 'functions of a public nature' under section 6(3)(b).[42] More importantly for present purposes, however, the conclusion that private bodies remain non-governmental organisations when performing public functions debunks the rights-stripping idea. Hybrids enjoy Convention rights under the HRA, even when performing public functions.

3.3 The chameleonic model

Acknowledging that hybrid public authorities enjoy Convention rights in their public capacities is one thing; protecting their Convention rights is another. For the most part the courts should not find this a difficult task. All they need to do is recognise that the performance by a hybrid

---

40 *Contra* Quane, who interprets Strasbourg's ruling in *Costello-Roberts* as a governmental organisation ruling because she believes the ruling to be instructive in determining the meaning of 'functions of a public nature' under s. 6(3)(b), having earlier argued that Strasbourg's positive obligation jurisprudence can never be relevant to the domestic courts' treatment of that provision: see Quane, 'The Strasbourg Jurisprudence', pp. 108 and 110. In response to the view that the positive obligation jurisprudence can never be relevant to interpreting s. 6(3)(b), see Williams, 'A Fresh Perspective on Hybrid Public Authorities', pp. 147–8.

41 *Ibid.* at [26]. The Strasbourg court in *Storck v. Germany* (2006) 43 EHRR 6, and Lord Mance in *YL* at [95], also saw *Costello-Roberts* as a positive obligations case.

42 This serves as a rebuttal, therefore, to the views of the judges and academics at n. 31 above.

of public functions has no bearing on its ability to make Convention claims in court. So, for example, if a local authority applies to revoke a private care home's operating licence without adequate notice of the proceedings with the result that the operator's business is destroyed, the operator should be able to allege under the HRA that the local authority has breached its rights under Article 1 of the First Protocol (P1–1) and Article 6.[43] The fact that the operator's business may consist of delivering contracted-out residential care services, and that in the light of section 145 of the HSCA the operator is performing public functions under section 6(3)(b) of the HRA when doing so, will be irrelevant to its ability to make that claim. The same would also be true if the hybrid sought to rely defensively on its Convention rights against a public authority by way of collateral challenge,[44] or if the hybrid sought to use the common law horizontal effect mechanism to advance its Convention rights against a private defendant. All the courts need to do is allow the hybrid to advance those claims notwithstanding that it might be doing so during the discharge of its public functions.

In one respect the situation is more problematic, however, which is why the hybrid scheme should be read as generating *chameleonic* horizontal effect. On its face, by labelling private bodies performing public functions as public authorities, the hybrid scheme intends to treat hybrids in the same manner as core public authorities, such as local authorities or government ministers, in court. If a claimant brings an Article 8 claim against a local authority, for example, the court assessing the merits of that claim will work through the standard analysis of deciding whether there has been an interference by the local authority with the claimant's *prima facie* right and, if so, whether that interference is prescribed by law and has a legitimate aim according to Article 8(2). At this stage the local authority can rely on applicable Convention qualifications by claiming that it interfered with the claimant's right for the protection of the rights and freedoms of others, or for the prevention of disorder or crime and so on. But complications arise if hybrids are treated in the same way as core public authorities and the court works through the same analytical process with a hybrid defendant performing public functions. While

---

43 These were the facts of *Jain* v. *Trent Strategic Health Authority* [2009] UKHL 4, [2009] 1 AC 853, but the claimants were unable to make the Convention argument because the facts arose before the HRA entered into force.

44 Section 7(1)(b) of the HRA allows the victim to rely on their Convention rights in proceedings which are already underway.

hybrids might be able to avail themselves of certain Convention qualifications in isolated situations – private prison operators could claim that they were acting for the prevention of disorder or crime by routinely intercepting prisoners' communications, for example[45] – they will generally find it hard to do so. As Stanley Burnton J observed at first instance in *Leonard Cheshire*, 'the justifications referred to in Article 8(2) are all matters relevant to government, and not of any non-public body' such as a care home operator.[46] It is difficult to see how a private care home operator could claim that it was acting for the 'economic well-being of the country', for instance, when attempting to serve notice on residents to quit as in *Leonard Cheshire* and *YL*. Most importantly, it is difficult to see how it – or any other hybrid – could claim to be acting for the protection of the rights of *others* when seeking to advance its *own* right, say, to respect for property under P1–1. If insufficient account is taken of the private nature of the hybrid defendant and hence the necessarily *horizontal* nature of the dispute, the risk arises that hybrids are unable to deploy their own Convention rights defensively against private claimants through the 'rights of others' qualification. This is problematic because the HRA, through the Strasbourg scheme, requires hybrids to be able to rely on the Convention regardless of whether they perform public functions at the time.

Contrast the position of hybrid defendants under a purely 'vertical' reading of the hybrid scheme with that of ordinary private defendants in the parallel common law horizontal effect context. In the common law context, private defendants *can* deploy their own Convention rights through the Convention qualifications if a claimant seeks to use the Convention against them. This is because Convention rights are deployed by a claimant *indirectly* in the common law context; that is, against the court, if its duty as a public authority requires it to develop existing causes of action in a Convention-friendly fashion in order to safeguard the claimant's rights.[47] If the defendant considers that developing the common law in this way would infringe its own rights, it can plead those rights as a defence to the claimant's claim because the court, as a public authority, can claim that *it* is acting for the protection of the rights and

---

45 C. Donnelly, *Delegation of Governmental Power to Private Parties: A Comparative Perspective* (Oxford University Press, 2007), p. 261.

46 *Leonard Cheshire* at [71]. See also Oliver, 'Functions of a Public Nature', pp. 343–4; R. Buxton, 'Private Life and the English Judges', *Oxford Journal of Legal Studies*, 29 (2009), 413 at 416.

47 See Chapter 2.

freedoms of 'others' (that is, the defendant's Convention rights) by doing so.[48] The court then balances the competing rights to see which should prevail.

So, if the claimant deploys his or her Convention rights indirectly, against the court, the defendant has no difficulty asserting its own Convention rights in response. To avoid the risk of rights-stripping hybrids by failing to attach sufficient weight to the horizontal nature of the hybrid scheme, the hybrid scheme should be interpreted in the same way. This is the 'chameleonic' reading of the hybrid scheme. Although the scheme creates an ostensibly vertical framework of rights protection against a private body by designating it a public authority, the framework switches to take on a more horizontal character when the dispute gets underway. When in court, the claimant should be taken, as in the common law context, to assert their rights through the court rather than directly against the hybrid defendant itself.

3.4 Why the model works

Not only does the chameleonic model fully guarantee the ability of hybrid public authorities to rely on the Convention; it also exposes the hybrid scheme as giving rise to a form of horizontal effect similar to that which seems to operate in the parallel common law context.

The hybrid scheme, properly understood, contains elements of vertical and horizontal effect. It is vertical in the sense that it generates a statutory cause of action against an ostensibly public body. It is directly horizontal in the sense that the defendant hybrid public authority is in reality a private individual. In substance, the scheme also resembles one of *indirect* horizontal effect. Not perfectly so, because an indirectly horizontal scheme applies Convention rights to the *law* rather than generating a cause of action directly against the defendant itself, as the hybrid scheme does.[49] But common law indirect horizontal effect bears an additional defining characteristic, which *is* shared by the hybrid scheme once the dispute reaches court – that the claimant asserts their rights *through the court*, which sits at the apex of the dispute and balances the competing rights of

---

48 Because unqualified Convention rights cannot be balanced against the rights of others, the defendant could advance their Convention rights only if the claimant relied on a *qualified* right against them.

49 S. Gardbaum, 'Where the (State) Action Is', *International Journal of Constitutional Law*, 4 (2006), 760 at 764.

the claimant and defendant. The switch that occurs in the rights protection framework under the chameleonic model therefore represents a shift from an ostensibly vertical framework to one which can be described as roughly indirectly horizontal in nature.

The hybrid scheme, as a scheme of horizontal effect, broadly conceived, is not unlike the scheme of horizontal effect that the courts apply in the common law. This, too, is one of indirect horizontal effect. The courts do not appear to regard themselves as bound to create brand new Convention-based causes of action.[50] Their view, instead, is that they must develop *existing* causes of action in a Convention-friendly fashion. There is little evidence to suggest that the courts subscribe to the 'weak' model of indirect horizontal effect that requires them simply to consider and balance the values contained in the Convention against existing common law factors.[51] Rather, judges seem to regard themselves as *bound* to develop those causes of action consistently with Convention rights. In other words, they *apply* those Convention rights,[52] which supplant the existing law with Convention norms,[53] between the claimant and defendant to the dispute.[54] In *A v. B Plc*, for instance, Lord Woolf CJ stated in the breach of confidence context that the court's duty under section 6 should be discharged by 'absorbing the rights which articles 8 and 10 protect into the [existing cause of action]...so that it accommodates

---

50 Baroness Hale gave a clear statement to that effect in *Campbell* v. *MGN* [2004] UKHL 22, [2004] 2 AC 457 at [132]. It is clear also from the courts' approach in the common law privacy cases – where they develop the existing breach of confidence action – that they have rejected the idea that they must fashion brand new Convention-based causes of action. See Chapter 7 for Gavin Phillipson's response to the contrary view advanced by T. Bennett, 'Horizontality's New Horizons – Re-examining Horizontal Effect: Privacy, Defamation and the Human Rights Act', *Entertainment Law Review*, 21(3) (2010), 96 (Pt 1) and 145 (Pt 2).

51 Lord Nicholls's remarks in *Campbell* at [17], could be taken to endorse the weak model, however. For general discussion of the varied *dicta* in *Campbell*, see G. Phillipson, 'Clarity Postponed: Horizontal Effect after *Campbell*', in H. Fenwick, G. Phillipson and R. Masterman (eds.), *Judicial Reasoning under the UK Human Rights Act* (Cambridge University Press, 2007), pp. 143–73 at pp. 157–67.

52 This is the view commonly thought to be advanced by M. Hunt, 'The "Horizontal Effect" of the Human Rights Act', *Public Law* (1998), 423. In fact, Hunt seems to have envisaged s. 6 requiring more gradual, incremental development of the common law: see p. 442.

53 Morgan criticises the view that the courts must *apply* Convention rights to all existing causes of action on the basis that it effectively requires the content of the cause of action to be ignored and the Convention's content simply 'poured' in: J. Morgan, 'Questioning the "True Effect" of the Human Rights Act', *Legal Studies*, 22 (2002), 259, 271.

54 It is not entirely clear whether the courts regard themselves as bound to develop the law only *incrementally*, however. For further discussion see Chapter 2.

the requirements of those articles'.[55] Further support for this view can be found in more recent cases. Thus, Buxton LJ stated in *McKennitt* v. *Ash* that 'in order to find the rules of the English law of breach of confidence we now have to look in the jurisprudence of articles 8 and 10'.[56] Echoing the remarks of Lord Woolf CJ in *A* v. *B Plc*, his Lordship then described those articles as 'not merely of persuasive or parallel effect but . . . the very content of the domestic tort that the English court has to enforce'. Similarly, Eady J stated in *Mosley* v. *News Group Newspapers Ltd* that the HRA required the values expressed in Articles 8 and 10 to be 'acknowledged *and enforced* by the courts'.[57]

In the common law as well as the hybrid context, then, the court applies the Convention rights between the parties and balances competing rights, if necessary, to determine which should prevail. This is significant. In both the common law and hybrid contexts, Parliament has been unclear about *when* it expects Convention rights to apply between individuals. There are various linguistically plausible interpretations of the term 'functions of a public nature' under section 6(3)(b) and, as seen above, various plausible interpretations of the scope and effect of the court's duty to develop the common law in a Convention-friendly fashion. Judges are likely in both contexts to be resolving the issues with at least some reference to their own 'feel' for how far Convention rights should be permitted to infuse the private sphere. If the judges are prepared to endorse something akin to the strong indirect horizontal effect model in the common law context, they should not be too unhappy with the chameleonic reading – which is substantially similar – of the hybrid public authority scheme.

This is not to suggest that the chameleonic model is identical in nature and scope to the model adopted by the courts in the common law context, however. First, it is clear that the remedial provisions differ under each scheme. The court's remedial powers are governed by section 8 under the hybrid scheme, whereas the court awards remedies according to its own domestic precedents in the common law context.[58] Second, the scope of each scheme, that is, *when* a claimant can assert their Convention rights against the defendant, also differs. Under the common

---

55 *A* v. *B Plc* [2002] EWCA Civ. 337, [2003] QB 195 at [4].

56 *McKennitt* v. *Ash* [2006] EWCA Civ. 1714, [2008] QB 73 at [11].

57 [2008] EWHC 1777 (QB), [2008] EMLR 20 at [8] (emphasis added). Discussed further in Chapter 7.

58 For criticism of the courts' approach to damages under the HRA see Chapter 11.

law scheme, the claimant cannot assert their Convention rights against the defendant unless they can convince the court that the state would be liable in Strasbourg if their Convention rights were left unprotected in the circumstances in question – if the state would not be liable in Strasbourg, the claimant's rights are already protected and the court will not be acting unlawfully by refusing to develop the common law.[59] Claimants in the hybrid context need not demonstrate that the state would be liable in Strasbourg, however, because by necessary implication the hybrid scheme generates Convention remedies in domestic law which *expand* on those available against the state. This is because a particular body can engage the state's responsibility in only one of two ways in Strasbourg,[60] and Parliament has provided for domestic remedies in each situation using other schemes of liability under the HRA. If the claimant's rights are interfered with by what Strasbourg would regard as an emanation of the state, the claimant can pursue a direct claim against that body as a core public authority under section 6 of the HRA.[61] If the behaviour emanates instead from a private person whose behaviour the state is under a positive obligation to regulate, the claimant can pursue a remedy through the common law horizontal effect mechanism, as seen above. Provided that the subject matter of the claimant's complaint falls within the scope of an applicable Convention right, in the hybrid context it is not necessary for the claimant to show that the state itself would be liable in Strasbourg if he or she were left without a remedy in domestic law.

Domestic courts have considerable room to expand their definition of a public function before the hybrid scheme can be said to overburden private defendants. It should be remembered that claimants can assert their Convention rights only against private defendants who perform public functions under the hybrid scheme. Even on a broader construction of section 6(3)(b) that included the delivery of contracted-out public services, the vast majority of activities undertaken by private bodies would still fall outwith the definition of a public function, with the result that private defendants would be largely shielded from liability under the hybrid scheme. This contrasts with the relatively claimant-friendly

---

59 See Chapter 1.   60 See above, pp. 54–55.

61 The governmental organisation and core public authority categories seem to be coterminous: see above, p. 53 and *Aston Cantlow* at [6]–[7] *per* Lord Nicholls, [47] *per* Lord Hope, [160] *per* Lord Rodger, [129] *per* Lord Scott and [87] *per* Lord Hobhouse.

position in the common law horizontal effect context – all the claimant needs to do here is present a cause of action which is 'relevant' to the nature of the Convention claim made.[62] The extent to which the courts have been prepared to stretch the breach of confidence action to ensure compatibility with Article 8 demonstrates the relative ease with which claimants can assert their rights in at least some common law contexts.[63]

3.5 Conclusion

While it previously appears to have gone unrecognised, hybrid public authorities do in fact enjoy Convention rights of their own under the HRA during the performance of public functions. The prevailing academic and judicial assumption that a hybrid is somehow 'stripped' of Convention rights in its public capacity is a myth. Not only does this confirm that hybrids can use their Convention rights to mount challenges against other public authorities when acting publicly; it also opens up a valuable line of defence to hybrids who find themselves on the receiving end of Convention claims in court. In order to ensure that hybrids can make use of this defence, however, the hybrid scheme should be read as generating chameleonic horizontal effect.

Properly understood in this way and juxtaposed against the courts' treatment of the horizontality issue in the parallel common law context, the hybrid scheme is far riper for expansion in scope than the judges appear to believe. The courts' own case law in the common law context indicates that they should not regard expanding section 6(3)(b) to include contracted-out public services as causing undue harm to hybrid defendants. The width of the term 'functions of a public nature' under section 6(3)(b) is not the only factor responsible for determining the defendant's liability in court. Even if a claimant succeeds in demonstrating that a private defendant performs public functions, the claimant must then show, if the hybrid asserts its own Convention right in response, that *the claimant's* Convention right should prevail. It is at this stage that the court will be able to conduct an intricate and context-sensitive balancing

---

62 *Campbell* at [132] *per* Baroness Hale.
63 Judges in more recent cases have even referred to the newly-developed aspects of the law as a tort of misuse of private information in recognition of the nature and extent of that development: see, e.g., *McKennitt* v. *Ash* at [86] *per* Longmore LJ, and *Murray* v. *Express Newspapers Plc* [2008] EWCA Civ. 446, [2009] Ch 481 at [24] *per* Sir Anthony Clarke MR.

exercise between the competing rights.[64] This is the forum in which judges should air and accord due weight to any concerns that they might harbour about the impact on the defendant if the claimant's claim is upheld. Foreclosing the issue at the threshold stage by construing the meaning of a public function unduly narrowly is not the answer.

64 A defence based on the right to respect for property under P1–1 is likely to be a strong one: see Chapter 12.

4

Statute law: interpretation and declarations of incompatibility

JAN VAN ZYL SMIT[*]

The impact of the HRA on statute law appears at first glance to be relatively straightforward compared with its impact on the common law. In relation to statutes the HRA provides specific mechanisms for giving effect to Convention rights, so courts have not had to fashion their own methods under section 6 as they have done in common law cases. There are two mechanisms provided: courts have a duty to render statutes compatible with the Convention by interpretation 'so far as it is possible to do so' (section 3), and where interpretation fails they have the power to issue a declaration of incompatibility (section 4). Although declarations of incompatibility do not affect the validity of legislation, Parliament has generally responded by repealing or amending the statute in question. The HRA thus provides a relatively clear grounding for the constitutional role of the courts when Convention rights are invoked in cases involving statutes, unlike common law cases in which the courts have had to resolve this role for themselves to a greater extent.

Important questions of judicial technique remain, however. The courts are fleshing out their constitutional role by developing new techniques of statutory interpretation in order to give effect to Convention rights, and by delineating the circumstances in which they will issue a declaration of incompatibility. These new techniques have brought far-reaching changes which are of interest to both public and private lawyers. Sir Jack Beatson has observed extracurially that section 3 'makes statutory provision more like common law doctrine', due to the relative decline in importance of the statutory text and the increased importance of Convention case law in determining the interpretation that a court ultimately adopts.[1] Beatson

* I am grateful to Derek O'Brien for helpful comments on an earlier version of this chapter.
1 'Common Law, Statute Law and Constitutional Law' (2006) 27 Statute LR 1 at 11.

argues that this development may render statutes more 'opaque' to the ordinary litigant.[2] These remarks raise important themes for this chapter, as they draw attention to the need for courts to strike a balance between the protection of Convention rights and the value of legal certainty when private legal relationships are conducted within a statutory framework. Parliament shares responsibility with the courts for maintaining this balance, as the legislature is expected to respond to declarations of incompatibility by enacting a new or revised statutory framework to provide for the Convention rights that have been affected; indeed, Parliament may also respond to section 3 interpretations by revising the statute. Dialogue of this kind between the courts and the legislature is an important aspect of the impact of the HRA on statute law. This chapter aims to provide an overview of the impact on statutes in private law cases. The chapter is in three parts: the first deals with questions of mapping and situates statute law in relation to other forms of private law affected by the HRA; the second considers the judicial approach to issuing declarations of incompatibility and the legislative response thereto; and the third examines the extent to which the courts have modified existing doctrines of statutory interpretation in order to give effect to Convention rights in cases between private parties.

4.1 Mapping the impact of the HRA on statute law

In order to characterise the HRA's effect on statutes in private law cases, this chapter will use three of the classifying questions posed in Chapter 2.[3] The first question is the *source* of the impact on statutes, and in particular whether sections 3 and 4 of the HRA apply to statutes in litigation between private parties. The second, related question is the extent to which the Convention is *horizontally applicable* to relations between private parties under legislation. Third, there is the question of whether the courts are to give effect to Convention *rights* or *values* when faced with an offending statute. In all three respects the impact of the HRA on legislation differs significantly from its impact on common law.

The source of the HRA's impact on primary legislation – which will be the focus of this chapter so as to avoid complications relating to subordinate legislation – is found in the twin provisions of section 3 (interpretation) and section 4 (declarations of incompatibility). The drafters of

2 *Ibid.* at 13.
3 See Chapter 2; and refer to that chapter for the terminology used here.

the HRA took care to ensure that primary legislation would be insulated from the general duty that section 6 imposes on public authorities not to act incompatibly with Convention rights. Thus, Parliament does not act as a public authority when it enacts legislation,[4] and public authorities including the courts do not act unlawfully when they enforce a statute that cannot be rendered compatible with the Convention by interpretation.[5]

The courts have applied section 3 or section 4 to legislation irrespective of whether the parties to the case are private or public bodies. The justification for doing so has not been explored in great detail in the case law, but the main reasons do emerge. The relevant HRA provisions are broadly worded in most respects, and there are no stated exceptions for legislation on private legal relations. In X v. Y,[6] the Court of Appeal examined this question and held that section 3 was applicable to a statutory unfair dismissal claim against a private employer, arguing that it would be anomalous for the same legislation to be interpreted differently depending upon whether a public or private employer was involved. In Wilson v. First County Trust Ltd (No. 2),[7] a case concerning legislation on consumer credit agreements, the House of Lords had accepted obiter that both sections 3 and 4 were applicable, although in this case they did not apply retrospectively. The House of Lords applied section 3 without comment in Ghaidan v. Godin-Mendoza,[8] where it held that a private landlord was obliged to grant a statutory tenancy to the same-sex partner of the deceased tenant under a provision of the Rent Act 1977, which referred to a person 'living with the original tenant as his or her wife or husband'.[9]

Private litigants also need to establish the horizontal applicability of the Convention in the circumstances of their case.[10] This is the first-level question that is familiar in common law cases, as the UK courts have asked themselves whether the state has a positive obligation under a particular Article to protect individuals from the actions of other private persons.[11] The enquiry may seem unnecessary in section 3 cases, since the state has already intervened by enacting legislation which governs the situation. The Ghaidan decision also appeared to pass rapidly over this question, as

---

4 HRA, s. 6(3).
5 HRA, s. 6(2)(a): see Wilson v. First County Trust Ltd (No. 2) [2003] UKHL 40, [2004] 1 AC 816 at [25] ('Wilson').
6 [2004] EWCA Civ. 662, [2004] ICR 1634 at [57]. Also discussed in Chapter 16.
7 [2003] UKHL 40, [2004] 1 AC 816. Discussed further in Chapter 13.
8 [2004] UKHL 30, [2004] 2 AC 557 ('Ghaidan').   9 Schedule 1, para. 2(2).
10 See Chapter 1, pp. 7–11.   11 See Chapter 7 for further discussion.

the House of Lords found the provisions of the Rent Act engaged Article 14 read with Article 8, and proceeded to consider whether the statute was discriminatory.[12] What enabled the House of Lords to do so, however, was a Strasbourg ruling on precisely this point in which Austrian legislation was found to be discriminatory because it granted succession rights in private tenancies to opposite-sex partners only.[13]

In general it remains necessary for a UK court to enquire into the applicability of the Convention to private legal relations. As Gavin Phillipson puts it, this issue 'must be investigated in *all* cases, *including* those involving statutes, since the question here is whether there are any Convention obligations in play at all, not yet how the court is to give effect to them'.[14] This conclusion rests in part on the decision of the UK courts to treat Strasbourg case law as a 'ceiling' when determining the content of Convention rights, especially in cases concerning legislation.[15] A court might exceed this ceiling in a section 3 case if it were to forgo the enquiry into whether the Convention imposes obligations on the state to protect private persons from one another in the subject matter regulated by the statute. Nonetheless, the presence of a statute makes some difference to this enquiry, both in Strasbourg and domestically, as it brings negative as well as positive Convention obligations into play: for example, landowners challenging adverse possession statutes have invoked the negative obligation that Article 1 of the First Protocol imposes on states not to deprive persons of their possessions.[16]

The HRA case law illustrates that courts will establish that the Convention is horizontally applicable before invoking section 3 in a private law case. In *X* v. *Y*,[17] the court investigated Strasbourg case law on Article 8 to assess the extent of the state's obligations to protect an individual's privacy from incursions by other persons.[18] The claimant ultimately failed to show that it was a breach of this right for the statute to allow his employer to dismiss him on the basis of a criminal conviction for having sex in a

---

12 *Ghaidan* at [8]–[24].   13 *Karner* v. *Austria* (2004) 38 EHRR 24.

14 G. Phillipson, 'Clarity Postponed: Horizontal Effect after *Campbell*', in H. Fenwick, R. Masterman and G. Phillipson (eds.), *Judicial Reasoning under the UK Human Rights Act* (Cambridge University Press, 2007), p. 150 (emphasis in original).

15 See Chapter 5, pp. 92ff.

16 *Beaulane Properties* v. *Palmer* [2005] EWHC 817 (Ch), [2006] Ch 79; *Pye* v. *United Kingdom* (2008) 46 EHRR 45, discussed in Chapter 12, p. 271.

17 *X* v. *Y* at [51]–[52], [60]–[62]. The Court of Appeal reasoned that unless the conviction itself breached the right to privacy, there was no Convention difficulty about dismissing the claimant for the commission of a criminal offence.

18 *X* v. *Y* at [37]–[42].

public toilet (the court noted that the applicant did not challenge this conviction on Convention grounds). Moreover, before *Ghaidan* reached the House of Lords, the Court of Appeal had already noted that while Article 14 read with Article 8 was applicable to private relations between landlord, tenant and occupier in this case, other Convention rights might not be.[19]

The power to issue declarations of incompatibility under section 4 is also available in cases between private parties, likewise on condition that the court finds that an Article of the Convention is applicable and has been breached. The House of Lords had indicated obiter in *Wilson* that a declaration of incompatibility could be issued in a case between private parties; *Bellinger* v. *Bellinger*[20] was the first case in which it did so, declaring that the Matrimonial Causes Act 1973 breached Articles 8 and 12 by preventing transsexual persons from marrying in the acquired gender. Notably, *Ghaidan*, *Wilson* and *Bellinger* all originated as cases between private parties, but the final appeals in each case saw substantial arguments being presented by Ministers of the Crown. Section 5 obliges a court that is considering making a declaration of incompatibility to give the Crown an opportunity to intervene, which confirms that declarations of incompatibility are designed to be available in cases between private parties. In practice, however, there is a risk that the arguments for the Crown may distort the conduct of the case, particularly when, as in *Wilson*, none of the original parties participates in the final appeal. There is a clear risk of undermining legal certainty if the Crown concedes that a highly strained interpretation is 'possible' under section 3, perhaps in an effort to avoid the political fall-out associated with a declaration of incompatibility.[21] Counsel for the Secretary of State made such a concession in the event that the court should find a *prima facie* breach of Convention rights in *Ghaidan*,[22] and this may have encouraged the House of Lords to make bold use of section 3 here.

Having established that sections 3 and 4 are available in a case between private parties, the next mapping question to consider is what *effect* these

---

19 *Ghaidan* [2003] Ch 380 at [5].   20 [2003] UKHL 21, [2003] 2 AC 467 ('*Bellinger*').

21 The political pressures associated with declarations of incompatibility are discussed at p. 76 below. Lord Scott criticised government counsel for conceding a s. 3 interpretation in *Secretary of State for the Home Department* v. *F* [2009] UKHL 28, [2010] 2 AC 269, a case dealing with statutory control orders in respect of persons suspected of terrorism.

22 *Ghaidan* v. *Godin-Mendoza* [2004] UKHL 30, [2004] 2 AC 557 at 563.

provisions can achieve in cases where a statute appears *prima facie* to breach the Convention. Together, these sections provide a more comprehensive set of judicial responses to statutory breaches of the Convention than section 6 alone does in common law cases. Because there is no equivalent of the declaration of incompatibility in common law cases, judges may find themselves confronted with the issue of whether a breach of Convention rights is beyond their incremental powers of common law development to remedy.[23] By contrast, if a statutory breach of Convention rights cannot be remedied by interpretation under section 3, the courts will usually exercise their power to issue a declaration of incompatibility under section 4. In certain narrow circumstances they have declined to do so, notably when the breach of a Convention right could not be attributed to particular provisions of a statute, but rather reflected a lacuna in the law.[24] This approach ensures that the declaration of incompatibility does not become a mechanism for prompting Parliament to reform areas of the common law, although the courts remain free, as they always have been, to call for legislative reforms.[25]

The types of effect that sections 3 and 4 have on statutes are quite different, of course. A declaration of incompatibility has no legal effect on the validity of a statute, and if it is regarded as having a practical effect of inducing Parliament to amend the offending statute – a question which is discussed in the next part of this chapter – then this would be an intermediate horizontal effect. On the other hand, the interpretative function of courts under section 3 produces an indirect horizontal effect: the courts do not claim that the Convention rights override legislation, which would be direct effect; instead, they seek to protect Convention rights via the interpretation of particular provisions in a statute.[26] This, in turn, raises the question of whether interpretation results in the protection of Convention *rights* or *values*. So far, legislation and the common law seem to have fared differently in this respect. Courts often present their common

---

23 Phillipson, 'Clarity Postponed', p. 150, and see Chapter 6 for further discussion of this point.

24 *In Re S (Minors) (Care Order: Implementation of Care Plan)* [2002] UKHL 10, [2002] 2 AC 291 at [84]–[86].

25 Indeed, after *In Re S* Parliament enacted provisions in the Adoption and Children Act 2002, which responded to the judicial concerns expressed in that case. See T. Hickman, *Public Law after the Human Rights Act* (Oxford: Hart, 2010), p. 96.

26 The House of Lords emphasised, *In Re S* at [41], that a court 'should identify clearly the particular statutory provision or provisions' on which a s. 3 interpretation was based.

law decisions as protecting the values reflected in, or underpinning, the Convention: this would be a weak indirect effect.[27] By contrast, courts use section 3 to produce a strong indirect effect by interpreting legislation so as to protect a particular Convention right or rights that they have already identified. For example, the House of Lords in *Ghaidan* produced a section 3 interpretation of the Rent Act 1977 that was designed to protect the rights of same-sex couples under Article 14 read with Article 8, and the leading judgment began by determining the content of these Convention rights in the circumstances of the case.

It may seem obvious that courts should use section 3 to give effect to particular rights in the Convention rather than its underlying values. This impression is strengthened by the arguments presented in section 3 cases, as parties often seek, in the alternative, a declaration of incompatibility in respect of specified Convention rights. But in principle there are other ways in which the Convention could inform the interpretation of statutes. Courts in the United States, for example, have developed rights-based techniques of statutory interpretation which are designed to avoid challenges to the constitutionality of legislation.[28] Avoidance doctrines are not a precise means of protecting particular constitutional rights, and tend to involve only an abbreviated form of rights review as the court will adopt any tenable interpretation that avoids conflict with a constitutional right. Transposed into the context of the HRA, an avoidance doctrine would protect Convention values rather than the precise content of Convention rights. There might be certain advantages if the courts were to use this approach in section 3 cases between private parties, since the focus on values may make it easier to balance competing Convention rights, for example a landlord's property rights under P1–1, which some commentators suggest the *Ghaidan* judgments did not properly address.[29]

It is, nonetheless, clear that the courts have decided to treat section 3 as a precise interpretative tool for giving effect to particular Convention rights, rather than a general licence to promote Convention values. Several factors may account for this approach. The most important of these is the current judicial attitude to the duty to 'take into account' Strasbourg

---

27 Chapter 2, pp. 39ff.
28 F. Schauer, '*Ashwander* Revisited', *Supreme Court Review* (1995) 71.
29 I. Leigh and R. Masterman, *Making Rights Real: the Human Rights Act in its First Decade* (Oxford: Hart, 2008), p. 256 and D. Mead, 'Rights, Relationships and Retrospectivity: the Impact of Convention Rights on Pre-existing Private Relationships following *Wilson* and *Ghaidan*', *Public Law* (2005), 459 at 466. It appears that the landlord did not invoke P1–1.

jurisprudence when interpreting the Convention.[30] As long as judges regard the Strasbourg case law as a 'ceiling', particularly in cases involving legislation, they will have reason to prefer interpretative methods that enable them to modify legislation precisely to the extent needed to comply with Strasbourg views on the content of particular Convention rights. This approach to section 3 appears more likely to ensure exact compliance than an interpretative avoidance doctrine that might err on the side of generosity in protecting Convention values. Moreover, it has been argued that the considerable body of Strasbourg case law provides greater legal certainty to litigants if it is closely adhered to than if the courts craft a domestic view of the Convention while interpreting legislation.[31] Finally, the courts have come to view their interpretative function under section 3 as the 'principal remedial measure'[32] in cases where legislation *prima facie* appears incompatible with Convention rights. Section 3 can hardly serve as a remedy unless it can be used to correct breaches of particular Convention rights. This view of section 3 has emerged from the cases in which courts have contrasted their interpretative function with their power to issue declarations of incompatibility, which is considered next.

4.2 Declarations of incompatibility

The declaration of incompatibility is best known as a mechanism that respects Parliamentary sovereignty, as the HRA stipulates that it has no legal effect on the validity of a statute.[33] Most commentators have focused on questions surrounding Parliament's response to declarations, including whether the legislature ought to comply by amending a statute to bring it into conformity with the judgment of the court, and whether a reliable practice of such compliance has, in fact, been established.[34] It

---

30 Section 2(1), discussed in Chapter 5.

31 P. Sales, 'A Comparison of the Principle of Legality and Section 3 of the Human Rights Act 1998', *Law Quarterly Review*, 125 (2009), 598 at 613–14.

32 *Ghaidan* at [39] *per* Lord Steyn.

33 The HRA stipulates that the declaration of incompatibility 'does not affect the validity, continuing operation or enforcement of any incompatible primary legislation' (s. 4(6)(a)) and 'is not binding on the parties to the proceedings' (s. 4(6)(b)).

34 On these questions see A. Young, *Parliamentary Sovereignty and the Human Rights Act* (Oxford: Hart, 2009); A. Kavanagh, *Constitutional Review under the Human Rights Act* (Cambridge University Press, 2009), ch. 11; M. Elliott, 'Parliamentary Sovereignty and the New Constitutional Order: Legislative Freedom, Political Reality and Convention', *Legal Studies*, 22 (2002), 340; F. Klug, 'A Bill of Rights: Do We Need One or Do We Already Have One?', *Public Law* (2007), 701.

is important not to overlook the interim consequences of declarations of incompatibility, however, particularly as they affect private parties: the continued enforcement of the statute does have the benefit of preserving legal certainty during this period, albeit at the expense of the Convention rights of the persons concerned. These interim consequences will be borne in mind when discussing the two main questions that are pertinent to declarations of incompatibility: first, whether they have a reliable practical effect of inducing Parliament to comply and, second, what the circumstances are in which a court will issue a declaration of incompatibility.

A number of scholars argue that declarations of incompatibility now have the practical effect of virtually compelling Parliament to comply by amending the legislation concerned.[35] The record shows a slow but consistent accumulation of amendments designed to comply with declarations of incompatibility.[36] It is true that long delays have sometimes occurred before Parliament, or the executive,[37] has made these amendments, but as yet neither institution has repudiated a declaration of incompatibility. The sample is still fairly small. In the period from October 2000 until January 2009,[38] the courts made seventeen declarations of incompatibility that became final in the sense that they were no longer subject to appeal. Three of these declarations related to legislation that had already been amended before proceedings were instituted, and in some of these cases there was no legislative response: for example, Parliament did not legislate to compensate widowers who had suffered discrimination in tax and welfare law.[39] Eleven of the remaining fourteen declarations led to

---

35 Elliott, 'Parliamentary Sovereignty'; Klug, 'A Bill of Rights'; H. Fenwick, *Human Rights and Civil Liberties*, 4th edn. (Oxford: Routledge-Cavendish, 2007), pp. 189–90.

36 For an overview of declarations of incompatibility issued since commencement, see *Joint Committee on Human Rights, Enhancing Parliament's Role in Relation to Human Rights: Fifteenth Report of Session 2009–2010* (2010 HC 455; 2010 HL 85) and Secretary of State for Justice, *Responding to Human Rights Judgments: Government Response to the Joint Committee on Human Rights' Thirty-first Report of Session 2007–2008*, Cm 7524 (2009).

37 HRA, s.10 empowers the executive to amend primary legislation by remedial order so as to bring it into conformity with a declaration of incompatibility. The executive used this power only once during the period from 2000 to 2009.

38 *Responding to Human Rights Judgments*, pp. 42–56 sets out declarations of incompatibility, legislation enacted in response thereto and the views of the government as at January 2009 on declarations to which there had not yet been a response.

39 The cases in which widowers won declarations of incompatibility were *R (Hooper)* v. *Secretary of State for Work and Pensions* [2005] UKHL 29, [2005] 1 WLR 1681, and *R (Wilkinson)* v. *Inland Revenue Commissioners* [2005] UKHL 30, [2005] 1 WLR 1718.

legislative changes, while the government was still considering its position in relation to the other three declarations.[40] The changes Parliament makes in response to declarations of incompatibility are sometimes extensive. In the private law context, for example, the Gender Recognition Act 2004 provides in detail for the Convention rights of transsexuals that were the subject of the declaration of incompatibility in *Bellinger* v. *Bellinger*,[41] although it should be noted that Parliament was already considering legislation on this topic at the time of the *Bellinger* decision, as the Strasbourg court had identified breaches of Convention rights in *Goodwin* v. *United Kingdom*.[42] The Act establishes an administrative mechanism that enables transsexual persons to marry after obtaining a certificate of acquired gender, and also amends other areas of law including property and succession.

The legislative response to declarations of incompatibility is often severely delayed, however. It is not uncommon for more than a year to pass before amending statutes are brought into force; more than five years elapsed between the declaration in *R (M)* v. *Secretary of State for Health*,[43] and the entry into force of the Mental Health Act 2007 which modified the problematic definition of 'nearest relative',[44] which in *M*'s case applied to her adoptive father who had abused her. Particularly problematic are the delays that occur while the government considers its position, since in these cases the litigant has no idea what to expect. A notorious example of this is the protracted controversy about extending the voting rights of prisoners.[45] There is also the declaration in *Baiai*,[46] which concerns statutory provisions that make it harder for persons subject to immigration control to marry unless they do so in the Church of England. Although this appears to be a mere technicality, Parliament had not yet altered the legislation at the time of writing, more than two years after the House of Lords declared it incompatible. The Joint Committee on Human Rights has criticised the government for its delays in deciding

---

40 *Responding to Human Rights Judgments*, p. 41.
41 [2003] UKHL 21, [2003] 2 AC 467.   42 (2002) 35 EHRR 18.
43 [2003] EWHC 1094 (Admin), [2003] ACD 95.   44 Mental Health Act 1983, s. 26.
45 The Court of Session in *Smith* v. *Scott* [2007] CSIH 9, 2007 SC 345 issued a declaration of incompatibility in respect of s. 3(1) of the Representation of the People Act 1983. The Strasbourg court had earlier found the United Kingdom to be in breach of Art. 3 of the First Protocol in the Grand Chamber judgment in *Hirst* v. *United Kingdom* (2006) 42 EHRR 41.
46 *R (Baiai)* v. *Secretary of State for the Home Department* [2008] UKHL 53, [2009] 1 AC 287.

what legislative proposals to introduce in response to declarations of incompatibility, and has called for such decisions to be made within six months of a declaration being issued.[47]

The Strasbourg court, too, has had occasion to comment on the effectiveness of declarations of incompatibility, holding that the declaration of incompatibility is not a domestic remedy that UK applicants are obliged to exhaust.[48] Thus, for an individual bringing a claim under the HRA, a declaration of incompatibility does not prevent a further claim to the Strasbourg court for relief by way of compensation in a particular case. The court left open the possibility that a 'long-standing and established practice'[49] of executive and legislative compliance might persuade it otherwise.

UK commentators have pointed out that Parliament and the executive are under special kinds of pressure which increase the likelihood that they will comply with declarations of incompatibility. Aileen Kavanagh summarises these pressures as follows:

> The *political* repercussions of resisting a judicial finding of a rights violation, combined with the *legal* repercussions in the (highly likely) event of an adverse finding in Strasbourg, set against the background of the traditional comity between the three branches of government and the public respect for the courts, means that a declaration of incompatibility will tend to be followed rather than ignored.[50]

Political pressures should not be underestimated: once the courts have made a declaration of incompatibility, political actors risk undermining public respect for the judiciary if they do not comply with it.[51] Moreover, it is plausible to argue that Strasbourg is likely to find against the United Kingdom after the domestic courts have issued a declaration of incompatibility: the likelihood of this is increased by the cautious approach of the UK courts in treating Strasbourg cases as a 'ceiling' when determining the

---

47 *Enhancing Parliament's Role*, para. 184.
48 *Burden* v. *United Kingdom* (2007) 44 EHRR 51. See further M. Amos, 'The Impact of the Human Rights Act on the United Kingdom's Performance before the European Court of Human Rights', *Public Law* (2007), 655.
49 *Burden* at [39].
50 Kavanagh, *Constitutional Review*, p. 287 (emphasis in original). See also Elliott, 'Parliamentary Sovereignty', pp. 348–9.
51 In practice Ministers have treated declarations of incompatibility as binding, and this has arguably enabled them to shift responsibility for unpopular legislative changes to the courts: see F. Davis, 'The Human Rights Act and Juridification: Saving Democracy from Law', *Politics*, 30 (2010), 91.

compatibility of legislation.[52] The question remains, however, whether these pressures are sufficient to force Parliament to comply with every declaration of incompatibility. Kavanagh does not put the likelihood of compliance so high, citing countervailing political pressures in controversial cases.[53] At the time of writing, it appeared that the disenfranchisement of prisoners might be such a case, as this declaration remained controversial and had not yet drawn any firm legislative proposals from the government.[54]

It is not yet safe to conclude that declarations of incompatibility will predictably lead to compliance by Parliament. This is not simply a question of political expediency in controversial cases. There are theorists who argue that Parliament would in certain circumstances be justified in ignoring a declaration of incompatibility, or passing new legislation at odds with it, as part of a democratic dialogue with the courts regarding the content of the Convention rights. Most starkly, some have argued that *all* declarations of incompatibility are merely provisional and that Parliament may ignore a declaration whenever it sees fit to do so.[55] Others argue that Parliament will sometimes be justified in doing so: for example, Alison Young argues that Parliament may take a different view from the courts in certain cases, including those that present 'contestable' rights issues.[56] By contrast, Tom Hickman offers a model of dialogue in which the courts play the leading role: Hickman argues that it is for the courts to determine the meaning of Convention rights, but that judges ought also to foster the acceptance of rights by the legislature and executive, and to this end should exercise the 'passive virtues' of adjudication by sometimes declining jurisdiction or giving narrow rulings.[57] Both Young and Hickman point out that dialogue can be conducted via section 3 as well as section 4, since Parliament may enact legislation in response to a section 3 interpretation with which it disagrees.[58]

---

52 Chapter 5.   53 Kavanagh, *Constitutional Review*, p. 291.

54 See cases cited in n. 45 above.

55 T. Campbell, 'Incorporation through Interpretation', in T. Campbell, K. Ewing and A. Tomkins (eds.), *Sceptical Essays on Human Rights* (Oxford University Press, 2002) and D. Nicol, 'Statutory Interpretation and Human Rights after *Anderson*', *Public Law* (2004), 274.

56 Young, *Parliamentary Sovereignty and the HRA*, pp. 125–7, 130–8.

57 Hickman, *Public Law after the HRA*, pp. 71–2, 83–7.

58 Young, *Parliamentary Sovereignty and the HRA*, pp. 142–3; Hickman, *Public Law after the HRA*, pp. 81–3. Kavanagh, *Constitutional Review*, pp. 130–1 also points out that Parliament can legislate in response to s. 3 interpretations, but does not characterise this as dialogue.

This point is an important one in relation to the second question that was posed at the outset of this discussion: namely, the circumstances in which the courts will issue a declaration of incompatibility. This question may be loosely described as the choice between section 3 and section 4, arising in cases where the court has determined that a statute, as ordinarily interpreted, breaches a Convention right. More precisely, the structure of the choice is that the courts must first exhaust their interpretative function under section 3.[59] The wording of section 3 imposes a duty, whereas section 4 confers a power to issue a declaration of incompatibility, although, as already noted, the courts will generally exercise this power unless the incompatibility is not attributable to the statute but rather reflects a lacuna in the common law.[60] Academic discussion of the choice between these sections has often focused on the institutional features of the courts and the legislature, such as their vastly different capacities for law-making.[61] The insight of Young and Hickman that dialogue can be conducted via section 3 as well as section 4 strikes an important note of caution in this regard, since it entails the point that the legislative capacity of Parliament cannot simply be reckoned as an advantage pertaining to declarations of incompatibility. Parliament can legislate in response to a section 3 interpretation too. In fact, it did so after the decision in *Ghaidan*, albeit only to clarify that persons living as civil partners were entitled to succeed to a statutory tenancy.[62]

The leading House of Lords decisions confirm that while Parliament's ability to carry out wide-ranging and precise law reform supports the issuing of a declaration of incompatibility, it is not a sufficient reason for doing so. In addition, there must be reasons *against* a section 3 inter- pretation. This is illustrated by *Bellinger*,[63] where the House of Lords considered that it was inappropriate to use the interpretation to accom- modate transsexuals within the statutory provision that parties to a mar- riage had to be 'respectively male and female'.[64] Lord Nicholls pointed out that such an interpretation would leave the law in a confused state:

---

59 *Wilson* at [14]–[16].   60 See p. 71.
61 See A. Kavanagh, 'The Elusive Divide between Interpretation and Legislation under the Human Rights Act 1998', *Oxford Journal of Legal Studies*, 24 (2002), 259 at 271–4; A. Young, '*Ghaidan* v. *Godin-Mendoza*: Avoiding the Deference Trap', *Public Law* (2005), 23 at 31–2.
62 The Civil Partnership Act 2004 amended Schedule 1, para. 2 of the Rent Act 1977 to enable 'a person who was living with the original tenant as if they were civil partners' also to inherit a statutory tenancy.
63 [2003] UKHL 21, [2003] 2 AC 467.
64 Section 11(c) of the Matrimonial Causes Act 1973.

there might be doubts about the scope of the interpretation as a precedent for other transsexuals who had undergone lesser degrees of gender re-assignment treatment than Mrs Bellinger, and also the many legal consequences that recognition of a transsexual marriage would have in other areas of the law.[65] Such disadvantages inevitably attach to a section 3 interpretation, even if an ample interpretative power is assumed, since courts are able to exercise that power only through precedential law-making.[66] In other cases where the courts have issued declarations of incompatibility the subject matter has likewise been where the incompatibility could not be adequately cured by interpretation, for example, where multiple provisions in a statutory scheme were incompatible with Convention rights.[67]

The time during which the adequacy of a section 3 interpretation should be compared with the effect of a section 4 declaration of incompatibility is the interim period, which lasts until Parliament amends the statute in question. Once Parliament has intervened, as we have seen that it may do in either case, the difference between sections 3 and 4 disappears. This brings into focus the advantage of declarations of incompatibility, which is that they preserve legal certainty for persons subject to the statute. Of course, certainty is secured only at the cost of delaying the legal protection of the Convention rights of the parties and others, but this was a choice deliberately made in the HRA to avoid the disruption that other jurisdictions experience when legislation is struck down. Moreover, responsibility for the length of the delay lies with Parliament and the executive, as the Joint Committee on Human Rights has pointed out.[68] Thus, the courts are able to enhance legal certainty by issuing declarations of incompatibility. On the other hand, their interpretative function under section 3 offers the opportunity to provide immediate protection of Convention rights, and the legal certainty implications of innovative interpretive techniques require further examination.

4.3 Interpretation of statutes as a remedy

Interpretation, unlike a declaration of incompatibility, does give legal effect to Convention rights. Courts have described section 3 as a 'remedy' insofar as it enables them to produce rights-compatible

---

65 *Bellinger* at [40]–[48].

66 See *International Transport Roth GmbH* v. *Secretary of State for the Home Department* [2002] EWCA Civ. 158, [2003] QB 728, discussed below, p. 86.

67 *Ghaidan* at [33].   68 *Enhancing Parliament's Role*, para. 184.

interpretations of statutes that would otherwise have been found to breach the Convention.[69] Examples of this approach at House of Lords level include the private law case of *Ghaidan* and many public law cases, including decisions which read in an exception to the bar on sexual history evidence in rape trials,[70] alleviated the reverse burdens imposed by certain statutory offences,[71] broadened the scope of inquests[72] and expanded the disclosure requirements in control order proceedings.[73] The main challenge in the remainder of this chapter is to determine the extent of, and the justification for, remedial interpretation in private law cases.

The remedial use of section 3 has been defended by a number of theorists, including Aileen Kavanagh,[74] Alison Young[75] and Tom Hickman.[76] As noted above, Young and Hickman rely on the remedial use of section 3 as one of the routes by which the courts can engage in dialogue with the legislature about the content of the Convention rights. Theorists who propose rival models of dialogue have thus far been the most prominent critics of the remedial use of section 3: they would strongly prefer it if courts were to rely solely on declarations of incompatibility to express a legally non-binding view that a statute breaches a Convention right, rather than using section 3 to give immediate legal effect to their view of the Convention right concerned.[77] Finally, there have been a few outright critics of the remedial use of section 3 who have called into question its impact on Parliamentary sovereignty and legislative intention, which are the foundations of traditional, pre-HRA doctrines of statutory interpretation.[78] The views of this last group deserve particular attention in the context of private law cases, since there are reasons to be concerned about how changes in interpretative technique will affect private persons.

---

69 *Ghaidan* at [46] *per* Lord Steyn.
70 *R* v. *A (No. 2)* [2001] UKHL 25, [2002] 1 AC 45.
71 *R* v. *Lambert* [2001] UKHL 37, [2002] 2 AC 545; *Attorney-General's Reference (No. 4 of 2000)* [2004] UKHL 43, [2005] 1 AC 264.
72 *R (Middleton)* v. *Western Somerset Coroner* [2004] UKHL 10, [2004] 2 AC 182.
73 *Secretary of State for the Home Department* v. *MB* [2007] UKHL 46, [2008] 1 AC 440; *Secretary of State for the Home Department* v. *F* [2009] UKHL 28, [2009] 3 WLR 74.
74 *Constitutional Review.*
75 *Parliamentary Sovereignty and the HRA*, chs. 5 and 6.
76 *Public Law after the HRA*, ch. 3.
77 Campbell, 'Incorporation through Interpretation' and Nicol, 'Statutory Interpretation and Human Rights after *Anderson*'.
78 G. Marshall, 'The Lynchpin of Parliamentary Intention: Lost, Stolen or Strained', *Public Law* (2003), 236 and R. Ekins, 'A Critique of Radical Approaches to Rights-consistent Statutory Interpretation', *European Human Rights Law Review*, 6 (2003), 641.

Commentators have pointed out that the use of section 3 may undermine legal certainty for private persons who enter into legal relationships that are wholly or partly regulated by a statutory framework. Concentrating on *Ghaidan*, Ian Leigh and Roger Masterman observe that the House of Lords neglected to explore the private law dimensions of this case.[79] A private landlord, Mr Ghaidan, was obliged by the House of Lords decision to grant a statutory tenancy to the same-sex partner of the deceased tenant. This result was hard to foresee from the wording of the statute, which refers to a person 'living with the original tenant as his or her wife or husband'.[80] Leigh and Masterman argue that 'from the point of view of legal certainty the decision in *Ghaidan* is open to criticism'.[81] As David Mead puts it, the decision 'diminishes the consensual element of the original relationship'.[82] Mead's criticism draws attention to the legal certainty needs of contracting parties who act on expectations as to the likely interpretation of statutes that have a bearing on their transaction.

The facts of *Ghaidan* do not raise particularly strong concerns regarding legal certainty, however. While the judicial expansion of tenancy succession rights from opposite-sex to same-sex couples introduces a degree of legal uncertainty, this should be seen alongside the factual uncertainty that was always present, as landlords could not predict whether their tenants would invite an opposite-sex partner to live with them. In this respect the Rent Act 1977 had simply not created a precise expectation upon which landlords could rely. To assess the wider significance of legal certainty concerns, it is necessary first to examine the extent to which remedial interpretation in section 3 cases differs from traditional statutory interpretation doctrines, and then to evaluate whether this has led to an unjustifiable diminution of legal certainty where precise statutory frameworks are in place in other areas of private law.

The idea of remedial interpretation is not without precedent in pre-HRA doctrines of statutory interpretation. Courts were already able to protect Convention rights when resolving ambiguities in legislation, since the Convention was an international treaty binding the United Kingdom.[83] The courts had employed this technique in cases between

---

79 Leigh and Masterman, *Making Rights Real*, pp. 252–6.
80 Schedule 1, para. 2(2) of the Rent Act 1977.
81 Leigh and Masterman, *Making Rights Real*, p. 253.
82 Mead, 'Rights, Relationships and Retrospectivity', p. 465.
83 *R* v. *Secretary of State for the Home Department, ex p. Brind* [1991] 1 AC 696.

private bodies, notably when interpreting defamation statutes.[84] The courts employ stronger presumptions to protect certain common law rights and principles: these presumptions operate as default legal rules unless the statute provides to the contrary by express words or necessary implication.[85] In the leading case of *Simms*,[86] Lord Hoffmann explained that a presumption of this kind, the 'principle of legality', enabled UK courts to protect common law fundamental rights, such as the rights of access to court and freedom of speech. Judicial insistence that these rights can be displaced only by express words or necessary implication serves to ensure, in Lord Hoffmann's words, that 'Parliament must squarely confront what it is doing and accept the political cost'.

The remedial aspect of presumptions concerning rights should not be overstated, however. Defenders of orthodox accounts of Parliamentary sovereignty argue that in most instances the use of these presumptions is consistent with legislative intention.[87] When a statute is ambiguous, or is merely silent on the issue of rights, courts are justified in giving effect to the common law fundamental rights presumption as it is part of the background against which Parliament legislates. Indeed, this is required by the contextual approach to legislative intention, according to which the content of an enactment is ascertained from the full text and the context in which it was enacted, including existing law dealing with the same subject matter. The contextual approach is firmly established in contemporary UK statutory interpretation.[88] Even a work that acknowledges theoretical critiques of the corporate legislative intention, *Cross on Statutory Interpretation*,[89] argues that the judicial practice of using the contextual approach to ascertain legislative intention is valuable, since it treats legislation as an act of communication and thereby promotes legal certainty and the rule of law.

---

84 *McCartan Turkington Breen* v. *Times Newspapers Ltd* [2001] 2 AC 277; *Rantzen* v. *Mirror Group Newspapers* [1994] QB 670.

85 J. Bell and G. Engle (eds.), *Cross on Statutory Interpretation*, 3rd edn. (London: Butterworths, 1995), pp. 165–7.

86 *R* v. *Secretary of State for the Home Department, ex p. Simms* [2000] 2 AC 115 at 130–1 ('*Simms*').

87 Sales, 'A Comparison of the Principle of Legality and Section 3 of the Human Rights Act 1998', pp. 604–7; R. Ekins, 'The Intention of Parliament', *Public Law* (2010), 709 at 719; J. Goldsworthy, 'Legislative Intentions, Legislative Supremacy, and Legal Positivism', *San Diego Law Review*, 42 (2005), 493 at 506–8.

88 F. Bennion, *Statutory Interpretation: A Code*, 4th edn. (London: Butterworths, 2002), pp. 405–14; D. Greenberg, 'The Nature of Legislative Intention and its Implications for Legislative Drafting', *Statute Law Review*, 27 (2006), 15.

89 *Cross on Statutory Interpretation*, pp. 26–31.

A few cases decided by reference to the common law presumption in favour of fundamental rights must be regarded as truly remedial, because they are hard to reconcile with the contextual approach. These are cases where the court effectively protects a common law right despite contrary indications in the text of the statute, for example, the statutory ouster clause in the case of *Anisminic*,[90] which the House of Lords did not regard as sufficient to restrict the right of access to court. Judicial reluctance to recognise contrary indications makes it difficult for Parliament to restrict those rights by paying 'the political cost', as Lord Hoffmann suggests it can,[91] and so the courts have confined this approach to protect only the most fundamental rights.[92] These rare cases may be classified together with the other forms of remedial interpretation that are currently recognised: namely, the avoidance of absurd results and the correction of drafting errors.[93] The latter two doctrines are regarded as strong forms of purposive interpretation, and must be distinguished from ordinary instances of purposive interpretation in which consideration of the statutory purpose assists judges in ascertaining the content of a statute from the text in its context.[94] The threshold for strong forms of purposive interpretation is high, as reflected in contemporary judicial notions of absurdity, and so remedial interpretations remain rare.[95]

When the courts began to apply section 3 they faced the question of whether it had expanded their capacity for remedial interpretation. The text of the HRA did not provide much guidance. The opening words of section 3, 'so far as it is possible to do so', indicate at the very least that courts should not diminish their efforts to protect Convention rights in statutory interpretation, but also envisage that they will not necessarily succeed in every case. The White Paper, *Rights Brought Home*,[96] shed some light on the purpose behind the clause that became section 3, which was said to be designed to go 'far beyond the present rule which enables the courts to take the Convention into account in resolving any ambiguity in a legislative provision'.[97] Together, sections 3 and 4 would

---

90 *Anisminic* v. *Foreign Compensation Commission* [1969] 2 AC 147.
91 *Simms* at [131].
92 Sales, 'A Comparison of the Principle of Legality and Section 3 of the Human Rights Act 1998', p. 607.
93 *Cross on Statutory Interpretation*, pp. 99–105.
94 *Cross on Statutory Interpretation*, p. 49.
95 J. Horder, 'Judges' Use of Moral Arguments in Interpreting Statutes', in T. Endicott, J. Getzler and E. Peel (eds.), *Properties of Law: Essays in Honour of Jim Harris* (Oxford University Press, 2006), pp. 86–91.
96 Cm 3782 (1997).   97 *Rights Brought Home* at [2.7].

serve the overall purpose of the HRA by making Convention rights 'more directly accessible' in domestic courts.[98] The respective contributions that each provision would make to this aim were debated in Parliament, and Ministers played down the need for declarations of incompatibility. Lord Steyn inferred from these debates that section 3 was the appropriate remedy for most breaches of Convention rights.[99] Although this inference has been cogently criticised, it is now part of the HRA case law.[100]

Lords Steyn and Rodger have also argued that the words 'so far as it is possible to do so' in section 3 are intended to refer to the *Marleasing* doctrine.[101] The *Marleasing* judgment uses the touchstone 'so far as possible'[102] to describe the extent to which domestic courts should seek an interpretation of domestic legislation that gives effect to an EU directive dealing with the same subject matter. In some cases, UK courts have used *Marleasing* effectively to write content taken from a directive into a domestic statute; many of these decisions have been given in cases between private parties, where the directive in question lacked horizontal direct effect and so could be enforced only via interpretation of the domestic legislation.[103] The circumstances in which the courts are willing to do so remain controversial, however, in both UK and EU case law.[104] Moreover, there is a significant difference between EU directives and Convention rights, since the former have a precise content that may lend itself to being read into a statute, whereas the Convention rights are phrased in more general terms, and often require a relationship of proportionality between the statutory provisions and a legitimate objective pursued by the statute. As a result, the courts have been able to extract little guidance from the *Marleasing* case law in section 3 cases, and, in fact, the reverse

---

98 *Rights Brought Home* at [1.18]–[1.19].

99 *R* v. *A (No. 2)* at [44] and *Ghaidan* at [46].

100 Marshall, 'The Lynchpin of Parliamentary Intention', pp. 238–9 and A. Kavanagh, 'Choosing between Sections 3 and 4 of the Human Rights Act: Judicial Reasoning after *Ghaidan* v. *Mendoza*', in H. Fenwick, R. Masterman and G. Phillipson (eds.), *Judicial Reasoning under the UK Human Rights Act* (Cambridge University Press, 2007), p. 131.

101 Case C-106/89, *Marleasing SA* v. *La Comercial Internacional de Alimentación SA* [1990] ECR I-4135 ('*Marleasing*'), cited in *Ghaidan* at [45] *per* Lord Steyn and [118] *per* Lord Rodger.

102 *Marleasing* at [8].

103 *Pickstone* v. *Freemans Plc* [1989] AC 66; *Litster* v. *Forth Dry Dock & Engineering Co. Ltd* [1990] AC 546; *Webb* v. *EMO Air Cargo (UK) Ltd (No. 2)* [1995] 3 WLR 1454, and see the cases discussed in Oliver, Chapter 10, nn. 66–8.

104 See K. Sawyer. 'The Principle of "*interprétation conforme*": How Far Can and Should National Courts Go when Interpreting Legislation Consistently with European Community Law?', *Statute Law Review*, 28 (2007), 165.

has happened as the Court of Appeal has referred to section 3 case law to guide its use of the *Marleasing* doctrine.[105]

The conclusion the House of Lords drew from the wording and legislative history of section 3 was that it authorised a two-stage approach to the interpretation of statutes, in which the second stage was distinctively remedial. Although the House of Lords had used the two-stage approach to achieve remedial results in previous section 3 cases,[106] their Lordships set out a more comprehensive explanation for this approach in *Ghaidan*,[107] which remains the leading authority. At the first stage of a section 3 case, judges have to consider whether the statute, as ordinarily interpreted, would breach a Convention right. If they find a breach they proceed to the second stage, where they seek to devise a new interpretation that renders the statute compatible with the right. The second-stage interpretation is explicitly remedial. Noting that the purpose of section 3 was to go beyond resolving ambiguities, Lord Nicholls argued that:

> it becomes impossible to suppose Parliament intended that the operation of section 3 should depend critically upon the particular form of words adopted by the parliamentary draftsman in the statutory provision under consideration.[108]

It followed that, at the second stage of section 3 analysis, an interpretation need not adhere to the language used in a statute, but only to the 'concept expressed in that language'.[109] The interpretation should give effect to the 'underlying thrust' of the statute,[110] or 'go with the grain' as Lord Rodger put it.[111] These metaphors offer little guidance in themselves. Their Lordships therefore went on to identify, using previous case law, two limits that would indicate when a court had exceeded its interpretative function: these were that a section 3 interpretation should not be inconsistent with a 'fundamental feature' of the statute, and it should not determine 'issues calling for legislative deliberation'.[112] The bulk of the passages in *Ghaidan* dealing with interpretation were devoted to

---

105 *Commissioners for HMRC v. IDT Card Services Ireland Ltd* [2006] EWCA Civ. 29, [2006] STC 1252 at [85]–[92].

106 See Kavanagh, *Constitutional Review*, ch. 2 on the development of s. 3 case law prior to *Ghaidan*.

107 *Ghaidan* at [25]–[35] *per* Lord Nicholls, [38]–[51] *per* Lord Steyn and [104]–[129] *per* Lord Rodger.

108 *Ghaidan* at [31].   109 *Ghaidan* at [31].   110 *Ghaidan* at [34].

111 *Ghaidan* at [121].   112 *Ghaidan* at [33].

explaining why an interpretation that included same-sex partners would not exceed these two limits.[113]

The two-stage approach outlined in *Ghaidan* is rather artificial and encourages courts to neglect the first stage, which is based on existing doctrines of statutory interpretation. Thus, the House of Lords quickly concluded that the statutory provision did not include same-sex partners. In doing so, it did not engage with the textual support that it might have relied on: the vagueness of the expression '*as* his or her wife or husband'[114] arguably left scope for a purposive interpretation that could have taken account of changed social views to include same-sex partners. Ironically, the House of Lords gave more careful consideration to this argument in a pre-HRA case, *Fitzpatrick*,[115] which confirmed that it was appropriate to take changed social views into account when interpreting the Rent Act; *Fitzpatrick* ultimately decided that a same-sex partner could not be included under this provision, although they were held to be part of the tenant's 'family' under another. This type of purposive interpretation, also known as updating construction, was not pursued in *Ghaidan*.

Does the second stage of *Ghaidan*'s two-stage approach shed any more light on the doctrinal basis for section 3 interpretation, insofar as it requires that the interpreter should not transgress the fundamental features of a statute and should not determine 'issues requiring legislative deliberation'?[116] The latter constraint has already been encountered as a trigger for declarations of incompatibility. It is a valid constraint, but is indifferent between particular doctrines of interpretation and, indeed, applies to common law development also: the principle merely requires that courts should not determine issues that they cannot adequately regulate by precedential law-making.[117] The former constraint, relating to fundamental features of a statute, is rather mysterious, since Parliament does not earmark certain features of a statute as fundamental. Aileen Kavanagh has argued that the fundamental features of a statute are those that are cumulatively beyond the reach of existing doctrines of interpretation.[118] For example, in the *Roth* case,[119] purposive interpretation might have

---

113 Lord Millett dissented, arguing that both limits would be exceeded.
114 Schedule 1, para. 2(2) (emphasis added).
115 *Fitzpatrick* v. *Sterling Housing Association* [2001] 1 AC 27.
116 *Ghaidan* at [33].   117 Above, p. 78.
118 Kavanagh, *Constitutional Review*, pp. 37–41.
119 *International Transport Roth GmbH* v. *Secretary of State for the Home Department* [2002] EWCA Civ. 158, [2003] QB 728. Lord Rodger cited this case to illustrate the fundamental features constraint in *Ghaidan* at [110]. Another example of a statutory scheme which the court could not reverse by s. 3 interpretation was found in *In Re S*, cited in *Ghaidan* at [34] *per* Lord Nicholls, [47] *per* Lord Steyn and [112]–[115] *per* Lord Rodger.

removed one or two of the several Convention breaches identified in a harsh scheme of reverse burdens and fixed penalties for transport operators who had unwittingly carried stowaways on board their vehicle, but no single interpretation could remove all the defects. Kavanagh argues that courts may stretch existing doctrines, however, where they consider it necessary to grant an immediate legal remedy for the breach of a Convention right: on this basis she defends the decision in *R* v. *A (No. 2)*,[120] a section 3 interpretation which made a statutory bar on sexual history evidence subject to an exception to safeguard the defendant's right to a fair trial. If the fundamental features limit is flexible in response to the merits of the case, then it does not preserve existing doctrines of statutory interpretation.

The second stage of the *Ghaidan* approach thus assumes a reservoir of interpretative power, which is subject only to limits on precedential law-making. Lord Rodger candidly presented the decision as a 'modest development' of the tenancy that the statute had granted to unmarried opposite-sex partners.[121] It would be wrong to deny that judges sometimes engage in law-making when they interpret statutes: this is evident at least in cases where the court has to resolve an ambiguity. But the difficulty in subjecting section 3 interpretation *only* to limits on precedential law-making is that it risks conflating remedial interpretation with the development of the common law. Sir Jack Beatson has written extracurially that section 3 'makes statutory provision more like common law doctrine'.[122] Beatson argues that even if courts remain within the limits of precedential law-making set out in *Ghaidan* and *Bellinger*, 'we are going to have statutes that simply do not mean what the words say. That is, it is submitted, not good for the law because it increases its opacity.'[123] The dangers of conflation between remedial interpretation and common law development are also evident in a hypothetical use of section 3 mooted by Kavanagh:

> If the House of Lords in *Ghaidan* had been faced with a Rent Act which had stated expressly that 'married couples and heterosexual cohabitees' could qualify for statutory tenancies, this would not *necessarily* preclude a section 3(1) interpretation to include same-sex couples.[124]

---

120 *R* v. *A (No. 2)*, discussed in Kavanagh, *Constitutional Review*, p. 132.
121 *Ghaidan* at [128].
122 'Common Law, Statute Law and Constitutional Law', *Statute Law Review*, 27 (2006), 1, 11.
123 Beatson, 'Common Law, Statute Law and Constitutional Law', p. 13.
124 Kavanagh, *Constitutional Review*, p. 107 (emphasis in original).

If the law on succession to tenancy was based on common law rather than statute, this conclusion would be easy to accept: it would matter less that the relevant precedent had used the words 'heterosexual co-habitees', since it is the ratio of a case that binds rather than the exact words of a judge. Statutory interpretation is different, however.[125] A novel common law precedent merely unsettles expectations in a particular area of common law, and the legislature retains the power to intervene in this area. Judicial innovation in statutory interpretation doctrines has a wider feedback effect, insofar as it hampers the ability of the legislature to exercise its law-making competence precisely and effectively.[126]

Legal certainty is an aspect of the rule of law: it is valuable to persons because it allows them to form expectations as to the content of the law and plan their conduct accordingly, including their transactions with one another which are governed by a statute.[127] On the other hand, the enactment of the HRA might be thought to have removed any expectations regarding the enforcement of legislation that may conflict with Convention rights; for every private defendant who invokes an orthodox interpretation of a statute, there may be a claimant who invokes a Convention right. This is to some extent a valid objection to legal certainty concerns, and it explains why Mead,[128] and Leigh and Masterman,[129] concentrate their critique of the use of section 3 on private law cases in which the parties formed their relationship before the entry into force of the HRA. Yet the HRA does not go as far as to remove expectations regarding the enforcement of *every* statute that is contrary to Convention rights, since enforcement will continue for some time in the event that the court issues a declaration of incompatibility. Unlike jurisdictions where courts are bound to strike down statutes that breach constitutional rights, the extent to which expectations will be unsettled here depends on the approach that UK courts take to statutory interpretation under section 3.[130]

---

125 For further discussion see Chapter 5, pp. 100ff., which argues that common law development is a judicial power which does not bring courts into conflict with Parliamentary sovereignty.

126 J. Raz, 'Intention in Interpretation', in R George (ed.), *The Autonomy of Law* (Oxford: Clarendon Press, 1996), p. 279.

127 J. Raz, *The Authority of Law* (Oxford University Press, 1983), pp. 220–1.

128 'Rights, Relationships and Retrospectivity', n. 29.

129 *Making Rights Real*, p. 256.

130 Similarly, G. De Burca, 'Giving Effect to European Community Directives', *Modern Law Review*, 55 (1992), 215 points out that the *Marleasing* doctrine does not completely

It appears from the section 3 case law that the courts have selectively sought to maintain legal certainty in certain areas of statute law, including some areas of private law. Outside the human rights context courts have sometimes taken different approaches to different areas of law: as Lord Steyn has remarked 'fiscal legislation may sometimes require a stricter approach than social welfare legislation'.[131] Areas in which the need for legal certainty is high include those in which private persons are likely to form and rely upon expectations as to the legal effect of statute law, for example the law of property. It is noticeable that despite the number of property law cases in which Convention arguments have been raised, few have resulted in section 3 interpretations.[132] This outcome is not solely due to the judicial approach to section 3 in these areas. Many cases have been resolved at the first level of HRA analysis, as the courts have generally found property legislation to be compatible with P1–1.[133] The courts have taken into account the value of legal certainty in holding some bright-line statutory rules to be proportionate interference with this qualified right, despite their harsh impact on common law rights.[134] For example, under the statute in *Wilson*[135] pawnbrokers lost their entire security if the loan agreement did not meet the prescribed statutory formalities. The protection of legal certainty in property law may be usefully contrasted to those areas of public law where highly remedial interpretations have been given under section 3, such as the law of criminal evidence and inquests.[136] It may be that courts do not consider that individuals plan their conduct based upon the statutory frameworks in these cases, and in any event these section 3 interpretations have revised the statutory framework against public authorities and in favour of the individual.

unsettle expectations in areas covered by a directive that lacks direct effect, because it does not override domestic statutes.

131 'Dynamic Interpretation Amidst an Orgy of Statutes', *European Human Rights Law Review*, (2004), 245 at 249.

132 The exception is *Beaulane Properties* v. *Palmer* [2005] EWHC 817 (Ch), [2006] Ch 79, where s. 3 was used to narrow the statutory conditions in which an adverse possession claim would succeed. The interpretation of P1–1 in this case was rejected, however, in *Pye* v. *United Kingdom* (2008) 46 EHRR 45. See further Chapter 12, p. 271.

133 See Chapter 12 for a full discussion.

134 P. Sales and B. Hooper, 'Proportionality and the Form of Law', *Law Quarterly Review*, 119 (2003), 426 argue that the Strasbourg jurisprudence on proportionality sometimes attaches greater significance to legal certainty in property cases than in other areas of law, notably family law where flexibility is considered more important in satisfying the proportionality test under Art. 8.

135 *Wilson* is discussed further in Chapter 13.   136 See cases cited in nn. 70–3 above.

Legal certainty cannot be ensured by dividing the law into different areas, however. Cases frequently arise that can be classified in more than one area. *Ghaidan* is such a case, as it concerns discrimination and the right to private life, on the one hand, and property, on the other. For this reason, legal certainty would be improved if the courts clarified the doctrinal basis of remedial interpretation under section 3, since the interpretative doctrine would apply across different areas of law. There are some traces of a purposive approach in *Ghaidan*, since Lord Nicholls argued that the 'social policy' of securing the tenancy of opposite-sex partners who made their home together applied equally to same-sex partners.[137] The current two-stage approach obscures the doctrinal foundation of section 3 interpretations, as this chapter has argued, by concentrating on the limits of precedential law-making at the second stage. It is submitted that if the courts were to clarify the doctrinal nature of statutory interpretation under section 3, and make use of declarations of incompatibility in cases that lie beyond purposive interpretation, they would be better able to maintain legal certainty for private persons while giving effect to the Convention rights.

---

137 *Ghaidan* at [35]. For a more detailed discussion of purposive elements of this decision, see J. van Zyl Smit, 'The New Purposive Interpretation of Statutes: HRA Section 3 after *Ghaidan v Godin-Mendoza*', *Modern Law Review*, 70 (2007), 294.

Precedent

ALISON L. YOUNG[*]

Section 2(1) of the HRA requires that courts and tribunals determining an issue concerning Convention rights must 'take into account' any 'judgment, decision, declaration or advisory opinion of the European Court of Human Rights'. It is clear, therefore, that, when issues of Convention rights arise in private law cases, account must be taken to decisions of the European Court of Human Rights (Strasbourg court) as to the definition of the Convention right. What is less clear, however, is the *extent* to which national courts are required to take these decisions into account. Two main issues arise which will be discussed in this chapter. First, we need to determine how far domestic courts should adhere to the definitions of Convention rights provided by the Strasbourg court. Second, we need to determine the extent to which the need to take decisions of the Strasbourg court into account has altered rules regarding precedent, allowing courts to follow decisions of the Strasbourg court as opposed to the binding precedent of a higher or coterminous domestic court.

It will be argued that the HRA has altered the way in which decisions of the Strasbourg court are to be regarded in private law. However, it has done so in a manner that has created greater flexibility than is found in public law. Private law courts are less likely to regard decisions of the Strasbourg court as providing a ceiling to the definition of Convention rights. As such, courts have regarded themselves as free to develop principles of the common law, even those based upon or which mirror Convention rights, beyond the definition of the right provided by the Strasbourg court. Decisions of the Strasbourg court are to be regarded more as a springboard than as a straitjacket. This can be explained due to the different constitutional positions of the court when developing principles of the common law as opposed to reading and giving effect to legislation, declaring legislation incompatible with Convention rights or concluding that a public authority has acted unlawfully by contradicting Convention

[*] The author wishes to thank Richard Danbury for his extremely helpful editing advice.

rights. Courts have long enjoyed an inherent jurisdiction to develop the common law. As such, no issue as to possible breaches of the separation of powers arises. In addition, there is no indirect challenge to parliamentary sovereignty. Parliament is free to overturn a development of the common law through the enactment of legislation.

In addition, the HRA has modified the rules on precedent, again in a manner that provides an element of greater flexibility. The House of Lords, now the Supreme Court, is free not to follow its own previous decisions and the existence of a contradictory later decision of the Strasbourg court can provide a strong justification for the Supreme Court to depart from precedent and protect Convention rights. The Court of Appeal would also appear to have the ability to refuse to follow its own previous decisions where they are contradicted by a later decision of the Strasbourg court. Where there is less flexibility is with regard to the ability of the Court of Appeal to refuse to follow a decision of the House of Lords/Supreme Court that is contradicted by a subsequent decision of the Strasbourg court. The Court of Appeal should normally follow the decision of the House of Lords/Supreme Court, drawing attention to the possible conflict and giving leave to appeal to the Supreme Court. Lower courts are encouraged to use the leapfrog provisions in these circumstances. Given the difficulties that can emerge when interpreting Convention rights and applying their provisions to domestic legislation and individual circumstances, this would appear to be a sensible compromise to achieve the required balance of a strong protection of Convention rights and legal certainty.

5.1 Section 2(1): a straitjacket for private law?

In a consistent line of case law, courts deciding judicial review cases that concern Convention rights originally developed what Lewis refers to as the 'mirror principle'.[1] This requires courts to ensure that their definitions of Convention rights mirror those provided by the Strasbourg court. As such, English law is not able to protect Convention rights to a lesser degree than that required by the Strasbourg court. This ensures that potential liability for a breach of Convention rights by the UK Government before the Strasbourg court is substantially reduced, if not completely removed. However, this also means that English law cannot develop a stronger protection of rights than that provided in Strasbourg. Recent

---

1 J. Lewis, 'The European Ceiling on Human Rights', *Public Law* (2007), 720 and '*In re P and others:* an Exception to the 'No more and certainly no less' Rule', *Public Law* (2009), 43.

developments have, however, questioned the extent to which decisions of the Strasbourg court restrict the ability of English courts to develop rights beyond the definition of the Convention in public law and the extent to which English courts are required to adhere to decisions of the Strasbourg court. Moreover, it is arguable that section 2(1) does not operate in the same manner in private law, providing greater flexibility for the courts to develop the common law to protect human rights to a greater extent than that required by decisions of the Strasbourg court.

The mirror principle has its origins in the *dicta* of Lord Bingham in *R (Ullah)* v. *Special Adjudicator*, which stated that:

> the House is required by section 2(1)... to take into account any relevant Strasbourg case law. While such case law is not strictly binding, it has been held that courts should, in the absence of some special circumstances, follow any clear and constant jurisprudence of the Strasbourg court: *R (Alconbury Developments Ltd)* v. *Secretary of State for the Environment, Transport and the Regions* [2003] 2 AC 295, para. 26. This reflects the fact that the Convention is an international instrument, the correct interpretation of which can be authoritatively expounded only by the Strasbourg court. From this it follows that a national court subject to a duty such as that imposed by section 2 should not without strong reason dilute or weaken the effect of the Strasbourg case law. It is indeed unlawful under section 6 of the 1998 Act for a public authority, including a court, to act in a way which is incompatible with a Convention right. It is of course open to member states to provide for rights more generous than those guaranteed by the Convention, but such provision should not be the product of interpretation of the Convention by national courts, since the meaning of the Convention should be uniform throughout the states party to it. The duty of national courts is to keep pace with the Strasbourg jurisprudence as it evolves over time: no more, but certainly no less.[2]

Lord Bingham provides three justifications for the mirror principle. First, he focuses upon the relative competences of domestic courts and the Strasbourg court. As Convention rights are found in an international treaty, it is for the Strasbourg court to determine the definition of Convention rights, to ensure that they are applied across the different states bound by the international treaty in the same manner. Domestic courts, therefore, should comply with the definitions of Convention rights found in decisions of the Strasbourg court, unless there are strong reasons to modify the content of Convention rights. Second, attention is paid to the duty of the courts, as public authorities, to act in a manner

---

2 [2004] UKHL 26, [2004] 2 AC 323 at [20] ('*Ullah*').

compatible with Convention rights. If English courts were to define Convention rights differently from the Strasbourg court, it is possible that they would thereby be acting unlawfully. Their decision would not be compatible with Convention rights to the extent that the court's definition of a Convention right differed from that provided by the Strasbourg court. This conclusion is conditional upon acceptance of the first reason: that it is for the Strasbourg court to define Convention rights. There is a third latent justification for Lord Bingham's position, focusing upon the relative competence of the judiciary and the legislature. It is for Parliament, as opposed to the courts, to modify the content of Convention rights beyond that provided by the Strasbourg court. This justification is confirmed by Baroness Hale.[3]

The obligation to follow decisions of the Strasbourg court appeared to be strengthened in *R (Al Skeini) v. Secretary of State for Defence*, where, after referring to Lord Bingham's dictum, Lord Brown added:

> I would respectfully suggest that last sentence could as well have ended: 'no less, but certainly no more'. There seems to me, indeed, a greater danger in the national court construing the Convention too generously in favour of an Applicant than in construing it too narrowly. In the former event the mistake will necessarily stand: the member state cannot itself go to Strasbourg to have it corrected; in the latter event, however, where Convention rights have been denied by too narrow a construction, the aggrieved individual *can* have the decision corrected in Strasbourg. *Ullah*, of course, was concerned with the particular scope of individual Convention rights, there Art. 9, in the context of removing non-nationals from a member state. Lord Bingham's cautionary words must surely apply with greater force still to a case like the present.[4]

Lord Brown's statement adds a further justification for the mirror principle: the impossibility of correcting an overly broad definition of Convention rights, given that states do not have the right to petition the Strasbourg court. Although his strengthening of the mirror principle appears to be of general application, as is evident in his explanation, it applies with greater strength to those instances where national courts are referring to decisions of the Strasbourg court that determine the scope of application of the Convention itself, as opposed to the definition of Convention rights. In *Al Skeini*, the court was required to determine the extraterritorial application of the Convention. It is easier to see how this

---

3 *R (Al Skeini) v. Secretary of State for Defence* [2007] UKHL 26, [2008] 1 AC 153 ('*Al Skeini*').
4 *Al Skeini* at [106].

is a matter best resolved by the Strasbourg court as opposed to domestic courts, as well as how this provides a greater problem if an overly broad interpretation of extraterritoriality cannot be corrected by the Strasbourg court. There is a greater need for uniformity across the states as to when the Convention applies than there is as regards the definition of Convention rights. It is possible, therefore, to argue that this stronger obligation does not apply to the definition of Convention rights, but to issues concerning the territoriality of the Convention and other issues related to the scope of its application.

The mirror principle does enable national courts to develop rights beyond the definition provided by the Strasbourg court when faced with 'special circumstances'. A possible example of such special circumstances can be found in *Re P (Adoption: unmarried couple)*, which concerned the Convention compatibility of regulations in Northern Ireland that prevented unmarried couples from adopting children.[5] There was no clear decision of the Strasbourg court confirming that such rules would be contrary to Articles 8 and 14. In addition, earlier decisions of the Strasbourg court appeared to provide for similar forms of discrimination in adoption laws to be justified. Three of their Lordships concluded that, if the issue were to go before the Strasbourg court, the court, following a consistent line in similar cases, would conclude that the law was unjustifiable discrimination, contrary to Articles 8 and 14.[6] This would provide a narrow possible exception to the mirror principle, allowing national courts to develop their interpretation of Convention rights further than that currently found in decisions of the Strasbourg court, where to do so would be to follow a consistent line of case law of that court.

There are also statements in *Re P* that appear to undermine the mirror principle further, suggesting either a larger range of possible exceptions to the principle or even its possible erosion. First, evidence can be found for a further possible exception to the mirror principle when an issue is within the margin of appreciation afforded by the Strasbourg court to the signatory states.[7] This builds on statements found in earlier judgments of

---

5 [2008] UKHL 38, [2009] 1 AC 173 ('*In re P*').

6 *In re P* at [21]–[29] *per* Lord Hoffmann, [53] *per* Lord Hope, [136]–[142] *per* Lord Mance. Baroness Hale was unsure whether the Strasbourg case law would develop in this manner, but recognised that, in such circumstances, the court was free to interpret Convention rights beyond current Strasbourg case law [120] and Lord Walker disagreed [79]. See Lewis, '*In re P*'.

7 *In re P* at [31] *per* Lord Hoffmann, [117]–[118], [120] *per* Baroness Hale and [126]–[129] *per* Lord Mance.

Lord Steyn[8] and Lord Mance.[9] The existence of a margin of appreciation, particularly concerning whether a breach of a Convention right can be justified, undermines Lord Bingham's justification regarding the relative authority of the Strasbourg court and national courts to determine the scope of Convention rights. Although it is for the Strasbourg court to determine the definition of a Convention right and ascertain whether a Convention right is engaged to ensure a uniform interpretation of Convention rights, this is no longer the case when determining the application of a Convention right to a situation within the margin of appreciation granted by the Strasbourg court. In these circumstances, the Strasbourg court is recognising that the extent to which a breach of Convention rights can be justified is culturally dependent, placing the responsibility with the national courts to authoritatively determine whether a Convention right has been breached. As such, the first justification for the mirror principle would appear not to apply to issues within the margin of appreciation.

Second, statements in *Re P* criticise the justification for the mirror principle. Lord Hope is conscious of its constraining effect, cautioning against decisions of the Strasbourg court operating as a 'straitjacket'.[10] Lord Hoffmann argues that a distinction can be drawn between Convention rights and their domestic interpretation, relying on the decision of *McKerr*,[11] which confirmed that rights incorporated into English law through the HRA were best regarded as domestic as opposed to international rights. As such, the obligation of a court under section 6 is to ensure that it acts in a manner compatible with Convention rights as defined by domestic courts, not by the Strasbourg court. Although courts should regard decisions of the Strasbourg court as guiding, this obligation does not derive from the relative authority of the Strasbourg court to determine the scope of Convention rights, but from the standard interpretative presumption that statutes should be interpreted so as to ensure that the United Kingdom does not breach its international obligations and should, for reasons of comity, respect decisions of the Strasbourg court.[12] Although recognising the distinction between domestic and international rights, Lord Mance and Baroness Hale did not appear to go as far as Lord

8 *R (LS)* v. *Chief Constable of South Yorkshire Police* [2004] UKHL 39, [2004] 1 WLR 2196
   at [27].
9 *M* v. *Secretary of State for Work and Pensions* [2006] UKHL 11, [2006] 2 AC 91, [130]–
   [131].
10 *In re P* at [50].
11 [2004] UKHL 12, [2004] 1 WLR 807 ('*McKerr*').   12 *McKerr* at [33]–[36].

Hoffmann, potentially limiting their observations to those situations in which a margin of appreciation is granted by the Strasbourg court.[13]

If followed, Lord Hoffmann's dictum has the potential to undermine the mirror principle. However, even Lord Hoffmann recognised that it would be a 'rare occurrence' for dialogue to occur between the national courts and the Strasbourg court concerning the definition of a Convention right.[14] Two further decisions of the Supreme Court have referred to the need for dialogue. In *R v. Horncastle*, Lord Phillips, giving the judgment of the court, referred to 'valuable dialogue' between the two courts, such that, on rare occasions, it would be open to the Supreme Court to 'decline to follow' a clear line of Strasbourg authorities, providing reasons for this course of action.[15] Here, concerns were raised as to whether a decision of the Strasbourg court 'sufficiently appreciates or accommodates particular aspects of our democratic process', providing the court with a good reason not to follow a clear line of Strasbourg authority. In *Manchester City Council v. Pinnock*, Lord Neuberger, giving the opinion of the court, first recognised that the Supreme Court is not bound to follow every decision of the Strasbourg court; although the Supreme Court normally will follow a clear and consistent line of cases, it is both impractical and inappropriate to follow the Strasbourg court where it would destroy the ability of the Supreme Court to engage in 'constructive dialogue' with the Strasbourg court. He summarised the law as follows:[16]

> Where . . . there is a clear and constant line of decisions whose effect is not inconsistent with some fundamental substantive or procedural aspect of our law, and whose reasoning does not appear to overlook or misunderstand some argument or point of principle, we consider that it would be wrong for this court not to follow that line.

It would appear, therefore, that Lord Hoffmann's weakening of the mirror principle is restricted to those instances where the domestic court is acting within the margin of appreciation granted by the Strasbourg court, or where Strasbourg case law appears to be inconsistent with a fundamental aspect of English law, or where it overlooks or misunderstands a point of principle. Although this is a wider range of exceptions, it is still the case that the Supreme Court will normally adhere to decisions of the Strasbourg court.

---

13 *McKerr* at [117]–[118] *per* Baroness Hale and [128]–[129] *per* Lord Mance.
14 *McKerr* at [36].   15 [2009] UKSC 14, [2010] 2 AC 373 at [11].
16 [2010] UKSC 45 at [48] ('*Pinnock*').

Not only has the mirror principle been questioned, but it would appear that it does not apply to private law cases where courts develop principles of the common law to reflect Convention rights or the values underpinning these rights. The House of Lords appears to be willing to develop Convention rights beyond decisions of the Strasbourg court. A clear example of this can be found in *Campbell* v. *MGN Ltd.*[17] What is remarkable about the case is that the House of Lords was willing to apply Article 8 to horizontal situations, requiring a private media organisation to protect Ms Campbell's right to privacy, even though there was no clear case law of the Strasbourg court requiring that Article 8 should have horizontal applicability in this manner. Nor was there a clear line of case law indicating that the Strasbourg court was prepared to move in this direction – although the Strasbourg court did, later, extend Article 8 to apply in horizontal situations in *Von Hannover* v. *Germany*[18] (a case which has been regarded as anything but uncontroversial).[19]

Although three of their Lordships in *Campbell* referred to decisions of the Strasbourg court in their judgments, none of them discussed section 2(1), or appeared to regard the decisions of the Strasbourg court as constraining their development of Convention rights.[20] Lord Hoffmann even noted that the Strasbourg court did not require Article 8 to be interpreted so as to apply to horizontal situations, arguing instead that section 6(3)(a) required the court to recognise the values underpinning Convention rights, which then influence the development of the common law. Lord Hoffmann did not see why the values of autonomy and dignity which underpinned Article 8 would apply so as to restrain actions of the state, but not so as to restrain actions of private individuals.[21] The case is all the more remarkable, as it is arguable that determining whether a Convention right creates positive as opposed to merely negative obligations, thus meaning that the right is horizontally applicable, is not resolved merely by determining the content of a Convention right. It also raises issues as to the scope of application of the Convention, in the same manner

---

17 [2004] UKHL 22, [2004] 2 AC 457 ('*Campbell*').
18 [2004] (App. No. 59320/00), (2004) 16 BHRC 545.
19 N. Moreham, 'Privacy in Public Places', *Cambridge Law Journal*, 65 (2006), 606; B. Rudolf, 'Case Comment: *Von Hannover v Germany*', *International Journal of Constitutional Law*, 4 (2006), 533; and N. Hatziz, 'Giving Privacy its Due: Private Activities of Public Figures in *Von Hannover v Germany*', 16 *King's College Law Journal*, 16 (2005), 143.
20 *Campbell* at [49]–[50] *per* Lord Hoffmann, [86], [107]–[110], [117]–[120] *per* Lord Hope, [145] *per* Baroness Hale.
21 *Campbell* at [49]–[50].

as issues of extraterritoriality. As such, it is an issue even more suited to determination by the Strasbourg as opposed to domestic courts, to ensure a uniform application of the Convention.

Campbell is not the only example of English courts developing provisions of the common law beyond the scope of decisions of the Strasbourg court. Evidence can also be found of a willingness of the courts to develop the common law beyond the requirements of the decisions of the Strasbourg court in cases involving the right to freedom of expression, most notably through the development of the defence of reportage in defamation law. The recognition of the need to protect freedom of expression has led the courts to modify the content of private law; by prohibiting local authorities from bringing defamation actions[22] and through adapting the defence of qualified privilege to include circumstances in which the media communicates information to the public at large, provided that, in doing so, it complies with the standards of responsible journalism (the *Reynolds* privilege).[23] In applying the *Reynolds* privilege, the court has developed the defence of reportage. In order to satisfy the requirements of the *Reynolds* privilege, publishers normally need to demonstrate that they have taken reasonable steps to verify the truth of the information contained in the defamatory article. However, the reportage defence allows a publisher to benefit from the *Reynolds* privilege without the need to verify the truth of the allegations that it is reporting.[24] The defence applies when publishers provide an accurate report, on a matter of pressing public interest, normally involving political controversy,[25] of the fact that allegations have been made and may even include a unilateral report of one side of a particular argument.[26] This protection of freedom of expression goes beyond the requirements of Article 10, potentially in a manner that would breach Article 8.[27] Moreover, it seems to contradict established principles of defamation law, most notably the repetition rule, which treats an accurate repetition of a defamatory statement in the same way as the original publication of the statement.[28]

---

22 *Derbyshire CC* v. *Times Newspapers Ltd* [1993] AC 534 ('*Derbyshire CC*').
23 *Reynolds* v. *Times Newspapers Ltd* [2001] 2 AC 127 ('*Reynolds*').
24 *Al-Fagih* v. *HH Saudi Research and Marketing (UK) Ltd* [2001] EWCA Civ. 1634, [2002] EMLR 13.
25 *Flood* v. *Times Newspapers* [2010] EWCA Civ. 804.
26 *Roberts* v. *Gable* [2007] EWCA Civ 721, [2008] QB 502 and *Charman* v. *Orion Publishing Group Ltd* [2007] EWCA Civ. 972, [2008] 1 All ER 750.
27 G. Busuttil, 'Reportage: A not Entirely Neutral Report', *Entertainment Law Review*, 20 (2009), 44, 49–50.
28 Busuttil, 'Reportage', p. 48.

There are two possible and related explanations for this divergence. The first rests on constitutional concerns, in particular the principle of the separation of powers and the sovereignty of parliament. Courts are wary of performing a legislative function. This concern is found in the latent third justification provided for the mirror principle by Lord Bingham; if Convention rights are to be developed further than the definition provided by the Strasbourg court then this is for Parliament as opposed to the courts. A similar concern is found in *Re P*. Even in areas within the margin of appreciation, there is still an issue as to whether the courts or the legislature are best placed to develop Convention rights. In *Re P*, their Lordships reached opposite conclusions as to whether the legislature or the court was better placed to remedy the Northern Ireland adoption regulations to ensure that they no longer discriminated against unmarried couples. Lords Hoffmann and Hope felt that it was for the court to remedy the lack of compatibility between the adoption regulations and Convention rights.[29] Lord Walker reached the opposite conclusion, based upon the lack of clarity surrounding whether the Strasbourg court would develop Convention rights in the direction suggested by the English courts, thus rendering it contrary to Convention rights to discriminate against married and unmarried couples for the purposes of adoption; the need for a democratically elected body to decide whether UK law should move beyond Convention rights; and the practical repercussions that might ensue from merely declaring the adoption regulations incompatible with Convention rights.[30]

Such concerns do not arise in cases where courts develop the common law to reflect the content of Convention rights. The court has an inherent jurisdiction to develop the common law, to which it is perfectly well suited. Courts were developing the common law to protect fundamental human rights even prior to the HRA. This can be illustrated in particular by the way the courts modified the common law to protect the fundamental right to freedom of expression.[31] Such modifications are suited to development by the court through the incremental development of the law on a case-by-case basis. This may not be the case when courts are required to interpret legislation to ensure its compatibility with Convention rights for the purposes of section 3.

In a similar manner, the reluctance found in public law cases to develop Convention rights beyond the decisions of the Strasbourg court can be

---

29 *In re P* at [37] *per* Lord Hoffmann and [55]–[56] *per* Lord Hope.
30 *In re P* at [81]–[83] *per* Lord Walker.
31 See, in particular, *Derbyshire CC* and *Reynolds*.

explained by a desire to maintain parliamentary sovereignty. One expression of the will of Parliament is found in the HRA, which empowers courts to strike down actions of public authorities that are contrary to Convention rights. However, it is frequently the case that Parliament has granted discretionary powers to public authorities, which could extend to a power to determine the content of Convention rights. Moreover, it is not clear whether, when referring to Convention rights, Parliament intended courts to ensure that public authorities did not act contrary to Convention rights as defined by the Strasbourg court, or whether courts were able to provide their own definition of Convention rights, guided by the decisions of the Strasbourg court. Consequently, if courts are to define Convention rights for themselves, there is a potential for them to act contrary to the wishes of Parliament in two distinct ways. First, they may override the will of Parliament which granted the power to a public authority to determine the content of Convention rights. Second, they may contradict the will of Parliament by defining Convention rights in a manner different from that found in decisions of the Strasbourg court.

These concerns are not present when the court is called upon to develop the common law to reflect the content of Convention rights, where there is no possibility that the courts are contradicting the will of Parliament. If Parliament disagrees with any particular development, it can overturn this through legislation. Evidence of the relative restraint of the courts in public law as opposed to private law cases can be found in judicial statements: for example, Lord Bingham in *Ullah*,[32] Lord Brown[33] and Baroness Hale in *Al Skeini*[34] and *R (Animal Defenders International)* v. *Secretary of State for Culture, Media and Sport*.[35] All refer to the ability of both Parliament and the courts, through the development of the common law, to develop a protection of rights that is stronger than that provided by the Convention. However, they regard the role of the courts in public law cases as restricted to following the definition of Convention rights as provided by the Strasbourg court, ensuring that legislation or the actions of public authorities have not contravened the Convention.[36]

The second explanation rests on the difference between a duty and a power. A clear exposition can be found in the statement of Baroness Hale:

---

32 *Ullah* at [20].   33 *Al-Skeini* at [105]–[106].
34 *Al-Skeini* at [90].   35 [2008] UKHL 15, [2008] 1 AC 1312 at [53].
36 See J. Wright, 'Interpreting Section 2 of the Human Rights Act: Towards an Indigenous Jurisprudence of Human Rights', *Public Law* (2009), 595, 606–13.

> If Parliament wishes to go further, or if the courts find it appropriate to develop the common law further, of course they may. But that is because they choose to do so, not because the Convention requires it of them.[37]

When determining whether legislation or actions of a public authority are contrary to Convention rights, courts are fulfilling their duty under the HRA. As public authorities themselves, they are required to ensure that they act in a manner compatible with Convention rights. The same argument applies when courts modify the common law to ensure its compatibility with Convention rights. However, when developing the common law further than Convention rights, using Convention rights as an impetus for further developments of the fundamental principles of the common law, courts are exercising a power as opposed to executing their duty. In exercising such a power, there is also a clearer division between Convention rights and domestic human rights and, therefore, it is for the domestic courts and not the Strasbourg court to determine the content of these rights. Thus, the justifications for the mirror principle do not apply: there is no issue about parliamentary sovereignty.

5.2 Precedent and decisions of the European Court of Human Rights

5.2.1 Supreme Court

Following the Practice Direction issued on 26 July 1966, the House of Lords, now the Supreme Court, is free to depart from its previous decisions.[38] However, the House of Lords consistently explained that it would depart from previous decisions only when there are good reasons to do so. It is clear that the Supreme Court is prepared to depart from its own decisions when they are contradicted by a later decision of the Strasbourg court. This can be illustrated by *R (Purdy)* v. *Director of Public Prosecutions* concerning the law on assisted suicide.[39] Ms Purdy was suffering from primary progressive multiple sclerosis, for which there was no known cure. Ms Purdy believed that there would come a time when she would find her life unbearable and wished, when that time came, to take her own life. However, she would not be in a position to do so unassisted, and wanted to travel to Switzerland, where assisted suicide was lawful, with the help of her partner. She sought a declaration as to

---

37 *Al Skeini* at [90].
38 *Practice Statement (Judicial Precedent)* [1966] 1 WLR 1234.
39 [2009] UKHL 45, [2009] 3 WLR 403.

whether it would be an offence under section 2(1) of the Suicide Act 1961 for her partner to help her to travel to a country where assisted suicide was permitted and there help her to terminate her own life.

A similar issue had arisen in the case of *Pretty*, where Mrs Pretty, who was suffering from motor neurone disease, sought clarification from the Director of Public Prosecutions as to whether it would be unlawful for her husband to assist her to end her life in this country.[40] When deciding this issue, a majority of their Lordships concluded that Article 8 was not engaged; it did not extend to the right to choose the way in which to terminate your own life. However, the Strasbourg court reached the opposite conclusion, relying upon the dissenting judgment of Lord Hope that Article 8(1) was engaged. In *Purdy*, Lord Hope concluded that the importance of the protection of human rights provided a good justification for the House of Lords to depart from its own previous decision in order to follow a later, contradictory decision of the Strasbourg court.[41] He was joined in this conclusion by Lords Neuberger[42] and Brown.[43]

This conclusion is uncontroversial,[44] although, as discussed above, issues may arise as regards identifying both the existence and the extent of a contradiction between decisions of the Supreme Court and the Strasbourg court. Moreover, there may also be the possibility of dialogue between the Strasbourg court and the Supreme Court when determining the definition and application of a Convention right. In these circumstances, there may be a justification for adhering to the previous decision of the House of Lords or Supreme Court, particularly where this provides for a stronger protection of the Convention right than that found in the decision of the Strasbourg court.

5.2.2 Court of Appeal and below

5.2.2.1 Conflict between the Strasbourg court and the House of Lords or Supreme Court

The Court of Appeal and lower courts are bound to follow decisions of the House of Lords and the Supreme Court, even when these contradict subsequent decisions of the Strasbourg court, unless exceptional circumstances exist. This requirement derives from the House of Lords' decision

---

40 *R (Purdy)* v. *Director of Public Prosecutions* [2002] 1 AC 800 and *Purdy* v. *United Kingdom* (2002) 35 EHRR 1 ('*Purdy*').
41 *Purdy* at [34]–[39].   42 *Purdy* at [95].
43 *Purdy* at [87].   44 Confirmed recently in *Pinnock*.

of *Kay* v. *Lambeth LBC*.[45] When the case was heard by the Court of Appeal the court was faced with two apparently conflicting decisions, one of the House of Lords and a later decision of the Strasbourg court. In written submissions, the organisations Liberty and Justice argued that the Court of Appeal and below should be free to disregard precedent in favour of the decision of the Strasbourg court if four conditions were followed:

(i) the decision of the Strasbourg court was subsequent to the decision of the House of Lords;
(ii) the decision of the Strasbourg court created a clear and authoritative precedent that demonstrated a sound understanding of English law;
(iii) there was a clear inconsistency between the decision of the House of Lords and the Strasbourg court; and
(iv) this inconsistency could not be explained through the operation of primary legislation that would place the decision in question within the scope of section 6(2).

Lord Bingham rejected this argument. First, as evidenced by the case before the House of Lords, the issue as to whether there was clear inconsistency between the decision of the House of Lords and of the Strasbourg court was frequently contestable. Consequently, to enable precedent to not be followed under the conditions proposed by Liberty and Justice would give rise to possible uncertainty in the law. This would defeat the purposes of the system of precedent which is justified through its ability to promote legal certainty.[46] Second, Lord Bingham relied upon the relationship between the Strasbourg court and national courts. Although it is for the Strasbourg court to determine the definition of Convention rights, the determination as to how Convention rights are to be applied in 'the special context of national legislation, law, practice and social and other conditions' is within the, frequently wide, margin of appreciation granted to national authorities.[47] This includes rules regarding precedent. As such, there is no requirement for national courts to modify rules of precedent in order to fulfil their obligations as a public authority to act in a manner compatible with Convention rights.

Lord Bingham did allow one narrow exception, deriving from the example of *D* v. *East Berkshire Community NHS Trust*,[48] where the Court of Appeal departed from the previous House of Lords' decision of *X (Minors)* v. *Bedfordshire County Council*[49] in favour of a later,

---

45 [2006] UKHL 10, [2006] 2 AC 465 ('*Kay*').   46 *Kay* at [43].
47 *Kay* at [44].   48 [2004] QB 558.   49 [1995] 2 AC 633.

inconsistent decision of the Strasbourg court. The following features were used by Lord Bingham to establish the exceptional nature of a possible departure from precedent: first, the decision of the Strasbourg court undermined the policy underpinning the contradictory decision of the House of Lords; second, the decision of the House of Lords was taken before the enactment of the HRA; third, the decision of the House of Lords did not refer to Convention rights; fourth, the conflict was between a decision in the House of Lords and the Strasbourg court that concerned the same applicants on the same facts; and, fifth, the applicants had received substantial damages from the Strasbourg court.[50]

It is clear from *Purdy* in the Court of Appeal that these criteria are cumulative and that they are interpreted narrowly.[51] In *Purdy* the Court of Appeal was faced with *Pretty*, a conflicting decision of the House of Lords and the Strasbourg court in the same case. It was argued that the Court of Appeal should be free to disregard the precedent of the House of Lords in favour of the subsequent decision of the Strasbourg court, emphasising that the two contradictory cases concerned the same applicant and the same facts. Judge CJ disagreed, arguing that, although it was important that the contradictory cases in question did concern the same applicant and the same facts, this was not sufficient to establish the requirement of exceptionality necessary to justify departing from a decision of the House of Lords. Here, there was no evidence that the decision of the Strasbourg court had undermined the policy underpinning the earlier decision of the House of Lords. In addition, *Pretty* had been decided in the House of Lords following the enactment of the HRA and had referred to the Convention. Moreover, it was not clear that the decisions of the House of Lords and the Strasbourg court were contradictory; different opinions had been expressed as to both the existence and the extent of the contradiction between the two cases.[52]

5.2.2.2 Conflict between the Court of Appeal and the Strasbourg court

The position concerning whether the Court of Appeal and lower courts are free to depart from a decision of the Court of Appeal that is

---

50 The rule that the Court of Appeal and lower courts are bound by precedent apart from this one narrow exception was confirmed by the House of Lords in *R (RJM)* v. *Secretary of State for Work and Pensions* [2008] UKHL 63, [2008] 3 WLR 1023 at [64] *per* Lord Neuberger ('*RJM*').

51 [2009] EWCA Civ. 92, (2009) 106 BMLR 170.   52 *RJM* at [52]–[54].

contradicted by a subsequent decision of the Strasbourg court is more difficult to delineate. Lord Neuberger in *R (RJM)* v. *Secretary of State for Work and Pensions* stated that he believed that the Court of Appeal is free, though not obliged, to depart from a decision of its own when this is contradicted by a later decision of the Strasbourg court.[53] He provided two, general, justifications for this conclusion. First, the Court of Appeal should be freer to depart from its own decisions than from decisions of the House of Lords or the Supreme Court. If the Court of Appeal were to wrongly decide to follow the decision of the Strasbourg court, there is the possibility of an appeal to the Supreme Court to correct this mistake. Second, the rules concerning the extent to which the Court of Appeal is bound by precedent were established by Lord Greene MR in *Young* v. *Bristol Aeroplane Co. Ltd,*[54] a case that was decided when English law was more of a closed legal system, without the obligation to be guided by different international courts such as the European Court of Justice or the Strasbourg court. Both of these justifications provide a reason for modifying existing rules of precedent. However, they do not provide a specific justification for modifying the rules on precedent in the manner suggested by Lord Neuberger.

A possible justification can be found in the more general concerns dictating whether the Supreme Court should be free to depart from its own previous decisions that are contradicted by a subsequent decision of the Strasbourg court; namely, a concern to protect human rights that may override the need for certainty. In addition, less danger arises when the Court of Appeal erroneously departs from its previous decision in order to follow a decision of the Strasbourg court, as this error can be corrected on appeal to the Supreme Court. In these circumstances, it could be argued that the Court of Appeal should err on the side of providing a stronger as opposed to a weaker protection of human rights, following the later decision of the Strasbourg court as opposed to its own earlier decision, unless there are good reasons not to follow the decision of the Strasbourg court. These reasons could derive from the existence of a broad margin of appreciation applied to the Convention right in question, or from situations in which it is clear that the Strasbourg court misunderstood English law when taking its decision.

Lord Neuberger's comments contrast with the position in *Kay* v. *Lambeth LBC*, where Lord Bingham suggested that, when the Court of Appeal

---

53 *RJM* at [65]–[67].   54 [1944] KB 718, [1944] 2 All ER 293.

is faced with a prior decision of its own that appears to be contradicted by the Strasbourg court, the Court of Appeal should follow its own previous decision, leaving it for the House of Lords to determine whether the earlier decision of the Court of Appeal could stand with a decision of the Strasbourg court.[55] In *Actavis UK Ltd* v. *Merck & Co. Inc.*[56] the Court of Appeal shared Lord Neuberger's concern that the rules in *Young* v. *Bristol Aeroplane* did not prescribe rules of precedent for our current legal system with its greater interaction with foreign judgments, thus recognising the ability to create new exceptions to the rules of precedent, in this case as regards decisions of the European Patent Office (EPO) Boards of Appeal. The Court of Appeal concluded that it was free, but not bound, to follow a consistent line of authority found in the decisions of the EPO Boards of Appeal as opposed to contradictory decisions of the Court of Appeal. However, the court considered, obiter, that the position was different in respect of the Strasbourg court, such that the Court of Appeal should follow its own decisions, even in the face of contradictory Strasbourg decisions, preferring Lord Bingham's approach.

There were several good reasons for drawing this distinction between the different international courts. First, the House of Lords had declared that it was bound to follow the decisions of the EPO Boards of Appeal, whereas the House of Lords has recognised that it is not bound to follow decisions of the Strasbourg court. Second, decisions of the EPO Boards of Appeal were more precise and less contentious than decisions of the Strasbourg court, particularly as regards the lack of a margin of appreciation, meaning that it is easier to discern whether a decision of the Court of Appeal can stand with a decision of the EPO Boards of Appeal than with a decision of the Strasbourg court. Third, patent decisions rarely reached the House of Lords, unlike the numerous decisions of the House of Lords and the Supreme Court concerning Convention rights. Consequently, there may be fewer opportunities for higher courts to correct injustice that may arise through the Court of Appeal following its own prior decisions as opposed to those of the EPO Boards of Appeal than would arise with regard to decisions of the Strasbourg court. Fourth, there was a greater need for certainty across Europe with regard to patents than there was as regards the definition of Convention rights, justifying a need for the Court of Appeal to follow decisions of the EPO Boards of Appeal

---

55 *Kay* at [43]–[44].   56 [2008] EWCA Civ. 444 ('*Actavis*').

as opposed to relying on the higher court to overturn the contradictory precedent of the Court of Appeal.[57]

Although the statements in *Actavis* v. *Merck* were obiter, the Court of Appeal appeared to take a similar view in *Manchester City Council* v. *Pinnock*, where it refused to discuss Strasbourg authority, despite possible contradictions of previous decisions of both the Court of Appeal and of the House of Lords by the Strasbourg court, concluding that it was 'bound by precedent to accept the binding indistinguishable authority of decisions of the House of Lords and the Court of Appeal unless and until the House of Lords decides differently'.[58]

This conclusion does not sit easily with the view that the Court of Appeal does have the power, in exceptional circumstances, to depart from a decision of the House of Lords or Supreme Court that is contradicted by a decision of the Strasbourg court. It is possible that the same exceptional ability to depart from the rules of precedent could be found as regards the duty of the Court of Appeal to be bound by its own prior decisions – if justification exists for the Court of Appeal to not follow precedents of the Supreme Court that are contradicted by the Strasbourg court then the same reasons would appear to apply, perhaps even more strongly, to its own decisions which are of a lower authority than those of the Supreme Court.

Two arguments could be proposed for accepting a smaller new exception to the rules of precedent found in *Young* v. *Bristol Aeroplane*. First, *Actavis* v. *Merck* discussed only a general as opposed to a specific modification to the rules of precedent. A rejection of a general power of the Court of Appeal to choose to follow a decision of the Strasbourg court as opposed to adhering to its own prior decisions need not also entail a rejection of a more specific ability to not follow its own prevision decision taken: (i) before the enactment of the HRA; (ii) without reference to Convention rights; (iii) in relation to the same parties as the Strasbourg decision it chooses to follow; (iv) where the parties in question obtained a large sum of damages from the Strasbourg court; and (v) the decision of the Strasbourg court does not undermine the policy of the decision of the Court of Appeal. This is reinforced by the fact that the court in *Actavis* v. *Merck* approved of the judgment of Lord Bingham in *Kay* v. *Lambeth*,

---

57 *Actavis* at [101]–[104]. Lord Neuberger was sceptical of these differences: see *RJM* at [67].

58 [2009] EWCA Civ. 852 at [33], [2010] 3 All ER 201.

where this narrower exception to the rules of precedent is found. Second, *Pinnock* merely states that the Court of Appeal is bound to follow its own decisions, without reference to either the dicta in *Actavis* v. *Merck* or the statement of Lord Bingham in *Kay* v. *Lambeth*. It is at least arguable, therefore, that *Pinnock* is also compatible with the Court of Appeal's adoption of the narrower exception to the rules of precedent discussed in *Kay* v. *Lambeth* as regards its own decisions as well as decisions of the Supreme Court; there is no clear intention expressed in the decision to rule out this possible interpretation of the rules of precedent.

6

Tort design and human rights thinking

RODERICK BAGSHAW

The principal theme of this chapter is that in pursuing the goal of making English tort law compatible with Convention rights, and the related goal of developing tort law so as to allow it to assist in protecting these rights, we should not lose sight of what makes a good tort duty. Lord Bingham commended the opinion that 'where a common law duty covers the same ground as a Convention right, it should, so far as practicable, develop in harmony with it'.[1] But this chapter aims to unsettle any assumption that such harmony requires the development of tort duties which *mirror* Convention rights, even in situations where the tort duties will be owed by public bodies. It is more important for newly developed duties to be harmonious with the goals of the law of torts than for them to replicate concepts used by the Strasbourg court.

The first two sections of the chapter explain how we ought to think about tort duties and the process of designing them. Subsequent sections describe some obstacles in the way of a conclusion that judges in England are obliged to design tort duties to mirror Convention rights, and identify some of the features of Convention rights which are most likely to cause difficulties if they are directly incorporated into tort duties.

6.1 Tort duties as compromises

Tort duties are compromises[2] between the security interests of potential claimants and the liberty interests of potential defendants.[3] Such

---

1 *Chief Constable of the Hertfordshire Police* v. *Van Colle; Smith* v. *Chief Constable of Sussex Police* [2008] UKHL 50, [2009] 1 AC 225 at [58], agreeing with the opinion of Rimer LJ in *Smith* v. *Chief Constable of Sussex Police* [2008] EWCA Civ. 39 at [53]. Lord Bingham was, of course, dissenting from the majority in the House of Lords as to the appropriate result.

2 This section and the next draw heavily on a similar introduction in R. Bagshaw, 'Privacy and Tort Design', in K. Ziegler (ed.), *Human Rights and Private Law: Privacy as Autonomy* (Oxford: Hart, 2007), ch. 7.

3 For the same point made using different terminology, see P. Cane, *The Anatomy of Tort Law* (Oxford: Hart, 1997), p. 15.

compromises are constructed using multiple (linked) elements: for instance, how the claimant's protected interest is defined; how the forbidden (or required) behaviour of the defendant is described; how the state of mind of the defendant sufficient for liability is described; and how the necessary link between the defendant's restricted (or required) behaviour and the claimant's damage[4] is defined. Obviously such definitions and descriptions can be complex amalgams of positive and negative elements.

Since tort law exists to achieve goals in the real world,[5] it is valuable to assess potential compromises against benchmarks that measure whether a legal duty recognised by tort law is good at achieving these goals. No doubt there is scope for argument about the best formulation of tort law's real-world goals, but most versions will require duties both to influence the behaviour of potential defendants and to play a role in settling any disputes that reach the legal profession, or even the courts. Thus, it will be useful to consider how far any particular compromise is likely to influence behaviour, and at what cost, and how costly it will be to clarify and enforce its demands when a dispute arises.[6] A tort duty that it is difficult for potential defendants to understand, and thus comply with, may be deficient on that ground. Likewise, a design for a tort duty may be sub-optimal if it stimulates defendants to respond in some way other than simple compliance, particularly where that response is deleterious to other important interests. For example, if a duty is defined as obliging a person to perform a task competently *if he or she chooses to perform it,* then the person's response may be deleterious to an important interest if it involves reducing the frequency with which he or she chooses to perform the task.[7] As a final illustration, a tort duty that is formulated so

4 I do not want to claim that all torts are incomplete in the absence of damage, rather that one possible element in the definition of a tort duty might be a particular connection between the defendant's restricted behaviour and its impact on the claimant.

5 Some commentators might object to this proposition and claim that the value of tort law is intrinsic. My arguments against this view are set out in R. Bagshaw, 'Tort Law, Concepts and What Really Matters', in A. Robertson and H. W. Tang (eds.), *The Goals of Private Law* (Oxford: Hart, 2009), pp. 239–59.

6 I am not offering to establish that some particular ratio of commitments towards the various goals is optimal. The judges, legislators, law reform commissions and academics who design tort duties are in practice more like experimenting chefs ('let's try a pinch more of this and a little less of that') than slaves to the measurements in a canonical recipe book. That said, I would argue that influencing potential defendants in advance is more important than settling disputes.

7 This problem is particularly prominent in cases involving public defendants, because there is often no market pressure to encourage them to provide services at a particular level, and

that its existence or application turns on factors that it will be impossible for a potential claimant to monitor, or that turns on factors that it will be costly to prove to a court, must be regarded as less attractive as a result. This might mean, for example, that a judge choosing between a duty owed by a defendant who is giving advice depending on the defendant *knowing* how the claimant intends to use the advice or depending on whether it would be *reasonable for the claimant to rely* on the advice given ought to take into account that it is far easier for a claimant to be sure about (and capable of proving) the defendant's knowledge (since this can be directly influenced by the claimant – he or she can *inform* the defendant) than about the reasonableness of reliance. Similarly, a defendant is more likely to know what he or she knows (though corporate defendants may challenge this proposition!) than whether it would be reasonable for a claimant to rely on advice in a particular way. Thus, a duty formulated in terms of the defendant's knowledge would tend to be preferable with regard to the purpose of reducing monitoring and proof costs.

In the light of the preceding examples and illustrations it must be clear that compatibility with these benchmarks is not an absolute matter, not parallel to a simple binary division between passing and failing, between a switch being on or off. Rather, different designs for compromises will achieve different patterns of scores when assessed against the various benchmarks, and each particular design's pattern will indicate how good such a duty will be at advancing the real-world goals of tort law.

Behind this discussion lurks the important claim that tort duties do not design themselves any more than do caravans or sewing machines: any judge or legislator asked to clarify or reform a tort duty must make choices, and those 'design choices' will rarely resemble mathematical calculations.[8] For example, the relevant choices may involve a distributive element: a duty which is intended to stimulate early intervention in situations where it is suspected that a child may be at risk of cruel treatment in the family home may benefit those children who were indeed at risk but only at the

---

political pressure may be an inadequate encouragement when the services directly benefit only a minority.

8 This is not intended to alienate those who believe that tort duties are *based on* ethical duties and that ethical duties are natural. Those who believe this, nonetheless, ought to accept that the process of deriving practical legal duties from competing versions of natural ethical duties is not mechanical. A parallel explanation might also serve to reassure those who believe that tort duties are based on ethical duties that can be proved empirically to be acknowledged by some section of a community.

expense of some children who were not, and their parents.[9] Such choices will also often turn on relative assessments of the merits of different legal institutions: for instance, a detailed code of duties and exceptions may reduce the power of trial judges but may also be difficult for citizens to understand without legal advice, while a broad and less specified duty may be easier for citizens to grasp but may require more from trial judges when disputes arise. There is no *demonstrably right general* answer to the question of how abstract or specific particular tort duties ought to be.[10] Indeed, it is likely to be reasonable to argue in favour of different degrees of specificity in different contexts.

It has sometimes been argued that tort duties do not need to be 'designed', since they simply reflect the *form* of 'rights' that have a more general presence in law.[11] But there are (at least) two reasons to reject this contention. First, the argument is not *sufficient* to establish that 'tort law's design benchmarks' have no legitimate part to play in influencing the *form* of more general legal rights; the roles that such rights may play in areas of the law beyond tort law may make *additional* goals influential, but this does not make benchmarks focused on the goals of tort law irrelevant. Second, the argument that 'tort duties reflect the form of rights which have a more general presence in the law' is difficult to extend into the fields where tort law imposes *positive* duties that appear to play a role only in tort law. It seems more difficult to claim that *these* duties reflect *broader-than-tort* rights, and the alternative claim that the designs of such duties are wholly specified by *consensual undertakings* seems over-extravagant.[12] The weakness of 'the rights thesis' in the area

---

9 Similarly, few will doubt that the class of people who regard privacy as valuable (and worth securing) is not identical to the class which most values free expression (and would thus prefer to preserve liberty to publish).

10 Similarly, there is no demonstrably right general answer to the question of how broad or specific the provisions of an international human rights convention should be. But brief consideration of the different functions of national tort law and an international human rights convention prompts the question of whether duties expressed at the same level of detail are likely to be equally well suited to both purposes.

11 To spell this out, it seems that the argument is that such 'rights' have a wider role than merely to give rise to tort duties, their *form* or *shape* derives from this wider role, and tort duties reflect these *forms* rather than being 'designed'.

12 For example, many of the positive obligations that attach to owners and occupiers of land, such as those recognised in *Goldman* v. *Hargrave* [1967] 1 AC 645 and those codified and modified by the Occupiers Liability Acts 1957 and 1984, are difficult to explain as deriving from either *broader-than-tort* rights of potential claimants or *consensual undertakings*. Even Robert Stevens, in his detailed account of 'the rights thesis', can offer little by way of explanation for the detailed *form* or *shape* of the positive obligations of landowners ('The

of *positive* duties is, of course, of particular significance when considering the development of tort law to better protect Convention rights, since one of the areas where the clamour for extending tort duties is loudest is where the existing duties do not go as far as the positive obligations that have been conjured from some Convention rights.

To summarise the points made in this section: good designs for tort duties ought to take into account the benchmarks that measure whether a particular formulation of the duty will be good at achieving the goals of tort law.

6.2 Tort design: the common law

Do English judges accept that when asked to clarify or reform a tort duty they must assess how good rival formulations might be at achieving the goals of tort law? It is difficult to identify any judge who has expressly acknowledged an obligation in these terms, though there are many examples of concerns about the practical effects of various formulations proving to be influential.[13] But values that are embedded in consistent institutional practices may not need to be acknowledged openly.

English institutional practices have traditionally reflected the view that the task of designing appropriate compromises within the law of torts is a task that should be undertaken by judges using the common law method unless and until Parliament steps in. The common law method is not one which would appeal to a legislator with a blank page; it is best suited to incremental refinement of rules, using arguments based on accepted values, common experience, analogy and coherence. The objection to judicial adoption of a more radical method, such as that which a legislator might regard as appropriate, is partly constitutional and partly institutional. The constitutional concern reflects the fact that choices between rival compromises involve a distributive element: a radical *judicial* revision of the law of torts might involve substantial redistribution (of wealth or power) by an unelected body. The institutional concern reflects the fact that procedures appropriate for the resolution of a bipolar

---

rights we have against landowners that they take positive steps to protect us are the quid pro quo for the law's protection of their rights to exclusive enjoyment', R. Stevens, *Torts and Rights* (Oxford University Press, 2007), p. 16), and even less for the *form* of many of the positive obligations of occupiers (*ibid.*).

13 Clear recent examples can be found in the speeches of Lord Hope at [77], and Lord Carswell at [109], in *Chief Constable of the Hertfordshire Police* v. *Van Colle* [2008] UKHL 50, [2009] 1 AC 225 ('*Van Colle*').

dispute deeply anchored to a specific set of facts are not equally suitable for the drafting of rules suitable for application across a wide range of future cases. For example, detailed evidence relating to policy concerns, or about the frequency with which particular fact patterns are encountered, is rarely presented in court, and even less rarely *generated* for the purposes of bipolar litigation.[14] In some areas of tort law these constitutional and institutional concerns have crystallised into legal doctrines, which regulate such judicial law-making as must inevitably (and can legitimately) occur.[15] Often, however, such concerns have been relied on to justify judgments taking the form of 'sympathetic refusal'.[16] Is it plausible to claim that by confining themselves to the 'incremental refinement of rules, using arguments based on accepted values, common experience, analogy and coherence' common law judges ensure that their tort designs respect 'the benchmarks which measure whether a particular formulation of the duty will be good at achieving the goals of tort law'? Three arguments point towards a positive answer. The first contends that as long as a

14 Certainly, most barristers charged with presenting ground-breaking cases before English appellate courts do not seem to have considered themselves obliged to organise the sort of consultation process that a law reform body or policy-maker would consider desirable. For instance, in *A* v. *B Plc* [2002] EWCA Civ. 337, [2003] QB 195 at [7]–[9], the Court of Appeal reported receiving three lever-arch ring-binders of case law and a further file of Press Complaints Commission material, again dominated by previous decisions. It seems unthinkable that a policy-maker considering drafting legislation on privacy would regard such a bundle as an appropriate foundation.

15 The present author has attempted to explain the doctrines known collectively as 'the test for a duty of care' in these terms: R. Bagshaw, 'The "Test" for a Duty of Care: Self-Regulation of Judicial Lawmaking', unpublished, delivered at a seminar at the Australian National University on 1 December 2005.

16 A famous example of 'sympathetic refusal' is provided by the speech of Lord Wilberforce in *Launchbury* v. *Morgans* [1973] AC 127 at 136–7:

> My Lords, I have no doubt that the multiplication of motor cars on our roads, their increasing speed, the severity of the injuries they may cause, the rise in accidents involving innocent persons, give rise to problems of increasing social difficulty with which the law finds it difficult to keep abreast. And I am willing to assume (though I think that more evidence is needed than this one case) that traditional concepts of vicarious liability, founded on agency as developed in relation to less dangerous vehicles, may be proving inadequate ... But I have come to the clear conclusion that we cannot in this House embark on the suggested innovation ... Assuming that the desideratum is to fix liability in cases of negligent driving upon the owner of the car (an assumption which may be disputable), there are at least three different systems which may be adopted: ... My Lords, I do not know on what principle your Lordships acting judicially can prefer one of these systems to the others or on what basis any one can be formulated with sufficient precision or its exceptions defined. The choice is one of social policy; there are arguments for and against each of them.

prototype design respects the benchmarks, then any new design produced by incremental development, analogy and coherence is also *likely* to respect the benchmarks. The same clearly could not be said if a judge produced a fresh design like a legislator with a blank sheet of paper. The second argument maintains that factors such as 'accepted values' and 'common experience' will often reflect 'what has proved a *useful* standard' for those subject to the duty, those with an interest in monitoring compliance and those involved in settling or adjudicating upon disputes. The third argument insists that the benchmarks also *influence* common law technique less overtly through playing a role in determining whether an analogy is thought to be compelling, or an incremental development justified. In other words, an analogy is more likely to be found to be compelling where the new duty will be *as* effective at guiding behaviour and as suitable for judicial application and enforcement as was the old duty.

No doubt the strength of these three arguments can be disputed. But anyone who believes that English judges have made no commitment, express or implied, to the benchmarks *may* still accept that judges *ought* to make such a commitment: tort duties ought to be designed to work in practice. If a commitment has been made, or ought to have been, then a tendency to develop tort duties simply so that they *mirror* Convention rights would be of concern, because it would clearly reduce the *possible* influence of the benchmarks.

6.3 The challenges from human rights thinking

In this section I discuss two issues. First, I seek to assess the authority behind the demand that there are areas where the common law approach to the development of torts, which I have claimed incorporates benchmarks that measure whether a particular formulation of a duty will be good at achieving the goals of tort law, must be left behind because the HRA *obliges* English courts to build torts to a particular template. Second, I catalogue some features of designs for torts mirroring human rights provisions which fit badly with basic elements within the existing common law of torts. In the final section, I make some brief observations relating to how far tort designs which have expressly incorporated Convention rights, in particular the post-*Campbell*[17] privacy tort,[18] fall short of

---

17 *Campbell* v. *MGN Ltd* [2004] UKHL 22, [2004] 2 AC 457 ('*Campbell*').
18 No doubt there is still some life in the objection that the relevant privacy-protecting duty in English law is not part of tort law, but part of the law of equitable obligations. But

showing appropriate respect for 'the benchmarks which measure whether a particular formulation of the duty is good at achieving the goals of tort law'.

6.3.1 The judicial obligation to build torts to a particular template

I do not intend to discuss whether judges may ever be obliged to develop the scope of tort law in order to prevent a violation of Article 6, which might otherwise result from the 'removal of the courts' jurisdiction to determine a whole range of civil claims'. Instead, I will assume[19] that the decision of the majority of the Strasbourg court in *Z* v. *United Kingdom*[20] successfully quelled the outbreak of *Osmania*[21] that threatened to reverse the basic proposition that Article 6 'does not itself guarantee any particular content for (civil) rights and obligations in the substantive law of the Contracting States'.[22] I also do not intend to provide a detailed summary of the debate between those who believe that the HRA has given Convention rights direct horizontal effect, those who believe that it ought to have had no effect on the obligations of private actors, and those who have adopted intermediate positions.[23] Instead, I will mention only *some* obstacles in the way of a conclusion that the HRA has created an obligation on judges to build common law[24] torts *to a particular template*. Thus, my focus is not directly on *whether* an obligation to develop tort law to a particular template *exists*, but rather on three specific questions

---

any strategic advantage that the courts may have gained from developing protection for privacy within the existing cause of action for breach of confidence has now dissipated: development of privacy protection has required the creation within that cause of action of a separate strain of wrong based around distinct conditions of liability and defences. The strategy of cuckoos does not make their offspring into blackbirds. In any case, the precise classification of the duty does not affect the basic argument about its design.

19 I make this assumption primarily to limit the scope and length of the chapter. The question when, if ever, a restriction on the substantive scope of a common law right might violate Art. 6 is clearly a matter that deserves detailed analysis, though it may not yield a definitive answer: see *Matthews* v. *Ministry of Defence* [2003] UKHL 4, [2003] 1 AC 1163, Lord Walker at [141], 'The uncertain shadow of *Osman* v. *UK* still lies over this area of the law.'

20 [2001] 2 FLR 612.

21 See *Osman* v. *United Kingdom* (1998) 29 EHRR 245, [1999] 1 FLR 193.

22 Reiterated in *Z* v. *United Kingdom* [2001] 2 FLR 612 at [87].

23 Alison Young, in Chapter 2 of this volume, identifies four possible forms of weak indirect effect and seven different versions of strong indirect effect: see above, pp. 39–47.

24 Thus, I want to leave aside the question of how far the HRA and considerations of what makes a good tort duty are relevant when interpreting statutes which impose tort duties. Chapter 4 in this volume discusses the constitutional and institutional limits on statutory interpretation in private law cases.

that ought to confront anyone inclined to ask whether it exists. The issues that I discuss are: (i) how the obligation comes to be an obligation to develop *tort law*; (ii) how it is imposed on *judges*; and (iii) how it specifies a particular template ('mirror the Convention') for the tort duties which must be introduced.

6.3.1.1 A duty to develop the law of torts

It is helpful at this stage to highlight the distinction between an obligation to develop tort law so as to ensure better protection for substantive Convention rights, and one to develop tort law so as to provide an adequate remedy for violations of Convention rights. This distinction is important because different evidence will be necessary to satisfy claims that tort law must be developed to achieve each of these purposes. To spell this point out, if the claim is only that tort law must be developed in a particular way to ensure that an adequate remedy is available for violations of human rights, then we might expect to find evidence that the Convention demands a particular *type of remedy* for human rights violations, this is a type of remedy that can be provided through tort law, and this is a type of remedy that is not already being provided to victims in some other way. By contrast, if the claim is that tort law must be developed in a particular way so as to provide better protection for substantive human rights,[25] then we might expect to find evidence that the Convention makes demands about what steps must be taken to reduce the extent of non-compliance.

Anyone inclined to treat the HRA as having created an obligation to develop tort law in order to achieve some required end must surely think that there is evidence that developing *tort law* would assist in achieving that end. To give an easy example: if there was already a satisfactory procedure for obtaining an adequate remedy for a particular type of violation it is hard to imagine why the law would impose an obligation to develop tort law (even in cases where such judicial innovation would be constitutionally tolerable) in order to provide a *further* route to an adequate remedy.[26] Of course, many lawyers would accept that an obligation to innovate in order to produce an unnecessary duplicate is absurd. But in order to reconcile this acceptance with an obligation on *every state*

---

25 To avoid misunderstanding, protection of substantive human rights would be improved by a tort duty *if* the tort duty led to more people refraining from acting inconsistently with human rights. Thus, instead of providing remedies tort law would reduce the number of people who might need remedies.

26 The point made is merely about an *obligation* to develop tort law. No doubt the absence of obligation does not establish the absence of prudential reasons for developing tort law.

institution to do what it can to help (discussed in the next section), it is necessary to posit that the obligation of *every* state institution is fulfilled once *any* institution has done enough.

If the judicial obligation was to develop tort law in order to *provide* an adequate remedy, then it may be safe to conclude that this obligation has now evaporated in cases involving public defendants, because the development of the tort law duties of public bodies and officials will be pointless duplication: satisfactory – from the perspective of the Convention – remedies can already be obtained against such defendants by claims based directly on the HRA. If this is correct, then any continuing judicial obligation to develop tort law in a case with a public defendant *must be* based not on the aim of providing remedies – satisfactory remedies already exist – but on the aim of achieving better substantive compliance. But even here, when any tort duty developed will be owed by public defendants, it is not easy to see how it will provide an extra incentive to respect human rights since it will *duplicate* the (implied)[27] statutory duty not to act incompatibly with a Convention right. Perhaps it could be argued that although the *form* of a new tort duty would duplicate the pre-existing duty not to act incompatibly, the prospect of *tort process* and *tort remedies going beyond adequate remedies*[28] would increase the likelihood of compliance with the duty. Leaving aside empirical plausibility, we must note that (since any obligation imposed by Parliament on the judiciary is related to compatibility with the Convention) the argument supposes that the Convention imposes obligations to take steps *prospectively* to achieve some minimum level of attainment of respect for Convention rights, such an obligation not being fulfilled by the provision of satisfactory remedies for violations. To draw a parallel, the argument is similar to contending that some measure of damages is an adequate remedy for some wrong, but a duty backed by such a remedy is not sufficient to reduce wrongdoing to an appropriate level, so an additional remedy ought to be available. There is no logical flaw in this argument. But anyone seeking to rely on it as underpinning a judicial obligation to develop tort law must convince themselves that the Convention requires that states secure a degree of compliance *beyond* what can be achieved by the imposition of duties and adequate remedies for their breach.

So far I have considered what consequences might follow a concession that there cannot be a duty to develop tort law where to do so would

---

27 Implied because s. 6 of the HRA does not expressly impose a duty not to act incompatibly.
28 For example, exemplary or punitive damages.

involve a pointless duplication of duties and remedies. But might a broader concession be required? For example, should we interpret Parliament as having imposed an *obligation* to develop tort law even where it is clear that doing so is not likely to be the most efficient or effective method of advancing the purpose concerned? For instance, if the goal is that in future there should be better protection of the lives of prosecution witnesses who are threatened,[29] then it is not self-evident that the threat of costly civil litigation to establish the precise facts of a past case so that the 'new' tort duty can be retrospectively applied to them is likely to be the best way of achieving this goal. The method may be relatively costly. Further, there must be doubts as to whether such a threat will be felt by those public officials best placed to take whatever internal steps, perhaps through altering training or guidance, are most likely to further the relevant goal. Perhaps those inclined to recognise a judicial obligation to develop tort law will insist that this obligation extends even to requiring the use of a relatively inefficient and ineffective method of securing future compliance. But would they press this to the extent of requiring the development of tort duties where there is a significant risk that ongoing tort litigation would actually *impede* other initiatives intended to secure better future compliance with Convention rights?[30] Would it make sense for a legal system to acknowledge an obligation to develop tort law to enhance compliance with Convention rights that extends to circumstances where such a development is likely to reduce compliance?

This may be an appropriate point at which to introduce the issue of the appropriate constitutional limits on judicial innovation in tort law. In other words, even if the HRA has imposed an obligation on judges to use a relatively inefficient and ineffective way of securing an improvement in future human rights compliance,[31] there remains the question of whether the likely utility of any development of tort law is a relevant factor in deciding whether it would be constitutionally appropriate for a judge to innovate to the necessary extent. Might the constitutional freedom of judges to innovate in the law of torts be relative to the perceived utility of their innovations? If so, this provides a basis for insisting that the benchmarks remain relevant.

---

29 See *Van Colle*.
30 For example, those charged with designing an internal response might benefit from candour as to what caused the shortfall, but the prospect of tort litigation may inhibit that candour.
31 At least where development in tort law will not amount to no more than wasteful duplication and will not positively impede the project.

6.3.1.2 A duty on judges

Those who adopt intermediate positions that postulate a *limited* duty on judges to develop common law torts better to secure behaviour compatible with human rights, for instance postulating a duty to do so to such an extent as it is constitutionally legitimate for judges to develop the common law of torts, commonly concentrate on the *negative* restrictions on such a duty. This has led them to focus on questions such as how innovative an alteration to tort law can be before it becomes one which it is constitutionally inappropriate for a *judge* to introduce,[32] with degrees of innovation investigated through inquiries such as whether a change is 'more than an incremental development', whether the product of the change is a 'new cause of action', and how such a change relates to precedent.[33] But while such concentration on the negative restrictions is understandable it sidelines the prior question of how such a positive obligation comes to be imposed on *judges* in the first place. To put the point bluntly, even if we ought to assume that there may sometimes be an obligation on the United Kingdom to develop the law of torts this does not explain how such an obligation binds *judges*.

Obviously, it is generally accepted that section 6 of the HRA makes it unlawful for judges to act in a way that is incompatible with a Convention right, and this clearly provides a good basis for arguing that judges may be obliged to make some changes to tort law; for instance, so as to avoid granting remedies which would be incompatible with a Convention right. Moreover, section 6(6) of the HRA provides that 'a failure to act' is 'an act' for the purposes of the obligation imposed by section 6. But there are two ways in which a duty to avoid judicial 'acts' that might be incompatible with Convention rights might be distinguished from a duty to avoid 'failing to act'.

The first distinction stems from the fact that on any particular day many different state institutions may have 'failed to act' to protect a claimant's Convention rights. For example, Parliament clearly has the power to develop the law of torts, and some public officials may have the power to treat themselves as subject to obligations even without legislative or judicial action. This means that *judicial* development usually

---

32 Clearly, a significant issue is that such innovations will apply retrospectively; liability will depend on the law as determined in the judgment rather than on the law as commonly and reasonably understood at the date of the behaviour.

33 These are the variables used by Alison Young in presenting her seven varieties of strong indirect horizontal effect.

cannot be considered the *only* way of developing legal obligations so as to achieve human rights goals, but, at best, merely *one way* of doing so. The second possible point of distinction between 'incompatible acts' and 'incompatible omissions' is that the potential victim of an 'act' will often be more imminent and identifiable than the potential victim of a judicial failure to create new duties within tort law. Indeed, it will often be impossible to say of a particular victim that his or her Convention rights would probably have been respected if only a judge had previously developed a duty within the common law of torts.

The two points raised in the previous paragraph are, of course, related, in that *sometimes* an omission to develop the law of torts *will* have a direct and identifiable victim and it will be easy to see why a *judge* might be best placed to ensure respect for that victim's Convention rights; for example, when the right at stake is 'privacy', a defendant has manifested an immediate intention to publish material that will violate that right, and is only delaying because of an interim injunction. By contrast, the suggestion that judges must extend the scope of tort law in a case where there is no prospect of a remedy *protecting* the immediate claimant's right, for example, where a defendant allegedly failed to take any steps to rescue an unconscious claimant from an otherwise innocuous hazard,[34] involves a situation where the judicial alteration to the law could only ever protect the *rights to life* of some unidentified future class (those who in future fall unconscious into shallow puddles near people inclined to be motivated by the law of torts and the like), and where the same class could be equally benefited by a whole host of other public officials (the legislature, those in charge of police deployment, etc.). No doubt an obligation on *every state institution to do whatever it can* to protect as yet unidentified individuals in the future is a *theoretical* possibility. But can such an obligation – *every state institution must do what it can to help protect classes of unidentified individuals against future risks* – be found within the Convention?

One argument that should be swiftly set aside might claim that the exclusion of the Houses of Parliament and failures to introduce proposals for legislation from the scope of section 6 of the HRA[35] establishes that Parliament has imposed a duty on judges to do whatever *they* can in such cases. It must be set aside because the fact that section 6 does not oblige Ministers (or back-benchers) to introduce bills, nor Parliament to pass them, does not establish that legislative powers should be ignored as

---

34 Such as a shallow puddle.
35 The exclusions are found in ss. 6(3)(b) and 6(6) of the HRA.

an alternative, and often superior, way of creating law to achieve human rights goals when considering what the Convention requires.

My opinion is that the Convention does not contain a general requirement that every emanation of a state must do whatever it lawfully can in order to increase the likelihood that there will be fewer violations of Convention rights in the future. Consequently, the duty imposed on judges by section 6 of the HRA does not create a *general* obligation to make changes to tort law for the benefit of future classes, even if such changes would be constitutionally legitimate. My primary goal, however, is not to defend this opinion, but merely to identify obstacles in the way of a conclusion that the HRA has created an obligation on judges to build common law torts to a particular template. Thus, my claim here is simply that the need to find specific obligations imposed by the Convention to develop private law *to help protect classes of unidentified individuals against future risks* will often be such an obstacle.

One further concern about *incremental* judicial development can be expressed relatively briefly, although this should not be treated as a measure of its complexity: if tort duties are developed to protect Convention rights, then it will become necessary to check that a restriction to *incremental* developments does not lead to any unjustifiable discrimination as to the extent to which Convention rights are protected. A concrete example may help to anchor this point. Consider, for example, the incremental development of property torts to protect privacy (and other aspects of Article 8) indirectly. In this context there might be a tension between arguments that property torts should be incrementally expanded in various ways to protect the Article 8 rights of those with a particular degree of association with the property, and a rival argument based on Article 14 that it is discriminatory to link Article 8 protection to particular forms of association with private property. Perhaps a further obstacle facing anyone inclined to identify a judicial obligation to develop tort law in a particular way will be to demonstrate that such obligations will not discriminate in favour of those who enjoy interests which are already well protected by the common law.

As a final observation in this section it is worth noting that so far as the Convention *does* impose an obligation on *every state institution to do what it lawfully can,*[36] then this must apply to a far wider range of

---

36 A nice point might be whether this obligation extends to requiring institution A to use its power to extend the lawful powers of institution B. For example, might the UK Parliament be obliged to legislate so as to relax any constitutional limits on judicial law-making?

bodies than the judiciary. For example, it ought to apply to administrative bodies with power to make subordinate legislation. This might mean, for example, that any public authority with the power to create bye-laws for a public park will be acting unlawfully if it fails to pass bye-laws requiring park users to rescue others from ponds and puddles. Similarly, those with discretion to deploy public officials might be obliged to allocate them to patrolling ponds and puddles rather than carrying out non-mandatory tasks with no human rights dimension (for example, picking up litter). Likewise, those with discretion to spend public funds might be obliged to set up schemes offering rewards to incentivise those who might otherwise hesitate over pulling people from ponds and puddles. Perhaps we should anticipate someone arguing that the park authority does not have to pass bye-laws, the managers do not have to re-deploy public officials, and no one has to fund a reward scheme because no positive obligation can arise under the Convention until the obliged party ought to appreciate that some particular person, or identifiable class, is at *immediate* risk of death or serious suffering. But, if this argument is valid, it also serves to disarm any judicial obligation to 'develop' the common law so as to recognise a duty which will only help an unidentified class in the future.

6.3.1.3 A template for torts?

So far I have discussed how any obligation to develop tort duties might come to be an obligation to develop *tort law* and one which is imposed on *judges*. The third issue I want to confront is more directly relevant to the central theme of tort design: could any obligation of judges to develop tort law make it mandatory for them to develop only tort law duties which precisely mirror Convention rights? To make the issue more concrete, suppose that a particular Convention right is defined in such a way that a violation can be identified only *after* the degree of culpability of the actor and severity of the consequences have been assessed, but a tort duty which is based on a familiar and fixed degree of culpability whatever the consequences is likely to be more effective at securing fulfilment of this right than a duty precisely mirroring the Convention right;[37] would it not be odd if courts bound to develop tort law so as to reduce the

---

37 A fictitious non-tort example may help: if there was a human right to legal assistance when questioned by police 'except where denial is proportionate to reasons of state necessity' for denying this, then the right might be better fulfilled by a national legislature imposing on the police a duty to provide legal assistance 'unless there is convincing evidence that doing so will facilitate intimidation of witnesses, destruction of evidence . . . etc.' rather than a duty phrased in terms of 'proportionality' and 'state necessity'.

number of people whose Convention rights are infringed were bound to introduce a relatively ineffective tort duty precisely mirroring the form of the Convention right? Surely a duty '*to do whatever you can*' might instead demand the introduction of the tort duty which was likely to achieve the most by way of reducing the number of people whose Convention rights are infringed?

But here we must confront a dilemma that it is easiest to illustrate with a non-tort example. Suppose that the Convention requires states to take steps to prevent their citizens from starving to death. Suppose also in a particular state that a minister has a statutory power to give binding directions as to the distribution of the 'strategic food reserve'. Imposition of a legal duty on the minister to feed those known to be at immediate risk of starving to death would no doubt have some effect, but there will almost certainly be some citizens who still starve because of the difficulty of identifying those at risk. By contrast, a legal duty to provide minimal supplies to every citizen would be likely to lead to a greater reduction in the number of starving people, but only at the cost of delivering a benefit to a large number of people whose Convention rights were never in jeopardy, and perhaps also at the cost of providing an insufficient amount to *some* people who *would* have been helped more by a scheme which required the state to consider what it 'knows'. If the minister was subject to a provision identical to section 6 of the HRA, then which of these versions of his or her duty should the minister acknowledge?

If the choice is between an obligation to introduce a scheme precisely mirroring a Convention right and an obligation to introduce a scheme which does not precisely mirror a Convention right but is likely to achieve greater compliance it is hard to see why, from a human rights perspective, anyone would argue for the former. Indeed, that preference seems right even if some beneficiaries of the former scheme would not benefit from the latter, provided that the overall level of compliance improves.[38] But if this is the case, then can there be any objection to the development of tort duties which are not precisely parallel to human rights provisions, but might be more *effective* at improving overall compliance?[39] Perhaps in

---

38 Of course, this assumes that the awkwardness cannot be avoided by reframing the choice as being between the former scheme and a scheme that combines both the former and latter: I stipulate that the 'strategic food reserve' is too small to enable both schemes to be carried out.

39 No doubt there *can be* good reasons for anchoring a tort design to the terms that have been used to define a human right; for instance, such anchoring will, if performed competently, forestall future arguments that the new tort design needs still further modification to

some cases an objection might arise from the tension between the design that will best improve future compliance and the design that will best deliver satisfactory remedies to past victims who *require* them. But even in this rare situation it is not self-evident that priority should be given to the formulation that delivers remedies most accurately. Moreover, where an adequate remedy is provided through a non-tort route doubts about the effectiveness of mirrored designs seem a clear obstacle in the way of any conclusion that judges are obliged to build torts that perfectly reflect Convention rights.

The practical significance of the points in the previous paragraph may, perhaps, be best illustrated by working through a rather superficial example. Let us assume that all family members enjoy a human right that their residence should not be subjected to certain severe forms of pollution, and that a judge is considering whether he or she is obliged to develop the tort of private nuisance to better secure fulfilment of this right. Such a development would be likely to require an alteration of the rule from *Hunter* v. *Canary Wharf Ltd*[40] as to who may bring a claim in private nuisance, in other words, to whom the duty not to unreasonably interfere with the use and enjoyment of a particular plot of land is owed. But surely the judge should not consider that his or her only options are to leave the law untouched or make an alteration as to who can sue that will only apply in cases of such severe pollution as to involve a human rights violation (making the tort *precisely* shadow the human rights obligation). One further option that ought to be considered is to change the rule as to who can sue *for all cases of private nuisance*, not just those involving such severe pollution as to involve a human rights violation. This said, the consequences of altering the rule as to who can sue for *minor* private nuisances might be thought to be too great, and this might lead to a preference for the option of developing the tort of private nuisance so that one class could claim for minor nuisances and another class for severe ones. But if such a distinction is to be introduced it might be better, from the perspective of influencing behaviour or efficient settlement of disputes, to rely on distinguishing factors other than those directly invoked in human rights cases. The purpose of the example is not, of course, to advocate any particular alteration to the tort of private

achieve better compatibility. But my argument is *not* that these reasons should be ignored; rather, they should be weighed alongside other factors which ought to influence the design of tort duties.

40 [1997] AC 655.

nuisance, but merely to establish that an obligation that insists on alterations that will precisely shadow Convention rights may lead to law which is sub-optimal by way of its capacity to alter behaviour and the cost of settling disputes.

Of course, there are at least two reasons why judges might *prefer* to develop tort duties as precise shadows even if their obligation does not specify a template. First, using such a model might be thought to establish a constitutional basis for the particular form of the innovation. Second, a judge confronted with a choice between different possible developments might ask, wholly understandably, how the common law method provides a basis for choosing between them, especially if those that are likely to be most effective might be those that are least obviously 'incremental'. The principal theme of this chapter, however, is to caution against any lazy assumption that Convention rights are templates for good torts. The judge who asks 'How should I choose between designs?' should be told to consider both how far a particular formulation of the duty will really increase compliance with human rights and the benchmarks that measure whether the formulation will be good at achieving the goals of tort law, as well as the constitutional limits on judicial innovation.

6.3.1.4 Straw men?

Do the concerns raised in this section have any *real* target, or are they thrusts against a 'straw man', an imaginary menace? Perhaps the best answer is to sketch the target and leave readers to consider whether the result is an exaggerated caricature or a plausible photo-fit. The primary target might be a judge who accepts an invitation to induce from cases decided by the Strasbourg court 'what Strasbourg holds it is the duty of the State to do in such a situation', and then directly translates this into a duty (recognised by national law) expressed in identical terms on some potential defendant, usually a public official or authority, which will give rise to remedies in tort if it is broken, pausing on the way merely to consider if the innovation is too radical to fall within *judicial* competence. Fortunately, the number of English judges whose behaviour has in any way resembled the sketch is low. But the secondary target comprises those academic lawyers who write and think as if judges should be encouraged to behave in accordance with this sketch. The negative sketch can be contrasted to a positive role model: such a judge, would consider what advantages might be achieved by imposing a duty in tort law – in addition to the provisions of the HRA – whether there is really a *obligation* on him or her to develop tort law to achieve these advantages or merely *reasons* for doing so, and how any duty he or she might develop in national law can best be designed in order to achieve these advantages.

6.3.2 Challenging features of Convention rights

Under this heading I catalogue some features of Convention rights that might conflict with established elements within the structure of the common law torts. The catalogue is not intended to be exhaustive, but simply to add some substance to the claim that it would be inappropriate to assume that tort duties that *mirror* Convention rights would work effectively and efficiently as tort duties. In the next section I go on to suggest, briefly, why I believe that torts that have directly incorporated Convention concepts, such as the post-*Campbell*[41] privacy tort,[42] are unlikely to be optimal at achieving the goals of tort law.

6.3.2.1 Acts and omissions

An acceptable summary of orthodox negligence doctrine relating to public actors might be: (1) if a public actor performs a task which *creates* a reasonably foreseeable risk of physical damage to the claimant's person or property then the public actor will *usually*[43] come under a duty (breach of which will amount to the tort of negligence) to perform the task with reasonable skill and care; (2) if a public actor has the capacity to intervene in order to *reduce* a risk to the claimant's person or property, and it is reasonably foreseeable that if the actor fails to intervene then the claimant will be harmed, then the public actor will only *exceptionally*[44] come under a duty (breach of which will amount to the tort of negligence) to make a competent decision as to whether to intervene or to demonstrate

---

41 *Campbell.*

42 My response to objections to the use of the word 'tort' in this context is above, at n. 18.

43 There are exceptions: for instance, where the task involves the pursuit of military objectives in wartime (see, e.g., *Shaw Savill and Albion Co. Ltd* v. *The Commonwealth* (1940) 66 CLR 344), some tasks related to the investigation of crime (see, e.g., *Brooks* v. *Chief Constable of Police for the Metropolis* [2005] 1 WLR 1495) and some tasks where a duty to one class of claimants might divert focus from the primary purpose of protecting another class (see, e.g., *JD* v. *East Berkshire Community NHS Trust* [2005] 2 AC 373).

44 The most common exception is where the public actor has 'assumed responsibility' *to the* claimant for reducing the risk, for instance, by 'undertaking' to provide a professional-style risk-control service *to* the claimant.

reasonable skill and care in ensuring that the intervention is effective in reducing the risk. The distinction between *creating* a reasonably foresee-able risk and failing to intervene to *reduce* a risk, which is often presented (at the risk of considerable confusion) as the distinction between *acts* and *omissions*, is one which reflects a *foundational* concept within the law of torts.[45] To put the same point another way, the question of whether a situation involves *creation* of a risk or *failure to reduce* one does not depend on whether the defendant is a public or a private actor.

If the positive obligations directly imposed by the Convention were to be mirrored by tort law, then the new duties would bind only public defendants.[46] For instance, if English tort law had been developed in the *Smith* case so as to hold that when 'a member of the public (A) furnishes a police officer (B) with apparently credible evidence that a third party whose identity and whereabouts are known presents a specific and immediate threat to his [A's] life or physical safety, B owes A a duty to take reasonable steps to assess the threat and, if appropriate, take reasonable steps to prevent it being executed',[47] then this duty would not be similar to any duty owed by private defendants. Surely, no such duty would be owed by B in such circumstances if he were a *private* gangland enforcer, even if he had greater power than the police to prevent a threat from being carried out in a particular community.

Would treating public and private defendants as subject to different tort duties reduce the efficiency or effectiveness of tort law? Clearly, one concern might be that there would be an additional degree of uncertainty, and cost of litigating, as to whether particular defendants were on the 'public' side of the line. But such uncertainty would parallel what already exists with regard to the duty under section 6 of the HRA. A further concern might be that to introduce such a distinction into tort law would bring the law of torts into disrepute. How could it be explained, for example, that a pupil would have greater *private law* entitlements against a teacher in a state-funded school learning of severe bullying by a particular

---

45 Claiming that the concept is *foundational* is not, of course, the same as claiming that all situations can be classified uncontentiously.

46 The question of whether there could be a judicial obligation to impose a duty on private individuals is briefly discussed above, pp. 118–24. It is noted there, however, that there are considerable obstacles in the way of recognising a judicial obligation to impose *positive obligations* on private individuals.

47 This was Lord Bingham's formulation of the duty (which he referred to as 'the liability principle') in *Smith* v. *Chief Constable of Sussex Police* [2008] UKHL 50, [2009] 1 AC 225 (heard alongside *Chief Constable of the Hertfordshire Police* v. *Van Colle*). The majority of the House of Lords rejected such a duty.

perpetrator than against a similar teacher in a school funded by privately-paid fees or against a youth leader in a club run on a voluntary basis by a charity?[48] So far as the HRA incorporates such a distinction any difference in the duties and availability of remedies contained in the Act can be attributed to the choice of Parliament; but could a judge defend developing private law entitlements in this uneven way? Perhaps it might be argued that the ideal solution would be for a judge to develop the common law so as to impose a mirroring obligation on public actors *and* extend a similar obligation to private actors as well. But such an extension would conflict with the reasoning that has previously been relied on to explain the general absence of duties to intervene to reduce risks created by others, or their consequences.[49] Moreover, such a solution would magnify the problems assessed in section 6.3.2.2 below.

6.3.2.2 Liability turning on some degree of fault (or severity of damage)

Creating tort duties to mirror the positive obligations directly imposed by Convention rights might also cause problems as far as they impose standards other than objective reasonable care, and liabilities that are conditional on a breach leading to a particular degree of personal injury or property damage. Clearly, one concern here is that any proliferation of different standards of care within the tort of negligence is likely to increase uncertainty and settlement costs, particularly if the new standards incorporate elements that are peculiarly costly for potential claimants to monitor and prove, such as a defendant's state of mind or the 'severity' of a misinterpretation of the law. A further concern must be that any liability that depends on damage of a particular degree of severity having been suffered may prove to be less effective at altering behaviour (and securing compliance) than a simpler duty: indeed, where liability depends on some composite assessment of the defendant's degree of culpability and the severity of the claimant's harm it may be impossible to express the duty with which the defendant ought to comply in practical terms.[50]

---

48 Suppose, e.g., that the public defendant acted reasonably to discharge its obligation by notifying a private agency then the private agency failed to act effectively.

49 See, e.g., the speech of Lord Hoffmann in *Stovin* v. *Wise* [1996] AC 923.

50 Of course, some scholars who write about tort law would not see this as a matter for concern, since they believe that tort law's 'duties' are fictitious, and are referred to in propositions about the law only as some sort of shorthand for circumstances where *liability* may result. On this, see the discussion in N. McBride, 'Duties of Care: Do they Really Exist?', *Oxford Journal of Legal Studies*, 24 (2004), 417.

6.3.2.3 Proportionality

In the next section I discuss in more detail the difficulties that have been caused by incorporating 'proportionality' into the newly recognised privacy tort. Here it is sufficient simply to note that potential defendants are likely to struggle to comply with a duty that requires them to make a case-by-case assessment of the value of another's interests.

6.4 Torts which purport to incorporate human rights

In the following section I seek to explain, briefly, why I believe that torts, such as the 'extended form of breach of confidence', which have been designed so as to incorporate provisions of the Convention, have failed to pay sufficient respect to 'the benchmarks which measure whether a particular formulation of the duty is good at achieving the goals of tort law'.

Imagine that a private claimant sues a newspaper defendant for libel and the defendant responds that the existing common law rules, which might appear to make it liable, ought to be altered because they amount to a disproportionate restriction on freedom of expression. Where a claim based on Article 10 takes the classic form of a claim against the state then clearly the state takes the burden of justifying the restriction, and must demonstrate that it is necessary in a democratic society, that is, proportionate to a pressing social need. Thus, the state will seek to demonstrate that the social need exists and that the limitation is proportionate: in particular, that no measure that limits the right to a lesser extent can be expected to satisfy the need. This process is not straightforward. There is no single recipe for a sufficient justification, and courts (consciously or unconsciously) determine what sort of evidence the state is required to muster or generate in the course of the legislative or decision-making process in order to establish a justification.[51]

---

51 It is surely obvious that the sort of material that must be produced to justify a restriction 'in the interests of national security' will be very different from the sort of material that must be produced to justify a restriction in the interest of 'the economic well-being of the country'. Equally, it might be thought obvious that the sort of material likely to be required to justify general legislation will be very different from the sort of material likely to be required to justify an individual decision. It may be worth noting that much of the discussion of proportionality as a standard of review in English administrative law has apparently overlooked the fact that, by determining what sort of evidence the state must produce in order to justify a decision, the courts will be indirectly determining how legislative and decision-making *processes* must be structured and, indirectly, the sorts of measures and decisions that can be contemplated.

Clearly, this approach to justification cannot be straightforwardly translated to the context of claims between private parties: surely, private individuals seeking to protect their reputations should not have an obligation equivalent to a state's to generate evidence demonstrating that no less extensive limitation on free expression than the rules of libel law which currently exist will sufficiently meet this need?[52] Even if it is thought that individuals involved in litigation over the rules of libel law should have to produce *some* evidence about the effects of alternative versions of the law, surely they cannot be expected to generate the same sort of evidence that the state might be expected to generate in order to justify legislation defining the tort or defences to it. The obvious problem stems from the fact that the claimant in such a case did not *make* the rule that he or she invokes. Indeed, when the rule is a product of the incremental common law process, nobody who might plausibly be described as the rule-maker is likely to be a party to the litigation or even capable of intervening.[53] Moreover, where a rule predates widespread discussion of human rights concerns, and many of the common law rules relating to libel and its defences do, it is generally the case that the judgments in which such rules were formulated or refined will not even contain any discussion of the proportionality of the rule and the reasons why alternatives ought to be rejected.

A further dimension of proportionality inquiries may also be worth consideration. In deciding cases involving rules or policies made by the legislature or elements of the executive the courts have been inclined to assess the expertise of the relevant institutions in assessing their views as to factors concerned and the balance between them. Where a rule or policy has been made by an institution with a higher degree of expertise this has been treated as justifying the courts treating its views with a higher degree of deference.[54] But what is the appropriate degree of deference where

---

52 Similarly, can it really be supposed that a media defendant seeking to resist the expansion of a tort to protect privacy must generate evidence demonstrating that any further curtailment of free expression will restrict that value to a greater extent than can be justified by the project of protecting privacy?

53 Who ought to intervene to demonstrate that the rule of privilege developed by the House of Lords in *Reynolds* v. *Times Newspapers Ltd* [2001] 2 AC 127 strikes the appropriate balance between protection of reputation and free expression?

54 No doubt this simplifies a complex and controversial area. Some judges regard the language of 'deference' as unhelpful, some have been inclined to take into account the constitutional legitimacy of the institution's claim to make such decisions (as well as its expertise) when assessing such matters, and a strong academic case has been made for considering not just the institution's innate expertise, but also whether its *processes* on the particular occasion suggest that the expertise was suitably deployed.

what is under scrutiny is a common law rule that has been developed incrementally by generations of judges? And should there be any difference in approach depending on whether an expert or inexpert litigant[55] seeks to invoke, and therefore defend, the rule?

When it is claimed that the state has made some rule or policy that is incompatible with human rights it has become commonplace to describe the staged processes operating between judiciary and state whereby it is determined whether a justification has been sufficiently established as a 'dialogue': courts are aware that if they castigate a legislative or decision-making process as inadequate in public law proceedings, then the consequence will often be that the matter is reconsidered using an improved process, and, if necessary, the product of this reconsideration can be considered by the courts. But there is no equivalent of 'dialogue' in a private law claim: a decision in the context of a libel claim that no sufficient justification has been provided for the particular liability rules that the claimant was invoking will either preclude liability, or, at the very least, give rise to an awkward procedural question.[56]

The discussion in the previous four paragraphs has assumed a situation where the proportionality of a particular *rule* is challenged. Similar problems are likely to arise, however, where a tort duty is designed to shadow precisely a qualified Convention right, so that the definition of the tort requires proportionality to be expressly assessed with regard to the specific facts of the case. An example of this may be provided by the newly developed privacy tort (or, for those who prefer, newly extended sub-species of breach of confidence), which appears to impose liability for publication of private material where such a restriction on free expression is necessary in a democratic society in order to protect privacy and it is not necessary to sacrifice the protection of privacy to preserve a sufficient degree of free expression.[57] In order to apply such a liability rule

---

55 It does not seem implausible to suppose that some private litigants, for instance, newspapers, may have greater insight into the effects of libel law on freedom of expression (expertise) than some other private litigants (for instance, television celebrities or professional footballers).

56 An awkward procedural question can arise where, for instance, the court finds that the claimant has not mustered the evidence necessary to establish that the restriction on the defendant's free expression was justified, but is unable to determine whether the evidence could have been mustered had the claimant been aware of what was likely to be required at an early enough stage in proceedings.

57 This double balance reflects the fact that neither right (privacy or free expression) takes priority: *Campbell* at [140] *per* Baroness Hale. See also [113] *per* Lord Hope and [167] *per* Lord Carswell.

it seems that the questions as to whether the claimant's privacy could be sufficiently protected without such a restriction on free expression and whether the defendant's free expression can be sufficiently exercised without such harm to privacy are both relevant.[58] In the privacy context it seems that the English courts have silently accepted that a tort duty phrased in the terminology used to define a Convention right will, nonetheless, not require the same sort of evidence that might be required in a review of state action for compatibility with the same right. Certainly, no English judge has compelled a privacy claimant to *demonstrate* that no imaginable measure that limits freedom of expression to a lesser extent than a claim for damages, including damages for distress, can be expected to protect his or her privacy sufficiently.[59]

If we focus directly on 'the benchmarks that measure whether a particular formulation of the duty is good at achieving the goals of tort law' then a key question must be whether a duty reflecting the 'balance' between the competing Convention rights is likely to be effective at regulating behaviour. Here it is worth considering how frequently potential defendants will be poorly placed to assess the value from a free speech perspective of what they are contemplating publishing and the value from a privacy perspective of not doing so. Clearly, if the only potential defendants are newspapers with the resources to consult expert human rights lawyers, and the only potential claimants are a relatively homogeneous group of 'celebrities' who provided fairly clear indications of what aspects of their lives they were willing to share with a mass audience, then the duty might be effective. But the scope of the duty is not limited in this way: a wide range of people in a wide range of contexts 'publish' material about other people, and frequently have to consider whether they are at liberty to do so where there is no realistic prospect of consulting a human rights lawyer.

---

58 In the *Campbell* case the House of Lords does seem to have regarded the newspaper defendant as having some special expertise as to what might be necessary in order to communicate a legitimate story effectively, but does not seem to have credited the claimant with any parallel expertise as to what degree of privacy might be necessary in order to live as a recovering drug addict.

59 This is not, of course, to claim that sufficient evidence could not be marshalled to demonstrate that no alternative measure can be expected to protect privacy sufficiently without restricting free expression to the same extent. But a few moments spent considering how one might go about generating appropriate evidence might help to bring home the magnitude of the task.

6.5 Conclusion

It has not been argued in this chapter that tort law has no useful role to play in better securing Convention rights. Rather, the primary argument has been that it should not be assumed that the best way for tort law to play a useful role is by the development of tort duties that precisely shadow such rights and incorporate the concepts that the Strasbourg court has found useful. In rare cases such innovations could actually impede the human rights project or be no more useful than the production of a wasteful duplicate. More often, however, such an assumption may prevent consideration of different designs for new tort duties, which may be both more efficient and effective. In any case, where concepts used in the definition of substantive human rights are transposed into tort duties the different procedural contexts mean that the concepts may have to be applied differently. The design of torts may be a craft similar to the building of medieval cathedrals, but its values should not be neglected even when pursuing a project as important as seeking to secure protection of Convention rights.

7

Privacy: the development of breach of confidence – the clearest case of horizontal effect?

GAVIN PHILLIPSON

Soon after the Human Rights Act came into force, one commentator suggested that 'horizontal effect [will] perhaps have its greatest impact in the field of privacy',[1] and this prediction appears to have been fully vindicated: it is generally acknowledged that it is in the development of breach of confidence into a species of privacy tort that common law horizontal effect has been at its clearest and strongest. Statements by Law Lords in *Campbell* v. *MGN Ltd*[2] that 'The essence of the tort [of breach of confidence] is better encapsulated now as misuse of private information',[3] followed by the Court of Appeal in *Douglas* v. *Hello! Ltd* acknowledging this transformation in bold terms by referring to the 'action formerly described as breach of confidence',[4] have had commentators reaching excitedly for their pens to celebrate the new birth. The author has been one of those who have insisted upon the significance of the developments, arguing that they have seen the discarding of one of the key limbs of breach of confidence and the transformation of the other, resulting in at least a *de facto* new right to privacy.[5] The use of birth metaphors is not just a sign of academic over-excitement, judges have used them too: Jack J in *A* v. *B* referred to 'the law of confidence' as 'like a mother swollen with the child of privacy' who had now 'given birth and the umbilical cord

---

1 J. Morgan, 'Privacy, Confidence and Horizontal Effect: "Hello" Trouble', *Cambridge Law Journal* (2003), 444 at 467 (Morgan, '"Hello" Trouble').
2 [2004] 2 WLR 1232 ('*Campbell*').
3 *Campbell* at [17].
4 *Douglas* v. *Hello! Ltd (No. 3)* [2005] EWCA Civ. 595, [2006] QB 125 at [53] ('*Douglas III*').
5 G. Phillipson, 'The "Right" of Privacy in England and Strasbourg Compared', in A. T. Kenyon and M. Richardson (eds.), *New Dimensions in Privacy Law* (Cambridge University Press, 2006) (Phillipson, 'Right of Privacy').

cut',[6] although we should immediately note that the typical common law qualifier that this 'may be' was added. Perhaps even more significant than this 're-christening'[7] of breach of confidence is the approach taken in the most recent Court of Appeal case, *Murray* v. *Express Newspapers Plc*,[8] in which the court, while purportedly dealing with a common law action, appeared to define its key tests in entirely Convention right terms.[9]

On the other hand, and apparently paradoxically, we have the phenomenon of the judges firmly disclaiming any notion that they are creating a new general right to privacy. Most importantly, of course, in *Wainwright* v. *Home Office*,[10] the House of Lords unanimously declined to hold that there was any tort of invasion of privacy, as such, in English law. The Court of Appeal in the same case saw formidable 'definitional difficulties and conceptual problems in the judicial development of a "blockbuster" privacy tort',[11] and thought the creation of such a tort, even if desirable, as being clearly a task for Parliament, not the judiciary.[12] Instead, Mummery LJ said that the judges preferred 'the promising and well trod path . . . of incremental evolution'.[13] Similarly, Woolf CJ, speaking *obiter* in *A* v. *B Plc* strongly steered the lower courts away from considering the development of a free-standing tort of privacy,[14] while Lindsay J, invited in *Douglas* v. *Hello! Ltd*[15] to declare a general right to privacy, firmly declined the opportunity.

The aim of this chapter is not to argue for a particular interpretation of the court's duty under the HRA, something I have attempted elsewhere.[16] Rather, its purpose is to make use of the rigorous taxonomy of different degrees of horizontal effect set out in Chapter 2 to investigate how far these admittedly important developments in the field of breach of confidence disclose a conscious application of any particular horizontal effect model – or set of models – by the judiciary. However, although it will not take issue with the model of 'full' or 'direct' horizontal effect originally advanced by

---

6 These dicta are from the initial judgment of Jack J in *A* v. *B*, 30 April 2001, unreported at [16]–[17].
7 As Buxton LJ referred to it in *McKennitt* v. *Ash* [2006] EWCA Civ. 1714, [2008] QB 73 at [8] ('*McKennitt*').
8 [2008] EWCA Civ. 446, [2009] Ch 481 ('*Rowling*').
9 See further below pp. 150–3.   10 [2003] 3 WLR 1137 ('*Wainwright*').
11 [2002] QB 1334, 1351 *per* Mummery LJ.   12 *Wainwright* at 1365.
13 *Wainwright* at 1365.   14 [2002] EWCA Civ. 337, [2003] QB 195 at 206.
15 [2003] 3 All ER 996 at [229(iii)]. This was the trial of the action.
16 G. Phillipson and A. Williams, 'Horizontal Effect and the Constitutional Constraint', (2011) *Modern Law Review* (forthcoming).

Sir William Wade,[17] but set out in more sophisticated form by others,[18] it will seek to refute the view recently advanced by three scholars[19] that the courts have actually recognised this model in recent privacy cases as the correct interpretation of their duty under the HRA. It will seek to explain the apparent paradox of the creation of a new tort accompanied by vehement denials of such activity, and will also provide a tentative answer to the important question: why is it in this area that horizontal effect has seemingly been at its strongest? In this way, it will seek to bring fresh perspectives both to the horizontal effect debate itself and to the question of how far judicial attitudes to horizontal effect in this particular area of law can be taken as a general template for the judicial view on horizontality overall.

It is necessary very briefly to explain the recent development of breach of confidence. Perhaps the most useful summary is to be found in the Court of Appeal's judgment in *Douglas III*. The court accepted that the basis of the action is now the notion of a 'reasonable expectation of privacy' and went on to say succinctly:

> Megarry J in *Coco* v. *A N Clark* identified two requirements for the creation of a duty of confidence. The first was that the information should be confidential in nature and the second was that it should have been imparted in circumstances importing a duty of confidence. As we have seen, it is now recognised that the second requirement is not necessary if it is plain that the information is confidential, and for the adjective 'confidential' one can substitute the word 'private'.[20]

The first change – the disappearance of the second limb – came, of course, from *Campbell*. While cases such as *Shelley Films*,[21] and, more recently *Douglas* v. *Hello!*, had provided for relief in breach of confidence against those who took snatched photographs, even though there was no

17 W. Wade, 'Horizons of Horizontality', *Law Quarterly Review*, 116 (2000), 217.
18 J. Morgan, 'Questioning the "True Effect" of the Human Rights Act', *Legal Studies*, 22 (2002), 259 and '"Hello" Trouble' and S. Pattinson and D. Beyleveld, 'Horizontal Applicability and Horizontal Effect', *Law Quarterly Review*, 118 (2002), 623.
19 N. Moreham, 'Privacy and Horizontality: Relegating the Common Law', *Law Quarterly Review*, 123 (2007), 373 (Moreham, 'Privacy and Horizontality'); T. Bennett, 'Horizontality's New Horizons – Re-Examining Horizontal Effect: Privacy, Defamation and the Human Rights Act', *Entertainment Law Review*, 21(3) (2010), 96 (Pt 1) and 145 (Pt 2) (hereafter, Bennett, 'Horizontality's New Horizons'). K. Hughes, 'Horizontal Privacy', *Law Quarterly Review*, 125 (2009), 244 (Hughes, 'Horizontal Privacy'), suggests that direct horizontality is evident in one recent judgment.
20 *Douglas III* at [83].
21 *Shelley Films Ltd* v. *Rex Features Ltd* [1994] EMLR 134.

agreement of confidentiality or previous relationship between the parties, nevertheless, in such cases there had been clear indications that the scene was intended to be confidential, such as warning signs forbidding photography (*Shelley Films*), or the elaborate security precautions to prevent photography taken at the Douglases' wedding. None of these factors were present in *Campbell*, in which the complained-of photographs were taken in the street. In fact, the only factor that could impose the obligation of confidence in relation to the photographs was the obviously private nature of the information itself – the fact that it concerned therapeutic treatment. *Campbell* was also the first case in which relief had been given in respect of *personal information* – as opposed to information of commercial value – taken in this way. This was then the first time that an English appellate court had imposed liability for unauthorised use of personal information, in the absence of any circumstances imposing the obligation save for the nature of the information itself. And if it is the private nature of the information that can itself impose the obligation, then the second limb of confidence effectively ceases to exist: there has to be information of a private nature to fulfil the first limb in any event, so the second limb no longer has any independent content. 'Breach of confidence' thus became an action that protects against unauthorised publicity given to private facts.

7.1 Applying Convention rights or Convention values/principles?

Before going on to analyse how horizontal effect has been applied in the cases, it is necessary to look a little more closely at the nature of Article 8 and its associated jurisprudence. In the very precise typology in Chapter 2, a distinction is drawn between models that regard the court as obliged to act compatibly with the rights themselves and those in which they are bound only to apply, or have regard to, Convention values.[22] However, certainly in relation to Article 8, it may be doubted whether this distinction is of real significance in practice. In my view, Article 8 can function in the private sphere only as a broad value, or set of principles. This point becomes clearer when we consider the nature of Article 8, as a generally qualified right, in contrast to narrower and more precise rights, such as Articles 2, 3 or 5, for example. Because of the breadth of the wording both of the primary guarantee ('respect for private life') and of the exceptions to it (the 'protection of morals', 'the rights of others'), it is generally not

---

22 See pp. 39ff.

possible to argue that Article 8 mandates particular outcomes in particular circumstances: it is under-determinate; that is, open to a range of plausible interpretations. It will be only extremely rarely, if at all, that the bare text of Article 8 *itself* will plainly demand a specific change in the common law. This is because of the wording of Article 8(2), which means that, absent the Strasbourg case law, it is not clear that Article 8 requires state intervention in private relations at all. Article 8(2), it will be recalled, states that there shall be no interference *by a public authority* with the right to respect for private life, except in pursuit of the stated exceptions. If one wants to argue (contrary to the surface reading) that states, in fact, must not only refrain from interference with privacy, but also intervene to offer positive protection against interference by private actors, then one will need the Strasbourg jurisprudence to make the case: the Article itself is silent on the matter.[23] In short, the horizontality of Article 8 requires the positive obligations doctrine in the Strasbourg jurisprudence; and that cannot be found to follow from the bare text of the Article itself. Thus, specific demands are likely to come only from the Convention case law – which, of course, is not binding, according to the plain terms of section 2(1) of the HRA: courts must only take it 'into account'. Thus, the fact that the HRA only makes the rights binding, not the Strasbourg case law, in practice therefore empties out most of the content of any theoretically *absolute* obligation to develop domestic law compatibly with Convention rights.

A possible counter-argument would contend that the above relies on too sharp a distinction between sections 6(1) and 2(1) of the HRA, setting up a misleading view of the HRA in which the courts have a duty to act compatibly with the Convention rights, while the Strasbourg jurisprudence must merely be taken into account. Such a critic would point out that courts never have approached their section 6(1) task, whether in public law or horizontal situations, by deciding *de novo* what the Convention rights mean, while merely 'noting' the Strasbourg view. Rather, they have accepted, as Lord Bingham put it in *Ullah*,[24] that 'the correct interpretation of [the Convention] can be authoritatively expounded only by the Strasbourg court'. In general, therefore, it may be said that the courts accept that the Convention means what Strasbourg says it means.[25] Thus, in carrying out their duty under section 6(1), courts, in effect, follow

23 Strasbourg has, of course, found that Art. 8 may require such intervention: see *X and Y v. The Netherlands* (1986) 8 EHRR 235 and numerous other authorities including *Von Hannover* v. *Germany* [2005] 40 EHRR 1.
24 *R (Ullah)* v. *Special Adjudicator* [2004] UKHL 26, [2004] 2 AC 323 at [20].
25 *R (Alconbury Developments Ltd)* v. *Secretary of State for the Environment, Transport and the Regions* [2001] UKHL 23, [2003] 2 AC 295 at [26] *per* Lord Slynn.

the Strasbourg jurisprudence, since to do otherwise might well place the United Kingdom in breach of the Convention, as Lord Bingham observed in *Animal Defenders*.[26] In response, it may be pointed out that the above does not, of course, mean that courts have accepted a duty slavishly to follow all particular Strasbourg decisions: rather, as noted in Chapter 5, they have left themselves various exit routes from the general obligation,[27] and we have some examples of specific refusals to follow such decisions[28] and other instances in which the House of Lords has in effect refused to follow Strasbourg, while pretending obedience.[29] In particular, courts may decline to follow a particular Strasbourg judgment that would require a particular result that they think would be mistaken or inconsistent with basic constitutional principles, such as the separation of powers.[30] It is also a matter of clear law that the courts *must* decline to follow Strasbourg decisions where these are inconsistent with post-HRA precedents of the House of Lords or Supreme Court on the interpretation of Convention rights, even where the Strasbourg decision was decided *after* the domestic precedent in question.[31] Therefore, there can be no absolute obligation to give effect to the Convention rights *as constituted by the Strasbourg case law* in domestic law: for that to be so, the courts would have to be bound always to follow all principles laid down in the Strasbourg case law in all circumstances. That is not so.

Thus, the obligation to give effect to Article 8 would, without its associated jurisprudence, in most cases be an obligation devoid of specific content in the private sphere – one that would in practice beat the air. Once it is accepted that concrete content requires the Strasbourg jurisprudence, it cannot be argued that the courts have an absolute obligation to give effect to that content. Moreover, while courts *can* decide to give Article 8 concrete content independent of Strasbourg, this is unlikely to happen more than occasionally and, as Young argues in relation to *Campbell*, would amount essentially to the exercise of a power rather than the implementation of an obligation.[32] In practice, therefore, I contend that the horizontal applicability of the Convention rights turns into an

---

26 [2008] UKHL 15 at [37].   27 Chapter 5, pp. 92–102.
28 *R v. Horncastle* [2009] UKSC 14, [2010] 2 WLR 47.
29 In *Animal Defenders*, the House of Lords plainly declined to follow *VgT Verein gegen Tierfabriken v. Switzerland* (2001) 34 EHRR 159, while making a very implausible argument that another case, *Murphy v. Ireland* (App. No. 44179/98, (2003)), was more relevant.
30 *Alconbury* at [76].
31 *Kay v. Lambeth LBC* [2006] UKHL 10, [2006] 2 WLR 570; see Chapter 4, p. xxx.
32 Chapter 5, pp. 98ff.

obligation to apply broad values and principles, with an essentially discretionary ability to develop more concrete rules. Therefore, the following models set out in Chapter 2 cannot be applicable to Article 8 (or in reality impose no concrete obligations): direct horizontal effect; unlimited (or full) indirect horizontal effect; and all seven models of 'strong indirect effect', which talk of an obligation to apply 'Convention rights'.[33] To put it another way, those models could be applicable, but would have to have the caveat added: 'save that the obligation does not apply where a court is unable or properly unwilling to apply an obligation deriving from the Strasbourg case law'. In general terms, I would suggest that one would expect the courts to be unwilling to apply an obligation deriving from Strasbourg in the common law where to follow it would require them to make changes to the law that go beyond the incremental, since to go further than this would arguably be at odds with 'the distribution of powers in the British constitution' as Lord Hoffmann put it in *Alconbury*. I would not, therefore, expect the courts to follow any of the Young models that require more than incremental development: this obviously includes direct, unlimited indirect (full) and all versions of strong indirect that do not include the limitation of incremental development. Later in this chapter, I will argue that the case law to date in this area bears this suggestion out, recent suggestions to the contrary notwithstanding.

In the next section, I seek to show that the courts have in fact been reluctant to apply in full a particular Strasbourg decision, on the grounds that this would radically expand the limits of privacy protection. This section also serves to introduce readers to the recent case law.

7.2 *Von Hannover* and the domestic courts: accommodation and resistance

The Strasbourg court, in its groundbreaking judgment in *Von Hannover v. Germany*,[34] finally provided comprehensive guidance as to the applicability of Article 8 in relations between private parties and its scope. This section briefly considers the evolving inter-relationship between this decision and the developing English common law action for 'misuse of private information'. *Von Hannover* appeared to set out an extremely broad scope for Article 8, particularly in relation to the publication of non-consensual photographs, such that it now seems that, as far as Strasbourg is concerned, *any* picture taken without the consent of someone in

---

33 Chapter 2, pp. 39–47.   34 [2005] 40 EHRR 1.

their everyday (as opposed to 'official' life) seemingly engages Article 8 and requires countervailing justification. As the court baldly observed in a recent decision: 'The concept of private life includes elements relating to a person's right to their image and the publication of a photograph falls within the scope of private life.'[35] However, the *Von Hannover* decision is open to more than one interpretation, and I have previously put forward an argument[36] that the English courts would be unlikely to accept the above 'absolutist' reading of it, since such a development would have the effect of broadening enormously the reach of the common law; the latter seems limited to protecting information that relates to a specific aspect of private life, as more narrowly understood, such as health, sexuality, private finances, family life and the like. The difference is neatly captured in a well-known comment by Baroness Hale in *Campbell*:

> We have not so far held that the mere fact of covert photography is sufficient to make the information contained in the photograph confidential. *The activity photographed must be private.* If. . . [Naomi Campbell] pops out to the shops for a bottle of milk . . . there is nothing essentially private about that information nor can it be expected to damage her private life.[37]

Similar comments were made by other members of the House of Lords in that case.[38] The issue of the protected scope of private life is also related to the issue of location or 'public domain': English courts are less inclined to treat activity taking place in the street as private, simply because it is generally harder to argue that one has a reasonable expectation of privacy in a busy street than in the home – another way in which the Strasbourg approach seems broader than that taken under the common law.

Accepting *Von Hannover* in full would therefore have the effect of broadening enormously the reach of the common law: the former action for 'breach of confidence' would, in the space of a few years, have morphed into a right to one's image. Hence, I put forward a possible interpretation

---

35 *Eerikäinen v. Finland* (2009) (App. No. 3514/02) at [61]. See the like finding in *Sciacca v. Italy* (2006) 43 EHRR 20, *Reklos and Davourlis v. Greece* (2009) (App No. 1234/05); *Egeland and Hanseid v. Norway* (2010) 50 EHRR 2.

36 *Media Freedom Under The Human Rights Act* (Oxford University Press, 2006), pp. 680–2, 763–9.

37 *Campbell* at [154] (emphasis added).

38 Lord Hoffmann: 'In the present case, the pictures were taken without Ms Campbell's consent. That in my opinion is not enough to amount to a wrongful invasion of privacy. The famous and even the not so famous who go out in public must accept that they may be photographed without their consent, just as they may be observed by others without their consent': *ibid.* at [73].

of *Von Hannover* that would have allowed English courts to 'read down' that decision, so that it stood for the proposition that the systematic and persistent pursuit and photographing of a person going about their everyday life and the publication of those photographs in mass circulation newspapers can give rise to a breach of Article 8. This argument was put to the court by the media parties in *McKennitt*, hoping thereby to limit the scope of *Von Hannover*, as applied in English law. In response Buxton LJ quite clearly rejected this interpretation.[39] However, I argue that the English courts, while purporting explicitly to reject this narrower reading, have not yet embraced *Von Hannover* fully. I have already made that argument in relation to cases up to and including *McKennitt*,[40] and do not repeat it here.

Since that decision, the English courts have – with one ambiguous exception – broadly confined the new tort to instances in which obviously sensitive personal information has been published – such as the *Mosley* case,[41] or there has been a clear breach of confidence in the old-fashioned sense (*McKennitt* and *HRH Prince of Wales v. Associated Newspapers Ltd*).[42] In contrast, when celebrities have brought cases concerning anodyne photographs of them in public in instances in which there is no plausible argument of media harassment, they have not, so far, been successful. Thus, in *John v. Associated Newspapers Ltd*,[43] Sir Elton John applied for an injunction restraining the *Daily Mail* from publishing a photograph of him, showing him standing with his driver in a London street outside the gate to his home. Mr Justice Eady dismissed the application in short order, noting that the photographs disclosed no private information and that English law does not require consent to take photographs.[44]

A very similar claim was brought by J. K. Rowling recently; the two decisions so far generated by that litigation in the High Court[45] and Court of Appeal have not, it must be said, done much to aid resolution of this issue. The case concerned a photograph, taken covertly by a photographer

---

39 *McKennitt* at [41].

40 See 'The Common Law, Privacy and the Convention', in H. Fenwick, G. Phillipson and R. Masterman (eds.), *Judicial Reasoning under the UK Human Rights Act* (Cambridge University Press, 2007), pp. 240–4 (hereafter, Phillipson, 'The Common Law').

41 *Mosley* [2008] EWHC 1777 (QB), [2008] EMLR 20 ('*Mosley*'). For comment, see Hughes, 'Horizontal Privacy'.

42 [2006] All ER (D) 276 (Mar).

43 *John v. Associated Newspapers Ltd* [2006] EWHC 1611 (QB), [2006] EMLR 27.

44 *Ibid.* at [15] and [21].

45 *Murray v. Express Newspapers Plc* [2007] EWHC 1908 (Ch).

using a long-range lens without consent, of J. K. Rowling's son and herself in a public street in Edinburgh. It showed the son being pushed along in a buggy by his father, with his then pregnant mother walking alongside. It was subsequently published by the *Express*.[46] At first instance, Platten J considered himself bound by the reasoning in *Campbell*; he found that *Von Hannover* could be either distinguished or simply not followed. He plainly recognised the major implications for English law of giving full effect to *Von Hannover*, describing it as amounting to the recognition in effect of a right to one's image; he was clearly hostile to this development, and the extremely broad approach to Article 8 that lies behind it; he therefore struck the case out, as disclosing no reasonable cause of action. However, the Court of Appeal then overturned this judgment, reinstating the plaintiff's case so that it could go to trial; the case subsequently settled, depriving us of a definitive legal resolution of the issues it raised. Two main notions emerge from the Court of Appeal's judgment. The first is that the court seemed more predisposed to the view that the publication of a photograph of someone engaged in everyday activities *might* engage Article 8, depending on the facts.[47] The second is that the protection of the privacy of children is of particular importance,[48] a point considered further below.[49] It may well be that the result of this case will be that children, but not adults, in such situations may be protected and there is plenty in the court's judgment to steer a lower court to that conclusion.

Meanwhile, when the *Douglas* case reached the House of Lords, Lord Walker took the opportunity to reassert firmly and in pure common law style:

> Nor can anyone (whether celebrity or nonentity) complain simply of being photographed. There must be something more: either that the photographs are genuinely embarrassing ... (*Theakston* v. *MGN Ltd*) or that their publication involves a misuse of official powers (*Hellewell*) or that they disclose something which merits temporary protection as a commercial secret (*Shelley Films*).[50]

Presumably his Lordship saw the privacy part of the *Douglas* case as falling within the last of these categories.

---

46 It will be noted immediately that the facts of this case are virtually identical to the New Zealand decision of *Hosking* v. *Runting* [2005] 1 NZLR 1.

47 *McKennitt* at [55], [56].   48 *McKennitt* at [57].   49 At p. 157.

50 *OBG Ltd* v. *Allan; Douglas* v. *Hello! Ltd (No. 3)* [2007] UKHL 21, [2008] 1 AC 1 at [293] (case refs omitted). The decision in the House of Lords was concerned with the dispute as between *OK!* and *Hello!* not the initial privacy claim.

In short, then, on one of the key issues concerning the scope of the privacy action, English courts have *not* so far given full effect to the scope of Article 8 as interpreted by Strasbourg; this shows how the stronger abstract models of indirect horizontal effect in practice lose their force through the distinction between the Strasbourg case law and the rights themselves. In the following section, I consider how the courts have dealt with the issue of horizontality more generally. In doing so, I will refer to two of the more moderate interpretations of the court's duty[51] in this respect, as well as the views of the direct and full horizontalists referred to earlier.[52]

7.3 Horizontal effect in the case law

7.3.1 The cases up to and including Campbell

It is not necessary for present purposes to analyse this in detail.[53] In short, the courts have ruled out the Buxton thesis that denies any horizontal effect at all,[54] and (generally speaking) the Wade view[55] of full or unlimited indirect effect. But they have then not sought to clarify which variant of indirect effect is correct: at times they have endorsed different varieties, from weak 'value infusion'[56] to a clear endorsement of Hunt's strong indirect approach.[57] More striking still, there have been dicta apparently embracing the 'outer' positions also. Thus, there has been apparent support for the Wade view,[58] and, at the other end of the spectrum, doubts expressed as to whether the HRA affects substantive law at all, as opposed

---

51 The more moderate interpretations are those of M. Hunt, 'The "Horizontal Effect" of the Human Rights Act', *Public Law* (1998), 423 and G. Phillipson, 'The Human Rights Act, "Horizontal Effect" and the Common Law: a Bang or a Whimper?', *Modern Law Review* 62 (1999), 824.
52 See notes 17 and 18 above.
53 For full discussion, see G. Phillipson, 'Clarity Postponed: Horizontal Effect after *Campbell*', in Fenwick, Phillipson, and Masterman (eds.), *Judicial Reasoning under the UK Human Rights Act* (Phillipson, 'Clarity Postponed').
54 See, e.g., dicta of Butler-Sloss P in *Venables & Another* v. *News Group Newspapers Ltd* [2001] 1 All ER 908, 916.
55 *Douglas III* at [50] *per* Lord Phillips MR; *Campbell* at [132] *per* Baroness Hale; *Wainwright*.
56 *Campbell* at [17] and [18] *per* Lord Nicholls; *Douglas* v. *Hello! Ltd* [2001] QB 967 at 993–4 *per* Brooke LJ and 1012 *per* Keene LJ.
57 *Douglas* at 998 *per* Sedley LJ; *Campbell* at 132 *per* Baroness Hale; *Douglas III* at [52] *per* Lord Phillips MR.
58 *McKennitt*; *Re S (A Child) (Identification: Restriction of Publication)* [2004] UKHL 47, [2005] 1 AC 593 at [23] *per* Lord Steyn.

to procedures and remedies;[59] most strikingly of all, have been judicial statements that nothing has yet been decided, and that nothing may ever be.[60] Particularly noteworthy was *Campbell*,[61] in which their Lordships not only produced widely divergent – even contradictory – dicta, but also – with the honourable exception of Baroness Hale[62] – failed properly to confront, still less resolve, the issue.[63] Moreover, none of their Lordships even *began* to engage with the first level of the horizontal effect inquiry[64] – the question of whether Article 8 itself and its associated jurisprudence *requires* the protection between private parties that the *Campbell* judgment provided, for the first time, in English law – a point I will return to later.

But there is an issue arising from *Campbell* requiring clarification that is more important than mere consideration of the specific dicta it contains on the issue. What should we make of the fact that, on one interpretation, *Campbell* has created a new tort – 'misuse of private information', and that, as one commentator puts it:

> It is the very creation of this new tort that is the most important aspect of *Campbell*. If the creation of new causes of action is a *hallmark* of direct horizontal effect, impossible as it is under indirect horizontal effect, then such a creation is the clearest endorsement of [the adoption of full or direct horizontal effect by the courts].[65]

In order to be clear about what the courts have been up to in terms of horizontal effect, it is important to recognise the mistakes here on a number of levels. First, this assertion leaves out of account the important fact that the House of Lords has an inherent ability at common law to fashion new causes of action, as do all top common law courts.[66] It is in this respect that the New Zealand Court of Appeal's recent 'finding' of a new tort of invasion of privacy in *Hosking* v. *Runting*[67] is of such clear significance. In *Hosking*, there was no possible obligation under the

---

59 *R (Wooder)* v. *Feggetter* [2003] QB 219 at [48] *per* Sedley LJ; *Kay* v. *Lambeth LBC* [2006] 2 WLR 570 at [61] *per* Lord Nicholls; *Campbell* at [49] *per* Lord Hoffmann.
60 *Kay*; *X* v. *Y* [2004] ICR 1634 at [45].
61 For the full analysis, see Phillipson, 'Clarity Postponed', pp. 157–8.
62 *Campbell* at [132].
63 See, e.g., Lord Hope at [113], Lord Nicholls at [17] and [18], Lord Hoffmann at [49]–[51]. Lord Carswell does not mention the issue.
64 See Chapter 1, p. 8.   65 Bennett, 'Horizontality's New Horizons', p. 100.
66 A classic example of the use of such power by the House of Lords is the creation of the modern law of negligence in *Donoghue* v. *Stevenson* [1932] AC 562.
67 [2005] 1 NZLR 1.

New Zealand Bill of Rights Act 1990 (NZBORA) for such a bold move, since the NZBORA does not incorporate Article 17, the privacy guarantee of the International Covenant on Civil and Political Rights.[68] But despite this seemingly negative indication by the legislature towards the creation of privacy rights, the New Zealand Court of Appeal went ahead and created the new tort anyway, relying on comparative common law jurisprudence from English and US law and the well-accepted need to develop the common law in order to answer to changing social needs and circumstances. This decision therefore indicates that even if the House of Lords *did* create a new tort in *Campbell*, this in itself would provide no evidence of full or direct horizontal effect, since the New Zealand court most certainly created a new tort, yet were clearly under no obligation at all to do so from their relevant Bill of Rights. The mistake is plain when Bennett states baldly that 'under indirect horizontal effect, the courts cannot and do not create any new causes of action';[69] to be accurate, this would have to be re-phrased to read: '*the courts are not obliged to create any new causes of action, but may choose to do so as a result of their ordinary constitutional powers*'. Moreover, it is a mistake to assert that all indirect effect models rule out an obligation to create new causes of action.[70] Rather, what all but Wade's model deny is that courts are under an obligation *immediately* to create new causes of action; Hunt explicitly allows for the creation of new causes of action as a result of development over time,[71] and Young allows for various kinds of duties in relation to new causes of action in her various models.[72]

It is also strongly arguable that Bennett's thesis is wrong on a more basic level. Whether or not the House of Lords' 'development' of breach of confidence went as far as to give rise, in effect, to a new tort,[73] it is plainly *not* the case that their Lordships' reasoning proceeded on that basis – that they were fashioning a new cause of action *de novo* rather than merely modifying the existing action in breach of confidence. It is perhaps surprising that Bennett should so readily assert the contrary,

---

68 Article 17 provides: (1) No one shall be subjected to arbitrary or unlawful interference with his privacy, family, home or correspondence, nor to unlawful attacks on his honour and reputation. (2) Everyone has the right to the protection of the law against such interference or attacks. Its omission from the NZBORA is discussed in *Hosking* at [181].

69 Bennett, 'Horizontality's New Horizons', p. 102.   70 Chapter 2, pp. 39–47.

71 Hunt, *Horizontal Effect*, p. 442.

72 Chapter 2; see also the new model advanced by Phillipson and Williams, cited in n. 16 above.

73 As I have previously argued (Right of Privacy), though I offered a more cautious view elsewhere: Phillipson, 'The Common Law', pp. 227–32.

given the clear rejection by the House of Lords in *Wainwright* v. *Home Office* of the existence of any general tort of invasion of privacy, and Lord Nicholls' confirmation in *Campbell* itself that: 'In this country, unlike the United States of America, there is no over-arching, all-embracing, cause of action for "invasion of privacy".'[74] Aside from the fact that none of the Law Lords in *Campbell* expressed the view that they were giving full or direct horizontal effect to the Convention, and, indeed, that this was explicitly denied at least by Baroness Hale,[75] careful attention should also be paid to what Lord Nicholls himself said in *Campbell,* at paragraph 14:

> This cause of action has now firmly shaken off the limiting constraint of the need for an initial confidential relationship. In doing so it has changed its nature. In this country this development was recognised clearly in the judgment of Lord Goff of Chieveley in *Attorney-General* v. *Guardian Newspapers Ltd (No. 2)* [1990] 1 AC 109, 281. Now the law imposes a 'duty of confidence' whenever a person receives information he knows or ought to know is fairly and reasonably to be regarded as confidential. Even this formulation is awkward. The continuing use of the phrase 'duty of confidence' and the description of the information as 'confidential' is not altogether comfortable. Information about an individual's private life would not, in ordinary usage, be called 'confidential'. The more natural description today is that such information is private. The essence of the tort is better encapsulated now as misuse of private information.

Lord Nicholls thus makes clear that in his view, one of the key developments in the law had happened well before the HRA, and that the House was merely continuing this process of evolution. Indeed, in *Douglas* v. *Hello! Ltd* in the Lords, it was said by Lord Walker that Lord Goff's dictum in *Spycatcher* amounted to 'the most important single step in the course of the law's recent development'.[76] Lord Nicholls' dictum above is but one example of a number of passages that suggest that the Law Lords did not see this particular case as raising new issues of principle, or breaking new ground,[77] and which stress continuity with previous case law.[78]

While it is true that their Lordships in some of these passages do appear either to be concealing, or not fully appreciating, the full significance of the development they were engineering,[79] by no stretch of the imagination can their Lordships be taken to be consciously creating a new cause of action, although it may be argued that the effect of the changes they

---

74 *Campbell* at [11].   75 *Campbell* at [132].
76 *Douglas III*, HL at [272].   77 See, e.g., Lord Hoffmann at [47], [48].
78 Lord Hoffmann at [50], Lord Hope at [85], Lady Hale at [145] and [147] and Lord Carswell at [163].
79 Phillipson, Right of Privacy.

introduced was the equivalent. The key point is this: while there may be academic argument about whether and when development of an existing cause of action tips over into *de facto* creation of a new one, the House of Lords did *not*, as the full or direct horizontal effect models require, consider that they were *obliged* to create a new cause of action as a result of the HRA. This point is further illuminated by the clear contrast that the New Zealand Court of Appeal drew in *Hosking* v. *Runting* between their own approach – to strike out boldly and actually create a new privacy tort – and the more cautious approach taken by the House of Lords in *Campbell* of developing breach of confidence to do the job of protecting privacy.[80]

7.3.2 Case law from McKennitt v. Ash onwards: direct/full horizontal effect?

We may now turn to the cases since *Campbell*, which will allow us to consider the view of some scholars[81] that the courts *have* at least in these recent cases given full or direct effect to the Convention rights – in other words, that they have not just developed breach of confidence, but have straightforwardly replaced it with a new cause of action deriving directly from the Convention. The leading privacy scholar Nicole Moreham and Tom Bennett have both argued that the Court of Appeal's decision in *McKennitt* v. *Ash* represents an acceptance of direct horizontal effect. Moreham puts it thus:

> In *McKennitt*, Buxton LJ applied Arts 8 and 10 directly to the dispute between McKennitt and Ash and relegated the common law to a supporting role – rather than providing the framework for the privacy action, it merely assisted the court to determine the content of Arts 8 and 10. The HRA was therefore given 'direct' horizontal effect.[82]

Relying on this, and his own analysis, Bennett concludes that the case 'has made clear beyond doubt that the HRA, and the Convention rights it protects, is being given direct horizontal effect'.[83] Bennett points out that the most striking phrase in *McKennitt* – that Articles 8 and 10 'are now not merely of persuasive or parallel effect but are . . . the very content of the domestic tort that the English court has to enforce . . .'[84] – was

---

80 *Hosking* at [45] and [110].
81 Bennett, 'Horizontality's New Horizons'; Moreham, 'Privacy and Horizontality'.
82 Moreham, ibid., at p. 375.   83 Bennett, 'Horizontality's New Horizons', p. 99.
84 *McKennitt* at [11].

echoed by Sir Anthony Clarke MR in the *Rowling* case.[85] These are indeed the dicta that come closest to suggesting judicial endorsement of full or direct horizontal effect[86] and, particularly given that they were delivered in the two most recent Court of Appeal decisions, they are worthy of close attention. The full quote from Buxton LJ appears in paragraphs 10 and 11 of his judgment in *McKennitt* v. *Ash*. There, his Lordship states clearly in paragraph 10 that he is seeking to summarise 'the effect of . . . guidance' from previous cases, which he says consists of dicta from Baroness Hale in *Campbell* [132], Lord Phillips in *Douglas III* at [53], 'and in particular' *per* Lord Woolf CJ in *A* v. *B Plc*:

> under section 6 of the 1998 Act, the court, as a public authority, is required not to act 'in a way which is incompatible with a Convention right'. The court is able to achieve this by absorbing the rights which articles 8 and 10 protect into the long-established action for breach of confidence. This involves giving a new strength and breadth to the action so that it accommodates the requirements of those articles.[87]

It is quite clear therefore that Buxton LJ was simply summarising the effect of previous dicta from senior judges on this point. Since he, indeed, states that this is what he is doing, it is not possible to use his dicta to contradict those he cites. And once the cited dicta are examined, any suggestion of full or direct horizontal effect falls away. First, it is clear from the passage cited that Lord Woolf CJ was *not* talking about direct, but indirect, horizontal effect, since he is referring to developing an existing action by 'giving [it] new strength and breadth', *not* replacing it with a new tort. It is also particularly hard to defend *A* v. *B Plc* as a decision embracing any strong form of horizontal effect, direct or indirect, since there was no citation of any Strasbourg case law. Moreover, it is not at all clear from the judgment whether the developments represented by the decision are thought to be (a) merely a rationalisation of existing common law authority, (b) *required* by a strong indirect horizontal application of Article 8, or (c) merely a desirable step, which the court is either (i) *free* to make as part of the normal process of developing the common law or (ii) *encouraged* to take by the reception of Article 8 as a general legal value into English law.

---

85 *Rowling* at [27]; Bennett, 'Horizontality's New Horizons', p. 102.
86 Save for those in *Re S (A Child)* [2005] 1 AC 593 at [23] *per* Lord Steyn; but see the analysis of these by Phillipson, 'Clarity Postponed', pp. 167–9, and A. Young, 'Horizontality and the Human Rights Act 1998', in K. Ziegler (ed.), *Human Rights and Private Law: Privacy as Autonomy* (Oxford: Hart, 2007), pp. 42–3.
87 [2003] QB 195 at [4].

In other words this single dictum could correspond to several of Young's models.

The other two passages referred to by Buxton LJ in fact *rule out* full horizontal effect. Thus, in the dictum by Baroness Hale in *Campbell* referred to by Buxton LJ in *McKennitt* v. *Ash* she states:

> The [HRA] does not create any new cause of action between private persons. But if there is a relevant cause of action applicable, the court as a public authority must act compatibly with both parties' Convention rights.[88]

The dicta of Lord Phillips MR in *Douglas III*[89] merely summarise Lady Hale's view, although his Lordship mistakenly also attributes it to Lord Nicholls in *Campbell*, who in fact only spoke of 'the *values* embodied in articles 8 and 10' as being applicable in the case, while declining 'to decide whether the duty imposed on courts by section 6 [HRA] extends to questions of substantive law as distinct from questions of practice and procedure'.[90] In short, then, this purported announcement in favour of full or direct horizontal effect by Buxton LJ in *McKennitt* and Sir Anthony Clarke MR in *Rowling* merely amounts to Sir Anthony repeating an inaccurate summary by Buxton LJ of previous dicta, which in fact rule out direct and full horizontal effect. It should also be noted that Lord Bingham appears to have subsequently disapproved any such notion in *Von Colle*, saying that: 'It seems . . . clear . . . that the existence of a Convention right cannot call for instant manufacture of a corresponding common law right where none exists', citing *Wainwright* for the proposition.[91]

What, then, is the real meaning of these dicta in *McKennitt* and *Rowling*? It is, of course, true that in *McKennitt* and other privacy cases, the courts appeared to have engaged in some kind of novel fusion of common law and Convention principles, by their finding that common law liability depends upon the engagement of Convention rights. Thus, in *Rowling*, as the court put it, the 'two key questions which must be answered in a case where the complaint is of the wrongful publication of private information' are:

> first, whether the information is private in the sense that it is in principle protected by Article 8 (i.e., such that Article 8 is in principle engaged) and,

---

88 *Campbell* at [132].   89 At [52].   90 *Campbell* at [18].
91 *Chief Constable of the Hertfordshire Police* v. *Van Colle* [2008] UKHL 50, [2009] 1 AC 225 at [58] ('*Van Colle*').

secondly, if so, whether in all the circumstances the interest of the owner of the information must yield to the right to freedom of expression conferred on the publisher by Article 10.[92]

There are three reasons, I would suggest, why such statements – and indeed such a methodology in privacy cases – do not disclose acceptance of full or direct horizontal effect by the courts. First, and most importantly, if direct or full horizontal effect applies, then it must apply across the board; and yet it is only in privacy cases that we have seen this fusion occur. In other words, as argued further below, the English courts have not accepted the force of Articles 8 and 10 into this area because they accept a *general* obligation to apply Convention rights in private law, but because in this area they wanted in any event to plug a gap in English law that had become embarrassing.

The second point is the fact that, despite the statements made above, the English courts do *not* in practice simply accept that if the information in question falls within Article 8 then there is a *prima facie* cause of action. Indeed, courts have been very clear that it is not just the nature of the information that is determinative. The overall test is now whether there was 'a reasonable expectation of privacy',[93] a question decided by examining a number of factors.[94] While the nature of the information, and particularly whether it is 'obviously private', is the most important factor,[95] others will often also be relevant or even decisive in determining whether a reasonable expectation of privacy exists. These include:

(1) the location in which the information was acquired and/or whether it had already entered the public domain;[96]
(2) the conduct of the defendant: for example, use of intrusive means, such as a telephoto lens, recording devices or of trickery or deceit to obtain the information; whether a breach of confidence was involved;[97] and the manner of publication; and

---

92 *Van Colle* at [27]. Hughes, 'Horizontal Privacy', above, argues that this is also the methodology used by Eady J in the *Mosley* case; but see, in relation to this, pp. 154–6 below.
93 See, e.g., Lord Nicholls in *Campbell* at [22].
94 Below, n. 98.   95 See Lord Hope, *Campbell* at [96].
96 See the comments of the Court of Appeal in *Douglas III* at [105].
97 See, e.g., *HRH Prince of Wales* v. *Associated Newspapers Ltd* [2006] All ER (D) 276 (Mar), esp. [71].

(3) the conduct of the claimant: whether he or she previously publicised personal information in the same category as that complained of here.[98]

It is by no means clear that all these factors would be relevant to a pure Article 8 inquiry. In particular, it is noteworthy that in relation to the last issue, the English courts have continued, albeit inconsistently, to treat the previous attitude of the claimant towards publicity as highly relevant to whether they now have a reasonable expectation of privacy. This was treated as decisive in the 2005 decision of *A* v. *B*,[99] but was also seen as highly relevant by the Court of Appeal in *Rowling*: the fact that his parents had always shielded their child David from publicity was repeatedly stressed. Presumably, had the converse been the case, then David would have enjoyed a lesser expectation of privacy – perhaps none in the particular context. In short, this factor continues to be applied despite there being no clear endorsement of it at Strasbourg and strong doubts as to its compatibility with Article 8.

Similarly, the courts continue to treat obligations of confidentiality as in many ways *more important* than 'mere' privacy rights. For example, in *McKennitt*, both High Court and Court of Appeal thought that it was 'of great importance in the present case [that] the complaint here is of what might be called old-fashioned breach of confidence by way of conduct inconsistent with a pre-existing relationship'.[100] Indeed, the Court of Appeal, when considering the accusation that the findings made by Eady J at first instance '*went far beyond anything previously decided*', first of all doubted the conclusion, by reference to *Douglas* and *Campbell*, but then went on to say that: 'there is a *much more formidable reason* why this assault on Eady J's conclusions must fail . . . [namely] the nature of the relationship between the . . . claimant and . . . defendant'.[101] In other words, the common law value of confidentiality continues to play a strong role in the cases, again inconsistently with the suggestion of direct or full horizontal effect. Third, we may note the considerable resistance displayed

---

98 The Court of Appeal in *Rowling* said that relevant factors included: (1) the attributes of the claimant; (2) the nature of the activity in which the claimant was engaged; (3) the place at which it was happening; (4) the nature and purpose of the intrusion; (5) the absence of consent and whether it was known or could be inferred; (6) the effect on the claimant; and (7) the circumstances in which and the purposes for which the information came into the hands of the publisher.

99 [2005] EWHC 1651, [2005] EMLR 36. See the critical commentary by Phillipson, 'The Common Law', pp. 244–9.

100 *McKennitt* at [8].   101 *McKennitt* [14] and [15].

towards *Von Hannover* noted above, which also suggests that the courts do not in practice make themselves mere conduits of Strasbourg case law.

Finally in this section, we should ask whether the cases since *Campbell* have advanced the *substance* of the law radically in a way that would suggest the application of full or direct horizontal effect. Despite the argument that they have 'expanded the range of circumstances in which relief will be given for interference with an individual's privacy',[102] on closer examination, none have broken new ground, save perhaps for the Court of Appeal decision in *Rowling*, which was, after all, only an appeal from a strike-out. Three of them, *Mosley* v. *News Group Newspapers Ltd*, *McKennitt* v. *Ash* and *HRH Prince of Wales* v. *Associated Newspapers Ltd*,[103] concerned pre-existing relationships, sufficient for the courts in all these cases to conclude that liability could be made out on 'old-fashioned' confidence grounds.[104] It is also fairly clear that *Mosley* broke no new ground conceptually. Eady J had no hesitation in finding that the publication of detailed accounts – and videos – of Max Mosley, then President of F1, engaging in group sex sessions of a sado-masochistic nature, with five sex workers, in private, residential property, fell within the scope of his private life. But as the judge also found, the information and images provided by a sex worker engaged by the claimant could plainly have been said to have been provided to the newspaper in breach of an implied obligation of confidentiality.[105] It is true that in both *A* v. *B*[106] and *Theakston* v. *MGN Ltd*[107] it was doubted whether fleeting sexual encounters – particularly with prostitutes – could attract an obligation of confidentiality. If *Mosley* could be clearly shown to have departed from these findings, it could perhaps be instanced as an example of direct application of the Convention, *in preference* to domestic precedents. However, this is not the case: in neither of the previous two cases did the court *rule out* protecting information about such encounters. Rather, the finding was that lesser weight should be attached to short-term sexual relationships than to marriage. Thus, Lord Woolf said that 'the more stable the relationship, the greater will be the significance which is attached to it'.[108] He found that there was a 'significant difference' between the confidentiality of stable relationships and transitory ones,[109] and went on to quote with approval Ouseley J's views in *Theakston* to like effect.[110] In other words, at that

---

102 Bennett, 'Horizontality's New Horizons', p. 100.
103 [2006] All ER (D) 276 (Mar).   104 *Mosley* at [7].   105 *Mosley* at [105]–[108].
106 [2003] QB 195.   107 [2002] EWHC 137 (QB), [2002] EMLR 398.
108 *A* v. *B* at 551H.   109 *Ibid.* at 560D–G.   110 *Theakston* at [59].

point, the judges saw such information as *protectable* under the law, but as attracting a relatively low weight.[111] But there was no clear doctrinal barrier to protecting such relationships: what we saw between *A* v. *B* and *Theakston*, on the one hand, and *Mosley*, on the other, was a shift in *values* – from notions of confidentiality and 'clean hands', to privacy, dignity and autonomy. In other words, this was a subtle shift, which could be accounted for by almost any model of indirect effect, since it is the *values* underpinning the law that changed. Certainly, Eady J did not think he was breaking new ground. As he put it: 'the matter is by no means outside the scope of existing authority', citing the injunction granted against any photographs of the brothel encounter in *Theakston* itself.[112] Bennett further says that *Mosley*:

> constituted the clearest indication that has been given in a single case that Art. 8 rights are directly horizontally enforceable. Eady J's decision is peppered with references to the 'new privacy tort' and its applicability between private parties.

I have dealt with this issue above: such assertions conflate the *fact* that a new *de facto* tort has been created with its supposed *cause*. And, indeed, the most that Eady J had to say about the creation of a new tort was the guarded comment that Lord Nicholls in *Campbell* 'may have intended to convey that infringements of privacy should now be regarded as an independent tort uncluttered by any limitations deriving from its equitable origins'.[113]

---

111 For critical analysis of this point, see G. Phillipson, 'Transforming Breach of Confidence? Towards a Common Law Right to Privacy under the Human Rights Act', *Modern Law Review*, 66(5) (2003), 726, 747–8.

112 *Mosley* at [23].

113 *Mosley* at [182] (emphasis in original). Hughes ('Horizontal Privacy', pp. 246–7) also draws attention to one reason put forward in this case by Eady J for rejecting the award of exemplary damages, that the cause of action, in the judge's words: 'involves direct application of Convention values and . . . jurisprudence as part of English law [and] that it would be somewhat eccentric to graft on to this . . . an alien anomaly from the common law in the shape of exemplary damages' (*Mosley* at [196]). Hughes argues that this shows Eady J's acceptance 'that Convention jurisprudence directly applies, and that it constitutes a part of English law which is independent from common law principles'. But first, as she acknowledges, the use of the term 'Convention values' muddies the water; indeed, the somewhat contradictory notion of 'direct application of Convention values' is plainly far from the notion of direct horizontal effect as used by scholars. Second, while it is true that these dicta rather strikingly characterise the Convention jurisprudence as the core of the action and additions from the common law as possible 'alien anomalies' to it, this author believes this to be merely an example of a judge reaching for an argument by counsel to assist in rejecting a particular conclusion that he was clearly loath to reach (that courts ought to allow awarding of exemplary damages

We have considered the *Rowling* case above, but need now to take a closer look at it: since it did not concern a situation in which there was any pre-existing relationship, and concerned anodyne photographs taken in public, it alone of the cases since *Campbell* could at first sight be seen as extending liability beyond the *Campbell* situation, in which the photographs generated liability only because they revealed information relating to Campbell's treatment at Narcotics Anonymous. Bennett asserts that the finding in *Rowling* that 'the law should indeed protect children from intrusive media attention . . . without parental consent',[114] is highly significant:

> Clearly, the court does not feel it is particularly constrained by the rules of the new tort as laid down by the *Campbell* case. If they are not adequate to provide protection in these circumstances, the court will modify, extend and re-mould the tort to ensure the child is protected. This approach cannot possibly be described as *indirect horizontal effect*. It is completely *direct*.[115]

This conclusion is erroneous for three reasons. First, full horizontal effect does not consist in modifying, extending or remoulding a common law tort: it consists in recognising a *wholly new tort*, depending only on section 6 and the Convention. Second, it is simply not the case that the Court of Appeal plainly departed from *Campbell*. There are dicta in that case ruling out liability for photographs that do not reveal particularly sensitive information,[116] or portray a humiliating experience[117] – but none dealing with photographs of children, as the Court of Appeal observed.[118] The court in the *Rowling* case was thus addressing a new situation, concerning the particular rights of children. It is recognised by, among others, the Press Complaints Commission that the privacy of children is a special case.[119] In this respect, the Court of Appeal referenced the United Nations Convention on the Rights of the Child, to which the United Kingdom is a party.[120] Moreover, the court expressly stated that, 'this was at least arguably a very different case from that to which Baroness Hale referred . . . of Ms Campbell being photographed while popping out

---

in privacy cases). Since the privacy cases, including judgments of Eady J himself (e.g., *A v. B*, n. 99 above), contain many applications of common law principles, it is simply not plausible to read the above as suggesting that all such applications constitute improper grafting of 'alien anomalies' onto the pure Convention jurisprudence.

114 *Rowling* at [57].   115 Bennett, 'Horizontality's New Horizons', p. 102.
116 *Campbell* at [154] *per* Baroness Hale.   117 *Campbell* at [73] *per* Lord Hoffmann.
118 *Rowling* at [47].   119 Editors' Code of Practice, clause 6.
120 *Rowling* at [45].

to buy the milk', because in *Rowling* there had been a pattern of systematic intrusion by the defendants.[121] At most, therefore, *Campbell* was distinguished, in classical common law fashion, in response to a new set of circumstances. Finally, what Bennett appears to be suggesting here – that the Court of Appeal was refusing to follow a post-HRA House of Lords authority and preferring the Strasbourg decision of *Von Hannover* v. *Germany* – is something that does not, and cannot, legitimately occur even under the *vertical* effect of the HRA.[122] Bennett, therefore, appears at this point to be arguing that the disputed horizontal effect of the HRA is actually stronger than its express vertical effect – a scarcely plausible position. In fact, reading the judgment, it is plain that as the Court of Appeal said, it focused on the *Campbell* judgment, gleaning from it the governing principles of the action;[123] in contrast, it declined to analyse *Von Hannover* in any detail, merely finding that it was 'permissible to have regard' to it.[124] This was because it expressly acknowledged that the Court was bound by *Campbell* but not *Von Hannover*.[125]

7.4 Why breach of confidence?

The final part of this chapter addresses the question posed at the beginning: why is it in *this* area of law that we have seen the clearest and strongest application of the Convention? I suggest that there are three reasons. The first is that there was, by the time the HRA came into force, a clear lacuna in English law, which was becoming embarrassing. The lack of a legal privacy remedy in respect of the non-consensual disclosure of personal information had long been bemoaned by the courts,[126] by official Reports[127] and by influential commentators.[128] However, it is possible that they would not have engaged in the developments they have had they thought that Parliament was going to step in to remedy the problem.

This gives us our second reason – clear indications that no legislative action was to be expected. Parliament, of course, cannot act on such a

---

121 *Rowling* at [18].   122 See Chapter 4, pp. 102–9.   123 *Rowling* at [21]–[36].
124 *Rowling* at [59].   125 *Rowling* at [20].
126 It was condemned by the Court of Appeal in *Kaye* v. *Robertson* [1991] FSR 62, CA, said to give rise to 'serious, widespread concern' by Lord Nicholls in *R* v. *Khan* [1997] AC 558, 582; and referred to as a 'glaring inadequacy' by the Law Commission: Breach of Confidence (Law Com. No. 110), para. 5.5.
127 See n. 129, below.
128 See, e.g., Basil S. Markesinis, 'Our Patchy Law of Privacy – Time to Do Something About It', *Modern Law Review*, 53 (1990), 802; 'The Calcutt Report Must Not Be Forgotten', *Modern Law Review*, 55 (1992), 118.

matter without full government backing for any Bill, and, while there had for many years been intermittent governmental interest in statutory protection for privacy[129] no government had actually grasped the nettle, doubtless partly due to the fear of press hostility.[130] Governmental deference to such hostility was most recently seen in the previous government's immediate rejection[131] of a recommendation in a Report of the Select Committee on Media Culture and Sport of legislation to protect individuals from media intrusion into their private lives.[132] It had also recently been made clear that self-regulation, so long the panacea lauded by the press, would not be considered adequate protection for privacy in Strasbourg terms: in *Peck* v. *United Kingdom*, the court found that a power to fine media bodies who breached privacy was not sufficient to protect Article 8 – there needed to be an ability to award damages.[133] Given that the Press Complaints Commission lacks any coercive powers at all, and, indeed, has jurisdiction only when newspapers choose to assent to it, the supposed 'remedy' in English law was pretty manifestly inadequate. Importantly, in the light of Bagshaw's cautionary remarks in Chapter 6 about the dangers of judges seeking to implement Convention rights through tort law, *Peck* clearly demonstrated that *a specific remedy* for this kind of breach of Article 8 – namely, damages – was required by the Convention; something that is generally provided by tort law. Thus, *Peck*, together with Parliament's persistent inaction, provided important evidence, not only that the United Kingdom was obliged to provide further protection for Article 8, but that this obligation could in practice be discharged *only* by common law development. Thus, two critical conditions were in place: first, long-standing and

---

129 The Younger Committee (Report of the Committee on Privacy (1972 Cmnd 5012), Calcutt Committee on Privacy and Related Matters (1990 Cm 1102), Review of Press Self Regulation (Cm 2135), *Fourth Report of the National Heritage Select Committee on Privacy and Media Intrusion*, Appendix 24, HC 294-II (1993) and a Lord Chancellor's Green Paper (CHAN J060915NJ.7/93) had all proposed the introduction of statutory measures to protect privacy.

130 See, e.g., S. Rasaiah, 'Current Legislation, Privacy and the Media in the UK', *Communications Law*, 3(5) (1998), 183.

131 *The Government's Response to the Fifth Report of the Culture, Media and Sport Select Committee on 'Privacy and Media Intrusion'*, HC 458-1 (2002–3), Cm 5985, esp. at [2.3].

132 *Fifth Report Privacy and Media Intrusion*, HC 458 (2002–3), esp. at [111].

133 *Peck v. United Kingdom* (2003) 36 EHRR 41 at [109]. 'The Court finds that the lack of legal power of the [Regulators] to award damages to the applicant means that those bodies could not provide an effective remedy to him. It notes that the [Regulator's] power to impose a fine on the relevant television company does not amount to an award of damages to the applicant.'

serious dissatisfaction with the absence of proper protection in the existing law; second, clear evidence that the government was most unlikely
to bring forward legislation to provide the particular remedy required,
so that common law development was the only realistic way of doing
the job.

This then takes us to the third factor, which has already been touched
on: namely, that the area of law in question, breach of confidence, had
already been subject to incremental development that had brought it
into a fairly inchoate state, leaving it ripe for further judicial reform.
Bennett contends that the *Mosley* case demonstrates that 'the *strict rules*
of the common law of torts' are 'no longer . . . the most important aspect
of this type of claim' compared with the imperative of giving effect to
Article 8.[134] But this misses the important point that breach of confidence
was *not* a tort with 'strict rules' at all: it was at least in origin an equitable
action – and one which, certainly by 2000 when the HRA came into force,
was highly flexible, based on broad concepts such as the duty to be of
good faith and not to act unconscionably. Previous stricter requirements
of prior relationships of confidence and identifiable detriment had already
been jettisoned. As Keene LJ put it in the first *Douglas* judgment, 'breach
of confidence is a developing area of the law, the boundaries of which
are not immutable'.[135] Indeed, reviewing the state of the law just before
the HRA came into force, in an article written with Helen Fenwick,
we asked the question what role there was for the Convention to play in
the development of the law 'given that the judges already apparently have
to hand a serviceable tool with which to tackle invasions of privacy?' Our
suggestion was that it could help to resolve uncertainties in the confidence
action and 'provide the normative impetus for the consolidation of the
developments' that had already taken place.[136]

In this respect it is important to note that we had pointed out as
far back as 1996 that the action in confidence was already by then in a
much more advanced state of development, and able to protect privacy,
than was generally recognised.[137] Therefore, to suggest that the courts
post-HRA have wholly re-written the action in confidence is to over-
simplify the case. The fact is that the hard edges to the doctrine had been

---

134 Bennett, 'Horizontality's New Horizons', p. 101 (emphasis added).
135 Note 56 above, at p. 1011.
136 G. Phillipson and H. Fenwick, 'Breach of Confidence as a Privacy Remedy in the Human
     Rights Act Era', *Modern Law Review*, 63 (2000), 660.
137 H. Fenwick and G. Phillipson, 'Confidence and Privacy: a Re-examination', *Cambridge
     Law Journal*, 55 (1996), 447.

blurring for many years in a way that had often gone largely unnoticed. For example, some commentators were surprised by, or critical of, the decision in *Douglas* v. *Hello! Ltd* because they appeared to think that it was still clear law at that point that a pre-existing confidential relationship was required. Commenting on the first *Douglas* decision, Mulheron stated that:

> Given that there was absolutely no antecedent relationship of confidence between celebrity claimants and photographer defendant, the second element of the cause of action is stretched at best, and completely ignored at worst, by the outcome in this decision.[138]

This requirement had in fact been dispensed with as far back as 1984, in *Francome* v. *Mirror Group Newspapers*.[139] Indeed, the whole point of the 1996 article was to show that the law had already developed to the point at which breach of confidence was far more able to protect privacy than was generally recognised.

In this respect, it is worth noting that the HRA has had a much more dramatic effect upon breach of confidence than upon defamation.[140] It is suggested that one reason for this may well be the prosaic but important one that the latter is very well established and contains a number of quite detailed rules based on a very extensive case law; in contrast, breach of confidence was already in a state of evolution well *before* the HRA, was consequently in a much more inchoate state, and therefore had a much more pressing need – and ability – to seek strong guidance from the Convention. In defamation, on the other hand, it is much harder to see clear rules being overturned. For example, one long-established and hard-and-fast rule is that deriving from *Bonnard* v. *Perryman*, that no injunction may be issued where the defendants intend to plead justification. At present, despite considerable pressure from Article 8-based arguments, the courts are holding firm to this old common law rule.[141] It may be hazarded that only the Supreme Court will feel able to overrule it, if indeed that ever happens.[142]

---

138 R. Mulheron, 'A Potential Framework For Privacy? A Reply To *Hello!*', *Modern Law Review*, 69(5) (2006), 679–713.

139 [1984] 2 All ER 408. The information in this case was obtained from an unlawful telephone tap: no previous relationship of confidence existed. Other cases involving surreptitious taking of information in the absence of such relationships, such as *Shelley Films*, had also made this clear well before *Douglas* was decided: see p. 145, above.

140 See further Chapter 9.   141 *Greene* v. *Associated Newspapers Ltd* [2005] QB 972.

142 See further Chapter 5.

There were then three conditions[143] in place that allowed for the particularly strong impact of the Convention on the common law: first, a clear
gap in human rights protection; second, an absence of likely intervention
from Parliament; and third, prior developments that rendered the law
very open to Strasbourg influence. Interestingly, as noted in Chapter 4,[144]
what might be expected to be the fourth condition – a clear imperative
from Strasbourg to furnish a remedy not currently available – was *not* the
case at the time that *Campbell* was decided.[145] There were, however, some
fairly clear indications that both particular cases and underlying Convention principles pointed in this direction;[146] moreover, the decision in *Peck*
v. *United Kingdom* gave a fairly strong indication that non-consensual
disclosure of personal images by private bodies would engage the UK's
responsibility, although in that case an organ of the state was involved.[147]
Alternatively, as pointed out in Chapter 5, courts have a power – though
not a duty – to develop the law beyond the strict requirements of the
Convention as currently interpreted,[148] and cases such as *Campbell* may
be best explained this way.

It is contended further that the above explanation takes us towards
an answer to the seeming paradox identified in the introduction to this
chapter, of the creation of at least a *de facto* new privacy tort, accompanied
by vehement denials by senior judges that any tort of privacy is being
created. It may be tentatively suggested that the reason for this lies in
a basic tension: that the UK judiciary has both wanted to make use of
Article 8, while being simultaneously wary of it. On the one hand, the
judges saw Article 8 as the normative source from which they could
draw inspiration in order to fill the 'signal shortcoming' in English law
so glaringly evidenced in *Kaye* v. *Robertson*:[149] hence, the dynamic use
of Strasbourg jurisprudence to develop breach of confidence. On the

---

143 A further reason why confidence has been subject to more radical development may
be that, as Ivan Hare has pointed out, injunctions are the primary remedy, and the
jurisdiction to grant them has traditionally been seen as practically unlimited: I. Hare,
'Vertically Challenged: Private Parties, Privacy and the Human Rights Act', *European
Human Rights Law Review* (2001), 526, 534. This may partly explain the way in which,
in some cases in which injunctions to protect privacy have been sought, the courts have
shown relatively little concern about the precise role of the Convention rights in the case
before them: in particular, it may help explain the confusing dicta in *Re S (A Child)*: see
n. 86, above.

144 See p. 103.   145 *Von Hannover* was decided *after Campbell.*

146 Fenwick and Phillipson, 'Confidence and Privacy'.

147 Namely, the local authority that released the CCTV images to the media bodies.

148 Chapter 5, pp. 92–102.   149 [1991] FSR 62 at 71 *per* Leggatt LJ.

other hand, it is well known both that Article 8 has a uniquely broad scope in the Convention[150] and that English law has never recognised any general right to privacy. Hence, the judges have been keenly aware that to declare Article 8 as being horizontally applicable across the board would have the potential both for unsettling large areas of common law and also for requiring a degree of judicial law-making – the creation of the general 'blockbuster' tort of invasion of privacy – that they consider plainly beyond their constitutional and institutional capacities. Hence, the pattern of the *partial* use of Article 8, accompanied by denial that respect for privacy is, or can be, a 'general' or 'high level principle' of English law,[151] giving rise to a 'blockbuster tort'. This, it is contended, provides a final, cogent reason why we should *not* treat the cases this chapter has surveyed as providing a general template for common law horizontality. It also helps to explain the ambiguous and contradictory dicta on horizontal effect noted in this chapter[152] and in Chapter 1.

7.5 Conclusion

There is no doubt that, as the Introduction to this book puts it, breach of confidence has been radically remodelled to protect privacy. Academics love to generalise and theorise, and it is tempting, as we have seen, to suggest that the Convention-driven transformation that has occurred in this area of law provides a general answer to the broader question surrounding the acceptance of horizontal effect on the common law at large. Hence, the argument that the developments in this area of law 'prove' acceptance of the full or direct horizontal effect of Convention rights by the judiciary. This chapter has sought to show, first, that even in this area of law, no such acceptance has occurred, despite the *prima facie* appearance of some judicial dicta, while the creation of a new tort – if that is what we have seen – provides no kind of touchstone in this respect. Importantly also, it has provided an explanation of *why* the judiciary has accepted such strong use of the Convention in this area of law, which, arguably, convincingly demonstrates that it has *not* flowed from the clear acceptance of any general model of horizontal effect by the courts. Rather,

---

150 Noted in Chapter 18, p. 379, citations at n. 1. See further on Article 8, D. Feldman, 'Secrecy, Dignity or Autonomy? Views of Privacy as a Civil Liberty', *Current Legal Problems* 47(2) (1994), 42.

151 *Wainwright*, per Lord Hoffmann at [19]; see generally his speech at [15]–[35].

152 See pp. 146–7, above.

the judges have used the Convention to solve a particular problem in the law – the embarrassing gap highlighted by *Kaye* v. *Robertson* – acting only when it was fairly clear that no solution was to be expected from Parliament. Moreover, much of the developmental work required to do the job had been undertaken before the HRA came into force, giving the judges a very flexible tool that was already close to what was required, and ripe for further development. Such a prosaic explanation is doubtless less dramatic than extrapolating a general theory of horizontality from one set of cases, but is, I believe, considerably closer to the truth. It is also in harmony with judicial instincts about the limits of the common law's creative role in the UK constitution. Finally, it helps to solve the seeming paradox surrounding the judicial attitude to a 'right to privacy' identified at the start of this chapter.

8

Nuisance

DONAL NOLAN[*]

With the exceptions of defamation and privacy, private nuisance is probably the area of tort law in which the HRA has had the most influence so far. One of the notable aspects of the relationship between nuisance law and the HRA has been the co-existence of both the 'vertical' and the 'horizontal' effect of the HRA in this context, so that in the case law we can find examples of claimants bringing common law nuisance actions against public authorities alongside direct actions under the HRA, and examples of cases in which it has been argued that the nuisance analysis may itself be affected by human rights considerations. The purpose of this chapter is to explore all these different aspects of the relationship between nuisance and the HRA.

The chapter is divided into three main parts. In the first part, I consider the 'vertical effect' of the HRA in environmental nuisance cases, looking first at the relevant Articles of the Convention, then at the case law of the Strasbourg court, and then at the English case law since the HRA came into force. In the second part of the chapter, I consider the relationship between the vertical effect of the HRA and the law of nuisance. In particular, I identify the advantages and disadvantages for a claimant of the two possible routes to redress, and the inter-relationship between the two types of claim when they arise on the same set of facts. Finally, in the third part of the chapter, I consider the possible 'horizontal effect' of the HRA on the law of nuisance itself, looking in particular at the standing rules and the statutory authority defence.

8.1 The vertical effect of the HRA

In this part of the chapter, I seek to identify the circumstances in which a claim can be brought under the HRA with respect to the kinds of

---

[*] A draft of this chapter was presented to the Torts subject section at the Society of Legal Scholars annual conference at the University of Southampton in September 2010. I am grateful to the participants for their comments.

environmental interferences[1] that ground actions in the common law of nuisance. I begin by considering the relevant Convention rights in outline, before going on to consider the Strasbourg case law. I then complete my survey of the HRA's vertical effect in this context by looking at the English cases.

8.1.1 Article 8 and Article 1 of the First Protocol

There are two Articles of the Convention that are of potential relevance to the law of nuisance:[2] Article 8, which protects the right to respect for private and family life, the home and correspondence; and Article 1 of the First Protocol ('P1–1'), which protects the right to the peaceful enjoyment of one's possessions. The most important of the two in this context is Article 8, according to which 'everyone has the right to respect for his private and family life, his home and his correspondence'. It is customary to divide the Article 8 right into a number of component elements, one of which is the right to respect for one's home. It is this element of the right with which we are concerned here. As we shall see, the right to respect for one's home encompasses peaceful enjoyment of the home, so that serious interferences with the use and enjoyment of a person's home by environmental factors such as toxic emissions, noise and smells can amount to violations of Article 8.

The right to respect for one's home is not a property-based right; as Lord Millett has observed, a person's home is an 'important aspect of his dignity as a human being, and is protected as such and not as an item of property'.[3] By contrast, Article P1–1 is a right to peaceful

---

1 For a helpful survey of the impact of the Convention on environmental nuisances, see S. Praduroux, 'The European Convention and Environmental Nuisances', *European Review of Private Law* (2008), 269.

2 In extreme cases of environmental pollution and other environmental hazards, Art. 2 (the right to life) may also come into play, as in *Guerra v. Italy* (1998) 26 EHRR 357, where it was argued that the state's failure to provide information about the risk of arsenic poisoning from toxic factory emissions violated Art. 2; and *Öneryildiz v. Turkey* (2004) 41 EHRR 325, where Art. 2 was found to have been violated when nine members of one family were killed after a landslide from a rubbish tip engulfed their home. However, since personal injury and death are not actionable in the tort of nuisance (see *Hunter v. Canary Wharf Ltd* [1997] AC 655 at 696 *per* Lord Lloyd, at 707–8 *per* Lord Hoffmann) ('*Hunter*'), Art. 2 falls outside the scope of this chapter.

3 *Harrow LBC v. Qazi* [2003] UKHL 43, [2004] AC 983 at [89] ('*Qazi*'). See also at [8] *per* Lord Bingham ('Article 8 is not directed to the protection of property interests') and at [69] *per* Lord Hope (Art. 8 'does not concern itself with the person's right to the peaceful enjoyment of his home as a possession or as a property right').

enjoyment of one's possessions as items of property,[4] which requires that no one be deprived of his or her possessions 'except in the public interest and subject to the conditions provided for by law and by the general principles of international law'. This Article has been held to protect against interferences by the state that seriously affect the economic value of property, on the grounds that these amount to a partial taking.[5] It follows that Article P1–1 can potentially be invoked where environmental factors significantly diminish the economic value of a person's land,[6] and it is in such cases that the potential overlap with the law of nuisance arises. Compared with Article 8, Article P1–1 has both advantages and disadvantages for the claimant in a nuisance-type case. The advantages are, first, that Article P1–1 is not limited to interference with a person's home, but extends to interference with real property rights in general; and, second, that there might be cases in which a nuisance which is not serious enough to amount to an Article 8 violation nevertheless diminishes the value of the claimant's land sufficiently to bring Article P1–1 into play. Conversely, the disadvantages of Article P1–1 are that it probably does not protect a person without a proprietary interest in their home, and that it can be invoked only if the nuisance affects the economic value of the affected land, no matter how serious its other consequences.

8.1.2 The Strasbourg case law

Any assessment of the impact of these two Articles on claims under the HRA in respect of environmental nuisances must begin with the case law of the Strasbourg court and the Commission. This case law is, of course, much more extensive than the English case law, and in any case when applying the HRA the English courts are obliged to 'take into account' the Strasbourg jurisprudence (even if they are not obliged to *follow* it).[7]

The first decisions by the Strasbourg institutions on environmental nuisances concerned aircraft noise generated by planes flying out of Heathrow and Gatwick airports. During the course of the 1980s, a number of settlements were reached in such cases following decisions of the Commission

---

4 On Art. P1–1 in general, see D. Anderson, 'Compensation for Interference with Property', *European Human Rights Law Review* (1999), 543.

5 *Rayner* v. *United Kingdom* (1986) 47 DR 5, at 14.

6 See, e.g., *S* v. *France* (1990) 65 DR 250 (Commission), discussed below at pp. 168–70.

7 HRA, s. 2. See further Chapter 5.

that the applicants' complaints were admissible.[8] At the same time, the Commission made it clear that it would not be easy to establish that a noise nuisance amounted to a possible interference with either Article 8 or Article P1–1. Only if such a nuisance were 'intolerable and exceptional'[9] would the Convention come into play, and even then such a nuisance could not be considered to constitute an unreasonable burden for the individuals concerned if they had 'the possibility of moving elsewhere without substantial difficulties and losses'.[10] The first case of this kind to reach the Strasbourg court was *Powell and Rayner* v. *United Kingdom*,[11] where the court held that although aircraft noise could violate Article 8 because it could affect a person's physical well-being and their enjoyment of the amenity of their home, on the facts any interference was justified under Article 8(2) because the airport's operation was necessary for the economic well-being of the country and the relevant authorities had taken reasonable steps to control noise levels by reducing flight numbers and dividing the area into two different sectors. This early decision demonstrated that the potential significance of Article 8 in this context was not limited to cases in which a public authority itself created the interference, as the airport was not owned or operated by the state; any violation of Article 8 would therefore have arisen as a breach of the state's *positive* obligation to protect its citizens against interference by other private parties.

Two early decisions of the Commission also demonstrated the potential significance of Article P1–1 in this context. In its decision on admissibility in the *Rayner* litigation, the Commission made it clear that although Article P1–1 did not 'in principle guarantee a right to the peaceful enjoyment of possessions in a pleasant environment',[12] a noise nuisance of sufficient gravity could so seriously affect the value of real property as to amount to a partial taking. On the facts, however, there was no evidence that the value of the applicant's property had been substantially diminished by the aircraft noise. In its later decision in *S* v. *France*,[13] which concerned the construction of a nuclear power station opposite a house owned by

---

8 *Arrondelle* v. *United Kingdom* (1980) 19 DR 186, (1982) 26 DR 5 (settlement of £7,500 in respect of noise at Gatwick); *Baggs* v. *United Kingdom* (1985) 44 DR 13, (1987) DR 29 (settlement of £24,000 in respect of noise at Heathrow).

9 See, e.g., *Vearncombe* v. *United Kingdom and Germany* (1989) 59 DR 186, where the Commission declared inadmissible an application concerning noise generated by a military firing range in West Berlin.

10 *Rayner* v. *United Kingdom* at [13].   11 (1990) 12 EHRR 355.

12 *Rayner* v. *United Kingdom* at [14].   13 65 DR 250 (1990).

the applicant on the banks of the Loire, the Commission reiterated its analysis in *Rayner*. And while the Commission once again declared that there had been no violation of Article P1–1, this time this was not because the market value of the property had not been seriously affected (it had been halved), but because compensation had been paid to the applicant following litigation in the domestic courts which was reasonably related to the loss of value sustained.

The first case in which an Article 8 claim based on an environmental nuisance was successful before the Strasbourg court was *López-Ostra v. Spain*,[14] where the applicant's complaint concerned gas fumes, smells and contamination produced by an unlicensed waste management plant operated by a group of tanneries a few metres from her home. Although the plant was not operated by a public authority, Article 8 was engaged because of the failure of the relevant authorities to close the plant down. The court held that 'severe environmental pollution may affect individuals' well-being and prevent them from enjoying their homes in such a way as to affect their private and family life adversely', while noting that 'regard must be had to the fair balance that has to be struck between the competing interests of the individual and of the community as a whole'.[15] On the facts, the court considered that notwithstanding the considerable margin of appreciation enjoyed by the state, it had failed to strike the correct balance between the economic well-being of the local area and the applicant's rights under Article 8.

The court also held that there had been a violation of Article 8 in the later case of *Guerra v. Italy*,[16] which concerned the risks created by the operation of a chemical factory close to the town where the applicants lived. The court took the view that because the toxic emissions from the factory had a direct effect on the applicants' right to respect for their private and family life, Article 8 was applicable, and that by failing to provide timely information about the risks associated with the factory's activities, and thereby depriving the applicants of the opportunity to assess for themselves the dangers of continuing to live in the vicinity, the authorities had failed to fulfil their Convention obligations. Like *López-Ostra*, *Guerra* was a positive obligations case, since the factory was operated by a private company, but the court emphasised that although the object of Article 8 was essentially that of protecting the individual against arbitrary interference by public authorities, it did not merely compel the state to abstain

---

14 (1994) 20 EHRR 277 ('*López-Ostra*').   15 *López-Ostra* at [51].
16 (1998) 26 EHRR 357 ('*Guerra*').

from such interference and there might also be positive obligations inherent in effective respect for private and family life.[17] In this connection, the court emphasised that by failing to provide the information in question, the relevant authorities were in breach of their statutory obligations under Italian law.

In the same year that *Guerra v. Italy* was decided, the Commission in *Khatun v. United Kingdom*[18] declared inadmissible an application by the residents of London's Docklands, whose nuisance claims had previously been rejected by the House of Lords in the leading case of *Hunter v. Canary Wharf Ltd*.[19] The application centred on a nuisance caused by dust generated by the construction of the Limehouse Link Road. Since the focus was on Article 8, the Commission accepted that – unlike in the domestic nuisance context – applicants without a proprietary interest in their homes had standing, and considered that the fact that they could not open windows or dry laundry outside for a period of three years 'severely impaired their right to enjoy their homes and private or family lives',[20] and so amounted to an interference under Article 8(1) which required justification under Article 8(2). However, the Commission went on to hold that the interference had been justified, since the construction of the road had been essential to the regeneration of the local area and pursued the legitimate aim of the economic well-being of the country; and that, bearing in mind that the dust did not seem to have given rise to health problems and that the interference had been limited to the period of the works, a fair balance had been struck between the interests of the applicants and those of the community as a whole.

A number of more recent decisions of the Strasbourg court have further clarified the extent of the state's Article 8 obligations with respect to environmental nuisances. In *Hatton v. United Kingdom*,[21] the Grand Chamber concluded by twelve votes to five that the UK Government's policy on night flights out of Heathrow did not violate Article 8, because it struck a balance that fell within the margin of appreciation, and the procedure adopted in arriving at the policy had not been fundamentally flawed. Three points about *Hatton* are of particular note. The first is that the court held that in cases involving state decisions relating to environmental matters, there were two aspects to the inquiry that might be carried out by the court: first, the court might assess the substantive merits of the decision under attack to ensure its compatibility with Article 8; and,

17 *Guerra* at [58].   18 (1998) 26 EHRR CD 212.   19 [1997] AC 655.
20 (1998) 26 EHRR CD 212, 215.   21 (2003) 37 EHRR 611 ('*Hatton*').

second, the court might scrutinise the decision-making process to ensure
that due weight had been accorded to the interests of the individuals
affected.[22] The second point of note is that the court denied that the Convention accorded environmental rights any special status.[23] And the third
noteworthy aspect of *Hatton* is that while the court acknowledged that the
state's responsibility in environmental cases might arise from its failure
to regulate private industry in a manner securing proper respect for the
rights enshrined in Article 8, it also noted that in both the *López-Ostra* and
Guerra cases the finding of a breach of the state's positive obligations had
been predicated on the authorities' failure to comply with an aspect of the
domestic legal order. By contrast, this 'element of domestic irregularity'
was absent in *Hatton*, where the night-flying scheme had been found to
be compatible with national law.[24]

The second such case was *Moreno Gómez* v. *Spain*,[25] where the court
held that Article 8 had been violated when high levels of night noise were
generated by nightclubs and bars in the vicinity of the applicant's flat,
which had been given permission to operate there by the local council.
An important feature of this case was the fact that the court found that
although the council had adopted measures that would have been adequate to secure respect for the applicant's rights, it tolerated the repeated
flouting of the rules it had itself established, with the result that on a
number of occasions the maximum permitted noise levels were exceeded.
The authorities' failure to take action to deal with the noise meant that the
applicant suffered a serious infringement of her rights under Article 8.

In *Fadeyeva* v. *Russia*,[26] the court held that the failure of the state
to protect the applicant from toxins emitted by a nearby steel plant
had violated her Article 8 rights. The court stressed that the adverse
effects of pollution must attain a certain minimal level if they were to
fall within the scope of Article 8. The assessment of that minimum was
relative and depended on all the circumstances, such as the intensity and
duration of the nuisance, its physical or mental effects and the 'general

---

22 *Hatton* at [99].
23 *Hatton* at [122]. In this respect, the reasoning of the court was consistent with its earlier
   decision in *Kyrtatos* v. *Greece* (2005) 40 EHRR 390, where it made clear (at para. 52)
   that the Convention was not specifically designed to provide general protection of the
   environment as such, and that environmental pollution would interfere with rights under
   Art. 8(1) only where there was 'a harmful effect on a person's private or family sphere
   and not simply the general deterioration of the environment'.
24 (2003) 37 EHRR 611 at [120].   25 (2005) 41 EHRR 40.
26 (2007) 45 EHRR 10 ('*Fadeyeva*').

environmental context'.[27] The court noted that the pollution levels had been well in excess of domestic environmental norms, and attached particular significance to the fact that domestic legislation defined the area in which the applicant lived as unfit for habitation, and the fact that the domestic courts had recognised the applicant's right to be resettled. Since it was possible to conclude that the applicant's health had deteriorated as a result of the emissions, and that it made her vulnerable to various diseases, the detriment to her health and well-being reached a level sufficient to bring it within the scope of Article 8.

Finally, in *Giacomelli* v. *Italy*,[28] Article 8 was held to have been violated by persistent noise and harmful emissions from a waste treatment plant close to the applicant's home. The court noted that neither the decision to grant the operating licence for the plant nor the decision to authorise it to treat industrial waste by means of detoxification had been preceded by an environmental impact assessment, as required by the relevant domestic legislation, and that when such an assessment had eventually been carried out, it had been found that the operation of the plant breached domestic environmental regulations. Furthermore, the relevant state authorities had refused to enforce judicial decisions holding that the plant's operations were unlawful and ordering their immediate suspension.

Two general points can be made about the Strasbourg authorities. The first is that the general tenor of the case law is that only the most severe nuisances will bring Article 8 into play. In particular, it is noteworthy that in most of the cases in which Article 8 violations were identified, the applicants alleged that the interference was so grave that it had either already damaged their health or threatened to do so,[29] and that in two of the cases it was so grave that the authorities had either re-housed the applicant or undertaken to do this.[30] The second point is that although the court has

---

27 *Fadeyeva* at [69].   28 (2007) 45 EHRR 38.

29 In *López-Ostra*, the applicant alleged that the emissions from the plant caused her and her family serious health problems; in *Guerra*, 150 people had been hospitalised with acute arsenic poisoning following an explosion at the factory; in *Moreno Gómez*, the applicant alleged that the noise nuisance had caused her to suffer insomnia and other serious health problems; and in *Fadeyeva* the court concluded that the emissions might well have affected the applicant's health. Conversely, in *Khatun*, the fact that it was not alleged that the dust had given rise to any health problems was one of the reasons why the application was declared to be inadmissible by the Commission, and it was not alleged in *Hatton* that the government's night flights policy had affected any of the applicants' health.

30 In *López-Ostra*, the applicant had been re-housed at the state's expense for a period of a year, and in *Fadeyeva* a domestic court had accepted that the applicant had the right to be resettled outside the area most seriously affected by the pollution.

accepted that a failure by the state to intervene to secure respect for the rights recognised in Articles 8 and P1–1 may amount to a Convention violation – so that these Articles have 'horizontal applicability'[31] – in practice such violations have almost always been predicated on a failure by the national authorities to comply with some aspect of their own domestic legal order. As Tom Allen points out, it remains the case that 'the court is reluctant to intervene in cases where the state has adopted and adhered to a regulatory regime which may involve intrusion on some interests', so that the strongest cases are those 'where the individual is only seeking the enforcement of existing laws in respect of a clear default'.[32] He concludes that:

> Although both [Articles 8 and P1–1] do give rise to positive obligations regarding environmental or other interferences with the enjoyment of possessions or the home, it seems that the Court is unlikely to find that a fully considered, lawful decision to allow the interference to continue has upset the fair balance under either right.[33]

This focus on domestic legality calls into question the significance of the state's positive obligations under Articles 8 and P1–1 for claims under the HRA in respect of environmental nuisances. If on the Strasbourg jurisprudence the state's positive duties are largely confined to the enforcement of domestic legal norms, then successful claims under the HRA for breaches of such duties are likely to be few and far between.

8.1.3 The English case law

In a number of cases decided since the HRA came into force, the English courts have had to grapple with the issues raised by the application of Articles 8 and P1–1 to environmental nuisances. The first significant domestic authorities were the decisions at first instance, in the Court of Appeal and in the House of Lords in *Marcic* v. *Thames Water Utilities Ltd*.[34] Over a period of several years, the claimant's property in Stanmore had suffered from regular and serious incidents of external flooding as a result of the inadequacy of the defendants' sewerage system. He sought redress in common law nuisance, and also under the HRA (it having been conceded that the defendant was a 'public authority' for this purpose). At

---

31 See further Chapter 2.
32 T. Allen, *Property and the Human Rights Act 1998* (Oxford: Hart, 2005), p. 216.
33 Allen, *Property and the Human Rights Act 1998*, pp. 217–18.
34 [2002] QB 929, QB; [2002] EWCA Civ. 65, [2002] QB 929; [2003] UKHL 66, [2004] 2 AC 42 ('*Marcic*').

first instance, HHJ Richard Havery QC held that applying the special rules governing the liability of sewerage undertakers the nuisance claim failed, but that the defendants' failure to carry out works to alleviate the problem amounted to a violation of the claimant's rights under Article 8 and Article P1–1, and that he was therefore entitled to damages under the HRA. As regards Article P1–1, the judge pointed out that the value of the property must have been seriously affected by the flooding (the claimant alleged that it was unsaleable), and that this amounted to a partial expropriation. According to the judge, the key question was whether the interference with the claimant's rights could be justified in accordance with Article 8(2) and the qualifying words in Article P1–1. The burden of proof as to justification lay on the defendants, and they had failed to establish that the system of priorities they had adopted for dealing with such problems struck a fair balance between the claimant's interests and those of their other customers.

On appeal, the Court of Appeal dismissed the defendant's appeal on the human rights point, and allowed the claimant's cross-appeal on liability in nuisance. The court took the view that the decision to allow the cross-appeal rendered the HRA issue otiose, since under section 8(3) of the HRA, the claimant's common law damages amounted to just satisfaction in respect of any HRA claim. However, the court went on to hold that the defendant had failed to establish that the judge had been wrong to hold that there was a Convention violation, and Lord Phillips MR said that even if the defendants had established that they had taken reasonable steps to abate the flooding, it did not follow that they ought to have escaped liability. It was arguable that those who benefited from a sewerage system should be charged enough to cover the cost of paying compensation to the minority who suffered damage as a result of the system's operation, and one way of achieving this would be to hold that in such circumstances the payment of compensation was necessary to strike a fair balance between the competing individual and community interests for the purposes of the HRA.

On further appeal to the House of Lords, the House held that the claimant in *Marcic* had no remedy at common law or under the HRA. As regards the HRA claim, their Lordships accepted that 'direct and serious interference of this nature with a person's home' was *prima facie* a violation of Articles 8 and P1–1,[35] but they also held that applying Article 8(2) and the qualifying words of Article P1–1 the statutory scheme laid down in

---

35 *Marcic* [2003] UKHL 66, [2004] 2 AC 42 at [37] *per* Lord Nicholls.

respect of sewerage undertakers' drainage obligations in the Water Industry Act 1991 struck a fair balance between the interests of the individual and the community as a whole, and, hence, complied with the Convention. Under this scheme a general drainage obligation was imposed on sewerage undertakers, but the enforcement of this scheme was left to the industry regulator, whose decisions were subject to judicial review. According to Lord Nicholls, in establishing this scheme, 'Parliament acted well within its bounds as policy maker', and even though in the instant case matters had 'plainly gone awry', the malfunctioning of the statutory scheme on this occasion did not cast doubt on its overall fairness.[36] Lord Hoffmann emphasised that under the Convention national institutions were accorded a broad discretion in choosing the solution appropriate to their own society or creating the machinery for doing so.[37]

The second case of this kind to come before the English courts was *Dennis* v. *Ministry of Defence*,[38] where Buckley J held that noise from military jets flying over the claimants' stately home violated their rights under Article 8 and Article P1–1, and would have entitled them to damages under the HRA had an adequate remedy in damages for nuisance not also been available. The noise produced by a particular training exercise conducted directly above the claimants' estate was so loud as to make it impossible to pursue their ordinary activities. The judge also found that the noise had reduced the market value of the estate by some £4 million, and destroyed any possibility of using it for commercial entertaining. Buckley J said that while it was accepted that interference with the rights arising under Articles 8 and P1–1 could be justified by reference to a legitimate aim, any such interference would be disproportionate if it obliged a citizen to bear an unreasonable burden in the absence of compensation. The admissibility decision in *S* v. *France* and the words of Lord Phillips in the Court of Appeal in *Marcic*[39] were cited as authority for this latter proposition. On the facts, although the interferences with the claimants' Convention rights were in pursuit of the legitimate aim of national security, the extent of the burden was so great that only if compensation were awarded could a Convention violation be avoided.

---

36 *Marcic* at [43].
37 *Marcic* at [71]. See also at [87] *per* Lord Hope (referring to the 'margin of appreciation' that must be given to the legislature in a democratic system).
38 [2003] EWHC 793 (QB), [2003] Env. LR 34. For a helpful discussion of this case, see J. Hartshorne [2003] Conv 526 (note).
39 See p. 174. The judgment in *Dennis* was handed down before the decision of the House of Lords in *Marcic*.

Two other cases of significance on the scope of the Article 8 and Article P1–1 rights in this context are *Lough* v. *First Secretary of State*[40] and *Andrews* v. *Reading BC*.[41] In *Lough* it was argued that the decision to grant planning permission for a building development in the Bankside area of London violated local residents' rights under the two Articles. The Court of Appeal refused to quash the decision, arguing that the two Articles created no absolute right to amenities currently enjoyed, and had to be interpreted in the light of competing interests, including the right of other landowners to make beneficial use of their land and the needs of the community as a whole. On the facts, the planning inspector had struck an appropriate balance, bearing in mind the benefits of the proposed development. Relying on the Strasbourg authorities, Keene LJ said that 'Not every adverse effect on residential amenity will amount to an infringement of the right to respect for a person's home under Article 8(1)', and Pill LJ that only a 'substantial' degree of interference would bring Article 8 into play.[42] In *Andrews*, the Court of Appeal held that a significant increase in traffic noise audible from the claimant's home brought about by the defendant council's decision to close an alternative route to cars amounted to a violation of his rights under Article 8. According to Calvert-Smith J, the degree of interference following the change was substantial enough to trigger Article 8(1), and relying on *Dennis* v. *Ministry of Defence*, he reasoned that maintenance of a correct balance between individual rights and the public interest might in appropriate cases require compensation to persons directly affected by decisions justifiable on public interest grounds. This was such a case, and an award of modest damages under the HRA to help towards the cost of double glazing the property was appropriate.

Two points in particular can be made about the English cases. The first is that English judges are arguably taking a more expansive view of the protections afforded by the Convention in environmental nuisance cases than the Strasbourg institutions. Indeed, there is even evidence that sometimes the courts are mistakenly assuming that just because an interference amounts to a common law nuisance it must also be serious enough to amount to a potential violation of Articles 8 and P1–1.[43] One

---

40 [2004] EWCA Civ. 905, [2004] 1 WLR 2557 ('*Lough*').
41 [2005] EWHC 256 (QB).   42 *Lough* at [54] and [43].
43 See, e.g., *Pemberton* v. *Southwark LBC* [2000] 1 WLR 1672 at 1684, where Clarke LJ simply assumes that noise actionable in nuisance would also infringe an occupier's rights under Art. 8.

particular manifestation of this tendency is the approach taken towards Article P1–1 in this context. It seems to be customary to treat this Article almost as if it were co-extensive with Article 8, and to assume on the slim authority of the single admissibility decision in *S* v. *France* that it will be engaged by any substantial reduction in the value of real property attributable to a nuisance for which a public authority is responsible.[44]

The second point is that there is increasing evidence that the courts are using the HRA to move towards recognition of an English equivalent of the French public law principle of equality before public burdens (*égalité devant les charges publiques*), according to which compensation should be provided where a citizen is called upon to bear more than an equal share of a burden imposed for the common good.[45] The reasoning of Lord Phillips in the Court of Appeal in *Marcic* is particularly striking in this respect,[46] and the decisions in *Dennis* and *Andrews* were strongly influenced by this kind of argument; in *Dennis*, for example, Buckley J stated that in his view 'common fairness demands that where the interests of a minority, let alone an individual, are seriously interfered with because of an overriding public interest, the minority should be compensated'.[47] Again, however, it is questionable how much support there is for such a principle in the Strasbourg authorities,[48] and it raises a number of difficult questions, such as how serious the interference must be before compensation is merited, how much compensation must be paid to make the interference proportionate, and in what circumstances compliance with the Convention will require more than the mere payment of compensation.[49]

---

44 Cf. *Lough* at [51] *per* Pill LJ ('A loss of value in itself... does not affect the peaceful enjoyment of possessions').

45 On this principle, see D. Fairgrieve, *State Liability in Tort: A Comparative Study* (Oxford University Press, 2003), pp. 144–50.

46 In the House of Lords in *Marcic*, Lord Nicholls said (at [45]) that 'The minority who suffer damage and disturbance as a consequence of the inadequacy of the sewerage system ought not to be required to bear an unreasonable burden', although he clearly regarded this as a matter for the regulator to deal with under the statutory scheme rather than a basis on which to impose liability.

47 At [63]. See also *Andrews* at [93] *per* Calvert-Smith J ('In order to maintain a proper balance between the rights of the individual and the public the authority should be prepared in particular cases to compensate individuals who are directly affected').

48 'The fact that the Commission once viewed with approbation the payment of compensation to a French citizen, aggrieved at the arrival of a nuclear power plant, seems thin grounds for binding all statutory undertakers to one particular conception of distributive justice' (C. Miller, 'Environmental Rights in a Welfare State? A Comment on DeMerieux', *Oxford Journal of Legal Studies*, 23 (2003), 111, 121).

49 See Hartshorne [2003] Conv 526 at 532–3.

8.2 The relationship between the vertical effect of the HRA and the law of nuisance

In this part of the chapter I consider the relationship between the vertical effect of the HRA and the law of nuisance. I look first at the advantages and disadvantages for a claimant of the two possible routes to redress, and then I go on to consider the inter-relationship between the two types of claim when they arise on the same set of facts.

8.2.1 The advantages and disadvantages of the two possible routes to redress

A victim of an environmental nuisance may be faced with a choice between suing a public authority that is responsible for the nuisance under the HRA or at common law. What factors will determine which of these two possible routes to redress is more favourable?

All things being equal, a claimant is likely to prefer the nuisance claim, for five reasons. First, at least on the Strasbourg authorities, only the most serious of environmental nuisances are likely to qualify as interferences with Convention rights; in a nuisance action, by contrast, any substantial interference with a protected interest will be actionable. Second, while the Convention case law is littered with examples of *prima facie* interferences being justified on public interest grounds under Article 8(2) and the qualifying words of Article P1–1,[50] it is an established principle of nuisance law that the social utility of the defendant's activity is not a defence to an otherwise actionable interference, but at most a reason to award damages in lieu of an injunction.[51] Third, under the HRA damages are discretionary,[52] and to be awarded only if necessary to afford the claimant 'just satisfaction',[53] whereas in nuisance they are awarded as of right and they may in general terms (and quite apart from the subtleties of the damages issues raised by concurrent claims discussed below) be more generous than the damages that would be awarded under the HRA.[54] Fourth, the limitation period for actions in nuisance is six years,[55] whereas the default limitation period under the HRA is one year.[56] And a final

---

50 See, e.g., *Hatton*.
51 See, e.g., *Miller* v. *Jackson* [1977] QB 966; *Kennaway* v. *Thompson* [1981] QB 88; *Dennis*.
52 See *Anufrijeva* v. *Southwark LBC* [2003] EWCA Civ. 1406, [2004] QB 1124 at [55] *per* Lord Woolf CJ ('*Anufrijeva*').
53 Section 8(3).   54 See Chapter 11.   55 Limitation Act 1980, s. 2.
56 Section 7(5).

possible advantage of suing in nuisance is that while it is clearly not a defence to a nuisance action that the claimant 'came to the nuisance',[57] there are suggestions in the Strasbourg case law on environmental nuisances that the fact that the applicant either chose to move into the vicinity of the nuisance – or not to move away from it – may count against him or her. In *Rayner v. United Kingdom*, for example, the Commission emphasised that the applicant had taken the risk of choosing a home in an environment that was likely to deteriorate as local air traffic increased, and went on to say that a noise nuisance could not be considered to constitute an unreasonable burden for those concerned if they could move elsewhere without substantial difficulties and losses.[58]

An important additional distinction between the two types of claim is that the rules as to standing are different. To sue in nuisance, the claimant must have a proprietary interest in the land affected by the nuisance.[59] The same is probably true if a claim is brought under the HRA on the ground that the nuisance amounts to a violation of the right to peaceful enjoyment of possessions under Article P1–1, since (like the tort of nuisance) that Article is limited to the protection of property interests, in a broad sense.[60] However, the picture changes where the HRA action is based on Article 8, because it is well established that the concept of the 'home' underlying Article 8 is an autonomous one that is not tied to property rights in domestic law;[61] as Lord Millett has said, on the Strasbourg authorities it is neither 'necessary nor sufficient' that the applicant

---

57 See K. Oliphant (ed.), *The Law of Tort*, 2nd edn (London: LexisNexis Butterworths, 2007), para. 22.98.

58 (1986) 47 DR 5 at 13. See also *Hatton*, where the court said (at para. 127) that it was reasonable, in determining the impact of a general policy on individuals in a particular area, to take into account their ability to leave that area; and *Fadeyeva*, where it was said (at para. 120) to be 'material' that the applicant had moved to the location in question knowing the environmental situation to be unfavourable, and where consideration was also given to the ease with which she could move away from the affected area. Similar reasoning has been employed in the domestic case law as well: see *Marcic v. Thames Water Utilities Ltd (No. 2)* [2001] EWHC 394 (TCC), [2002] QB 929 at [12] *per* HHJ Richard Havery QC ('if a person chooses to go into occupation of a property known to be subject to flooding, I do not think that failure to alleviate the flooding could be regarded as an infringement of his human rights'). See further Miller, 'Environmental Rights in a Welfare State?', pp. 122–5.

59 *Hunter*. See further Oliphant, *The Law of Tort*, para. 22.59ff.

60 Note, however, that even where Art. P1–1 is concerned, the standing rules may be wider than in nuisance, since it could be argued that, e.g., a contractual licence to use land is a 'possession' for Art. P1–1 purposes, even though it is not a proprietary interest sufficient to ground a nuisance action: see Allen, *Property and the Human Rights Act 1998*, p. 210.

61 See *Khatun; Prokopovich v. Russia* (2004) 43 EHRR 167.

should have a proprietary interest in the premises concerned.[62] Instead, the claimant will have to show that the property counts as his or her home under the Convention case law, which treats the question as one of fact and requires the claimant to demonstrate the existence of a 'sufficient and continuous link'.[63]

Distinctions also emerge when we flip from the question of who can sue under the HRA and nuisance to the question of who can be liable. The main point here, of course, is that only 'public authorities' can be liable under the HRA.[64] Although that critical distinction will exclude the possibility of a HRA claim in many nuisance cases, there is also a category of case in which a particular defendant will not be liable in nuisance, but may be liable under the HRA. It is an established principle of the law of nuisance that a landlord out of occupation is liable for a nuisance emanating from the demised land only if he has authorised it, a strict test that requires either that the nuisance was expressly authorised, or that it was certain to result from the purposes for which the property was let.[65] Furthermore, it is also clear that a landlord will not be deemed to have authorised a nuisance created by a tenant because with knowledge of its existence he refrained from exercising his right to end the tenancy, or took no other active steps to prevent the continuation of the interference.[66] An example is *Hussain* v. *Lancaster City Council*,[67] where the claimants, who owned a shop on the defendant's council estate, had been subjected to a campaign of racial harassment by tenants on the estate. Their nuisance action against the defendant for not putting a stop to the abuse by evicting those responsible was struck out because the failure to evict did not amount to an authorisation. It is clearly arguable that in these

---

62 *Qazi* at [97].

63 See, e.g., *Gillow* v. *United Kingdom* (1986) 11 EHRR 335; *Buckley* v. *United Kingdom* (1996) 23 EHRR 101. For commentary, see D. J. Harris *et al.*, *Harris, O'Boyle and Warbrick's Law of the European Convention on Human Rights*, 2nd edn. (Oxford University Press, 2009), pp. 376–7. Note that the Strasbourg court has now accepted that in certain circumstances, Art. 8 protects the 'right to respect for a company's registered office, branches or other business premises' (*Société Colas Est* v. *France* (2004) 39 EHRR 17 at para. 41). In the leading English authority on the concept of 'home', *Harrow LBC* v. *Qazi*, Lord Bingham approved the description of a person's home as the place where 'a person lives and to which he returns and which forms the centre of his existence' (at [8], citing *Uratemp Ventures Ltd* v. *Collins* [2002] 1 AC 301 at [31] *per* Lord Millett).

64 Section 6. See further on the meaning of 'public authority' Chapter 2.

65 See Oliphant, *The Law of Tort*, para. 22.66.

66 See, e.g., *Malzy* v. *Eichholz* [1916] 2 KB 308; *Smith* v. *Scott* [1973] Ch 314; *Mowan* v. *Wandsworth LBC* (2001) 33 HLR 56.

67 [2000] QB 1.

circumstances, the claimants would now have an action against the council under the HRA for violation of their Article 8 rights. This possibility is, however, subject to three caveats. The first is that since it is not the council itself that is creating the nuisance, an HRA claim would lie only if in these circumstances Article 8 gave rise to a positive obligation on the authority's part to protect the claimant from interference by third parties. Second, on these facts, a claim under the HRA might fail if the claimant could achieve a similar outcome by proceeding directly against the tenants in nuisance, since in those circumstances there would arguably not be a sufficiently strong causal connection between the authority's inaction and the interference suffered by the claimant.[68] And finally, it would have to be borne in mind that in such a scenario, the eviction of the perpetrators of the nuisance might violate *their* rights under Article 8.[69]

8.2.2 The inter-relationship between the two types of claim

The next issue is the inter-relationship between the HRA claim and the nuisance claim when they both arise on the same set of facts. At this point it is worth pausing to note: (1) that no award of damages is to be made under the HRA unless, taking account of all the circumstances of the case, including any other relief or remedy granted, the award is necessary to afford just satisfaction to the claimant;[70] and (2) that when a court is deciding whether to award damages under the HRA, or the amount of such damages, account must be taken of the principles applied by the Strasbourg court in relation to the award of compensation under Article 41 of the Convention,[71] and it is therefore to be expected that the quantum of awards made under the HRA will roughly mirror the quantum of awards made in Strasbourg.[72]

---

68 In *Mowan*, Peter Gibson LJ said that the availability of injunctive relief against the creator of the nuisance meant that it was not necessary to modify the law of nuisance in order to give the tenant a remedy against the landlord in this scenario. On the possible 'horizontal effect' of the HRA in these circumstances, see p. 191.

69 In *Qazi*, the House of Lords made it clear that any attempt to evict a person from their home will engage Art. 8, and in *Connors* v. *United Kingdom* (2004) 40 EHRR 189, the Strasbourg court held that the eviction of the applicant's family from the caravan site where they lived for alleged anti-social behaviour violated his Art. 8 rights.

70 HRA, s. 8(3).   71 Section 8(4).

72 In *R (Greenfield)* v. *Secretary of State for the Home Department* [2005] UKHL 14, [2005] 1 WLR 673, Lord Bingham said (at [19]) that domestic judges 'should not aim to be significantly more or less generous than the [Strasbourg] court might be expected to be'. For criticism of this 'mirror approach', see Chapter 11.

Unlike in the case of an application to the Strasbourg court, it is not a condition of an HRA action that all other remedial possibilities have been exhausted. This is reinforced by the short time limit that applies to claims under the HRA, which makes it unrealistic to expect a claimant to await the outcome of common law proceedings before resorting to the Act. It follows that the fact that the victim of an Article 8 or Article P1–1 violation might also have an action against the relevant public authority in nuisance should not preclude him or her from suing the authority under the HRA, and that the *possibility* of a nuisance claim would not in itself mean that an award of HRA damages would not be necessary to afford him or her 'just satisfaction' applying section 8(3) of the HRA, which requires the court to take into account only remedies that have already been granted, and not remedies that may be available, but that the claimant has not yet sought.[73]

Nevertheless, for the reasons given above, in most cases such a person is likely to bring an action against the authority at common law either instead of, or in addition to, bringing a claim under the HRA. If the claimant chooses to sue only in nuisance, then, of course, no question arises as to the inter-relationship of the two actions. Issues may, however, arise when actions of both kinds are brought in respect of the same interference. In practice, the approach of the courts in such cases has been to consider the common law action first. If the court finds that there is no liability at common law, it simply proceeds to consider the HRA claim in the usual way (as happened both at first instance and in the House of Lords in *Marcic*), but complexities emerge when the court holds that there is liability in nuisance, as it then has to decide what implications the common law liability has for the HRA claim.

This was the position in which the Court of Appeal found itself in *Marcic*, where it was then simply assumed that the damages to which the claimant was entitled at common law would afford him just satisfaction for any violation of his Convention rights, so that it was unnecessary to proceed to consider his HRA claim in any detail. In the words of Lord Phillips MR, the claimant's 'right to damages at common law displaces any right that he would otherwise have had to damages under the Act', and so the HRA point became 'academic'.[74] A similar approach was taken by the Court of Appeal in the recent case of *Dobson* v. *Thames Water Utilities Ltd*, where Waller LJ said that since it was 'most improbable, if

73 See Law Com. No. 266, *Damages Under the Human Rights Act 1998* (2000), para. 2.24.
74 [2002] EWCA Civ. 65, [2002] QB 929 at [104].

not inconceivable' that damages at common law would be exceeded by an award to the same claimant for a violation of Article 8, a common law damages award would normally constitute 'just satisfaction' for HRA purposes and no additional award of compensation under that Act would therefore be necessary.[75]

A further question that arose in *Dobson* was the implication, if any, of an award of common law damages to someone with a legal interest in the affected land for a claim under the HRA by a person resident in the property but lacking any interest in it (and hence standing in nuisance). Previously, in *Dennis*, Buckley J had held that an award at common law of £950,000 to the owner of the stately home for the amenity damage caused by the noise nuisance provided just satisfaction in respect of both his *and his wife's* claims for violations of their Convention rights, even though she had no legal interest in the property, and was therefore a party neither to the nuisance action nor the damages award. The court in *Dobson* took a more nuanced view, concluding only that an award of damages in nuisance to a person with a proprietary interest in a property would be *relevant* to the question of whether a damages award was necessary to afford just satisfaction for a violation of the Article 8 rights of a person who lived in the same household, but had no interest in the property. According to Waller LJ, the vital question in such cases was 'whether it is *necessary* to award *damages* to another member of the household or whether the remedy of a declaration that Article 8 rights have been infringed suffices, alongside the award to the landowner, especially when no pecuniary loss has been suffered'.[76] Furthermore, if it is concluded that a separate award is necessary, the fact and amount of the award to the right-holder should be taken into account when assessing quantum.[77]

Two general points should be made before looking further at these questions concerning the relevance of an award of nuisance damages to an HRA claim in respect of the same interference. The first is that the House of Lords made it clear in *Hunter* v. *Canary Wharf Ltd* that even in cases of intangible nuisances, the injury is to the property rather than the occupiers, so that the loss to be compensated is the diminution in the utility value of the land, rather than the discomfort and inconvenience suffered by those using it.[78] It follows that in nuisance cases, the quantum

---

75 [2009] EWCA Civ. 28, [2009] 3 All ER 319 at [52] ('*Dobson*').
76 *Dobson* at [45] (emphasis in original).   77 *Dobson* at [46].
78 See *Hunter* at 696 *per* Lord Lloyd, at 706 *per* Lord Hoffmann, at 724–5 *per* Lord Hope. On the wider implications of this analysis, see D. Nolan, '"A Tort Against Land": Private

of damages does not depend on the number of people on the affected property,[79] but is governed instead by the objective qualities of the land, such as its size, commodiousness and value.[80] Unfortunately, however, this clear principle of objective assessment of nuisance damages was somewhat muddied in *Dobson*,[81] with the result that the court appears to have lost sight of the very different purposes served by nuisance damages and those awarded for Article 8 violations under the HRA: namely, that while the former compensate for the effect of the interference on the *land*, the latter compensate for its effect on the *individual*. The second general point is that when awarding damages under Article 41, the Strasbourg court has taken into account factors – such as the degree of the public authority's culpability – which would not be taken into account in assessing damages in nuisance.[82]

From these observations, certain conclusions follow. Looking first at the position of a claimant *with* a proprietary interest who has suffered an Article 8 violation, the Court of Appeal was doubtless correct to hold in *Dobson* that here the award of nuisance damages can normally be expected to afford her just satisfaction for the breach of her Convention rights, particularly when it is borne in mind that the Strasbourg court's approach to compensation for non-pecuniary loss has been parsimonious by domestic standards, and that this can therefore be expected to have a dampening effect on awards under the HRA.[83] Having said that, it is possible to envisage circumstances in which a co-owner of a property affected by a serious nuisance recovers a relatively small amount of damages at common law because the award is shared with the other co-owners, but as the only occupier of the property actually affected by the interference can reasonably expect a larger award for the violation of his or her

Nuisance as a Property Tort', in D. Nolan and A. Robertson (eds.), *Rights and Private Law* (Oxford: Hart, forthcoming).

79 'The reduction in amenity value is the same whether the land is occupied by the family man or the bachelor': *Hunter* at 696 *per* Lord Lloyd. See also at 706–7 *per* Lord Hoffmann, at 724 *per* Lord Hope.

80 *Hunter* at 706 *per* Lord Hoffmann.

81 Waller LJ departed from the *Hunter* analysis when he said (at [34]) that only nominal damages would be available in nuisance if the house was unoccupied throughout the nuisance and suffered no physical damage or other loss of value, and the owner no other form of pecuniary loss.

82 For recognition of the relevance of such factors by the English courts, see, e.g., *Anufrijeva* at [67] *per* Lord Woolf CJ ('the scale and manner of the violation').

83 See, e.g., *Johnson v. United Kingdom* (1997) 27 EHRR 296, where three years' detention of a mental patient in violation of his Convention rights resulted in an award of only £10,000 for non-pecuniary loss.

Article 8 rights. Furthermore, the solution proposed by the court in *Dobson* in such a case – that the application of the principles of equitable accounting between co-owners should mean that the co-owner in occupation can recover from the absentees any share of the nuisance damages to which the latter would otherwise be entitled – misses the point that applying the *Hunter* analysis the absentee co-owners are just as much entitled to damages in nuisance for the injury to the co-owned land as she is. It is also possible to imagine a case in which the nuisance damages are very low because the effect of the interference on the amenity of the land assessed objectively is minimal, but in which the actual effect on the claimant personally is much more significant, and here too the nuisance award may not be enough to afford just satisfaction for the Convention violation.[84]

If we then turn to the position of a claimant *without* a proprietary interest who has suffered an Article 8 violation, the extent to which his or her HRA claim should be affected by an award of damages in nuisance to the owner of the property where he or she lives is questionable. As Waller LJ pointed out in *Dobson*,[85] there is no support in *Hunter* for the view that the person who has standing in nuisance is recovering damages on behalf of the property's other occupiers, in which case it is difficult to see why the ability of those other occupiers to recover damages for the violation of their Convention rights should be prejudiced by the nuisance award. Suppose, for example, that the claimant is a lodger, or someone living in a residential home. In such a case, why should an award of damages to the property owner for a serious nuisance affecting the claimant's accommodation preclude her from suing the public authority responsible for damages under the HRA, or even serve to reduce the amount of the damages awarded, when the owner would almost certainly be under no obligation to share out the award?[86] Having said that, as a matter of common sense (and bearing in mind the discretionary nature of the damages remedy under the HRA), there is clearly a stronger argument for treating an award of nuisance damages to the owner as affording just satisfaction to the other occupiers for the violation of their Convention rights if they are members of the same family, who can be assumed

---

84 See R. Bagshaw, 'Private Nuisance and the Defence of the Realm', *Law Quarterly Review*, 120 (2004), 37, 41.

85 At [36].

86 It is possible, but unlikely, that if the licensee occupies the premises pursuant to a contract, then the terms of the contract would require a share of the damages to be paid to the licensee.

to have a common interest in the recovery of the nuisance damages.[87] The solution may therefore be for the courts to hold that an award of nuisance damages to a person with a legal interest in a property will usually afford just satisfaction to a partner, child or other family member of that person living in the same household, but that this would not generally be the case with regard to other types of occupier lacking a legal interest.[88]

Finally, we should note that difficulties of this sort ought not to arise where claims for violations of Article P1–1 are concerned, since there only someone with a legal interest in the affected property is likely to have standing under the HRA, and the quantum of damages for the Article P1–1 violation (the reduction in the economic value of the property attributable to the interference) should closely mirror the award in nuisance.

8.3 The horizontal effect of the HRA on the law of nuisance

In addition to providing a possible alternative cause of action to nuisance where a public authority is responsible for the interference, the HRA may also affect the law of nuisance itself by virtue of its 'indirect horizontal effect'.[89] The existing strength of private nuisance as a tort protecting the right to the use and enjoyment of land means that any changes brought about by the horizontal effect of the HRA are likely to be quite limited. The two areas where there is arguably the greatest divergence between nuisance law and the Convention regime are the right to sue and the defence of statutory authority. I will consider these first, and then look briefly at a few other aspects of the law of nuisance that might also be affected by the horizontal effect of the HRA.

8.3.1 The right to sue

In *Hunter* v. *Canary Wharf Ltd*, the House of Lords reiterated the long-standing rule that only those with a proprietary interest in the land affected have the right to sue in nuisance. This means that the claimant must

---

87 As one commentator on the *Dobson* decision puts it, the issue with a family member is 'whether the occupant can be meaningfully said to derive some benefit from the damages awarded in nuisance' (S. Tofaris, 'Damages for Sewage Smells in Nuisance and Under the Human Rights Act 1998', *Cambridge Law Journal* (2009), 273, 275).

88 A solution along these lines was hinted at in the judgment at first instance in *Dobson*: see [2007] EWHC 2021 (TCC), [2008] 2 All ER 362 at [209]–[210] *per* Ramsey J.

89 On indirect horizontal effect in general, see further Chapter 2.

either have a right to the land (for example, as its owner), or be in exclusive occupation of it,[90] and it follows that mere licensees – such as children living in their parents' home, lodgers, live-in staff and residents of residential homes – will not generally have the right to sue in nuisance in respect of interferences with their enjoyment of properties that would count as their 'homes' for the purposes of Article 8. It has been argued that the fact that nuisance law cannot be used by such a person to protect his or her right to respect for their home makes it incompatible with the Convention regime, and that the courts should therefore reconsider the rules on standing in the light of the HRA.[91] In his dissenting opinion in *Hunter*, for example, Lord Cooke drew upon Article 8 in support of his argument for the extension of the right to sue, and in the later case of *McKenna* v. *British Aluminium Ltd*,[92] Neuberger J held in strike-out proceedings that there was an arguable case that the limitation of the right to sue to those with an interest in the land affected violated the Article 8 rights of other household members:

> There is obviously a powerful case for saying that effect has not been properly given to Article 8(1) if a person with no interest in the home, but who has lived in the home for some time and had his enjoyment of the home interfered with, is at the mercy of the person who owns the home, as the only person who can bring proceedings.[93]

At the same time, however, Neuberger J accepted the strength of the argument that changing the *locus standi* rule would be inconsistent with the very nature of nuisance as a property tort. After all, as the House of Lords demonstrated in *Hunter*, the requirement of an interest in land is not a mere technicality, but goes to the very root of the cause of action in nuisance as a tort against land.[94] Changes to the rules on standing would therefore arguably introduce radical incoherence into the law of nuisance, and would inevitably have knock-on effects in other areas that are heavily influenced by the property tort analysis, such as the principles governing

---

90 *Hunter* at 468 *per* Lord Hope.
91 See, e.g., J. Wright, *Tort Law and Human Rights* (Oxford: Hart, 2001), ch. 8.
92 [2002] Env. LR 30.
93 *McKenna* at [53]. Note also that in *Pemberton*, Clarke LJ said (at 1684) that Art. 8 was a relevant factor in determining whether a tolerated trespasser had a right to sue in trespass or nuisance.
94 See *Hunter* at 698 *per* Lord Lloyd. See also at 702 *per* Lord Hoffmann ('Nuisance is a tort against land . . . A claimant must therefore have an interest in the land affected by the nuisance'), and at 723 *per* Lord Hope.

the assessment of damages.[95] It is unlikely that the horizontal effect of the HRA is powerful enough to require such a radical change to be made to a long-standing cause of action, and it is noteworthy that the limitation of the right to sue in nuisance to those with a proprietary interest was not questioned in the more recent decisions in *Dennis* and *Dobson*. All in all, it seems doubtful that the horizontal effect of the HRA will produce any change in that rule in the near future.

8.3.2 The defence of statutory authority

The area of nuisance law where the horizontal effect of the HRA may prove to be most significant is the defence of statutory authority. As we have seen, there is increasing support in the English case law for the view that compensation should be provided where an individual is called upon to bear more than an equal share of a burden imposed for the common good.[96] Of particular significance in this respect is the decision of the Commission in *S* v. *France* that although a nuisance caused by a nuclear power station interfered with the Convention rights of the applicant, the payment of reasonable compensation meant that the interference did not go beyond what was necessary in a democratic society and was therefore Convention-compliant. More generally, if a nuisance is serious enough to amount to a deprivation of possession under Article P1–1, the Strasbourg case law makes it clear that such a taking without payment of an amount reasonably related to the property's value will normally amount to a disproportionate interference, and that a total lack of compensation will be considered justifiable only in exceptional circumstances.[97] It follows that the domestic courts may well invoke Articles 8 and P1–1 to repel arguments to the effect that in nuisance cases private rights can be overridden by public interest considerations, unless adequate compensation is given

---

95 See A. Mullis and K. Oliphant, *Torts*, 4th edn (Basingstoke: Palgrave Macmillan, 2011), p. 257 (referring to the 'fundamental re-conceptualisation of private nuisance' that would be entailed by relaxation of the interest in land requirement).

96 See p. 177.

97 See Praduroux, 'The European Convention and Environmental Nuisances', pp. 271–2. English authorities applying this principle include *Dennis*; *Andrews*; and *R (London and Continental Stations and Property Ltd)* v. *Rail Regulator* [2003] EWHC 2607 (Admin). See also *Marcic* v. *Thames Water Utilities Ltd* [2002] EWCA Civ. 65, [2002] QB 929 at [118] *per* Lord Phillips MR (Strasbourg authority suggests that 'where an authority carries on an undertaking in the interest of the community as a whole it may have to pay compensation to individuals whose rights are infringed by that undertaking in order to achieve a fair balance between the interests of the individual and the community').

to those affected.[98] In the absence of statutory authorisation of the defendant's activity, this would merely reinforce the traditional common law approach to public interest arguments: namely, that they will not provide a defence to a nuisance claim if there is substantial interference.[99] However, such an approach might prove significant in cases where the defendant would previously have been able to call upon the statutory authority defence. In such cases, the legislation in question usually provides for compensation of those most seriously affected, but in the absence of such provision, or where the compensation provided is manifestly inadequate, there is every possibility that a court would refuse to apply the defence on the grounds that to do so would be incompatible with the claimant's Convention rights.

There are two possible routes that a court might take to arrive at such a conclusion, though the distinction between them is perhaps not a clear one. The first would be for the court to alter the content of the statutory authority defence itself, by holding that it does not apply in cases where the statute in question does not make provision for adequate compensation, a qualification on the operation of the defence that has been advocated by a number of eminent judges, going as far back as the nineteenth century.[100] It is clear, however, that under the existing law, the absence of a compensation provision is merely *evidence* that Parliament did not intend to exclude the right to sue at common law, and is not *conclusive* in this regard;[101] a rule reaffirmed by the House of Lords in the leading case of *Allen v. Gulf Oil Refining Ltd*,[102] where no provision

---

98 For criticism of this suggestion, see Miller, 'Environmental Rights in a Welfare State?', p. 121, arguing that 'the extent to which the common good should be attenuated by the need to compensate individuals who suffer in its pursuit is an inescapably political question' which should be left to Parliament.

99 See, e.g., *Miller*, *Kennaway*, *Dennis*.

100 See, e.g., *Hammersmith and City Rly Co. v. Brand* (1869) LR 4 HL 171 at 191–2 *per* Bramwell B; *Allen v. Gulf Oil Refining Ltd* [1980] QB 156 at 168–9 *per* Lord Denning MR. For more tentative suggestions of judicial disquiet at the operation of the defence in these circumstances, see *Marriage v. East Norfolk Rivers Catchment Board* [1950] 1 KB 284 at 308–9 *per* Jenkins LJ; *Schenck v. Ontario* (1981) 131 DLR (3d) 310 at 324 *per* Robins J.

101 See, e.g., *Metropolitan Asylum District v. Hill* (1881) 6 App. Cas. 193 at 203 *per* Lord Blackburn; *Guelph Worsted Spinning Co. v. Guelph* (1914) 18 DLR 73 at 80 *per* Middleton J; *Edgington v. Swindon BC* [1939] 1 KB 86 at 89–90 *per* Finlay LJ. See further on the relevance of compensation clauses, S. Kneebone, 'Nuisance and the Defence of Statutory Authority: Inferring the Intention of Parliament', *University of Adelaide Law Review*, 10 (1986), 472, 480–2.

102 [1981] AC 1001.

for compensation had been made in the private Act authorising the oil refinery alleged to be causing a nuisance. It must also be borne in mind that statutory authority is a general defence to a tort action, and that this is justified by reference to the sovereignty of Parliament; as Lord Halsbury LC once put it, 'the legislature is supreme, and if it has enacted that a thing is lawful, such a thing cannot be a fault or an actionable wrong'.[103] It is doubtful whether the horizontal indirect effect of the HRA will be sufficiently forceful to topple such a well-entrenched common law principle.

A potentially more fruitful way of arriving at the same position would be for the courts to read down any legislation that failed to make adequate provision for compensation in cases where the operation of the defence would be incompatible with the claimant's Convention rights. This could be done by reference to section 3(1) of the HRA, which requires the courts to read and give effect to legislation in a way that is compatible with the Convention rights 'so far as it is possible to do so'.[104] Since it now seems clear that this interpretative duty can apply in the case of litigation between private parties,[105] such an approach would not be limited to cases in which the defence of statutory authority was being relied upon by a public authority. This would therefore be an example of 'statutory horizontal effect'.[106]

A possible objection to either of these approaches is that if the defence of statutory authority is limited in this way, then in cases in which the statute provides for no (or inadequate) compensation, the claimant may be entitled not only to damages, but also to an injunction, with the result that the defendant's activity will not simply be made to pay its way, but potentially shut down altogether.[107] The solution to this difficulty is to hold that in such cases the statute gives the defendant a qualified privilege to infringe the claimant's rights, it being a condition of the privilege that the defendant pay for any loss caused.[108] It may follow that the court should award not only common law damages for past harm, but also damages in lieu of an injunction for future losses.[109]

---

103 *Canadian Pacific Rly Co.* v. *Roy* [1902] AC 220 at 229.
104 See further Chapter 4.   105 *X* v. *Y* [2004] EWCA Civ. 662, [2004] ICR 1634.
106 See Chapter 2.
107 *Allen* v. *Gulf Oil Refining Ltd* [1981] AC 1001 at 1013 *per* Lord Wilberforce, at 1024 *per* Lord Roskill ('a most curious, and as I venture to think, illogical result').
108 On qualified privileges of this kind, see R. Stevens, *Torts and Rights* (Oxford University Press, 2007), pp. 102–7.
109 *Allen* v. *Gulf Oil Refining Ltd* [1980] QB 156 at 169 *per* Lord Denning MR.

Two final points can be made. The first is that whatever happens in the standard statutory authority scenario, it is extremely unlikely that a court would decline to abide by a statutory provision expressly removing the right to sue at common law, such as section 76 of the Civil Aviation Act 1982, which gives the operators of civil aircraft immunity from nuisance liability if they comply with any applicable Air Navigation Order. In such a case, the most that a court could do would be to issue a declaration of the legislation's incompatibility under section 4. And the second point is that the significance of the HRA for the operation of the statutory authority defence obviously depends on the extent to which Parliament has made adequate provision for compensation of those affected by authorised nuisances. In that connection, it should be noted that under the Land Compensation Act 1973, there is a general right to compensation for a depreciation in the value of land caused by physical factors incident upon the operation of public works, where the common law right of action has been removed by statutory authorisation.

8.3.3 Other aspects of nuisance law

Any horizontal effect of the HRA might be thought to call into question three other aspects of the law of nuisance where the existing rules are arguably inconsistent with claimants' Convention rights. The first is the rule that a landlord is not deemed to have authorised his tenant's nuisance, because with knowledge of its existence he refrained from exercising his right to end the tenancy.[110] Where the nuisance is sufficiently serious to engage the claimant's Convention rights, there is a case for saying[111] that the courts should bring the position of landlords out of occupation into line with the position of occupiers of land, who are liable if they fail to take reasonable steps to abate the nuisance in this type of case.[112] Against this, however, is the fact (a) that the claimant will usually have a common law remedy against the perpetrators of the nuisance in these circumstances, which might be thought adequately to protect his or her Convention rights;[113] and (b) that if the landlord is a public authority,

---

110 See p. 180.   111 See, e.g., Allen, *Property and the Human Rights Act 1998*, p. 212.

112 See, e.g., *Page Motors Ltd* v. *Epsom and Ewell BC* (1981) 80 LGR 337; *Lippiatt* v. *South Gloucestershire Council* [2000] QB 51. See further, Oliphant, *The Law of Tort*, para. 22.65ff; S. Bright, 'Liability for the Bad Behaviour of Others', *Oxford Journal of Legal Studies*, 21 (2001), 311.

113 In the pre-HRA case of *Mowan*, Peter Gibson LJ argued that the availability of injunctive relief against the creator of the nuisance, coupled with the possibility of judicial review

the claimant may have a direct action against it for its inaction under the HRA in any case.[114]

The second additional area of nuisance law that might be affected by the HRA is the rule that the law of nuisance does not recognise a right not to have one's property overlooked. A good example is provided by an unreported case cited by Winfield in which a dentist in Balham was denied redress against neighbours who used an array of large mirrors in their garden to observe what was going on in his consulting-room.[115] The horizontal effect of the HRA has, of course, been most potent so far in the privacy context, and while the focus until now has been on the development of the tort of breach of confidence to provide adequate protection of the right to respect for private life under Article 8,[116] there is no reason why the same arguments could not be used to challenge this well-established (but hardly fundamental) rule of the law of nuisance.[117] It should be noted, however, that even if such a challenge were to be successful, a nuisance action would lie only if the surveillance was known about by the claimant at the time, since only then would it have been capable of interfering with his or her use and enjoyment of his or her property.

The final aspect of the law of nuisance that should be mentioned is the so-called 'common enemy' rule, which entitles an occupier to take steps to protect his or her property against an external threat, such as floodwaters, even if the effect is to divert the threat onto the land of another. A challenge to this rule as incompatible with Articles 8 and P1–1 was rebuffed by the Court of Appeal in *Arscott* v. *The Coal Authority*,[118]

---

proceedings against the council landlord, made it unnecessary to modify the law of nuisance in order to hold the council liable to the claimant in this scenario. Staughton LJ agreed that the law of nuisance should not be modified, saying (at [18]) that the relevant principles were 'too well established for that'.

114 See pp. 180–1.
115 P. H. Winfield, 'Privacy', *Law Quarterly Review*, 47 (1931), 23 at 27. See also *Victoria Park Racing and Recreation Grounds Co. Ltd* v. *Taylor* (1937) 58 CLR 479. See further Oliphant, *The Law of Tort*, para. 22.23.
116 See further Chapter 7.
117 For criticism of the principle, see the dissenting judgment of Evatt J in *Victoria Park Racing* (at 521), arguing that the right to spy on or overlook another's property was not absolute and unrestricted. Note also that in *Bernstein* v. *Skyviews & General Ltd* [1978] QB 479, Griffiths J suggested that constant aerial surveillance of a person's property, accompanied by the photographing of his every activity, might be actionable in nuisance (although this remark was *obiter*, and the relevant nuisance cases had not been cited).
118 [2004] EWCA Civ. 892, [2005] Env. LR 6.

on the ground that (subject perhaps to exceptional instances) it struck a reasonable balance between the interests of neighbouring occupiers.

8.4 Conclusions

The principal conclusions of this chapter can be summarised as follows:

(1) There is some evidence from the case law that English judges are taking a more expansive view of the protections afforded by the Convention in environmental nuisance cases than the Strasbourg institutions. There is a danger that this will lead to a 'false equivalence' problem, whereby English judges mistakenly assume that just because an interference amounts to a common law nuisance it must also be serious enough to amount to a potential violation of Articles 8 and P1–1.

(2) Although the Strasbourg authorities make it clear that Articles 8 and P1–1 may impose positive obligations on public authorities to protect citizens against interference with their home life and peaceful enjoyment of their possessions, it remains unclear what level of state involvement is required in such cases for there to be a sufficient nexus between the authorities and the interference to engage the Convention. One interpretation of the Strasbourg jurisprudence is that the state's positive duties under these Articles are largely confined to the enforcement of domestic legal norms, in which case such duties would be of limited significance in domestic litigation.

(3) There is some evidence that the English courts are using the HRA to develop a new principle of 'equality before public burdens' in nuisance cases, according to which compensation should be provided where an individual is called upon to bear more than an equal share of a burden for the common good. However, the full ramifications of this new principle have not been thought through, and so far its impact has been patchy.

(4) Where a claimant has a choice of suing in nuisance or under the HRA in respect of the same interference, there are distinct advantages in pursuing the common law remedy. However, an HRA claim will be useful to a claimant who lacks a legal interest in the land affected, and may enable pursuit of a local authority landlord who would not be liable in nuisance.

(5) Difficult issues may arise in cases of concurrent liability in nuisance and under the HRA. In particular, the implications of an award of

damages in nuisance for claims in respect of the same interference under the HRA have yet to be fully worked through.

(6) The horizontal effect of the HRA on the law of nuisance is likely to be very limited. The area of nuisance law most likely to be modified to reflect human rights concerns is the defence of statutory authority.

9

Defamation

KEN OLIPHANT[*]

The aim of this chapter is to assess the impact of the HRA on the law of defamation in the first ten years of its implementation by means of a short survey of cases in which the Convention rights have been relied upon in an effort to challenge established principles of defamation law, or otherwise to develop it beyond its previous state of existence.

Reputation is not an explicit Convention right, though it is an aspect of the rights protected by Article 8. It is also expressly provided in the Convention that the necessity for protecting reputation is capable of justifying interference with the right to freedom of expression under Article 10(2) (restrictions etc., 'necessary...for the protection of the reputation or rights of others').

In fact, as this chapter will seek to show, there has been a tendency in domestic law to rely on the Convention, not as a basis for liability, but to resist or reduce liability: to argue that the Convention right to freedom of expression requires, or at least allows, the introduction of new limitations on liability in the tort of defamation. This has applied both to common law aspects of the law of defamation, and to some instances where the law of defamation is regulated by statute. In the latter cases, of course, the courts have to apply the obligation under section 3 of the HRA to interpret legislation so as to give effect to the Convention rights.[1]

The methodology adopted in this chapter is that of a survey of defamation cases of the last ten years to consider where there has been an attempt to challenge or develop some key principle of defamation law using the

---

[*] Some sections of this chapter draw upon the author's *Current Legal Problems* lecture, 'European Tort Law: A Primer for the Common Lawyer', *Current Law Journal*, 62 (2009), 440. The author gratefully records his thanks to Ali el Haj for conducting the initial research on which this chapter is based, and to David Hoffman for his exceptionally helpful comments and suggestions.
1 Discussed in Chapter 4.

HRA.[2] It is not proposed to consider here cases where it was merely noted that the application of defamation and human rights principles led to the same result,[3] or referred to the Act or a Convention right in deciding whether or not to exercise a discretion,[4] or where a finding that a Convention right had been violated was treated as dispositive of an issue within the established framework of legal principle, for example, where a public authority's breach of the claimant's right to reputation under Article 8 precluded its assertion of a duty to publish, and so excluded the common law defence of qualified privilege.[5]

9.1 Reliance on the Convention right to reputation

The Convention right to reputation was relied upon, albeit without success, in the following cases in an effort to change or develop English defamation law in favour of claimants.

9.1.1 Greene v. Associated Newspapers Ltd

Greene v. *Associated Newspapers Ltd*[6] considered the effect of section 12 of the HRA on the well-known rule in *Bonnard* v. *Perryman*,[7] under which a defendant can successfully oppose the claimant's application for an interim injunction in respect of defamation by pleading a defence of

---

2 For completeness, this survey considered all cases that have been reported on the Westlaw database since the HRA came into force and showed up with the keyword 'defamation' as well as the HRA, and then filtered them for cases where it was sought to use the HRA to change or develop the law.

3 See, e.g., *Lowe* v. *Associated Newspapers Ltd* [2006] EWHC 320 (QB), [2007] QB 580 at [42] (defence of fair comment; commentator not to be confined to pleading facts stated in the words complained of). See now *Spiller* v. *Joseph* [2010] UKSC 53.

4 One may note in particular the courts' greater readiness to treat an action in defamation as an abuse of process if it does not serve the legitimate purpose of protecting the claimant's reputation, in view of their responsibility for keeping a balance between reputation and freedom of expression. See especially *Jameel* v. *Dow Jones & Co. Inc.* [2005] EWCA Civ. 75, [2005] QB 946 at [55], cited and followed by Tugendhat J on several occasions: see *Lonzim Plc* v. *Sprague* [2009] EWHC 2838 (QB); *Hays Plc* v. *Hartley* [2010] EWHC 1065 (QB); *Kaschke* v. *Osler* [2010] EWHC 1075 (QB); *Kaschke* v. *Gray* [2010] EWHC 1907 (QB). Cf. *Underhill* v. *Corser* [2010] EWHC 1195 (QB). See also *Brady* v. *Norman* [2010] EWHC 1215 (QB) (limitation); *Fiddes* v. *Channel 4 Television Corp.* [2010] EWCA Civ. 730, [2010] 1 WLR 2245 (mode of trial).

5 *Clift* v. *Slough BC* [2009] EWHC 1550 (QB), affd [2010] EWCA Civ. 1171.

6 [2004] EWCA Civ. 1462, [2005] QB 972. See also *Terry (or LNS)* v. *Persons Unknown* [2010] EWHC 119 (QB), [2010] EMLR 400 (the John Terry super-injunction case).

7 [1891] 2 Ch 26.

justification, fair comment or privilege, unless such defence is certain to fail. Section 12 directs the court to have regard to the Convention right to freedom of speech when considering the grant of any relief that might affect its exercise. Section 12(3) further specifies that, where injunctive relief is sought so as to restrain publication before trial, it is not to be granted 'unless the court is satisfied that the applicant is likely to establish that publication should not be allowed'. The Court of Appeal ruled that the 'likely' criterion in section 12 was intended to set a minimum requirement for the grant of interim injunctive relief where questions of free speech are at issue, whatever the cause of action, but does not water down the more substantial protection of free speech that is already provided in defamation actions by the rule in *Bonnard* v. *Perryman*.[8] The court rejected the claimant's argument that the rule runs roughshod over the right to reputation because it prevents the court weighing the competing rights in the balance and giving a proportionate response; on the contrary, the court considered the rule a necessary protection of free expression, while noting that the claimant's right could still be vindicated at trial.[9]

9.1.2 Buckley v. Dalziel *and* Westcott v. Westcott

In *Buckley* v. *Dalziel*[10] and *Westcott* v. *Westcott*,[11] the novel question for decision was whether a person making a complaint to the police is protected by absolute or merely qualified privilege in a defamation action against him or her by the person who is the subject of complaint. If the former, the privilege prevents an action in defamation even if the defendant made the statement with malice; if the latter, the defence is defeated by malice. The High Court in *Buckley* and the Court of Appeal in *Westcott* both came to the same conclusion:[12] a person who makes a complaint to

---

8 At [66]. The Court of Appeal distinguished the decision of the House of Lords in *Cream Holdings Ltd* v. *Banerjee* [2004] UKHL 44, [2005] 1 AC 253.

9 At [58] and [67]ff.   10 [2007] EWHC 1025 (QB), [2007] 1 WLR 2933.

11 [2008] EWCA Civ. 818, [2009] QB 407. See also *A* v. *K* [2008] EWHC 594 (QB), mentioned in *Westcott*, but not included amongst this survey as no transcript is available on either Westlaw or BAILII. Cf. *Gray* v. *Avadis (No. 1)* [2003] EWHC 1830 (QB), *The Times*, 19 August 2003 (absolute privilege in respect of complaint to the Office for the Supervision of Solicitors; the claimant raised no argument based on the HRA). Note also that, in *A* v. *United Kingdom* (2003) 36 EHRR 917 (App. No. 35373/97), the Strasbourg court rejected a challenge to the absolute privilege applying to statements in Parliament; as to which, see also *Reavey* v. *Century Newspapers Ltd* [2001] NI 187.

12 Refusing to recognise an exception based on Art. 8 to the absolute privilege attaching to statements made as part of the process of criminal investigation recognised in *Taylor* v. *Serious Fraud Office* [1999] 2 AC 177.

the police, thereby instigating a police investigation, can shelter behind the defence of absolute privilege if a claim is brought against him or her in defamation even if no prosecution ensues. In such cases, it is clear that a balance has to be struck between two competing demands: the necessity for the due administration of criminal justice that complaints of alleged criminal conduct should be capable of being made to the police free from fear that the person accused will subsequently involve the complainant in costly litigation; and the countervailing consideration that no one should have his or her reputation traduced without being afforded a remedy to redress the wrong.[13] A restriction on a person's right to reputation arising under Article 8 could therefore be justified by reference to the public interest in the administration of justice, this constituting a legitimate aim, and in the circumstances the restriction was not disproportionate.[14]

9.2 Reliance on the Convention right to freedom of expression

Following the implementation of the HRA, it has been argued on several occasions before the courts that the Article 10 right to freedom of expression requires, or at least permits, the introduction of new limitations on liability in the tort of defamation. These arguments have met with more success than those seeking to effect a change in the law in favour of claimants, though their impact has been mixed and relatively limited.

9.2.1 O'Shea v. MGN Ltd

The claimant in *O'Shea* v. *MGN Ltd*[15] bore a close resemblance to, and was mistaken for, a glamour model photographed in an advert, appearing in the defendant's newspaper, for an adult internet service. She alleged that those who read the words together with the photograph, and who knew or were acquainted with her, would reasonably have understood them to refer to her and to mean that she was appearing or performing on a highly pornographic website containing material of an explicit, indecent and lewd nature and had shamelessly agreed to promote this website and her own appearance on it in a national newspaper. The defendant applied for summary judgment on the basis that the claimant had no realistic prospect of success in her action, it being contrary to Article 10

---

13 See *Westcott* at [32].   14 *Westcott* at [38].
15 [2001] EMLR 943 (4 May 2001).

to impose strict liability for inadvertent defamatory reference to a claimant as a result of identification from a photograph of somebody else of similar appearance. Morland J noted that this was the first case of its sort in English law. Notwithstanding the normal strict liability rule for unintentional defamation at common law,[16] Morland J considered that the implementation of the HRA required a different approach. It would be contrary to Article 10 to impose strict liability for inadvertent defamatory reference to a look-alike. The imposition of strict liability would amount to an interference with the Convention right to freedom of expression, and there was no pressing social need for such interference such as would justify it under Article 10(2). The fact that no previous claim of look-alike libel had ever been made in English law was an indication that there was no pressing social need for the application of the strict liability principle for the protection of the look-alike's reputation. To apply the strict liability rule would be an unjustifiable interference with freedom of expression that was disproportionate to the legitimate aim of protecting the reputations of look-alikes.[17] In effect, the judge felt that the HRA required the recognition of a special look-alike rule by way of exception to the strict liability arising at common law. What is notable about the case for present purposes is that the basis on which Morland J gave effect to Article 10 was not any general theory about the HRA's horizontal effect but the obligation under section 12(4) of the Act to 'have particular regard to the importance of the Convention right to freedom of expression' when considering whether to grant any relief which, if granted, might affect its exercise.[18] The judge failed to explain how this rather vague obligation relating to remedies warranted a departure from an established and binding principle of substantive law.

9.2.2 Branson *v.* Bower (No. 2) *and* Lowe *v.* Associated Newspapers Ltd

Resolving what he considered to be previous uncertainty on the matter, Eady J in *Branson v. Bower (No. 2)*[19] ruled that the defence of fair comment requires only that the defendant's opinion was expressed honestly, and not that it was objectively fair. In his view, the correct approach was to have regard to the Strasbourg court's Article 10 jurisprudence, and, in reaching his conclusion, he emphasised the 'chilling effect' that would result from

---

16 See *Hulton v. Jones* [1910] AC 20.   17 See especially at [43]ff.
18 At [29].   19 [2002] QB 737 (15 June 2001).

the alternative approach.[20] The same judge subsequently reiterated this conclusion in *Lowe* v. *Associated Newspapers Ltd.*[21]

9.2.3 Berezovsky *v.* Forbes Inc.

The defendant in *Berezovsky* v. *Forbes Inc.*[22] argued that what constitutes a defamatory meaning has been altered by the HRA, and that the 'repetition rule' which denies a defence to a publisher who simply recycles a libel, and the 'conduct rule' by which an allegation of reasonable suspicion has to be defended by attributing it to the claimant's own behaviour, are incompatible with the Convention right to freedom of expression. Alternatively, section 5 of the Defamation Act 1952 – allowing a defence of justification where the defendant proves the truth of one or more, but not all, of a number of distinct charges, and the unproven charges do not materially injure the claimant's reputation having regard to the proven charges – should be interpreted so that 'distinct charges' included lesser meanings of the words complained of. The Court of Appeal ruled that the principle that justification must draw the sting of the defamatory imputation, and not a 'diminished version' of it, is not a disproportionate limit on freedom of expression. It meets the legitimate purpose, recognised by Article 10(2), of protecting people from the publication of damaging and unjustified falsehoods, and, having regard to the availability of the separate defences of fair comment and qualified privilege even in cases of exaggeration and error, does not do so disproportionately.[23] Essentially the same considerations stood against the defendant's fall-back argument based on section 5 of the Defamation Act 1952.[24]

9.2.4 Loutchansky *v.* Times Newspapers Ltd (No. 2)

The defendant newspaper in *Loutchansky* v. *Times Newspapers Ltd (No. 2)*,[25] argued that Article 10 requires the adoption of a 'single

---

20 See especially at [23].
21 [2006] EWHC 320 (QB), [2007] QB 580 at [73]. See now *Spiller* v. *Joseph* [2010] UKSC 53.
22 [2001] EWCA Civ. 1251, [2002] EMLR 1030 (31 July 2001).
23 See at [12].   24 See at [15].
25 [2001] EWCA Civ. 1805, [2002] QB 783. A subsequent application to the Strasbourg court also failed: *Times Newspapers Ltd* v. *United Kingdom* (App. Nos. 00003002/03, 00023676/03). At the time of writing, legislative reform was under active consideration: see Ministry of Justice, *Defamation and the Internet: The Multiple Publication Rule*, CP20/09, 2009; House of Commons Culture, Media and Sport Committee, *Press Standards, Privacy and Libel*, HC (2009–10) 362-I, para. 216ff.

publication rule' whereby an article stored in an Internet archive is published once and for all at the time of its initial posting, and therefore gives rise to only one cause of action no matter how many times it is accessed. The Court of Appeal disagreed, ruling that the established multiple publication rule did not have a chilling effect going beyond what was necessary and proportionate in a democratic society for the protection of reputation.

9.2.5 Chase *v.* News Group Newspapers Ltd

The Court of Appeal in *Chase* v. *News Group Newspapers Ltd*[26] ruled that the HRA made no difference to the continued validity of three established principles of the law of defamation relating to the defence of justification. First, in order to justify an allegation that there are reasonable grounds for suspecting the claimant of an offence, the defendant must be able to point to some conduct by the claimant giving rise to suspicion, or some other objectively reasonable grounds for such suspicion. Second, where the defendant repeats a defamatory statement by another person, a plea of justification will succeed only on proof that what was said was substantially true (the repetition rule). Third, the defendant may not generally rely on matters occurring after the date of the publication complained of in order to support a plea of justification, except in the case of general aspersions against the claimant's character. The court refused to accept that any of these rules was a disproportionate restriction on freedom of expression.[27]

9.2.6 Maccaba *v.* Lichtenstein

The question in *Maccaba* v. *Lichtenstein*[28] was whether the common law distinction between offices of profit and offices of honour has survived the enactment of section 2 of the Defamation Act 1952, under which the claimant, in contrast to the general rule applying to slanders, need not prove special damage in an action for slander for disparagement in an office, profession, calling, trade or business. Under the common law rule, an allegation of unfitness in an office of profit was actionable without proof of special damage, but for an office of honour it was generally necessary for the words complained of to impute a lack of integrity.

---

26 [2002] EWCA Civ. 1772, [2003] EMLR 218 (3 December 2002).
27 See at [64].   28 [2004] EWHC 1580 (QB).

The survival of the distinction was apparently accepted by Diplock J in *Robinson* v. *Ward*,[29] and considered arguable in previous editions of *Gatley* and *Duncan & Neill*.[30] Gray J was invited to construe section 2 in the light of Article 10, but found that the relevant words were so clear that they did not permit the proposed distinction: it was not possible to construe 'any office' as meaning 'any office other than an office of honour'. The HRA did not permit – far less, require – the construction for which the defendant contended.[31]

9.2.7 Jameel v. Dow Jones & Co. Inc.

In *Jameel* v. *Dow Jones & Co. Inc.*,[32] the Court of Appeal rejected a submission that the irrebuttable nature of the presumption of damage consequent on the publication of a libel was in conflict with Article 10. The court considered that English law had been well served by its established approach, and that it would not be right to abandon it in the absence of convincing evidence that it was in conflict with Article 10.[33] Only in rare cases was the presumption likely to be of significance, and the risk that a claimant who had in fact suffered no damage might bring a claim was better dealt with on an ad hoc basis – for example, by striking out the action as an abuse of process – than by a radical change in the law.[34]

9.2.8 Culnane v. Morris

In *Culnane* v. *Morris*,[35] Eady J declined to follow the Court of Appeal's established interpretation[36] of section 10 of the Defamation Act 1952,[37] which it construed as limiting the defence of privilege in respect of defamatory statements published by or on behalf of an election candidate. In the judge's view, it would be contrary to the Convention to deprive an election candidate or agent of the generally available defence of qualified privilege, and section 3 of the HRA required that the Defamation Act

---

29 (1958) 108 LJ 491.   30 See [2004] EWHC 1580 (QB) at [19].
31 See especially at [22].   32 [2005] EWCA Civ. 75, [2005] QB 946 (3 February 2005).
33 See at [37].   34 See at [39].
35 [2005] EWHC 2438 (QB), [2006] 1 WLR 2880 (8 November 2005).
36 *Plummer* v. *Charman* [1962] 1 WLR 1469.
37 This reads, so far as is material: 'A defamatory statement published by or on behalf of a candidate in any election . . . shall not be deemed to be published on a privileged occasion on the ground that it is material to a question in issue in the election'.

provision should not be interpreted that way, notwithstanding the Court of Appeal authority.

9.2.9 Jameel *v.* Wall Street Journal Europe SPRL

The defendants in *Jameel* v. *Wall Street Journal Europe SPRL*[38] sought a restatement of the law comparable with that effected by the House of Lords in *Derbyshire CC* v. *Times Newspapers Ltd*,[39] arguing that the HRA necessitates the introduction of a requirement of actual rather than presumed damage where a libel action was brought by a trading corporation. A bare majority of the House of Lords found that Article 10 required no such change, because the chilling effect of the existing rule was relatively insignificant, and because a company's reputation is something worth protecting.

9.2.10 Warren *v.* Random House Group Ltd

Warren v. *Random House Group Ltd*[40] addressed the court's discretion to permit a defendant, in exceptional circumstances, to resile from an offer of amends made and accepted under the Defamation Act 1996 so as to pursue a defence of justification. The defendant argued that the court was obliged by virtue of section 3 to read down the relevant sections of the 1996 Act so as to ensure compatibility with the Convention. It contended, in particular, that a construction that prohibited it from further defending the claim once the claimant had accepted its offer of amends interfered with its rights under Article 10. Rejecting these arguments, the Court of Appeal ruled that the offer of amends machinery did not constitute a disproportionate interference on the defendant's freedom of expression. Insofar as there was any interference, it arose from the claimant's acceptance of the defendant's own offer, and it was not materially different from the ordinary case of settlement between the parties. In any case, though the defendant had to pay compensation

---

38 [2006] UKHL 44, [2007] 1 AC 359. In *Wall Street Journal Europe SPRL* v. *United Kingdom* (2009) 48 EHRR 287, the Strasbourg court ruled the newspaper's challenge against other aspects of the law of defamation to be inadmissible.

39 [1993] AC 534. In *McLaughlin* v. *Lambeth LBC* [2010] EWHC 2726 (QB), Tugendhat J refused to extend the principle to prevent an action by persons engaged in the day-to-day management of a governmental body: the House of Lords in the *Derbyshire* case had clearly contemplated that such persons, if themselves defamed, might sue.

40 [2008] EWCA Civ. 834, [2009] QB 600.

under the statutory scheme, there was nothing to prevent it repeating the words complained of and pleading justification in any future defamation proceedings that the claimant might bring.[41]

9.2.11 Thornton v. Telegraph Media Group Ltd

In *Thornton* v. *Telegraph Media Group Ltd*,[42] Tugendhat J ruled that the definition of what is defamatory must be qualified by a minimum threshold requirement of seriousness, excluding trivial claims. The judge gave two reasons for his conclusion.[43] First, it accorded with Lord Atkin's intention in *Sim* v. *Stretch*[44] in establishing the test that would subsequently gain general currency (though Lord Atkin's celebrated formulation of the test – 'would the words tend to lower the plaintiff in the estimation of right-thinking members of society generally?' – makes no mention of such a requirement), as well as with other tests that have from time to time been employed. Second, the threshold of seriousness was required by Article 10. The decision builds upon previous decisions of the same judge relating to the discretion to dismiss trivial claims as an abuse of process,[45] but it appears to be the first time that he has adopted a threshold of seriousness as a substantive element of the tort.

9.3 Conclusions

The post-HRA changes to the law of defamation have been more subtle and less extensive than the monumental changes that have occurred in the law of privacy.[46] Defamation law is of considerably greater antiquity, and it constitutes a much more developed compartment of law. There have only been two cases, both at first instance, in which the Act has been relied upon to expressly overturn established principles: *O'Shea* and *Culnane*. Notably, *Culnane* was a case of statutory interpretation, so there was no need to consider the methodology by which the HRA applied: the judge applied the interpretative obligation in section 3.[47] Conversely, *O'Shea* was a case at common law between private actors, so the precise basis on which the Convention right to freedom of expression was applicable was not so straightforward. In fact, the court's approach was founded

---

41 See at [35]ff.   42 [2010] EWHC 1414 (QB), [2010] EMLR 609.
43 See at [90].   44 [1936] 2 All ER 1237 at 1240.   45 See n. 4 above.
46 Discussed in Chapter 7.   47 At [32] in particular.

exclusively on section 12(4) of the HRA,[48] rather than any general theory about the Act's horizontal effect, and the judge simply assumed that the rather vague obligation imposed (to 'have particular regard to' the right's importance) was sufficient basis for departing from an established common law rule (strict liability for unintentional defamation).

In a small number of other cases (*Branson, Lowe* and *Thornton*), the HRA and the Convention rights were relied upon in support of a proposed resolution of perceived uncertainty. None of these decisions can be said to have effected a dramatic change in the law.

Ironically, it appears that recognition of the importance of the Convention rights may have led to more radical changes in defamation law in the years *prior to* the Act's implementation, as is apparent from the three landmark cases of *Derbyshire CC* v. *Times Newspapers Ltd*,[49] barring defamation claims by democratically elected organs of government; *John* v. *MGN Ltd*,[50] amending practice in respect of jury determinations of damages in order to preclude unduly high awards; and *Reynolds* v. *Times Newspapers Ltd*,[51] on qualified privilege and the media. In each case, the new rule was presented as the natural development of existing principles, rather than as directly stemming from the Convention, though the accord between common law and human rights jurisprudence was frequently noted with satisfaction.[52]

Perhaps the most interesting observation that can be made is that, of those rare cases in which reliance on the Convention rights can be said to have contributed to a change or development of defamation law, all were cases in which freedom of expression trumped the right to reputation, rather than vice versa. To that extent, the implementation of the HRA may be said to have effected a small shift in the law of defamation's centre of gravity.

---

48 See at [29]. In truth, section 12 creates a form of indirect remedial horizontality: see Chapter 2, p. 19.
49 [1993] AC 534.
50 [1997] QB 586. See previously *Rantzen* v. *Mirror Group Newspapers (1986) Ltd* [1994] QB 670.
51 [2001] 2 AC 127.
52 *Derbyshire* v. *Times* at 551 *per* Lord Keith; *John* v. *MGN* at 619 *per* CA ('reinforcing and buttressing' the court's conclusions); *Reynolds* at 207 *per* Lord Steyn.

10

Discrimination law

HAZEL OLIVER

The United Kingdom has a comprehensive range of statutory discrimination laws, the majority of which are founded in European Union law, as recently consolidated into the Equality Act 2010. There is clear scope for the influence of human rights arguments on the development of these laws through statutory interpretation under section 3 of the HRA, particularly as these statutory provisions are continually being interpreted and developed by courts and tribunals in any event.

The HRA itself also contains a number of provisions that are directly relevant to discrimination law issues. The most obvious of these is Article 14, which provides a general non-discrimination provision as follows: 'The enjoyment of the rights and freedoms set forth in this Convention shall be secured without discrimination on any ground such as sex, race, colour, language, religion, political or other opinion, national or social origin, association with a national minority, property, birth or other status.' Other rights have also been used to challenge particular types of discriminatory treatment – most notably, Articles 8 (the right to respect for private life) and 10 (freedom of expression) in relation to sexual orientation discrimination, and Article 9 (the right to freedom of thought, conscience and religion) in relation to discrimination on grounds of religion or belief.

However, although at first sight there is ample scope for discrimination claims between private parties to be influenced by the HRA, in practice it has had only a limited impact on the development of the law. There are no leading private law cases in discrimination law that have grappled directly with the extent of the courts' powers of statutory interpretation under section 3. Neither has there been any detailed analysis of level one questions in such cases, although a number of claims involving freedom of religion have stalled on the question of whether there has been an interference with a Convention right at all. There are a variety of reasons for this, as discussed in more detail below. As a starting point, Article 14 itself has inherent limitations, due to the need to combine it with another right before it can be used in UK law. However, perhaps the most significant reason is the fact that the existing regime of discrimination legislation is so comprehensive and largely based on EU law. Following the full implementation of the Equal Treatment Framework Directive in the United Kingdom,[1] in the sphere of employment law at least there was little need for the HRA to intervene to ensure that key minority groups are protected. The harmonisation of discrimination legislation into the Equality Act in October 2010 also consolidated comprehensive protection from discrimination in goods and services.[2] This still leaves some role for the HRA in interpretation of the existing law and the possible development of new types of prohibited discrimination, but not as great a role as might be expected from such a significant piece of human rights legislation. The extent of this role in the future will depend on how strong a version of statutory indirect horizontality the courts are willing to use in interpreting statutory provisions in line with human rights principles.

10.1 Limitations of Article 14

Article 14 provides a wide and general non-discrimination provision. The use of the words 'or other status' at the end of a list of specific grounds of discrimination means that this is an open rather than a closed list, meaning that new groups that are not specifically listed may also be protected if they share the same essential characteristics.[3] The specified list of types of protected status is also considerably wider than those currently protected in either UK or EU law, which are limited to sex, marital status, pregnancy or maternity, gender reassignment, race, sexual orientation, disability, religion or belief and age.[4] As discussed further below, this suggests that Article 14 may have some role to play in expanding the scope of discrimination law in the future.

However, the key limitation on the use of Article 14 is that this is not a free-standing prohibition of discrimination. Instead, it is a principle of non-discrimination in relation to the other rights and freedoms

---

1 EC, Council Directive 2000/78/EC of 27 November 2000 establishing a general framework for equal treatment in employment and occupation, [2000] OJ L 303/16.
2 With the exception at the time of writing of protection from age discrimination in goods and services, implementation of which has been put on hold by the Coalition government.
3 See, e.g., *Salgueiro Da Silva Mouta* v. *Portugal* (1999) 31 EHRR 1055 in relation to the inclusion of sexual orientation.
4 See the Equality Act 2010.

guaranteed by the HRA, meaning that it is necessary to engage another one of the rights under the HRA before Article 14 can be brought into play. The United Kingdom has chosen not to ratify Protocol 12 of the Convention,[5] a stand-alone provision relating to discrimination law that prohibits discrimination in relation to any right set forth in the law.

Although it is necessary to link the use of Article 14 with the engagement of another one of the protected rights under the HRA, this has been interpreted relatively widely. In *Ghaidan* v. *Godin-Mendoza*,[6] the House of Lords confirmed that it was not necessary to establish a definite breach of another right in order to bring in Article 14, but rather to establish that the provision under scrutiny falls 'within the ambit' of that right.[7] In this case, the right in question was the right to respect for a person's home, under Article 8, in the context of a same-sex partner's ability to inherit tenancy rights under the Rent Act 1977. This is in line with the approach of the Strasbourg court, which has confirmed on a number of occasions that Article 14 has no independent existence, but requires the facts at issue to fall within the ambit of another Convention right.[8]

However, this need for another right to at least be potentially engaged does limit the ability of Article 14 to push UK discrimination law beyond its current scope. Before full implementation of the Equal Treatment Framework Directive into UK law, Articles 8 and 9 provided a route through which sexual orientation and freedom of religion could be protected, and Article 14 could assist in such cases (as in *Ghaidan*). However, now that these two forms of discrimination are expressly prohibited by domestic law, it is difficult to find another right in the HRA that could be used to create a new form of discrimination that is not already covered. By way of example, Article 14 includes 'social origin' in its list of protected characteristics. This is a type of discrimination that is not expressly prohibited in UK law, and there are no current plans to do so.[9] However, there is no obvious scenario in the private sphere where an act of discrimination on grounds of an individual's social origin would engage another protected right in a way that would enable Article 14 to become

---

5 The wording of Protocol 12 is identical to that of Article 14, save that it refers to 'the enjoyment of any right set forth by law' rather than 'the enjoyment of the rights and freedoms set forth in this Convention'.
6 [2004] 2 AC 557, discussed further in Chapters 4 and 12.
7 *Per* Lord Nicholls, *ibid.* at 566–7.   8 See, e.g., *Haas* v. *Netherlands* [2004] 1 FLR 673.
9 Section 1 of the Equality Act 2010 requires specified public authorities to have regard to socio-economic status when making decisions, but at the time of writing the Coalition government has announced that it will not be bringing this provision into force.

relevant. If an employee is discriminated against in the workplace because he or she comes from a disadvantaged social background, this is clearly discrimination based on social origin, but which other right under the HRA will be engaged? It is possible that this could be seen as an Article 8 issue involving the employee's private life, but this is far from clear, as social background could be seen as a type of status analogous to a person's race rather than a matter of private conduct or preference such as sexual orientation.[10] This seemingly 'obvious' example of discrimination on grounds of social origin has no obvious answer under the HRA.

Apart from the *Ghaidan* case, there are no significant examples of private law cases in the United Kingdom where Article 14 has played a determinative role. The key cases which are recognisable as examples of discrimination have, in fact, been based on other specific Articles of the HRA, generally combined with existing statutory discrimination law. If the United Kingdom did ratify Protocol 12 of the Convention, this would overcome the need for another Convention right to be engaged. However, any private law case would still require there to be an existing legal provision to which the non-discrimination right could attach through indirect horizontality. The most obvious provision would be the Equality Act 2010. This purports to be a comprehensive discrimination law statute, so leaving room for arguments that it is not compatible with the Convention in omitting specific protected grounds such as social origin – although there would then be a question as to whether this could be subject to statutory interpretation under section 3 of the HRA, or more properly a situation requiring a declaration of incompatibility under section 4.

10.2 Other articles and discrimination law

Despite the European Commission's affirmation that its social policy is intended to ensure 'equality of opportunity for all',[11] it was only in 2000 that legal enforcement of this principle within the EU extended beyond sex equality. The United Kingdom had separately chosen to prohibit race

---

10 For further discussion see R. Wintemute, '"Within the Ambit": How Big is the "Gap" in Article 14 of the European Convention on Human Rights?', *European Human Rights Law Review* (2004), 366, which considers the difference between 'choice' grounds for denial of an employment opportunity (such as sexual orientation or religion), which fall more easily within the ambit of existing rights, and 'non-choice' grounds (such as sex, race, disability or age), which often cannot be brought within another right.

11 EC, Commission, *European Social Policy – A Way Forward for the Union: A White Paper* (COM (94) 333), at p. 41.

and disability discrimination,[12] but this left an obvious gap in relation to discrimination on grounds of sexual orientation and religion. It is in these two areas that the HRA has had the greatest potential to influence the development of UK discrimination law, through Articles 8 and 9.

The right to respect for private life under Article 8 has been relied on successfully by employees claiming protection from discrimination on the basis of sexual orientation. The key decisions for the United Kingdom are those of *Smith and Grady* v. *United Kingdom* and *Lustig-Prean and Beckett* v. *United Kingdom*,[13] relating to claims brought by various members of the armed forces following their dismissal from the military on the grounds that they were homosexual. The Strasbourg court found that investigations by military police into the applicants' personal lives, and the applicants' subsequent discharge from the military on the sole ground of their sexual orientation, were an interference with the right to respect for their private lives.[14] The court then went on to find that the UK Government was unable to justify this infringement of the applicant's rights.[15]

This is an area of discrimination law in which the Convention provided a remedy where EU law had failed. The case of *Grant* v. *South West Trains*[16] involved an attempt to apply EU sex discrimination law to discrimination based on sexual orientation, in relation to a challenge to a workplace policy which provided travel concessions to opposite-sex partners of employees but not to same-sex partners. The Advocate-General's initial opinion found that the policy gave rise to sex discrimination, but the European Court of Justice ruled otherwise, on the basis that the requirement that an employee had to live with an opposite-sex partner in order to receive the benefit applied equally to both men and women. Until the new EU provisions on sexual orientation came into force, it was the right to respect for private life under Article 8 that provided UK citizens with some protection from sexual orientation discrimination.

However, the issue of how to apply this protection in the private law context remained problematic. In the absence of a domestic law prohibiting sexual orientation discrimination, there was no clear piece of legislation that could be made subject to Article 8 under statutory

---

12 Race Relations Act 1976, Disability Discrimination Act 1995.

13 Reported together at [1999] 29 EHRR 493 ('*Smith and Grady*').   14 *Ibid.* at 593.

15 The justification for the interference must come within one of the categories listed in Art. 8(2) of the Convention, and must also be 'in accordance with the law' and 'necessary in a democratic society'.

16 Case C-249/96 [1998] ECR I-621.

indirect horizontality. Before the HRA itself was in force, attempts to argue that the Sex Discrimination Act 1975 required the definition of 'sex' to be interpreted as including sexual orientation had proved unsuccessful. In the cases of *MacDonald* v. *Advocate-General for Scotland* and *Pearce* v. *Governing Body of Mayfield School*,[17] the House of Lords confirmed this approach. The judgments did not clarify what the outcome would have been if the HRA had been in force at the relevant time, and arguably Article 8 would have required a different reading of the legislation. However, it must be questionable whether a court would have been willing to read the Sex Discrimination Act, which is clearly based around a comparison between men and women, as covering sexual orientation. This would depend on which model of horizontality was being applied, but would potentially require one of the stronger models to override what appears to be clear statutory wording.[18] Arguably this would be outside the permissible scope of statutory interpretation, and require a declaration of incompatibility under section 4 of the HRA.[19] This point about interpretation in the face of clear statutory wording is discussed in more detail at the end of this chapter.

Even if there had been a reluctance to take a more radical approach towards statutory interpretation of sex discrimination laws under section 3 of the HRA, Article 8 could have had an influence on more blatant forms of sexual orientation discrimination through the need to interpret other statutory employment law provisions in line with this right, particularly the legislation relating to unfair dismissal. For example, if an employee were to be dismissed on grounds of sexual orientation, Article 8 would indicate that this should be regarded as unreasonable conduct by the employer and so an unfair dismissal.[20] This would at least have reversed a notorious decision from 1980 in which the Employment Appeal Tribunal found that it was fair to dismiss a handyman at a children's camp when it was discovered that he was homosexual.[21] However, it might be thought

---

17 *MacDonald* v. *Advocate-General for Scotland* and *Pearce* v. *Governing Body of Mayfield School* [2003] IRLR 512.

18 For a different approach arguing that sexual orientation discrimination can be analysed as sex discrimination if the correct comparator is used, see: D. Pannick, 'Homosexuals, Transsexuals and the Law', *Public Law* (1983), 279 at 281; and R. Wintemute, 'Recognising New Kinds of Sex Discrimination: Transsexualism, Sexual Orientation and Dress Codes', *Modern Law Review*, 60 (1997), 334 and 'Lesbian and Gay Inequality 2000: the Potential of the Human Rights Act 1998 and the Need for an Equality Act 2002', *European Human Rights Law Review* (2000), 603.

19 See Chapter 4.   20 Under s. 98 of the Employment Rights Act 1996.

21 *Saunders* v. *Scottish National Camps Association Ltd* [1980] IRLR 174, EAT.

that a court considering this issue in the year 2000 would have reached a different decision in any event. In fact, there were no significant cases of this nature in the period between the HRA coming into force and the introduction of the new legislation on sexual orientation discrimination, meaning that the scope of Article 8 to create a new form of discrimination was never fully tested.

The other provision that is most directly relevant to discrimination law is Article 9 of the HRA, which establishes a right to freedom of thought, conscience and religion. Like Article 8, this provision has also been used by employees seeking to challenge workplace practices which are potentially discriminatory. Key decisions include *Ahmad* v. *United Kingdom*[22] (concerning a Muslim schoolteacher who required time off on Fridays for prayer), *Stedman* v. *United Kingdom*[23] (concerning a Christian employee who did not wish to work on Sundays) and *Kontinnen* v. *Finland*[24] (concerning a Seventh Day Adventist who wished to leave work before sunset on Fridays).

In all of these cases, it was accepted that the right to freedom of thought, conscience and religion was potentially engaged. However, although Article 9 was relevant, none of the claims were ultimately successful. In each case, the Strasbourg court took a conservative approach to the question of what behaviour by an employer would 'infringe' an employee's freedom of religion, finding that it was not an infringement to require compliance with the employment contract. The applicants in these cases failed to get over even the first hurdle of showing that the right to freedom of religion was affected, meaning that it was not necessary for the employer to justify its workplace requirements. In *Stedman*, this was the case even though the employer was altering the employee's existing employment terms to require work on Sundays.

This is somewhat different from the approach taken by the Strasbourg court towards Article 8 in the context of sexual orientation, particularly as reflected in *Smith and Grady* where the court gave short shrift to the argument that there was no infringement because the individuals had agreed to the contractual terms and were free to work elsewhere. However, in the context of freedom of religion, this narrow approach suggests that Article 9 would not be of much assistance to individuals who feel that they have been discriminated against by workplace practices that come into conflict with their religious beliefs. Article 9 may be clearly infringed by direct discrimination, such as harassment or dismissal based simply on

22 (1982) 4 EHRR 126.   23 (1997) 23 EHRR CD 168.
24 (1996) 87 EHRR DR 68 (Commission).

the fact of an employee's religious views. However, many issues involving religion are actually examples of indirect discrimination, where workplace requirements come into conflict with religious requirements. Although Article 9 expressly includes the right to 'manifest' religion or belief, the approach that there is no interference with this right if an employee is free to resign and work elsewhere places substantial limitations on the right in practice.

There have been some more recent Strasbourg court decisions that recognise that there may be an interference with Article 9 rights where particular practices are restricted, even where the individual theoretically has a choice of alternatives, including *Sahin* v. *Turkey*, which considered a headscarf ban implemented by a Turkish university.[25] In addition, it would in theory be open to the UK courts to interpret Article 9 more widely. This is a question of level one analysis – is there a Convention right that needs to be given effect between private parties in this particular case?[26] However, when the issue has been considered in the United Kingdom, the decisions have tended to follow the earlier Strasbourg court cases and take the same limited approach. The majority of the Court of Appeal followed the Strasbourg court's decision in *Stedman* when deciding the case of *Copsey* v. *WWB Devon Clays Ltd*,[27] which concerned the requirement for a Christian employee to work on Sundays. Similarly, in *R (Begum)* v. *Headteacher and Governors of Denbigh High School*, a majority of the House of Lords took the view that there was no interference with a schoolgirl's Article 9 rights when she was excluded from school for failure to comply with the required dress code, on the basis that she could have attended three other schools in the area which would have permitted her to wear the jilbab.[28] In these cases the UK courts have followed the approach of confining themselves to treating the Strasbourg jurisprudence as a ceiling, rather than going any further than required by that jurisprudence, as is particularly prevalent in cases concerning statute rather than common law.[29] This means that, to date, Article 9 has not shown itself capable of providing clear protection to religious requirements and practices in the United Kingdom.

---

25 (2007) 44 EHRR 5. It should be noted that even in these cases, the Strasbourg court has been very ready to find that such restrictions are justified under Art. 9: see L. McColgan, 'Religion and (In)Equality in the Workplace', *Industrial Law Journal*, 38 (2009), 16.

26 This analysis is introduced in Chapter 1.

27 [2005] ICR 1789, Mummery LJ and Neuberger LJ, Rix LJ dissenting on this point.

28 [2006] UKHL 15, [2007] 1 AC 100, Lords Scott, Hoffmann and Bingham ('*Denbigh High School*').

29 See Chapter 5.

10.3 The HRA and current discrimination law

Although there was initially some scope for Articles 8 and 9 to introduce new forms of protection against discrimination into UK law, these developments have now been overtaken by specific EU legislation. The Treaty of Amsterdam,[30] which came into force in May 1999, introduced new powers for the EU to take action to combat discrimination based on racial or ethnic origin, religion or belief, disability, age or sexual orientation. This led quickly to a general anti-discrimination package, which resulted in two significant new directives: a directive on racial equality (adopted on 29 June 2000);[31] and the Equal Treatment Framework Directive (adopted on 27 November 2000), which introduced for the first time regulation of discrimination in the workplace on grounds of disability, age, religion or belief, and sexual orientation.[32] These new provisions were implemented in stages into UK law, with protection against discrimination in employment on grounds of sexual orientation and religion or belief coming into force on 1 December 2003.[33]

The obvious effect of this new legislation was that the HRA was no longer needed to create new types of prohibited discrimination in the areas covered by EU law, at least in the employment sphere. In addition, discrimination in the provision of goods and services is now prohibited in relation to all types of discrimination apart from age.[34] This leaves the HRA with a potential role in the interpretation and development of this new legislation through statutory indirect horizontality, and some areas where this may be relevant are discussed in the final section of this chapter. However, the fact that this comprehensive regime of discrimination legislation is based on EU law means that the European Court of Justice also has a key role in the shaping the law. As European Court of Justice rulings are directly binding on the United Kingdom, this provides an alternative external forum instead of the Strasbourg court, which can shape the development of UK discrimination law. A further related point

---

30 The Treaty of Amsterdam – Amending the Treaty on European Union, the Treaties establishing the European Communities and certain related Acts (Amsterdam, 2 October 1997).

31 EC, Council Directive 2000/43/EC of 29 June 2000 implementing the principle of equal treatment between persons irrespective of racial or ethnic origin, [2000] OJ L 180/22.

32 EC, Council Directive 2000/78/EC of 27 November 2000 establishing a general framework for equal treatment in employment and occupation, [2000] OJ L 303/16.

33 The Employment Equality (Sexual Orientation) Regulations 2003 (SI 2003/1661) and the Employment Equality (Religion or Belief Regulations) 2003 (SI 2003/1660).

34 See the Equality Act 2010, which consolidates the previous statutory provisions.

is the presumption established by the Strasbourg court that a country will not have departed from Convention rights when implementing legal obligations arising from membership of the EU.[35] Although this presumption falls away if the protection of Convention rights is 'manifestly deficient', this suggests that the courts may be slower to identify a breach of Convention rights in relation to the Equality Act 2010 than in relation to other statutes which are not based so squarely on EU law.

Another limiting factor, particularly in the context of the employment relationship, is that all of the relevant Convention rights allow for justification of infringements. Accordingly, none of the rights that may apply in the workplace are absolute, and the employer always has an opportunity to justify its actions. The reason put forward in justification must fall within one of the range of legitimate aims listed for each right, but these permissible aims are relatively wide. Articles 8 and 9 both refer to 'the protection of the rights and freedoms of others', which can encompass a range of employer objectives, including protection of the employer's reputation. In addition to there being a permissible aim, the infringement of the right must be 'necessary in a democratic society', a phrase that has been interpreted as meaning that it must be proportionate to the legitimate aim pursued.[36] However, a number of the cases that apply the HRA to the workplace suggest a willingness to accept employer justifications without overly strict scrutiny, including those relating to freedom of religion.[37]

In contrast, the Equality Act relies on the separate concepts of direct and indirect discrimination.[38] Direct discrimination cannot generally be justified,[39] unless this is based on an 'occupational requirement'. This is a narrow test that requires a particular characteristic to be an occupational requirement, and in addition the application of this requirement must be 'proportionate' in the particular case.[40] With the possible exception of direct discrimination on grounds of sexual orientation, as discussed further below, this limited form of justification seems to provide stronger protection from direct discrimination than is afforded by the HRA.

It is possible under the Equality Act to justify indirect discrimination (whereby a seemingly neutral rule disadvantages a particular group), the

---

35 *Bosphorus Hava Yollari Turizm ve Ticaret Anonim Sirketi* v. *Ireland* (2006) 42 EHRR 1.
36 *Beldjoudi* v. *France* (1992) 14 EHRR 801.
37 See, e.g., *Sahin* v. *Turkey* (2007) 44 EHRR 5.   38 See ss. 13 and 19.
39 Except for age discrimination, where general justification of direct discrimination is permitted under s. 13(2).
40 Schedule 9, Pt 1.

statutory test being whether the discriminatory practice is a 'proportionate means of achieving a legitimate aim'.[41] At first sight, this seems very
similar to the proportionality test under the HRA. However, the test for
justification of indirect discrimination as formulated by the European
Court of Justice requires the practice under challenge to correspond to
a 'real need' and be 'necessary' to that end.[42] Although it may be questionable whether the UK statutory test and its application by the courts
complies with the standard required by the European Court of Justice, the
'necessity' test suggests that the standard of justification is at least as strict
as that required by the HRA, and potentially more so.[43] In addition, the
concept of indirect discrimination in the sphere of religious belief avoids
the problems that have arisen under Strasbourg court cases as to whether
there is an 'infringement' of Article 9 where an individual is prevented
from manifesting religious beliefs or practices. The issue of an individual's choice to work elsewhere is irrelevant to the question of whether a
workplace practice is indirectly discriminatory.[44]

10.4 Scope for the HRA to influence the future of discrimination law

Although the HRA may not have the potential to change the structure of
UK discrimination law radically, there are a number of areas where it may
have influence as the relatively new types of discrimination develop.

There are certainly aspects of discrimination on grounds of religion or
belief where the HRA may be particularly relevant. The first of these is
the definition of a 'philosophical belief' for the purposes of the law. The
original regulations were amended by the Equality Act 2006 to remove
the requirement that a philosophical belief needed to be 'similar' to a
religious belief in order to be protected, and the courts are currently
grappling with the issue of what types of belief should be protected.[45] The

---

41 Section 19(2)(d).   42 *Bilka-Kaufhaus* Case C-170/84 [1987] ICR 110 at 126.

43 See A. Baker, 'Proportionality and Employment Discrimination in the UK', *Industrial Law
Journal*, 37, (2008), 305, who argues that the proportionality test applied by the Strasbourg
court is stricter than that used by the UK courts in relation to indirect discrimination,
but recognises that the approach taken by the European Court of Justice requires an even
more rigorous standard.

44 Even those who criticise the width of the statutory protection of religious practices still
argue for some protection in addition to that afforded by Art. 9: see McColgan, 'Religion
and (In)Equality in the Workplace'.

45 The current definition in s. 10(2) of the Equality Act simply states that 'Belief means any
religious or philosophical belief and a reference to belief includes a reference to a lack of
belief'.

test as formulated by the EAT in the case of *McClintock* v. *Department of Constitutional Affairs* is that of whether beliefs have 'sufficient cogency, seriousness, cohesion and importance and are worthy of respect in a democratic society'.[46] This was developed further by the EAT in *Grainger Plc* v. *Nicholson*, in holding that, in principle, a belief in climate change was capable of being protected by the legislation.[47] The EAT drew on previous human rights cases to formulate a list of guidance as to when a belief will be protected, including: it must be a belief as to a weighty and substantial aspect of human life and behaviour; it must be worthy of respect in a democratic society; it must not be incompatible with human dignity; and it must not conflict with the fundamental rights of others.[48]

There may well be further scope for both Article 9 (framed relatively widely as the right to freedom of thought, conscience and religion) and Article 10 (the right to freedom of expression) to influence the extent to which non-religious belief is protected by the law. This includes the thorny issue of whether political beliefs should be covered, including those of extreme political organisations.[49] In *Nicholson*, the EAT took the view that, while 'support of a political party' would not of itself amount to a philosophical belief, a belief in a political philosophy or doctrine, such as socialism, Marxism or free-market capitalism, could do so.[50] This remains to be developed further by the courts, but is an area where Article 14 (which expressly refers to political opinion) could potentially be combined with Articles 9 and 10 to require the Equality Act 2010 to be interpreted as covering all types of political opinion. Although the protection of the most extreme political groups could be constrained by the requirement that the beliefs are worthy of respect in a democratic society and do not conflict with the fundamental rights of others,[51] there is clear scope for the HRA to shape the development of protection of political beliefs in discrimination law. This is particularly suitable for court interpretation

---

46 [2008] IRLR 29 at 33.

47 *Grainger Plc* v. *Nicholson* [2010] IRLR 4, EAT ('*Nicholson*').

48 *Nicholson* at 8. This included reference to *Campbell and Cosans* v. *United Kingdom* (1982) 4 EHRR 293, and *R (Williamson)* v. *Secretary of State for Education and Employment* [2005] 2 AC 246, HL, both of which considered whether beliefs about the use of corporal punishment in schools were protected by Convention rights.

49 To date attempts by British National Party members to rely on protection from discrimination based on religion or belief have failed before the Employment Tribunals: see *Baggs* v. *Fudge* ET 1400114/05 and *Finnon* v. *ASDA Stores Ltd* ET/2402142/05.

50 *Nicholson* at 9.

51 Although it must be questionable whether this analysis could be applied to the British National Party, which is a lawful political party in the United Kingdom.

under section 3 of the HRA, as the concept of 'philosophical belief' is already being shaped by the courts, and so any concerns about altering the meaning of clear statutory language and consequent legal uncertainty will be limited.[52]

The other area of obvious relevance relates to the test for indirect discrimination and how this interacts with the requirements of a particular religion. Indirect discrimination requires there to be a 'provision, criterion or practice' that applies equally irrespective or religion or belief, but is to the disadvantage of those sharing the particular religion or belief of the claimant.[53] This is particularly relevant to manifestations of belief, such as clothing requirements, food rules and time off for prayer. Indirect discrimination requires some form of group disadvantage, so a difficult question arises where an individual claims to manifest his or her belief in a certain way that is not shared by other adherents of the relevant faith. This issue was considered by the Court of Appeal in the case of *Eweida* v. *British Airways Plc*,[54] the issue being whether a claim of indirect discrimination arose where a Christian employee was prohibited from wearing a visible jewellery cross in contravention of the employer's uniform policy. Ms Eweida had not produced evidence to show that other Christians would feel disadvantaged by not being able to wear the cross openly, and the Court of Appeal followed the previous EAT decision in holding that solitary disadvantage was not sufficient: 'some identifiable section of a workforce, quite possibly a small one, must be shown to suffer a particular disadvantage which the claimant shares'.[55] Although the Court of Appeal did not specify what size of group was necessary to show the required disadvantage, it is clear from this decision that a court or tribunal needs to be satisfied that some group within a religion shares a particular belief, and this may involve an investigation into the requirements of different faiths.

This is in contrast to the approach taken by the House of Lords in the *Denbigh High School* case when applying Article 9 of the HRA to the claimant's wish to wear the jilbab. Although the majority found that her right to manifest her religion had not been infringed, they also noted that it was sufficient for her religious belief in the requirement to wear the jilbab to be sincerely held, and there was no need for her to show that it was a requirement of her Muslim religion that was followed by particular numbers of others – Lord Bingham stating that it was no less a

---

52 Discussed further in Chapter 4.   53 Section 19 of the Equality Act 2010.
54 [2010] IRLR 322 ('*Eweida*').   55 *Eweida per* Sedley LJ, *ibid.* at 324.

religious belief because it was 'shared by a small minority of people',[56] and Lord Hoffmann commenting 'the fact that most other Muslims might not have thought it necessary is irrelevant'.[57] This appears to be inconsistent with the UK equality legislation. Article 9 was considered by the Court of Appeal in *Eweida*, in a brief four paragraphs,[58] but it was not found to require any different interpretation of the law. Sedley LJ referred to the *Denbigh High School* case and the case of *Kalaç* v. *Turkey*[59] as support for the proposition that not all manifestations of belief should be protected by law, but did not engage with the argument that Article 9 potentially protects individual manifestations of belief as well as the underlying belief itself. It is therefore possible that Article 9 could be used in future cases to influence the development of indirect discrimination based on religion or belief, and, in particular, the issue of what type of group is needed to set up the required disadvantage. This could even go as far as an argument that the group limitation should be removed from the indirect discrimination test altogether. However, such an interpretation would be in the face of clear statutory wording to the contrary in both the Equality Act 2010 and the Equal Treatment Framework Directive, and so arguably the appropriate remedy would be limited to a declaration of incompatibility.

The HRA may also have some influence on the scope of 'occupational requirements' in relation to justification of direct sexual orientation discrimination. As discussed above, these appear to impose a stricter test than the justification of infringement of privacy or free expression rights permitted under the HRA. However, the Strasbourg court did take a particularly strict line in the case of *Smith and Grady*. In defending these cases, the government was effectively putting forward an occupational requirement relating to sexual orientation in order to justify its policy of dismissing homosexuals from the armed forces, based on 'the maintenance of the morale of service personnel and, consequently, of the fighting power and the operational effectiveness of the armed forces'.[60] The court made it very clear that this did not satisfy the proportionality test and so was not 'necessary in a democratic society'. In particular, they took the view that the policy affected a most intimate aspect of an individual's private life, and therefore particularly serious reasons by way of

56 *Denbigh High School per* Lord Bingham at [21].
57 *Denbigh High School per* Lord Hoffmann at [50].
58 *Eweida* at 325.   59 *Kalaç* v. *Turkey* (1997) 27 EHRR 522.
60 *Smith and Grady* at 525.

justification were required.[61] The court found the interferences to have
been particularly grave because the investigation process was exceptionally intrusive, the administrative discharge of the applicants effectively
ended their careers, and because the policy had an absolute and general
character.[62] They considered that the alleged threat to fighting power and
operational effectiveness was founded on the negative attitude of heterosexual personnel towards homosexuals, and noted that there was a lack
of concrete evidence to substantiate the alleged damage that would be
caused by a change in the policy.

This analysis suggests that the HRA will require occupational requirements relating to sexual orientation to be subject to a high level of scrutiny
by the courts. It could be said that the above cases were 'easy', balancing
very intrusive behaviour and the effective destruction of the applicants'
careers against the expression of negative and prejudicial attitudes by het-
erosexuals. However, this does suggest that the negative attitudes of third
parties cannot be used to justify a discriminatory policy. The court also
particularly criticised the absolute nature of the policy, which failed to
take into account individual circumstances. Although the occupational
requirement test requires proportionality in the 'particular case', the HRA
could be seen as taking this further, requiring account to be taken of the
individual's own circumstances and attributes as well as the requirements
of the specific post. Finally, the court also expected particularly serious
reasons by way of justification because the policy affected such an intimate part of a person's private life.[63] Again, this suggests that the UK
courts should require compelling reasons from employers when assessing
the validity of an occupational requirement relating to sexual orientation
in order to act compatibly with the requirements of Articles 8.[64] As with
the definition of 'philosophical belief', this is a matter of defining the scope
of a valid 'occupational requirement', and so is more easily susceptible to
interpretation under section 3 of the HRA than clearly incompatible
statutory wording.

10.5 A more radical approach to statutory interpretation?

The examples discussed above of areas where the HRA may influence the
development of discrimination law are important individual issues, but do

---

61 *Smith and Grady* at 530.   62 *Smith and Grady* at 530–1.
63 *Smith and Grady* at 533–4.
64 See further H. Oliver, 'Sexual Orientation Discrimination: Perceptions, Definitions and
    Genuine Occupational Requirements', *Industrial Law Journal*, 33 (2004), 1.

not represent a major change in the scope and coverage of discrimination rights between private parties. There remains a question as to whether the courts can go further and, in reliance on the HRA, introduce entirely new grounds of discrimination or overturn established legal tests in the face of clear statutory wording to the contrary. One example touched on above is removing the requirement for group disadvantage in the test for indirect discrimination in relation to manifestations of religion, based on Article 9. More major changes could also be possible if a broad approach is taken to Article 14 and its overlap with other rights, such as introducing a new ground of discrimination on grounds of caste or class, based on a link with Article 8 and the right to respect for private and family life. However, there is no indication in the discrimination law cases so far that the courts are moving towards this more radical approach to statutory interpretation in applying the HRA.

In fact, there have recently been some more innovative developments in the interpretation of UK employment law statutes based on EU provisions, rather than the HRA. Under the *Marleasing* principle, in applying an EU directive which does not have direct effect, national courts are required to interpret national law 'so far as possible, in the light of the wording and the purpose of the directive in order to achieve the result pursued by the latter'.[65] The wording 'so far as possible' has historically been seen as constraining the ability of the UK courts to push the concept of 'interpretation' too far, allowing a purposive interpretation of what is contained in the statute, but not a total disregard for clear wording. However, in some recent employment law cases the courts have been prepared to go much further than this, effectively rewriting statutory provisions in order to achieve compliance with EU law. In *EBR Attridge LLP v. Coleman (No. 2)*,[66] the EAT upheld a tribunal's decision to read additional words into the Disability Discrimination Act 1995 to cover discrimination on grounds of a third party's disability, following a European Court of Justice ruling in the same case that this type of discrimination was prohibited by the Equal Treatment Framework Directive. The existing statutory wording was clear in only covering persons who were actually disabled themselves. However, Underhill J was prepared to insert additional wording into the HRA in order to achieve this result – an entirely new section 3A(5A) providing that, 'a person also directly discriminates against a person if he

---

65 Case C-106/89 *Marleasing SA v. La Comercial Internacional de Alimentación SA* [1990] ECR I-4135; for further discussion see Chapter 4, p. 84.
66 [2010] IRLR 10 ('*Coleman*').

treats him less favourably than he treats or would treat another person by reason of the disability of another person', and a similar new section 3B(3) dealing with harassment.[67] Similarly, an employment tribunal has recently been prepared to add additional wording to the Working Time Regulations 1998 in order to allow for carry-over of holiday in cases of absence due to sickness, again by drafting and adding a new paragraph to the legislation.[68]

Although it may be questionable how these developments fit with *Marleasing*, they provide a clear example of how a broad approach to statutory indirect horizontality could be used in conjunction with the HRA to add to or even to alter existing statutory discrimination law wording. Indeed, Underhill J's judgment in *Coleman* relied heavily on *Ghaidan* and principles of statutory interpretation under the HRA in deciding how far the courts could go in interpreting statutes in compliance with EU law. As there is already a precedent for a more radical approach to statutory interpretation in the field of discrimination law, this could be a natural area for the courts to take a similar approach in private law cases in the context of rights under the HRA – although there are differences between EU and Convention rights that may make a different approach appropriate.[69] There are no current examples of the HRA being used to draft substantial additional wording into an existing statute in quite this manner, and this certainly raises potential concerns about legal certainty and the correct extent of section 3 statutory interpretation, particularly given the alternative of a section 4 declaration of incompatibility. In reality, a combination of weaknesses in the protection offered by various rights under the HRA and the comprehensiveness of the EU-based UK legislation means that there has been little need generally for private parties to rely on the HRA when making a claim based on unlawful discrimination. However, there is still scope for this to be an area of law that leads the way in developing principles of statutory indirect horizontality.

---

67 *Coleman* at 17.
68 *Shah* v. *First West Yorkshire Ltd* ET/1809311/09, the new wording in this case being, 'save where a worker has been prevented by illness from taking a period of holiday leave, and returns from sick leave, covering that period of holiday leave, with insufficient time to take that holiday leave within the relevant leave year; in which case, they must be given the opportunity of taking that holiday in the following leave year'.
69 See Chapter 4, p 84.

11

Damages: private law and the HRA – never the twain shall meet?

JASON N. E. VARUHAS

Section 8 of the HRA imported the private law remedy of damages into the public law field of human rights. This chapter considers the approach that the English courts have taken to damages under the Act, and discusses the possible interaction between such damages and damages principles developed in the common law of tort.

So far the English courts have, in the relatively few damages cases decided under the HRA, sought to distance the approach to damages under the Act from that at common law, preferring to transplant the Strasbourg court's approach to monetary compensation under Article 41 of the Convention into the domestic context. It is argued that this 'mirror' approach is deeply flawed, and ought to be abandoned. It cannot be supported on the terms of the HRA, it makes little sense as a matter of principle, and judges have struggled to apply the Strasbourg jurisprudence given its lack of principle.

The chapter proposes an alternative vindicatory, tort-based approach to human rights damages, which draws on common law damages principles. The law of damages in tort, particularly that developed in the context of the torts actionable *per se*, provides an appropriate model for damages under the Act as a matter of principle. Unlike the current mirror approach, a tort-based approach would promote coherence and consistency across the English law of damages, while giving effect to the policy of protection of fundamental interests that underlies the creation of the primary rights in human rights law.

11.1 Damages under the HRA: the current 'mirror' approach

Section 8 of the HRA gives English courts the power to award damages for breaches of incorporated Convention rights.[1] According to the terms of section 8 an award of 'damages' can be made only if it is 'necessary' to afford 'just satisfaction'[2] to the victim, and if it is 'just and appropriate'[3] to do so. The mention of 'just satisfaction' in section 8 is an indirect reference to Article 41,[4] under which the Strasbourg court awards compensation for breaches of Convention rights.[5] Section 8(4) expressly refers to Article 41 and provides that in deciding whether to make a damages award and quantum 'the court must take into account the principles applied by the European Court of Human Rights in relation to the award of compensation under Article 41'.

The higher courts have decided only a handful of human rights damages cases to date. In those few cases both the Court of Appeal and the House of Lords have been quick to distinguish and dissociate the approach to damages under the HRA from that taken in tort law. Indeed, it has been said that damages under the HRA have 'nothing to do with tort or delict'.[6]

Initially a *sui generis* 'public law' approach to human rights damages was proposed by the Court of Appeal, which would have entailed the courts weighing the individual interest in provision of redress against the public interest in the continued funding of public services on a case-by-case basis in determining whether damages ought to be awarded and quantum.[7]

---

1 For an overview of the case law on damages under the Act see R. Clayton and H. Tomlinson, *The Law of Human Rights*, 2nd edn. (Oxford University Press, 2009), ch. 21; H. McGregor, *McGregor on Damages*, 18th edn. (London: Sweet & Maxwell, 2009), ch. 43.

2 Section 8(3).   3 Section 8(1).

4 Article 41 provides: 'If the Court finds that there has been a violation of the Convention or the protocols thereto, and if the internal law of the High Contracting Party concerned allows only partial reparation to be made, the Court shall, if necessary, afford just satisfaction to the injured party'; this reference to Art. 41 in s. 8(4) is 'curious' given that 'Article 41 is, in terms, directed to a situation in which domestic law fails to make adequate provision' for monetary reparation: Clayton and Tomlinson, *The Law of Human Rights*, para. 21.58.

5 This is in fact the only form of redress granted by the Strasbourg court under Art. 41 other than a finding of breach: A. R. Mowbray, 'The European Court of Human Rights' Approach to Just Satisfaction', *Public Law* (1997), 647, 658.

6 *Sommerville* v. *Scottish Ministers* [2007] 1 WLR 2734 at [127] *per* Lord Rodger ('*Sommerville*'); see also the dicta of Lord Mance at [184].

7 See *Anufrijeva* v. *Southwark LBC* [2004] QB 1124, particularly at [56] ('*Anufrijeva*'). Some remnants of this approach remain: see, e.g., *Dobson* v. *Thames Water Utilities Ltd* [2009] EWCA Civ. 28 at [42]. Note that a variant of this approach has recently been adopted in the context of damages under the Canadian Charter on Rights and Freedoms: see *City of Vancouver* v. *Ward* [2010] SCC 27.

The House of Lords have since ruled that domestic courts should look exclusively to the Convention jurisprudence for guidance in determining whether damages should be awarded and for guidance as to scales of awards. In the leading case of *Greenfield*, Lord Bingham, speaking for a unanimous House, rejected counsel's submissions that, *inter alia*, English courts should be free to depart from the scales of damages applied at Strasbourg and apply domestic scales of damages in exercising their power under section 8, and that in calculating awards for distress and frustration the courts of this country should use damages awards made in discrimination cases as a comparator.[8] Lord Bingham said that the HRA was not a 'tort statute', and that its objects are different and broader.[9] His Lordship gave two further, more substantial reasons for this decision. First, drawing on a passage in the White Paper that preceded the HRA,[10] Lord Bingham said that the aim of incorporating the Convention into municipal law 'was not to give victims better remedies at home than they could recover in Strasbourg but to give them the same remedies without the delay and expense of resort to Strasbourg'. Second, and crucially, he opined that the requirement in section 8(4) that courts take into account those principles applied by the Strasbourg court, was the clearest indication possible 'that courts in this country should look to Strasbourg and not to domestic precedents'.[11] The Law Lords' decision effectively overruled previous dicta of the Court of Appeal that, in assessing quantum of damages, courts could seek guidance from the levels of awards made in tort, as well as the levels of awards made/recommended by other bodies such as the Ombudsman.[12]

The effect of *Greenfield* has been that lower courts now apply a 'mirror' approach to assessing damages under the HRA – English courts have sought to ensure that the domestic jurisprudence reflects the approach taken at Strasbourg in terms of how the power to award damages is exercised and the scales of damages applied.[13] The corollary of this approach

---

8 *R (Greenfield) v. Secretary of State for the Home Department* [2005] 1 WLR 673 at [18]–[19] ('*Greenfield*').

9 *Greenfield* at [19].

10 *Rights Brought Home: The Human Rights Bill*, Cm 3782 (1997), para. 2.6.

11 *Greenfield* at [19].   12 *Anufrijeva* at [74], [77]–[78].

13 The mirror approach has similarly been applied to issues concerning substantive Convention rights: see, e.g., *R (Ullah) v. Special Adjudicator* [2004] 2 AC 323 at [20], discussed further in Chapter 5; in the damages context see J. Steele, 'Damages in Tort and Under the Human Rights Act: Remedial or Functional Separation', *Cambridge Law Journal*, 67 (2008), 606; R. Clayton, 'Damage Limitation: the Courts and the Human Rights Act Damages', *Public Law* (2005), 429.

has been that guidance that could be obtained from the English law of damages has been completely sidelined, and that a parallel approach to remedies is developing under the Act. For example, in *Van Colle* the Court of Appeal, in assessing damages for the fear and distress suffered by a victim in the lead up to his murder in the context of a breach of Article 2, refused to consider the level of awards in domestic personal injury cases.[14] The court cited *Greenfield* for the proposition that 'the guide to quantum is to be found in Strasbourg cases rather than English decisions'.[15] Similarly, in assessing damages for grief, anguish and distress suffered by the victim's relatives, because of their bereavement, the court refused to consider the amounts awarded domestically under the Fatal Accidents Act 1976.[16]

It is submitted that this 'mirror' approach – with its strict separation of HRA damages and damages at common law – is deeply flawed and ought to be abandoned forthwith.

11.1.1 The terms of the HRA

The approach taken in *Greenfield* and its progeny is patently inconsistent with the terms of the HRA. The courts have apportioned disproportionate weight to the direction in section 8(4). Parliament deliberately did not require domestic courts to treat the Strasbourg principles as binding, but rather directed that the courts merely 'take into account' those 'principles' developed by the Strasbourg court in deciding whether to make an award and quantum. Lord Bingham's interpretation of the Act transforms what is a relevant consideration into a sole determinative consideration, and effectively renders the rest of section 8 redundant.

Furthermore, the courts have not only mechanically applied the 'principles' developed by the Strasbourg court, they have also effectively treated its jurisprudence as binding precedent. As the Law Commissions have observed, there is a clear conceptual distinction between the 'principles' developed by a court and its 'practice' or 'jurisprudence': '"Principles" are normally understood to refer to the basic objectives of the system, as opposed to the application of those principles to assessing damages in individual cases'.[17] This key distinction between principles and practice

---

14 *Chief Constable of the Hertfordshire Police* v. *Van Colle* [2007] 1 WLR 1821 at [120] ('*Van Colle* CA') (overturned on the question of breach of the Convention: [2008] 3 WLR 593).
15 *Van Colle* CA at [104].   16 *Van Colle* CA at [121]; see Fatal Accidents Act 1976, s. 1A.
17 *Damages Under the Human Rights Act 1998*, Law Com. No. 266/Scot Law Com. No. 180 (2000), paras. 4.6–4.11. Cf. *Greenfield* at [19].

is made even clearer by the difference between the language used in section 8(4) and that in section 2(1) of the HRA. While section 8(4) makes reference only to the 'principles' applied by the Strasbourg court, section 2(1) requires domestic courts, in deciding questions pertaining to substantive rights, to 'take into account' any 'judgment, decision, declaration or advisory opinion' of the Strasbourg court.

On top of this, the term used for the monetary award under the HRA is 'damages',[18] which is quintessentially a common law term of art that is unfamiliar in the Strasbourg context.

The terms of the statute are clear. However, if one thought them ambiguous the parliamentary debates on the Human Rights Bill support the view that Strasbourg decisions were not to be afforded precedent value: the then Lord Chancellor posited that 'our courts must be free to try to give a lead to Europe as well as to be led'.[19] Also of interest is that in deciding not to incorporate Article 13 – the right to an effective remedy – the government placed emphasis on the fact that English courts are 'rich in remedies',[20] and that the English law of remedies 'is one of the most sophisticated and developed systems in the world'.[21] A key argument for incorporation was that 'British judges are denied the opportunity of building a body of case law on the Convention which is properly sensitive to *British legal and constitutional traditions*,' and that the HRA would 'give power back to British courts'.[22] This tends to indicate that there was an expectation that the courts would have at least some recourse to the long-established law of remedies in English law, and seek to rationalise their approach to HRA damages within the English legal tradition. As Burrows has recently said, '"To bring home" rights might be thought to require that rights are compensated in a way that home regards as appropriate'.[23]

This analysis indicates that the terms of the Act would permit a court to take a common law-based approach to the assessment of damages, and that the framers of the Act had an expectation that judges would

---

18 HRA, ss. 8(2)–(6), 9(3)–(4).

19 HL Deb., vol. 583, cols. 513–15, 18 November 1997, Lord Chancellor.

20 HL Deb., vol. 583, col. 479, 18 November 1997; vol. 584, col. 1266, 19 January 1998, Lord Chancellor.

21 HL Deb., vol. 583, col. 477, 18 November 1997, Lord Chancellor.

22 P. Boateng and J. Straw, 'Bringing Rights Home: Labour's Plans to Incorporate the European Convention on Human Rights into UK Law', *European Human Rights Law Review* (1997), 71, 71, 72 (emphasis added); but see the ambivalent statements regarding damages (at 77).

23 A. Burrows, 'Damages and Rights', paper presented at 'Obligations V: Rights and Private Law', Oxford, 14–16 July 2010, p. 22.

draw on the English law of remedies in fashioning the general approach to remedies under the Act, as long as the courts had regard to principles applied by the Strasbourg court. In this respect it is important to note that the central principle applied both at common law and by the Strasbourg court is the same, at least with regard to compensatory damages: *restitutio in integrum.*[24]

11.1.2 Distinguishing supranational and domestic context

The quantum awarded by the Strasbourg court, and the manner in which it exercises its power to grant compensation under Article 41, should not be treated as a best practice guide for domestic institutions. The Strasbourg court's award of monetary compensation under Article 41 is designed to afford 'just satisfaction', which is distinct from the relevant remedial obligation on states parties which is to guarantee an 'effective remedy' under Article 13.[25] It is pertinent to note that in the parliamentary debates on the Human Rights Bill, the then Lord Chancellor made clear that the remedial provisions were designed to enable the courts to provide effective remedies and thus fulfil the UK's obligations under Article 13.[26] Moreover, the Strasbourg court exercises its remedial jurisdiction in the light of the established principle of subsidiarity, which holds that the protection of rights and provision of remedies is first and foremost the responsibility of domestic institutions and that the court acts only in a supervisory role.[27] Thus, what constitutes just satisfaction at the

---

24 See, e.g., *Kingsley* v. *United Kingdom* (2002) 35 EHRR 10 at [40]; Law Commissions Report on HRA Damages, paras. 3.19–3.21, 4.14.

25 This has been noted by the courts on a number of occasions, but less often in the damages context and was not mentioned in the leading cases of *Anufrijeva* and *Greenfield*. See *R* v. *Kansal (No. 2)* [2002] 2 AC 69 at [70]; *Brown* v. *Stott* [2003] 1 AC 681 at 715; *Re S* [2002] 2 AC 291 at [61]; *Re Attorney-General's Reference (No. 2 of 2001)* [2004] 2 AC 72 at [175]; *Sommerville* at [131].

26 HL Deb., vol. 583, cols. 475–81, 18 November 1997; vol. 584, cols. 1265–8, 29 January 1998; vol. 585, cols. 384–5, 19 January 1998, Lord Chancellor.

27 See, e.g., *Salah* v. *Netherlands* (2007) 44 EHRR 55 at [70] (awarding compensation is not one of the court's main duties); *Papamichalopoulos* v. *Greece* (1996) 21 EHRR 439 at [34] (*Papamichalopoulos*) (if the nature of the breach allows of *restitutio in integrum*, it is for the respondent state to effect it, the court having neither the power nor the practical possibility to do so itself); *Handyside* v. *United Kingdom* (1979–80) 1 EHRR 737 at [48]–[50]; *Z* v. *United Kingdom* (2002) 34 EHRR 3 at [103]; J. Beatson, S. Grosz, T. Hickman, R. Singh with S. Palmer, *Human Rights: Judicial Protection in the United Kingdom* (London: Sweet & Maxwell, 2008), pp. 620–2.

supranational level, when it is afforded by a supervisory and subsidiary institution, which is anxious not to impinge unduly on the sovereignty of states parties, will naturally and legitimately differ from what constitutes an effective remedy provided by a domestic institution that has principal responsibility for the provision of redress.[28] As the Strasbourg court has emphasised: 'Article 41 of the Convention does not provide a mechanism for compensation in a manner comparable to domestic court systems.'[29] In the light of this, Lord Bingham's observation in *Greenfield* that 'the focus of the Convention is on the protection of human rights and not the award of compensation' does not take one very far in the domestic context.[30]

On top of this, the court has regard to the standard of living in the defendant state in deciding upon quantum, meaning that awards in particular cases may not represent fair compensation given English domestic conditions.[31]

It is highly unlikely that an approach based on tort would run afoul of the requirements of Article 13 and require a claimant to travel to Strasbourg to vindicate their rights, given that the quantum of awards in tort is generally higher than those made by the Strasbourg court, which tend to be modest.[32] As Lord Woolf has said: 'The domestic approach to the quantum of compensation would certainly meet the requirements of the [Convention]'.[33]

---

28 See D. Feldman, 'Remedies for Violations of Convention Rights', in D. Feldman (ed.), *English Public Law*, 2nd edn. (Oxford University Press, 2009), para. 19.42.

29 *Varnava* v. *Turkey* (2010) 50 EHRR 21 at [156] (*Varnava*, 3rd Section); K. Reid, *A Practitioner's Guide to the European Convention on Human Rights*, 3rd edn. (London: Sweet & Maxwell, 2008), p. 605.

30 *Greenfield* at [9]. This statement also ignores the fact that provision of compensation for rights breaches would tend to promote the protection of rights.

31 D. J. Harris, M. O'Boyle, E. P. Bates and C. M. Buckley, *Harris, O'Boyle & Warbrick: Law of the European Convention on Human Rights*, 2nd edn. (Oxford University Press, 2009), p. 857.

32 The low levels of awards have been noted by several commentators: see, e.g., D. Fairgrieve, 'The Human Rights Act 1998, Damages and English Tort Law', in D. Fairgrieve, M. Andenas and J. Bell (eds.), *Tort Liability of Public Authorities in Comparative Perspective* (London: BIICL, 2002), p. 98; Reid, *Practitioner's Guide to the ECHR*, p. 605; Mowbray, 'Just Satisfaction', p. 658. The English courts have also noted the modesty of awards at Strasbourg: *Greenfield* at [17]; *R (Pennington)* v. *Parole Board* [2010] EWHC 78 (Admin) at [13](i), [20], [22] ('*Pennington*'); *Dobson* at [52]; *Watkins* v. *Secretary of State for the Home Department* [2006] 2 AC 395 at [26] ('*Watkins*').

33 Lord Woolf, 'The Human Rights Act 1998 and Remedies', in M. Andenas and D. Fairgrieve (eds.), *Judicial Review in International Perspective* (The Hague: Kluwer Law, 2000), p. 431.

11.1.3 Issues in application

Lastly, the mirror approach requires English courts to follow a jurisprudence that is riddled with problems. Commentators,[34] the Law Commissions[35] and the courts[36] are unanimous in their view that, apart from some broad general principles, such as the basic principle of *restitutio in integrum*, the Strasbourg court's approach to just satisfaction lacks consistency, coherence, predictability and principle.[37] Members of the court have even been quoted as saying that, when it comes to just satisfaction, they either have no principles, or do but do not apply them.[38] Commentators have advised that practitioners should avoid searching the case law for principles which do not exist.[39] The state of the jurisprudence is not altogether surprising given that the court takes a broad discretionary approach[40] to its remedial jurisdiction, which emphasises a flexible case-by-case methodology[41] and generally does not entail the court

---

34 See, e.g., Feldman, 'Remedies for Violations of Convention Rights', para. 19.42; Clayton, 'Damage Limitation', pp. 431–3; Clayton and Tomlinson, *Law of Human Rights*, para. 21.30; M. Amos, 'Damages for Breach of the Human Rights Act 1998', *European Human Rights Law Review* (1999), 178, 189; Mowbray, 'Just Satisfaction', pp. 658–9; Beatson *et al.*, *Human Rights: Judicial Protection*, para. 7–141; K. Starmer, *European Human Rights Law: The Human Rights Act 1998 and the European Convention on Human Rights* (London: LAG, 1999), paras. 2.44, 2.51; Woolf, 'The HRA and Remedies', p. 432.

35 Law Commissions Report on HRA Damages, paras. 3.4–3.15.

36 *Anufrijeva* at [52], [57]–[61], [71]; *Re P (A Child)* [2007] HRLR 14 at [64]; *R (Bernard) v. Enfield LBC* [2003] LGR 423 at [35]; *R (KB) v. South London and South and West Region Mental Health Review Tribunal* [2004] QB 936 at [24]–[25] ('*KB*'); *Dobson* at [43]; *R (Degainis) v. Secretary of State for Justice* [2010] EWHC 137 (Admin) at [18]; cf. *Greenfield* at [15].

37 Note that the court has taken some steps to try and ameliorate the problem of inconsistency: Beatson *et al.*, *Human Rights: Judicial Protection*, para. 7–102; Harris *et al.*, *Law of the European Convention*, pp. 856–7, 860.

38 D. Shelton, *Remedies in International Human Rights Law*, 2nd edn. (Oxford University Press, 2005), p. 2; although, given the emergence of some general principles, Shelton is more optimistic about the development of the jurisprudence compared to the first edition of her book: see *Remedies in International Human Rights Law* (Oxford University Press, 1999), p. 1.

39 Lord Lester, Lord Pannick and J. Herberg, *Human Rights Law and Practice*, 3rd edn. (London: LexisNexis, 2009), para. 2.8.4, n. 3.

40 *Dobson* at [43]. The problems associated with broad discretionary approaches are well known: see P. Birks, 'Three Kinds of Objection to Discretionary Remedialism', *University of Western Australia Law Review*, 29 (2000), 1; P. De Jersey, 'Discretion and Remedies', in C. E. F. Rickett (ed.), *Justifying Private Law Remedies* (Oxford: Hart, 2008), p. 69.

41 See *Varnava v. Turkey* (App. Nos. 16064/90–16073/90), 18 September 2009 at [224] ('*Varnava*, Grand Chamber').

rationalising its decisions by reference to past decisions and awards,[42] while the court generally does not explain the basis on which it decides whether or not to make an award or how it comes to quantum, only typically saying that it has done so on an 'equitable basis'.[43]

Predictably, the post-*Greenfield* domestic jurisprudence is replete with judicial observations as to the difficulty of interpreting and applying the Strasbourg case law. For example, in the recent case of *Savage* Mackay J said, 'it is far from simple to discern the principles which the [Strasbourg court] applies',[44] while in *Pennington* HHJ Pelling QC observed that 'it is not at all clear from the reports how the [Strasbourg court] arrived at particular figures'.[45] Similarly, in *Downing* Ian Dove QC said, 'This selection of authorities is typical of the proposition agreed between counsel that there are authorities from the European Court which go in either direction and, as I have already observed and as will be evident, it is hard to discern any hard and fast principles from those judgments.'[46] In the face of a problematic Strasbourg jurisprudence the English judges have been left in a difficult position. Some have responded by mirroring the Strasbourg court's 'parsimonious' approach to reasoning awards, conjuring a figure out of the ether.[47] Others, given the lack of guidance provided by Strasbourg decisions, have applied their own judgement and taken into account factors that in their view are relevant (but not sourced in the Strasbourg jurisprudence), while seeking to ensure that the final quantum is roughly consistent with the general scale of awards at Strasbourg.[48] It is unclear what judges should do when there is no applicable precedent.[49]

Given that neither section 8 nor the Convention require English courts to follow the jurisprudence under Article 41, or bar an approach informed

---

42 A notable exception is the recent case of *MAK* v. *United Kingdom* (2010) 51 EHRR 14 at [91]–[99].

43 Law Commissions Report on HRA Damages, para. 6.2; Harris *et al.*, *Law of the European Convention*, p. 860; *Greenfield* at [19]. This approach is partly explained by the fact that the court is exercising a subsidiary remedial jurisdiction, while it is perhaps understandable that a court composed of members from different legal traditions should express conclusions on damages in very general terms: *KB* at [25], R. Carnwath, 'ECHR Remedies from a Common Law Perspective', *International and Comparative Law Quarterly*, 49 (2000), 517, 519; Law Commissions Report on HRA Damages, paras. 3.6–3.11.

44 *Savage* v. *South Essex Partnership NHS Foundation Trust* [2010] EWHC 865 at [97] ('*Savage*').

45 *Pennington* at [16], and see [20].

46 *Downing* v. *Parole Board* [2008] EWHC 3198 (Admin) at [20], and see [14].

47 For example, *Savage* at [97].   48 For example, *Pennington* at [24]–[25].

49 For examples of situations where there is no Strasbourg precedent see *Dobson* at [43]; *Anufrijeva* at [60].

by domestic law, it is difficult to see why the courts have adopted a strong mirror approach when the common law provides a rich resource of relatively coherent and consistent rules, principles and precedents, which, as far as compensatory awards go, are consistent with the fundamental underlying principle of Convention jurisprudence, *restitutio in integrum*.

11.2 Deriving assistance from private law: a tort-based approach

The analysis in the last section showed that the current mirror approach to damages under the Act is fundamentally flawed as a matter of principle and as a matter of practice. Contrary to the dicta of the higher appellate courts, this section maintains that the law of damages developed in tort has much to offer in the human rights damages context. This was also the general conclusion of the English and Scottish Law Commissions in their in-depth report on damages under the Act, completed in 2000.[50]

This section makes a positive, albeit necessarily brief, case for a tort-based approach to damages under the HRA, founded on orthodox common law damages principles, to replace the current mirror approach. It is argued that an analogy with tort is sound as a matter of principle and that there are important benefits associated with such an approach. Importantly, this analogy with tort also serves to demonstrate the incoherence that adoption of the mirror approach to damages in the human rights context has caused across the English law of damages.

11.2.1 A tort-based approach as a matter of principle: an analogy with the vindicatory torts

The aim of this section is to show that despite the oft-made doctrinal distinction between tort law as a private law body of rules and human rights law as part of public law,[51] there are strong similarities between the two areas of law. This means that it would be logical, as a matter of principle, for the approach to damages in the human rights context to be analogous to that taken in the context of tort law, specifically in the context of the torts actionable *per se*.

---

50 See Law Commissions Report on HRA Damages, para. 4.26.

51 There are serious dangers in treating the public law–private law distinction as dispositive of legal issues: see, e.g., C. Harlow, '"Public" and "Private" Law: Definition Without Distinction', *Modern Law Review*, 43 (1980), 241; C. Harlow and R. Rawlings, *Law and Administration*, 3rd edn. (Cambridge University Press, 2009), pp. 18–22.

In *Qazi*, Lord Bingham said that the Convention 'was an attempt to identify the rights and freedoms most central to the enjoyment of human life in civil society and to give those rights and freedoms an appropriate measure of protection'.[52] Thus, one of the aims, if not the main aim, of the Convention, is to ensure the protection of fundamental rights through positive legal protection. Similarly, the Lord Chancellor, who sponsored the Human Rights Bill through Parliament, made clear that the aim of incorporation was to give as much protection to fundamental rights as possible.[53] This has also long been the aim of those torts that are actionable *per se*, such as trespass, battery, false imprisonment and defamation.[54] These 'vindicatory' torts afford strong legal protection to those interests considered fundamental to English civil society, such as property, liberty and reputation. They have long played a special constitutional role in protecting fundamental rights against intrusion by public officials,[55] with the application of such torts to both public official and private citizen alike being a core tenet of the rule of law in England.[56] As Samuels has said, 'decisions such as those involving the tort of trespass against public officials like the police are actually defining what, in a subjective rights structure, would be constitutional rights'.[57]

The common aim of protection is reflected in, and demonstrated by, the strong similarities between the internal legal structures of torts actionable *per se* and the rights enumerated in the Convention:

(1) while the relevant legal rights cast correlative duties, the *relative focus* of vindicatory torts and human rights provisions is on the rights of

---

52 *Harrow LBC* v. *Qazi* [2004] 1 AC 983 at [8]. See also Lord Lester, 'The European Court of Human Rights after 50 Years', *European Human Rights Law Review* (2009), 461, 463.

53 As far as that could be done consistent with parliamentary sovereignty: HL Deb., vol. 583, col. 808, 24 November 1997, Lord Chancellor.

54 See, e.g., J. Murphy, *Street on Torts*, 12th edn. (Oxford University Press, 2007), p. 4; T. Weir, *A Casebook on Tort*, 10th edn. (London: Sweet & Maxwell, 2004), pp. 7, 18; T. Weir, *An Introduction to Tort Law*, 2nd edn. (Oxford University Press, 2006), pp. 16–17, 133–5; A. M. Tettenborn and D. Wilby, *The Law of Damages*, 2nd edn. (London: LexisNexis, 2010), paras. 1.45–1.46, 2.08.

55 A classic example is *Entick* v. *Carrington* (1765) 95 ER 807.

56 A. V. Dicey, *Introduction to the Study of the Law of the Constitution*, 10th edn. (London: Macmillan, 1960), pp. 193–5, 202–3; Tettenborn and Wilby, *Law of Damages*, para. 2.08; Weir, *Casebook on Tort*, pp. 7, 322–3; C. Harlow, *Compensation and Government Torts* (London: Sweet & Maxwell, 1982), pp. 19–20, 40–1; C. Harlow, *State Liability: Tort Law and Beyond* (Oxford University Press, 2004) pp. 30–41.

57 G. Samuel, 'Governmental Liability in Tort and the Public and Private Law Division', *Legal Studies*, 8 (1988), 277, 288.

the claimant[58] (unlike in the context of, say, negligence, where the relative focus is on the duties owed by the defendant);[59]

(2) torts actionable *per se*[60] and Convention rights,[61] in contrast to other torts such as negligence and misfeasance in public office, for which damage is the 'gist'[62] of the action, are generally actionable without proof of actionable harm or special damage, meaning claimants need not demonstrate loss in order to vindicate their fundamental interests;

(3) liability is generally strict[63] not fault-based, with the defendant's conduct and blameworthiness not relevant to liability[64] and the court's inquiry focused firmly on whether the claimant's interests were interfered with;[65]

(4) countervailing interests are protected in both contexts – in tort, via defences and immunities and in human rights law through

---

58 Weir, *Introduction to Tort Law*, p. 30.

59 As Weir says, 'Language in terms of rights has not hitherto been characteristic of negligence discourse in England': *Casebook on Tort*, p. 323.

60 See, e.g., *Murray* v. *Ministry of Defence* [1988] 1 WLR 692 at 703 (false imprisonment); *Jameel* v. *Wall Street Journal Europe SPRL* [2007] 1 AC 359 at [91] (defamation); *Ashley* v. *Chief Constable of Sussex Police* [2008] 1 AC 962 at [60] (battery) ('*Ashley*').

61 In the human rights context the only requirement is that the claimant be a victim or potential victim of an alleged violation. This requires only that the claimant demonstrate that they were (or would be) 'directly affected by the specific act or omission': HRA, s. 7(1), (7); Lord Woolf, J. Jowell and A. Le Sueur, *De Smith's Judicial Review*, 6th edn. (London: Sweet & Maxwell, 2007), para. 2-048.

62 In respect of negligence see: *Sidaway* v. *Board of Governors of the Bethlem Royal Hospital* [1985] AC 871 at 883; *Gregg* v. *Scott* [2005] 2 AC 176 at [99]; *Lumba* v. *Secretary of State for the Home Department* [2011] UKSC 12 at [64]; J. Stapleton, 'The Gist of Negligence, Part 1: Minimal Actionable Damage', *Law Quarterly Review*, 104 (1988), 213. In respect of misfeasance in public office, see *Watkins* at [15], [79].

63 'Strict liability' in this context denotes that X can be held liable in tort for simply committing a voluntary act that infringes Y's protected interests, even though X may not have intended to interfere with Y's interests or acted negligently. For example, a person can be liable for trespass to land for walking onto another's property voluntarily, even if he did not know or had no reason to know it was someone else's and entered in good faith. Similarly, a defendant can be liable in defamation even if they did not know and had no reason to know that the statement they published was defamatory. See P. Cane, *The Anatomy of Tort Law* (Oxford: Hart, 1997), pp. 32–3, 45–6, 139; P. Cane, '*Mens Rea* in Tort Law', *Oxford Journal of Legal Studies*, 20 (2000), 533, 552. It is important to note that liability is not as strict across all of the vindicatory torts; liability rules may require something more than a mere voluntary act, such as the establishment of an intention to infringe another's protected interests.

64 The reasonableness of the actions taken by the state may be relevant to justification or damages, but generally the reasonableness or knowledge of the state actor will not be relevant to the question of whether the claimant's rights were infringed in the first place.

65 For example, *R* v. *Governor of Brockhill Prison, ex p. Evans (No. 2)* [2001] 2 AC 19 (in the context of false imprisonment) ('*Evans* HL'); Cane, *Anatomy of Tort*, p. 139 (discussing trespass).

limitation[66] and derogation[67] clauses – while in both contexts a rights-centric approach is taken with the primary rights of the plaintiff construed generously and justifications for interference interpreted narrowly;[68]

(5) the justifications for limiting primary rights will fail if exercised 'disproportionately' in the human rights context or 'unreasonably' in the tort law context, while purported justifications are scrutinised anxiously.[69] Thus, important countervailing interests can be accommodated, but they cannot impinge more than necessary upon the claimant's fundamental interests – another consequence of a rights-centric approach.[70] Furthermore, as in the context of the torts actionable *per se*,[71] once an interference with the relevant right is established the burden shifts to the defendant to prove that the interference was justified,[72] again reflecting 'the importance which the law places upon the security of the claimant's interests'.[73]

Given the similarities in function between torts actionable *per se* and Convention rights, as evidenced by their near identical internal legal structures, there is a powerful argument that, as a matter of principle, the approach to damages ought to be analogous in the two areas of law.[74]

The underlying vindicatory function of torts actionable *per se* is reflected in the established approach to compensatory damages.

---

66 For example, Arts. 2(2), 5(1)(a)–(f), 8(2).
67 Article 15 provides for derogations in times of public emergency that threaten the life of the nation.
68 Weir, *Introduction to Tort Law*, pp. 17, 135.
69 As the Strasbourg court has held, 'particularly convincing and weighty reasons' must exist 'by way of justification' for the interference with the applicant's right: *Smith and Grady* v. *United Kingdom* (2000) 29 EHRR 493 at [94].
70 Weir, *Introduction to Tort Law*, p. 135.
71 See, e.g., *Ashley* at [24] (in the context of assault and battery); *Lumba* at [65], [88] (in the context of false imprisonment); R. F. V. Heuston and R. A. Buckley, *Salmond and Heuston on the Law of Torts*, 21st edn. (London: Sweet & Maxwell, 1996), p. 15.
72 This is a fundamental departure from the traditional approach on judicial review under the *Wednesbury* head, where it is for the applicant to prove that the defendant public authority has acted unreasonably. See M. C. Elliott, *Beatson, Matthews and Elliott's Administrative Law*, 3rd edn. (Oxford University Press, 2005), ch. 9.
73 Heuston and Buckley, *Salmond and Heuston on the Law of Torts*, p. 15.
74 See further J. N. E. Varuhas, 'A Tort-based Approach to Damages under the Human Rights Act 1998', *Modern Law Review*, 72 (2009), 750. For judicial support for such an approach see the New Zealand case of *Dunlea* v. *Attorney-General* [2000] 3 NZLR 136 ('*Dunlea*') (but see now *Taunoa* v. *Attorney-General* [2007] NZSC 70).

Claimants can recover damages for the 'normative' damage to their underlying interests, be it loss of liberty in the false imprisonment context,[75]
or damage to reputation in the context of defamation.[76] This means that
damages are awarded for the interference with the right in and of itself,
notwithstanding whether the violation has specific psychological, emo-
tional or economic effects on the individual claimant. Such damage need
not be specifically pleaded or proven, and can never be too remote,[77]
since it is inherent in the violation. Awarding damages for the interference with the right, notwithstanding the impact of the violation on the
individual claimant, serves to ensure that the underlying interests are
afforded strong protection, and vindicates the relative normative importance of such interests within the legal order and that such interests have
an inherent value and worth. It is because such damages give effect to
the protective and vindicatory aims of that area of law that they are fairly
described as 'normative' in nature.[78]

Damages are also available to compensate for the specific effects of the
violation on the individual claimant. Damages for non-pecuniary losses
consequent on the violation, such as mental distress and humiliation suffered by the claimant, are readily recoverable and courts are generally
willing to presume or infer such losses on the facts. Pecuniary losses,
such as loss of earnings or damage to property, and consequential pecuniary losses, such as medical expenses, are also recoverable but must be
specifically pleaded and proved.

Importantly, in the context of the vindicatory torts, a wide range
of damages are available to fully vindicate and protect the underlying
rights, including nominal, compensatory, aggravated, gain-based[79] and

---

75 R v. *Governor of Brockhill Prison, ex p. Evans (No. 2)* [1999] QB 1043 at 1060 ('*Evans* CA');
    see also McGregor, *McGregor on Damages*, para. 37–011.
76 *John* v. *MGN Ltd* [1996] 3 WLR 593 at 607–8. For the proposition that the common
    law implies such damage where certain important rights are violated see, e.g., *Ratcliffe* v.
    Evans [1892] 2 QB 524 at 528, drawing on *Ashby* v. *White* (1703) 2 Lord Raymond 938 at
    955 ('*Ashby*'); see recently, *Lumba* at [195].
77 R. Stevens, *Torts and Rights* (Oxford University Press, 2007), p. 60.
78 Note that others describe such damages differently: e.g., Weir has referred to such dam-
    ages as providing a 'sanction' (*Casebook on Tort*, p. 7), while Stevens considers them
    'substitutive' for the right that has been violated (*Torts and Rights*, ch. 4(B)).
79 Although such damages are traditionally awarded for torts which safeguard propri-
    etary interests (for a recent affirmation of this principle see: *Devenish Nutrition Ltd* v.
    Sanofi-Aventis SA (France) [2008] EWCA Civ. 1086), a number of commentators main-
    tain that their availability could and should be expanded to torts that protect personal
    rights: McGregor, *McGregor on Damages*, paras. 12-021–12-022; J. Edelman, *Gain-based*

exemplary[80] (and possibly 'vindicatory')[81] damages. Notably, this range of damages is not available in the context of other torts, which are not geared towards the protection of fundamental interests.[82]

One difference between damages under the HRA and at common law is that damages are granted as of right where a tort is proved, whereas damages under the HRA may be granted only in the case of a violation if they are 'necessary'[83] and if it is 'just and appropriate'[84] to do so. It has been suggested that this difference is one important factor that indicates that damages under the HRA play, or should play, a different role from damages in tort.[85] This is not a convincing argument. First, that damages are not available as of right does not tell against taking a tort-based approach to assessment of damages where a court does decide to award damages. Second, that damages are not available as of right does not suggest that damages in human rights law should not, or cannot, play the vindicatory role that damages play in the context of the torts actionable *per se*. For example, that damages are not available as of right does not in itself suggest that a court is free to deny an award where a violation causes loss or damage and damages are the only remedy that can effectively remedy the right. The policy of protection of fundamental interests that underpins the primary rights in human rights law strongly suggests that ensuring vindication of the individual claimant's rights ought to be the principal consideration that guides a court's determination of whether it is necessary to make an award of damages in a particular case, which in turn suggests that it would be unusual for damages not to be awarded where they would be in an analogous tort context.

Such a vindicatory approach is supported by broader arguments of principle and law. Fundamental legal rights would be rendered hollow if interferences were not fully remedied, given that it is the function of a

Damages: Contract, Tort, Equity and Intellectual Property (Oxford: Hart, 2002), p. 145; A. Burrows, *Remedies for Torts and Breach of Contact*, 3rd edn (Oxford University Press, 2004), pp. 384–5; see also *Attorney-General* v. *Blake* [2001] 1 AC 268 at 283–284.

80 The Court of Appeal has specifically stated that exemplary damages are not available under the Act: *Anufrijeva* at [55]. However, the House of Lords left the question open when it was before them: *Kuddus* v. *Chief Constable of Leicestershire Constabulary* [2002] 2 AC 122 at [46] *per* Lord MacKay, [92] *per* Lord Hutton. But see: Watkins at [32], [64].

81 See the discussion in: *Lumba*; *Ashley* at [22], [28]–[29]; see also *Attorney-General of Trinidad and Tobago* v. *Ramanoop* [2006] 1 AC 328 at [18]–[19].

82 For example, aggravated damages are not available for the tort of negligence (*Kralj* v. *McGrath* [1986] 1 All ER 54 at 60–1), and exemplary damages have never been awarded in negligence, although they have been technically available since *Kuddus*.

83 Section 8(3).   84 Section 8(1).   85 *Anufrijeva* at [55], [74]

remedy 'to "realize" a legal norm, to make it a "living truth"'.[86] It would be odd indeed if damages were awarded routinely for interferences with lesser interests in tort, such as economic or contractual interests, but not for violations of the most fundamental of rights. On top of this, it is a long-standing principle of English law that where there is a right there ought to be a remedy (*ubi ius, ibi remedium*).[87] The principle is reflected in Article 13 of the Convention,[88] which prescribes that states parties must provide an effective remedy for violations of rights. The refusal to make an award in cases where damages would be the only effective remedy (or low levels of awards) could lead to a violation of Article 13,[89] as well as individual substantive rights.[90]

A vindicatory approach is also supported by the terms of the Act.[91] Section 8(3), which specifically addresses the court's power to award damages, provides that damages shall be awarded only if, 'taking account of all the circumstances of the case', a damages award is 'necessary to afford just satisfaction to the person in whose favour it is made'. As the Law Commissions have observed, 'These words direct attention to the needs of the victim.'[92]

This vindicatory approach to the award and assessment of damages, if applied in the context of human rights law, would ensure – as in the context of the vindicatory torts – that there is internal coherence as between the policy of protection that underlies the primary rights and the approach to relief for interference with those rights. As Birks has said, the full explanation for why certain consequences follow civil wrongs 'has to be completed in every case from the policies and values underlying the recognition of the primary duty which is in question'.[93] On a functional

---

86 P. Gewirtz, 'Remedies and Resistance', *Yale Law Journal*, 92 (1983), 585, 587.

87 *Ashby* at 953; see also Feldman, 'Remedies for Violations of Convention Rights', p. 827.

88 See *R (K)* v. *Camden and Islington Health Authority* [2002] QB 198 at [54].

89 See. e.g., *TP and KM* v. *United Kingdom* (2002) 34 EHRR 2 at [107] ('in appropriate cases, compensation for the pecuniary and non-pecuniary damage flowing from the breach should in principle be available as part of the range of redress'); *RK and AK* v. *United Kingdom* (2009) 48 EHRR 29 at [45]; *Wainwright* v. *United Kingdom* (2007) 44 EHRR 40 at [55]; *Burden* v. *United Kingdom* (2008) 47 EHRR 38 at [40], [43]; *Z* v. *United Kingdom* at [109].

90 See, e.g., *Armoniene* v. *Lithuania* (App. No. 36919/02), 25 November 2008 at [47]; *Biriuk* v. *Lithuania* (App. No. 23373/03), 25 November 2008 at [46] (both in respect of Art. 8).

91 The author has advanced a fuller version of this argument elsewhere: Varuhas, 'A Tort-Based Approach to Damages under the HRA', pp. 762–3.

92 Law Commissions Report on HRA Damages, para. 4.41; but see, e.g., *Brumarescu* v. *Romania* (2001) 33 EHRR 36.

93 P. Birks, 'The Concept of a Civil Wrong', in D. G. Owen (ed.), *Philosophical Foundations of Tort Law* (Oxford: Clarendon Press, 1995), p. 51.

level, a vindicatory approach to human rights damages makes sense in that it carries forward and gives practical effect to the underlying policy goal of ensuring strong protection for the underlying fundamental interests.

By contrast, the current approach to damages under the HRA lacks the core features of a vindicatory approach; it represents a restrictive approach that runs against the grain of the policy of protection that underlies the primary rights.

In terms of the range of damages available, only compensatory and possibly aggravated damages are recognised as available under the HRA.[94] The Strasbourg court only makes compensatory awards, does not award nominal,[95] aggravated[96] or punitive[97] damages, and has not awarded gain-based damages.[98]

Under the HRA no clear approach has emerged with regard to proof of non-pecuniary losses because of the small body of jurisprudence. However, in a number of cases the English courts have required proof of consequential non-pecuniary harm such as mental distress – being unwilling to infer such losses from the facts – and expressed scepticism about awarding damages for 'free-standing' non-pecuniary losses.[99]

Rather than adopt a vindicatory approach to the decision of whether to award damages under section 8, the English courts have sought to follow the Strasbourg court's more restrictive approach to the exercise

---

94 Regarding the possible availability of aggravated damages under the Act see: *KB* at [50]; Law Commissions Report on HRA Damages, para. 4.70, n. 132.

95 *Marckx* v. *Belgium* (1979–80) 2 EHRR 330 at [68]; *Lehideux and Isorni* v. *France* (2000) 30 EHRR 665 at [60]–[63]; cf. *Engel* v. *Netherlands* (1979–80) 1 EHRR 706 at [10].

96 See, e.g., *Selçuk* v. *Turkey* (1998) 26 EHRR 477 at [116]–[119] ('*Selçuk*'); *Mentes* v. *Turkey* (1998) 26 EHRR CD 1 at [18]–[21] ('*Mentes*'); *BB* v. *United Kingdom* (2004) 39 EHRR 30 at [36] ('*BB*').

97 See, e.g., *Selçuk*; *Mentes*; *BB*; *Varnava* (3rd Section) at [156]. Notably, some have argued that the Strasbourg court has at times awarded a 'disguised form of punitive damages': Fairgrieve, 'The Human Rights Act 1998, Damages and English Tort Law', pp. 92–4.

98 Law Commissions Report on HRA Damages, para. 4.77.

99 See *Amis* v. *Metropolitan Police Commissioner* [2004] EWHC 683 at [50]; *KB* at [71]–[73]; *R (Bernard)* v. *Secretary of State for the Home Department* [2005] EWHC 452 (Admin) at [54]–[62]; *R (Baiai)* v. *Secretary of State for the Home Department* [2006] EWHC 1035 (Admin) at [34]; *Degainis* at [18]. It may be that the current approach to proof changes in the light of the adoption of the mirror approach given that there is some precedent in the Strasbourg case law for the court inferring mental distress and other consequential non-pecuniary losses from the facts: see, e.g., *Greenfield* at [16] (in respect of mental distress caused by breach of Art. 6); *Pennington* at [24]–[25]; Law Commissions Report on HRA Damages, para. 3.26. Note, however, that the Strasbourg court's approach to the issue of proof is not consistent: Shelton, *Remedies in International Human Rights Law*, pp. 298, 316ff.

of its remedial discretion under Article 41. For example, the Strasbourg court often holds that a monetary award is not required, because the impact of the violation on the individual is not of such an intensity so as to warrant compensation[100] (although its practice in this respect is not entirely consistent),[101] and that a finding of breach of the Convention is enough to afford just satisfaction in such cases; the English courts have followed this practice, denying damages claims in the vast majority of cases.[102]

In many of these cases it is clear that some consequential non-pecuniary loss has been suffered, and the Strasbourg court has even acknowledged as much in denying awards.[103] A vindicatory approach would require such losses to be compensated; it hardly affords strong protection to rights if victims are left to bear the losses caused by a violation, and it hardly vindicates the fundamental importance of human rights if a claimant could recover such losses in the context of an interference with lesser or equivalent interests in tort, but not where their human rights are violated. While the Strasbourg approach *may* be a defensible one for a subsidiary, supranational institution, it is not an appropriate approach for domestic institutions that are charged with the primary responsibility for protecting rights. Even members of the Strasbourg court have questioned whether a finding of breach can afford just satisfaction in the supranational context, let alone an effective remedy in domestic courts.[104]

On top of this, making damages dependent on the impact of the violation on the individual completely ignores the normative dimensions

---

100 See, e.g., *Varnava* (Grand Chamber) at [224]; *Silver* v. *United Kingdom* (1983) 6 EHRR 62 at [10].

101 See, e.g., Law Commissions Report on HRA Damages, paras. 3.39–3.41; *Degainis* at [17].

102 In respect of a finding being just satisfaction see, e.g., *Greenfield* at [8]–[9], [19], [26], [29], [31]; *Re P* at [58], [71]; *R (H)* v. *Secretary of State for the Home Department* [2004] 2 AC 253 at [30]; *Austin* v. *Metropolitan Police Commissioner* [2005] EWHC 480 at [597]; *Downing* at [31]. In respect of degree of loss see: *R (Biggin)* v. *Secretary of State for Justice* [2009] EWHC 1704 (Admin) at [36]; *KB* at [73]; *Degainis* at [17]–[18]; *R (Bernard)* v. *Secretary of State for the Home Department* at [61]; *Baiai* at [37], [38]–[46], [49].

103 See, e.g., *Nikolova* v. *Bulgaria* (1999) 21 EHRR 64 at [76] (noting previous cases where 'the finding of a violation constituted sufficient just satisfaction in respect of any non-pecuniary damage suffered'). See also Fairgrieve, 'The Human Rights Act 1998, Damages and English Tort Law', pp. 91–2.

104 *Engel*, at 710, Judges Ganshof, Van Der Meersch and Evrigenis partly dissenting; *TW* v. *Malta* (1999) 29 EHRR 185 at 207–9, Judge Bonello partly dissenting, 209, Judges Tulkens and Casadevall partly dissenting; *Nikolova*, at 91–3 Judges Bonello and Maruste partly dissenting, 93, Judges Fischbach, Kuris and Casadevall partly dissenting, 93–4 Judge Greve partly dissenting.

of a violation. There is no discernible principle in the Strasbourg (or HRA) jurisprudence that a rights violation in itself imports normative damage that ought to be compensated regardless of the factual effects of the breach on the victim. In contrast, in the context of torts such as false imprisonment substantial damages are awarded for the 'normative' damage inherent in the denial of the fundamental right to liberty, notwithstanding the actual effects of the violation on the victim, and no matter how minor or serious the interference with the claimant's rights (although the seriousness of the interference will obviously affect quantum).[105] For example, the Court of Appeal recently affirmed that even in the case of a brief false imprisonment a court must award substantial (rather than nominal) damages given the fundamental importance of the protected interest of liberty, even if declaratory relief is granted.[106] Lord Neuberger MR, with whom the other judges concurred, expressly rejected the idea, adopted by the trial judge, that in the case of a brief false imprisonment a declaration that the victim had been falsely imprisoned afforded him substantial 'just satisfaction', meaning that substantial damages need not be awarded.[107]

11.2.2 Common functions, common interests and coherence

The argument that the torts actionable *per se* and human rights obligations share common bonds and underlying functions and should share a common approach to damages is strengthened by the point that both areas of the law, while not co-extensive in their coverage, protect very similar interests that are both fundamental and intangible. Indeed, the vindicatory torts have long protected many fundamental human rights 'albeit in a somewhat piecemeal and unsystematic way'.[108] And it is for this reason that 'In the great range of cases where a claim of a [human rights

---

105 One exception, where nominal damages are awarded, is where the claimant suffers an unlawful imprisonment but could and would have been subject to the same imprisonment with lawful justification: *Lumba*.

106 *Iqbal* v. *Prison Officers Association* [2010] 2 WLR 1054 at [44]–[49] *per* Lord Neuberger, [83]–[84] *per* Smith LJ, [104] *per* Sullivan LJ ('*Iqbal*'). For commentary see J. N. E. Varuhas, 'False Imprisonment of Prisoners: Lawful Authority, Omissions and Damages', *Cambridge Law Journal*, 69 (2010), 438. See also *Lumba* at [197]; *Karagozlu* v. *Commissioner of the Metropolis* [2007] 1 WLR 1881 at 1888.

107 *Iqbal* at [47].

108 See Murphy, *Street on Torts*, pp. 5–7; Weir, *Introduction to Tort Law*, pp. 16–17; Weir, *Casebook on Tort*, pp. 321–3; Lord Bingham, 'Tort and Human Rights', in P. Cane and J. Stapleton (eds.), *The Law of Obligations: Essays in Celebration of John Fleming* (Oxford: Clarendon Press, 1998), p. 1.

breach] is made there will also be a claim in tort.'[109] Thus, for example, the torts of false imprisonment and wrongful arrest and the Article 5 right to liberty and security of the person protect similar interests in liberty and freedom of movement. The torts of assault and battery and the Article 3 right not to be subjected to torture protect similar interests in personal safety and corporeal integrity. It would therefore be illogical and serve to disrupt the internal coherence of English law if the approach to damages varied greatly according to whether a case falls to be considered under the HRA or at common law. As Sir Anthony Mason has said in this context: 'One would expect the remedies to be concurrent.'[110]

Several recent English cases illustrate the incoherence that can result from parallel approaches to damages.

The case of *Mosley* involved an interference with the claimant's privacy interests.[111] Compensatory damages were assessed according to common law analogies because Mosley's privacy interests were protected horizontally through the private law action of misuse of private information.[112] However, had the claimant been able to bring a claim directly for a breach of Article 8, he would have received damages based on the jurisprudence of the Strasbourg court. The confusion and inconsistency that such a divided approach can cause was illustrated in *Mosley* itself. While taking a purely common law approach to compensatory damages, the court denied the claim for exemplary damages partly on the basis that the availability of such damages – 'not apparently familiar in Strasbourg' – would be anomalous in a context that involved the application of Convention values.[113]

---

109 *Dunlea* at [38].
110 A. Mason, 'Human Rights and the Law of Torts', in Cane and Stapleton (eds.), *The Law of Obligations*, p. 23.
111 *Mosley* v. *News Group Newspapers Ltd* [2008] EMLR 20 ('*Mosley*').
112 *Mosley* at [212]–[231]; see also *Campbell* v. *MGN Ltd* [2002] EWHC 499 at [130]–[170] (award of compensatory and aggravated damages upheld on appeal: [2004] 2 AC 457 ('*Campbell* HL')). It is not yet clear whether this cause of action is to be classified as a tort or a discrete form of the equitable action for breach of confidence, although it is increasingly common for judges to refer to the action as a tort: see *Campbell* HL at [14]; *McKennitt* v. *Ash* [2008] QB 73 at [8]; *Murray* v. *Express Newspapers Plc* [2009] Ch 481 at [24], [27]; cf. *Mosley* at [181]–[182]; *Douglas* v. *Hello! Ltd (No. 3)* [2006] QB 125 at [96]; see Chapter 7 for fuller discussion. If the action is a form of breach of confidence, then damages should not be awarded on a common law basis and should not be available as of right, given the equitable nature of the action: remedies in equity are discretionary, and monetary remedies would comprise equitable compensation or an account of profits.
113 *Mosley* at [196].

In the 2010 case of *Pennington* a prisoner had experienced an unjustified delay of just over three months between the date that the Parole Board ought to have made and communicated its decision to him that he was to be released on licence, and the date when the decision was in fact communicated.[114] This was held to constitute a breach of Article 5(4) of the Convention. Counsel for the claimant argued that damages ought to be assessed according to the approach in false imprisonment cases.[115] This would have been a sensible approach given that the interest protected both in false imprisonment and under Article 5 is that in liberty, and it was clear that because of the Parole Board's unjustified and unlawful delay the claimant spent three extra months in prison when he ought to have been out of prison, albeit on licence. Nonetheless, the judge rejected this approach based on the principle in *Greenfield* and sought to calculate damages according to the Strasbourg jurisprudence, despite observing that 'there is little in the [Strasbourg] cases that I have been referred to that assist in the assessment process other than that they illustrate the principle [that awards will be modest by English standards]'.[116] He awarded £1,750 in damages. On the other hand, according to submissions by counsel, a figure closer to £10,000 would have been awarded under a common law approach.[117] Counsel's submission does not seem far off the mark given guidance from the Court of Appeal,[118] and particularly given that in the case of *Ex parte Evans* an award of £5,000 was made for false imprisonment to a prisoner who had been kept in prison unlawfully for fifty-nine days beyond his release date.[119]

The problems of incoherence and inconsistency across English law are also demonstrated by a recent line of cases in which English courts have adopted the Strasbourg court's practice of denying damages on the basis of the social status or moral character of the victim.[120] Specifically in the context of successful claims by prisoners that the Parole Board

---

114 See *Pennington* at [1].
115 *Pennington* at [3] and the discussion from there onwards.
116 *Pennington* at [22].   117 See *Pennington* at [3].
118 See *Thompson* v. *Commissioner of Police for the Metropolis* [1998] QB 498.
119 See *Evans* CA at 1059–60, affd, *Evans* HL. Any comparison must account for inflation over the intervening ten-year period since *Evans* was decided.
120 See Shelton, *Remedies in International Human Rights Law*, pp. 312–15, 345, 346, 348. In some cases where damages have been denied partly or wholly on the basis of the claimant's wrongdoing, there has been a strong nexus or proximity between the wrongdoing and the loss (e.g., *McCann* v. *United Kingdom* (1996) 21 EHRR 97 at [219]); however, in other cases the link has been more tenuous: see Law Commissions Report on HRA Damages, paras. 3.54–3.57.

has failed to give them a speedy hearing as required by Article 5(4), domestic courts have denied damages partly on the basis that the victim was, at the time of the rights violation, serving a sentence for past serious criminal offending (although some judges have expressed doubts[121] about this emerging practice).[122] In domestic tort law an individual may be denied their ordinary rights in certain circumstances where the loss they are seeking to recover is linked to their own criminal wrongdoing.[123] However, given the seriousness of denying an individual their rights, there must generally be a strong nexus between the claimant's wrongdoing and the loss suffered – the relevant loss or damage must have been caused by the claimant's wrongful acts.[124] This is a very different proposition from denying a rights victim damages on the basis that they did something wrong at some point in the past, in circumstances that have no direct nexus with the human rights violation. The result is that if a prisoner seeks to vindicate their right to liberty in tort, their previous offending will not bear on whether they receive an effective remedy, whereas in human rights law this may well be a basis for denying them damages. Of course, the emergent practice in respect of prisoners under the HRA is not only objectionable because it causes incoherence across English law: as well as involving the judges in broad moral judgements,[125] making damages depend on the moral worthiness of the individual victim runs against the grain of the core rule of law principle of equality before the law, Article 14 of the Convention, the fundamental idea that human rights are universal in nature, and the modern trend towards the recognition of prisoner rights.

As a matter of principle the development of parallel approaches to damages is highly questionable. Whether an illegal deprivation of liberty is claimed at common law or under the HRA should make no difference to damages – the tort of false imprisonment and the right to liberty and security of the person protect the same underlying interests in liberty and freedom of movement, and the relevant damage suffered in the two

---

121 See *Degainis* at [19]–[20].   122 See *Biggin* at [35]; *Downing* at [29], [31].

123 See Murphy, *Street on Torts*, pp. 313–15; *The Illegality Defence*, Law Com. No. 320 (2010); Law Commissions Report on HRA Damages, para. 4.47.

124 *Gray* v. *Thames Trains Ltd* [2009] UKHL 33 at [53]–[54]. As Weir says 'if I run someone over in the street, it can hardly be relevant that he was on his way to or from a robbery': *Casebook on Tort*, p. 261.

125 See, e.g., the relatively broad range of considerations taken into account in *Biggin* at [35], in respect of the claimant's previous wrongdoing.

contexts is the same.[126] Why should these interests be considered less valuable and be less well protected, and recovery be subject to questionable considerations such as the moral status of the victim, because the claim is made under the HRA rather than at common law? Such an approach serves to disrupt the internal coherence of English law and also devalues fundamental interests that the common law has long served to protect and vindicate. As Stevens has said of the current approach under the HRA: 'Rights at common law are usually treated more seriously.'[127]

11.2.3 What tort can offer

As a matter of principle it makes sense that the approach to damages in the human rights field should be analogous to that taken in the context of torts actionable *per se*. In addition, an approach informed by tort law offers key benefits. This is not to say that the approach in tort is perfect, only that it has many benefits over other approaches, such as that based on the jurisprudence of the Strasbourg court.[128]

In contrast to the Strasbourg jurisprudence, tort law provides a reasoned and generally coherent, consistent and principled body of existing precedent, which can guide the award of damages in the human rights context, as well as an analytical approach and robust methodology that are characteristic of the common law method. As Stanley Burnton J has said: 'Our own jurisprudence and legal culture require a more analytical approach.'[129] The English law of damages offers an established and elaborate set of principles relating to various issues, including recoverable heads of loss, mitigation, proof, pleading, contribution, remoteness, causation, how to account for collateral benefits and how to assess quantum. These principles have been distilled over a number of centuries and represent the best efforts of common law judges to mould a common law of damages that is fair, coherent and rational; the common law is an authoritative source of principle in this area and ought not to be disregarded.

---

126 D. Oliver, 'The Human Rights Act and Public Law/Private Law Divides', *European Human Rights Law Review* (2000), 343, 350.

127 Stevens, *Torts and Rights*, p. 91; see also C. Harlow, 'Damages and Human Rights', *New Zealand Law Review* (2004), 429, 431.

128 Realistically it is likely to be impossible to devise a perfectly principled approach to damages, especially in the context of non-pecuniary loss: Carnwath, 'ECHR Remedies', p. 520.

129 *KB* at [25]; Lester *et al.*, *Human Rights Law and Practice*, para. 2.8.5.

The vast body of common law precedent provides significant and reasoned guidance as to scales of awards. The availability of such a corpus
of precedent is particularly important when it comes to assessing damages for non-pecuniary damage and loss, which will often be the only
harm suffered in the human rights context. Because there is no objective
method for calculating such damages, consistency and predictability are
at least as important as the actual quantum in ensuring the legitimacy
of awards.[130] Damages for non-pecuniary loss or damage suffered as a
result of the infringement of intangible interests, such as liberty, corporeal integrity and reputation, have long been awarded in the context of
torts actionable *per se*, meaning there exists a developed set of English
precedents to guide courts adjudicating claims in human rights law that
protects similarly fundamental and intangible interests.[131] Further, the
approach in tort has been improved in recent times through provision of
detailed tariff-style guidance from the courts[132] and the Judicial Studies
Board,[133] which is aimed at ensuring greater certainty and consistency in
levels of awards.

Some may ask what a court would do in a case with no tort law
equivalent, such as a case concerning breach of the right to freedom of
expression. The answer is the same as that given by the courts where
they have been required to assess damages in the context of new heads

---

130 Cane, *Anatomy of Tort*, p. 137.
131 It should be noted that damages in defamation and false imprisonment cases are generally assessed by juries at first instance. It does not necessarily follow that the general
levels of damages awards in those fields could not be relied upon to guide quantum in
new fields of liability. While some care should be taken with regard to past awards as it
is well documented that some such awards have been plainly excessive, particularly in
the defamation context (see McGregor, *McGregor on Damages*, paras. 39-023–39-026),
recent developments suggest that jury awards may now offer more reliable reference
points. In particular, there is now greater scope afforded to the trial judge (and counsel
in the defamation context) to suggest to the jury appropriate damages ranges or starting points, taking into account previous appellate decisions and the levels of awards
in personal injury cases (see *John*; *Thompson*). In any case some defamation and false
imprisonment claims are tried at first instance by a judge alone, while there exists a
body of appellate cases to draw on in which judges have scrutinised jury awards in detail
and proffered their own views on appropriate quantum (in the defamation context see
P. Milmo and W. V. H. Rogers (eds.), *Gatley on Libel and Slander*, 11th edn. (London:
Sweet & Maxwell, 2008), Appendix 3).
132 See *Thompson* (false imprisonment cases); *Heil* v. *Rankin* [2001] QB 272 (personal injury
cases); *Vento* v. *Chief Constable of West Yorkshire Police* [2002] EWCA Civ. 1871 at [65]
(injury to feelings in the discrimination context).
133 Judicial Studies Board, *Guidelines for the Assessment of General Damages in Personal
Injury Cases*, 9th edn. (Oxford University Press, 2008).

of liability. For example, in providing guidance for awards for injury to feelings in the discrimination context the Court of Appeal looked to previous awards made in discrimination cases and guidance provided in case law and by the Judicial Studies Board, and had reference to the general levels of awards in personal injury, malicious prosecution and defamation cases.[134] In *Mosley*, the court considered the practice in defamation and personal injury cases in elaborating the approach to damages for an infringement of the claimant's privacy interests, while also discussing the distinct character and nature of an infringement of privacy.[135] In the case of *KD* the court was faced with the novel task of assessing damages for a successful claim of harassment under the Protection from Harassment Act 1997.[136] In assessing a figure for injury to feelings and anxiety caused by the harassment the court drew on the Judicial Studies Board guidelines on personal injury awards, and the Court of Appeal's guideline judgments on damages in false imprisonment cases,[137] and damages in the context of anti-discrimination law.[138]

As these examples demonstrate, English courts have been able to successfully read across common law damages principles to new contexts. Experience in the law of tort and in new fields of liability where a common law approach has been taken suggests that if a tort-based approach were adopted in the human rights context there would, over time, 'emerge a more or less coherent framework of awards which would, while recognising the particular features of particular cases, ensure that broadly comparable cases led to broadly comparable awards'.[139]

11.3 Conclusion

A strong case can be made for departing from the current mirror approach employed by the English courts and for the adoption of a tort-based approach.

The HRA deliberately does not afford Strasbourg decisions precedent value. Further, the direct application of Strasbourg principles, developed by a subsidiary, supranational institution, in domestic cases is questionable as a matter of principle, and the lower court judges have struggled to apply the problematic Strasbourg jurisprudence.

---

134 *Vento* at [45]–[64].   135 *Mosley* at [212]–[231].
136 *KD* v. *Chief Constable of Hampshire* [2005] EWHC 2550 (QB), at [184]–[193].
137 *Thompson*.   138 *Vento*.   139 See *John* at 608.

The vindicatory approach to damages developed in the context of the torts actionable *per se* provides an appropriate model for damages under the Act as a matter of principle, as it is consonant with, and gives practical effect to, the policy of protection of fundamental interests that underlies the primary rights. Furthermore, tort provides an established and reasonably coherent and principled body of precedent to draw on, and a tort-based approach would promote coherence and consistency across domestic law. In contrast, the current approach to damages under the HRA not only undermines the protection of fundamental rights, but has also resulted in incoherence and inconsistency across the English law of damages.

12

Property and housing

AMY GOYMOUR[*]

In 1828 the Real Property Commission was tasked with making 'diligent and full inquiry' into the English law of property. Just one year later, the Commissioners reached the bold conclusion that property law, 'except in a few comparatively unimportant particulars, appears to come almost as near to perfection as can be expected in any human institutions'.[1] One can only conjecture, but, had the Commissioners been asked whether property law respects the values that are today enshrined in the Convention and the HRA, their answer would likely have been that, as a near-faultless human institution, it does.

It is the aim of this chapter to ascertain the effect of the HRA on property and housing law: is the domestic property system a bastion so perfectly formed that it is fortified against attacks on human rights grounds; or does it have weaknesses that expose it to such challenges? From the point of view of the property lawyer, the issue is whether property law needs to be relearned and property tomes rewritten on account of human rights, with the possible effect that the rules of property law become less stable and predictable. From a citizen's perspective, the importance lies in whether the current property rules determine their rights conclusively, or whether the HRA provides them with any greater or lesser proprietary entitlement against other citizens.[2]

This chapter puts forward the view that private property law ought to be susceptible to proper scrutiny against the Convention rights. Until very recently, the domestic judiciary – echoing the attitude of the Real Property Commissioners in 1829 – demonstrated a deep-seated reluctance to view

---

* I am enormously grateful to Mark Elliott, David Feldman, Sarah Nield and Stephen Watterson for their comments on an earlier draft.
1 Real Property Commission, *First Report* (1829), pp. 3 and 6.
2 As Wilson LJ has colourfully put it, the question is whether human rights 'represent a reservoir of entitlement' upon which a citizen can draw, e.g., in order to 'resist an order for possession when domestic law leaves him defenceless': *Pirabakaran v. Patel* [2006] EWCA 685 at [41] ('*Pirabakaran*').

property law as anything but a flawless system in the face of human rights challenges. In the face of growing criticism from Strasbourg, the immunity from human rights that property law seemed to enjoy could not be, and indeed should not have been, sustained. Greater scrutiny via the Convention lens should reveal that, while much of property law is already compatible with the Convention rights, small patches might not be and deserve consideration for reform. Thus understood, the Convention and the HRA will not ravage property law's system like a rampant, destabilising virus, but instead can be used to identify deficiencies in property law and thus fuel important reform.

12.1 Scope and structure of the analysis

This chapter considers both real and personal property, and – within real property – cases that involve housing law.[3] In a book on private law, the focus is necessarily on private property law, such as the rules governing the transfer of freeholds, the acquisition of easements or adverse possession. Notwithstanding the term 'private', it should be recognised that this body of law applies not only to citizens, but also to the state in its ordinary dealings with property, for example, when selling and transferring a freehold estate; indeed, many of the cases considered in this chapter concern the application of private property law to emanations of the state. But private property law must be distinguished from those rules of public law that allow the state to exert specific public powers over property, for example, compulsory purchase and planning laws. These are not the concern of this chapter.

Several Convention rights have the potential to impact on property law. Of particular significance are Article 1 of the First Protocol (P1–1), which protects the peaceful enjoyment of possessions, and Article 8, which ensures respect for one's private and family life and one's home. Being the most significant in the property context, these two Convention rights form the focus of this chapter. Articles 6 (the right to a fair trial), 10 (guaranteeing freedom of expression), 11 (guaranteeing freedom of assembly) and 14 (prohibiting discrimination) might also impinge on property law but, given the small amount of case law these rights have generated in this context, they are not considered here.[4]

---

3 Note that the term 'property law' in this chapter refers to both property and housing law.
4 For a discussion of the impact of Arts. 11 and 12, see S. Gray and K. Gray, 'Civil Rights, Civil Wrongs and Quasi-Public Space', *European Human Rights Law Review* (1999), 46.

Understanding the manner in which Convention rights impact on property law is like solving a puzzle of many parts, for it involves at least three different and overlapping variables. First, account must be taken of the fact that property law is made up of an intricate mixture of case law and statute. Second, cases involving the intersection of property law and human rights might arise in either a horizontal dispute between private parties, or, where the state is a party, a vertical dispute. To add a final variable into the mix, relevant cases arise both in the domestic courts and in the Strasbourg court. Key to having a proper understanding of this area of law is to adopt a structured analysis that is sensitive to these three different variables.

This chapter divides the analysis into two key issues. First, it identifies the sort of property disputes to which the Convention and HRA apply and have effect (the *applicability issue*);[5] and, second, it considers the extent to which property law is compatible with human rights in those disputes (the *compatibility issue*). The argument put forward is that, in order properly to test property law's *compatibility*, the Convention ought to be widely *applicable* in property disputes.

12.2 Applicability of Convention rights in property cases

Much academic ink has been spilt over the question of whether human rights are enforceable in private disputes.[6] This chapter does not seek to go over that well-trodden ground; instead, it focuses specifically on the courts' reactions to property disputes. It argues that, in the interests of treating all aspects of property law consistently, the Convention ought to apply widely.

Articles 8 and P1–1 were designed to protect the citizen against direct interferences by the state. In *Marckx* v. *Belgium*, for example, Sir Gerald Fitzmaurice said that the 'chief, if not the sole object of [P1–1] was to prevent the arbitrary seizures, confiscation, extortions, or other capricious interferences with peaceful possession that many governments are – or

---

Also see *CIN Properties Ltd* v. *Rawlins* [1995] 2 EGLR 130; *Porter* v. *Commissioner of Police of the Metropolis* [1999] All ER (D) 1129; *Anderson* v. *United Kingdom* (1998) 25 EHRR CD 172; *Appleby* v. *United Kingdom* (2003) (App. No. 44306/98).

5 See Chapters 1 and 2 for introduction of this analysis.

6 *Ibid.* See further R. Buxton, 'The Human Rights Act and Private Law', *Law Quarterly Review*, 116 (2000), 48; and G. Phillipson, 'Clarity Postponed: Horizontal Effect after *Campbell*', in H. Fenwick, R. Masterman and G. Phillipson (eds.), *Judicial Reasoning under the UK HRA* (Cambridge University Press, 2007), ch. 6.

frequently have been – all too prone to resort to'.[7] And in relation to
Article 8, Lord Hope has noted that 'the emphasis is on the person's
home as a place where he is entitled to be free from arbitrary interference
by the public authorities'.[8] At their core, Articles 8 and P1–1 provide a
check on the exercise of public powers and, thus, have clear relevance
in cases concerning *public* property rules, such as compulsory purchase
and planning regulation. Any impact that these rights might have on
private property law must therefore be understood as being outside the
core. The task of this chapter is to understand the extent to which human
rights might creep into the private property domain. Table 12.1 below
summarises the various formats a dispute concerning domestic *private*
property law might take.

Table 12.1

	Vertical disputes	**Horizontal disputes**
International law level	1	2
Domestic law level	3	4

Boxes 1 and 2 concern cases decided under the Convention, as an international treaty, by the Strasbourg court, itself an international institution.
Boxes 3 and 4 represent cases brought in the domestic courts in which the
Convention is implemented via the HRA. Clearly, the Convention has the
most potential to wreak havoc on private property law if it has an impact
in private disputes in the domestic courts (Box 4 – shaded grey).[9] In order
to ascertain the extent to which this might be the case, it is important
as a preliminary exercise to examine the cases decided under the treaty
in Strasbourg. There are two reasons for this. First, the HRA is parasitic
upon the Convention rights, for it provides mechanisms by which the
Convention rights can be enforced in the domestic arena. Understanding
the content of Articles 8 and P1–1 as a matter of international law is a
prerequisite for assessing their impact in domestic property law cases.[10]
Second, when the Strasbourg court decides that a particular state's rules

---

7 (1979) 2 EHRR 330 at [20]. See further T. Allen, *Property Law and the Human Rights Act
   1998* (Oxford: Hart, 2005), ch. 1.
8 *Harrow LBC* v. *Qazi* [2003] UKHL 43, [2004] 1 AC 983 at [50] ('*Qazi*').
9 The Convention's impact on *private* property law in domestic vertical disputes (Box 3)
   could also be significant. That is because the courts' interpretation of property law in
   such cases might impact on the application of those property rules when they are applied
   in a wholly private dispute.
10 See also Phillipson, 'Clarity Postponed', p. 149.

fall foul of the Convention, that state is likely to take swift measures to bring its domestic law into line with the Convention. In this manner, decisions of the Strasbourg court influence the future direction of domestic property legislation.

12.2.1 Property disputes at international level

(1) Types of dispute

In disputes brought to the Strasbourg court, the relevant state is the defendant. There are two ways in which a state might be sued in relation to its private property rules. First, and most clearly, the state might have taken direct action in relation to its property against a citizen in accordance with private property law (Box 1). It might, for example, terminate a citizen's lease, or evict a trespasser from its land. Because the state is directly involved, the Convention is clearly applicable whether or not it is found to have been violated. Second, the case might arise out of a domestic dispute between two private citizens where the losing party wishes to complain about the compatibility of the state's laws with the Convention (Box 2). For example, a private landlord who loses his freehold to his tenant under the domestic rules of leasehold enfranchisement might challenge the legality of those rules in Strasbourg.[11] For the purpose of examining the effect of the Convention on private property law, cases falling into the first category are interesting but of only limited use. This is because if the Convention is violated by a public authority exercising private law property rights, the violation could be explained either by the incompatibility of private property law or by the fact that the state was a direct participant in the conduct. This chapter is concerned only with the compatibility of private law itself. It is therefore more instructive to focus on those cases in the second scenario (Box 2) concerning horizontal disputes. The more willing the Strasbourg court is to apply the Convention in purely private cases, the greater the potential impact of the Convention on property law in domestic cases.

(2) State responsibility in relation to horizontal disputes (Box 2)

(a) **General rule** The Strasbourg institutions have made it clear that the Convention is inapplicable to property disputes between private parties unless the state is somehow implicated. This general rule was articulated by the Commission in *H* v. *United Kingdom*.[12] H jointly owned

---

11 See, e.g., *James* v. *United Kingdom* (1986) 8 EHRR 123 ('*James*').   12 (1983) 33 DR.

an oil concession in Libya with British Petroleum (BP). H and BP agreed that BP would bear the cost of investigating the oil reserves and in return would receive a greater proportion of any resulting profit if the project found oil. Oil was indeed discovered, and money started rolling in. However, the Libyan Government expropriated the concession, causing H and BP's contract to be frustrated. The House of Lords found that BP was entitled to recoup its $40 million development costs from H under the Law Reform (Frustrated Contracts) Act 1943.[13] H proceeded to argue in Strasbourg that his liability to pay such a huge sum interfered with the rights he should have been able to enjoy as a joint owner of the concession under P1–1. The Commission made it clear that domestic regulations on joint ownership 'are in the exclusive province of private law and outside the scope of the Convention, unless state responsibility is in some way involved in affecting their exercise'. State responsibility was not engaged on the facts.

The Strasbourg institutions have been reluctant to give clear rules on exactly what type of conduct will engage state responsibility. Nonetheless, as a rule of thumb, the Commission accepted in *Bramelid* v. *Sweden* that a state is responsible for ensuring that its private property rules do not allow one citizen arbitrarily to infringe the rights of another.[14] In relation to P1–1, for example, this means that the Convention is relevant in ensuring that 'the law [of a state] does not create such inequality that one person could be arbitrarily and unjustly deprived of property in favour of another'.[15] On a broad reading of this statement, states might owe a duty to ensure that no private citizen ever infringes another citizen's rights. Were this the case, the Convention would always apply in private property disputes. Subsequent decisions, however, reveal that states' duties are far narrower than this, and that only in certain circumstances are states accountable for the condition of their laws. Pinning down what those circumstances are, however, is not straightforward. Statute-based rules and the common law require separate consideration.

(b) **Statute law**   Take a hypothetical statute that sanctions a transfer of A's private home to private party B without compensation being payable. A, aggrieved by his loss, argues that the state is responsible for his loss of property under P1–1 and his home under Article 8. Early decisions displayed a reluctance to hold a state responsible for its property

---

13 *BP Exploration Co (Libya) Ltd* v. *Hunt (No. 2)* [1983] 2 AC 352.
14 (1982) (App. Nos. 8588/79, 8589/7) (Commission decision on admissibility).
15 Paragraph 1(d).

legislation. For example, in *Bramelid* v. *Sweden*, decided in 1982, Swedish legislation compelled the applicant to sell his shares to a private party for less than market value. The Commission found that state responsibility was not engaged and the Convention therefore inapplicable. *H* v. *United Kingdom*, discussed above, paints a similar picture. Again, the Commission found that the state was not implicated in the dispute, despite legislation being the reason why H had to pay BP. Nonetheless, the Commission contemplated that state responsibility might have been triggered had the frustrated contracts legislation been enacted *after* the parties had entered into their contract because, in such a scenario, the state would be responsible for interfering with and changing existing private relations.

Recent decisions have gone much further. It would now appear that states are responsible under the Convention for any legislation that might be 'activated as a result of the inter-actions of private individuals',[16] regardless of when it was enacted. Indeed, in direct contrast to the Commission's decision in *Bramelid*, the Strasbourg court decided in *Kanala* v. *Slovakia* that state liability would be engaged by the operation of a statute that allowed one co-owner a right of pre-emption against the other owner at below market value.[17] Similarly, legislation allowing leasehold enfranchisement by tenants has triggered state responsibility,[18] as has the operation of statutes that impose rent restrictions on landlords, or that confer security of tenure on their tenants.[19] And in *Pye* v. *United Kingdom*, the state was held responsible for those provisions of the Limitation Act 1980 that allow a squatter to acquire rights against private owners of land.[20]

(c) **Common law** Much of English property law is non-statutory, or at least a hotchpotch of statute and common law. An important, yet difficult, question is whether the state is responsible for the operation of common law property rules, such as the prescription of easements under the doctrine of lost modern grant, or the mortgagee's right to possession of mortgaged property. More difficult still: would the state be responsible

---

16 *Pye* v. *United Kingdom* (2008) 46 EHRR 45 at [57].

17 *Kanala* v. *Slovakia* (2007) (App. No. 57239/00).

18 See *James*. The state was responsible 'qua legislator'.

19 See, e.g., *Hutten-Czapska* v. *Poland* (2007) 45 EHRR 4 ('*Hutten-Czapska*') (although note that this was a case concerning a public sector landlord); *Ghigo* v. *Malta* (2006) (App. No. 31122/05); *Radovici* v. *Romania* (2006) (App. Nos. 68479/01, 71351/01, 71352/01).

20 For another example, see *Zehentner* v. *Austria* (2009) (App. No. 20082/02) ('*Zehentner*'), which concerned a judicial sale (pursuant to legislation) of private property to satisfy a private debt. It was considered that the state was responsible for ensuring adequate procedures were in place to protect the owner's Convention rights.

for the common law's enforcement of a private agreement relating to property, such as a lease?

The Strasbourg institutions have been slow to hold the state responsible for the common law. It would appear that the state is not automatically accountable for the operation of common law property rules, as it would be for statute-based rules; instead, the Strasbourg court asks whether the result reached by the law in a given situation is one that the Convention requires the state to take steps to guard against. In Convention jurisprudence, this is known as the doctrine of 'positive obligations'.[21] The doctrine is potentially far-reaching, for it exposes the state to liability not just for the condition of its common law rules, but also for any omissions or gaps in its legal framework. *Guerra* v. *Italy* provides a good illustration of the doctrine's application in the context of tort law. There, a private chemical factory in Italy had caused harm to local residents by emitting noxious gases. Having no redress against the chemical company under Italian law, the residents took their case to Strasbourg. They argued, successfully, that the state owed a positive duty, under Article 8, to protect one private party (the residents) against harm caused by another private party (the chemical company).[22]

The Commission decision in *Di Palma* v. *United Kingdom* illustrates how the doctrine might be relevant in a dispute concerning property law.[23] A private landlord forfeited his tenant's 99-year lease in accordance with the leasehold agreement for non-payment of the service charge. The County Court, having confirmed that the lease was properly forfeited, made a possession order in the landlord's favour. The order was later affirmed by the High Court and Court of Appeal. As the value of the long lease far exceeded the outstanding service charge debt, the tenant argued in Strasbourg that the forfeiture violated her rights to enjoy her lease under Articles 8 and P1–1. The Commission rightly recognised that it 'must first examine the way in which state responsibility arises'.[24] Because the dispute concerned a private leasehold agreement, the terms of which were governed by the common law not statute,[25] state responsibility was not engaged automatically. That was true even though the outcome of the dispute was determined by the state's courts, because the state's judicial

---

21 See generally A. Mowbray, *The Development of Positive Obligations under the ECHR by the European Court of Human Rights* (Oxford: Hart, 2004).

22 See also *Öneryildiz* v. *Turkey* (2005) 41 EHRR 20; this is discussed in more detail in Chapter 8.

23 (1986) 10 EHRR 149 ('*Di Palma*').   24 *Di Palma* 209.

25 *Di Palma* 210.

system 'merely provided the forum for the determination of the civil right in dispute' and did not itself interfere with the parties' rights. The Commission said that the state would be implicated only if it was 'under a positive obligation to protect the property rights of an individual in the context of their dispute with another private individual'.[26]

It is clear from this that the Convention's potential to impact on common law property rules depends on how widely drawn are the state's positive obligations. Unfortunately, the breadth of the duty is hard to pin down. Hypothetically, at its broadest, the state's duty could consist in ensuring that every citizen's Article 8 and P1–1 rights are respected by all other private citizens, thus giving the Convention extensive horizontal applicability. Conversely, the state's obligations might be more limited. The Commission in *Di Palma* favoured the restrictive interpretation and decided, on the facts, that because the forfeiture of the tenant's lease was governed by the terms of a purely private agreement, the state's liability was not engaged at all. The Commission declined to give any further guidance as to when a positive obligation might arise in future private property cases.

Subsequent decisions have given mixed signals. Some cases have indicated that private property disputes never engage the Convention.[27] However, more recently, the Strasbourg court has hinted that the state's positive obligations might reach into such disputes. In *Anheuser-Busche Inc.* v. *Portugal*, for example, the Strasbourg court observed that P1–1 entailed the state taking 'measures to protect the right of property' in litigation between private parties.[28] Similarly, in *Tudor Tudor* v. *Romania*, the court countenanced a state being responsible for the effect on private parties of its non-statutory rules of ownership.[29] And, in a similar vein, albeit in a domestic case, Wilson LJ recognised that the state might be under a positive obligation to provide legislation to protect a homeowner when his lease is forfeited under the common law by a private landlord.[30]

Any movement towards the Convention being applicable, via the doctrine of positive obligations, to common law as well as to legislation should

26 *Di Palma* 210.
27 See, e.g., *Skowronski* v. *Poland* (2001) (App. No. 52595/99) (a dispute concerning the sale of co-owned property); and *Kranz* v. *Poland* (2002) (App. No. 6214/02). See further Allen, *Human Rights*, pp. 231–2.
28 (2007) 45 EHRR 36 at [83]. See further *Ion Constantin* v. *Romania* (2010) (App. No. 38515/03) at [32].
29 (2009) (App. No. 21911/03). See similarly *Belchikova* v. *Russia* (2010) (App. No. 2408/06).
30 *Pirabakaran* at [45].

be welcomed. Property law in England and Wales consists in an 'inextrica-
ble tangle'[31] of both types of law. Indeed, Lord Walker has metaphorically
remarked that 'common law' rights in property are often 'surrounded on
all sides by statutory infrastructure, like a patch of grass in the middle of
a motorway junction'.[32] This being so, it would be manifestly arbitrary,
from the perspective of property law, to hold a state responsible under
the Convention for one type of law and not the other.

12.2.2 Property disputes at domestic level

The enforcement of human rights in domestic property disputes (Boxes 3
and 4 of the table) must now be addressed. As discussed above, the HRA
operates by bringing the Convention rights into domestic law, such that
they are directly enforceable in domestic courts. Two points follow from
this. First, and most obviously, the Convention can be enforced only in a
domestic property dispute to the extent that the provisions of the HRA
allow. Second, the HRA is parasitic upon the Convention, in the sense that
the HRA is merely the machinery for bringing the rights, created by the
Convention, into the domestic arena. As described above, the Convention
rights, emanating as they do from an international treaty, have meaningful
content only if they engage a state's responsibility. For the Convention to
apply in a domestic property dispute, the relevant facts must be such that
they would have engaged state responsibility had the facts arisen before the
Strasbourg court, because only then is a Convention right in play.[33] Thus,
there are two hurdles for a litigant to clear in order for the Convention
to be applicable to a domestic property dispute. First, that the state's
liability is engaged. It was argued above that state responsibility should
be cast widely, which would render the first hurdle easy to clear. Second,
the applicant must show that the HRA machinery allows the relevant
Convention right to be applied in the domestic arena. The following
analysis considers that second hurdle, and assumes that the first has been
cleared.

31 *Doherty* v. *Birmingham City Council* [2008] UKHL 57, [2009] 1 AC 367 at [96] *per* Lord
    Walker ('*Doherty* HL'). See further J. Howell, 'The Human Rights Act 1998: Land, Private
    Citizens, and the Common Law', *Law Quarterly Review*, 123 (2007), 618.
32 *Doherty* HL at [100].
33 See Phillipson, 'Clarity Postponed', p. 149; this is subject to the argument that the HRA
    might do more than replicate the Convention rights by making the courts 'public authori-
    ties' under s. 6, and so requiring the courts to apply the Convention in wider circumstances
    than those which would engage state responsibility in Strasbourg. See Chapters 1 and 2.

(1) Disputes between a public authority and a private citizen
(Box 3)

As discussed above, disputes concerning private property law arise frequently between public authorities and citizens. Examples include a public authority landlord, having terminated a lease according to the terms of the leasehold agreement, seeking to evict the former tenant; or an authority evicting a trespassing traveller; or a public authority adversely possessing a private citizen's land. In such circumstances, can the citizen rely on his Convention rights, via the HRA, to resist the consequences of domestic property law? In particular, does Article 8 – which guarantees respect for the home – offer a citizen who is dwelling on the property a defence to the local authority's possessory claim?

In theory, there is a good deal of scope for applying the Convention to such a scenario because, in addition to the other enforcement mechanisms of the HRA, section 6 specifically obliges public authorities to act compatibly with the Convention. In practice, however, until the recent Supreme Court decision in *Manchester City Council* v. *Pinnock*,[34] the domestic courts persistently – and, it is suggested, wrongly – prevented the Convention from having a significant impact on public authorities' private property rights. To appreciate the extent of the sea-change that *Pinnock* brought about, it is instructive to consider first the domestic courts' earlier, restrictive, approach to the Convention. The discussion here is limited to Article 8. Although not discussed expressly in the cases, it is likely that the same principles of 'applicability' would also be relevant to P1–1.[35]

(a) **The position prior to *Pinnock***   The question of the applicability of Article 8 arose three times before the House of Lords – in *Harrow LBC* v. *Qazi*,[36] *Kay* v. *Lambeth LBC; Leeds CC* v. *Price* (a conjoined appeal)[37] and *Doherty* v. *Birmingham City Council*.[38] In a parallel series of decisions, the Strasbourg court itself ruled on the same issue in three cases brought against the United Kingdom: *Connors*,[39] *McCann*[40] and *Kay*.[41] The two

---

34 [2010] UKSC 45, [2010] 3 WLR 1441. See also the subsequent decision of the Supreme Court in *Hounslow LBC* v. *Powell* [2011] UKSC 8, [2011] 2 WLR 287.

35 Of course, the substantive 'compatibility' issue will be dealt with differently under the two Convention rights.

36 [2003] UKHL 43, [2004] 1 AC 983.   37 [2006] UKHL 10, [2006] 2 AC 465 ('*Kay*').

38 [2008] UKHL 57, [2009] 1 AC 367.   39 (2005) 40 EHRR 9.

40 (2008) 47 EHRR 40.   41 (2010) (App. No. 37341/06).

courts adopted strikingly opposed views on the Convention's applicability: while the Strasbourg court embraced the Convention in property disputes, the Lords fought vigorously to defend property law from human rights interferences. The following analysis briefly chronicles the battle between the two courts, and advances the view that the Lords' insular view could not be justified and was unsustainable in the face of growing criticism from Strasbourg.

Qazi, the first in the trio of domestic cases, involved a local authority that had leased one of its apartments to a married couple jointly. Following the breakdown of their relationship, the wife moved out and unilaterally served a notice to quit on the landlord which, as a matter of domestic law, brought the joint tenancy to an end.[42] The local authority thereupon sought to recover possession from the husband who was by then a trespasser in the apartment. The House of Lords, by a bare majority, dismissed the husband's Article 8 defence, holding that 'contractual and proprietary rights to possession cannot be defeated by a defence based on Article 8'.[43] Accordingly, domestic law was deemed inherently compatible with the Convention. It should be noted that the *Qazi* decision was reached on the *compatibility* rather than the *applicability* issue; nonetheless, by their recognition that, as a blanket rule, proprietary claims comply with Article 8, the House of Lords by the same stroke effectively rendered the Convention right inapplicable in such cases.

A similar issue arose before the House of Lords in the conjoined appeal of *Kay; Price*. Their Lordships were asked to reconsider the position they had taken in *Qazi* in the light of the intervening decision of the Strasbourg court in *Connors*.[44] There, a local authority had licensed certain gypsies to stay on its land. The gypsies behaved anti-socially. Lawfully under domestic law, the authority terminated the gypsies' licence and sought to evict them. In their defence the gypsies established in the Strasbourg court that their rights under Article 8 had been violated. Significantly, this meant that, contrary to the opinion of the Lords in *Qazi*, as a matter of Convention law, domestic property law could not be regarded as inherently compatible with Article 8 and that for the United Kingdom to

---

42 *Hammersmith and Fulham LBC* v. *Monk* [1992] 1 AC 478.

43 *Qazi* at [84] *per* Lord Hope. Note, however, that Lords Hope and Millett (speaking in the majority) reserved their opinion in obiter dicta as to whether an Art. 8 argument might succeed in 'exceptional circumstances'. Unfortunately, it was unclear as to when the exception might apply and what it might entail.

44 (2005) 40 EHRR 9.

bring itself into line with the Convention, it was necessary to give Article 8 a voice in domestic cases. The House of Lords was presented with the opportunity of doing this in *Kay; Price*. Reflecting the importance of the issue, the House sat as a committee of seven. *Kay* is of most relevance here.[45] It concerned a local authority that, having lawfully terminated a lease, sought to evict former tenants from its land.[46] Their Lordships recognised a tension between the occupiers' rights to raise an Article 8 defence and the 'colossal waste of time and money' that would result if for every possession action of this sort the judge had to consider the Convention.[47] Accordingly, they carefully circumscribed the situations in which an occupier might raise Article 8 as a defence to a possession claim. A majority of four to three identified just two ways in which the tenants might challenge the eviction, neither of which was satisfied on the facts. Lord Hope, supported by the rest of the majority,[48] set out the breadth of these two 'Gateways', as subsequently they became known.[49]

First, Gateway (a) allowed the occupiers to challenge, via the mechanisms in the HRA, 'the law' that led to their eviction. For the tenants in *Kay*, this would entail establishing that the relevant rules on leases and recovery of possession were themselves – in the abstract and without reference to the occupiers' personal plight – incompatible with the Convention. Demonstrating that the abstract law violates the Convention is difficult, and is discussed in section 12.3 below. For the purposes of the applicability of the Convention rights, the recognition of Gateway (a) was significant for it provided, at least in theory, an outlet for directly attacking property law on Convention grounds, which the House of Lords in *Qazi* had ruled out.

Second, Lord Hope recognised that the local authority's 'decision' to evict the tenants and initiate possession proceedings would be susceptible to judicial review, for example, on grounds that the decision was 'arbitrary, unreasonable or disproportionate'.[50] Judicial review could be

---

45 For *Price*, see p. 290 below.

46 The occupier's 'tenancy' was of the type recognised in the case of *Bruton* v. *London and Quadrant Housing Trust* [2000] 1 AC 406, whereby the occupier's landlord was himself merely a licensee of the freehold owner. That licence was terminated, thus precipitating the simultaneous termination of the occupier's 'tenancy'.

47 *Kay* at [55].   48   *Kay* at [110].

49 *Doherty* v. *Birmingham City Council* [2006] EWCA Civ. 1739, [2007] HLR 32 at [22] *per* Carnwath LJ (*Doherty* CA). See also *Doherty* HL at [10] *per* Lord Hope.

50 *Kay* at [114].

initiated either by an application for review in the Administrative Court or, crucially, collaterally via Gateway (b), as a defence to possession proceedings in the County Court.[51]

Thus, the Gateways worked in tandem, providing the occupier with a seemingly strong, two-pronged defence against eviction. However, they fell short as effective guardians of an occupier's Article 8 rights: the majority in *Kay* considered that, while Article 8 – and by implication other Convention rights – was relevant to the Gateway (a) defence, it was wholly irrelevant to Gateway (b). Thus, the Convention could fuel a systemic attack on the *law* via Gateway (a), but was irrelevant when reviewing the local authority's *decision* to enforce its domestic property rights. Thus, Gateway (a) was to be the sole channel for human rights arguments. The minority, by contrast, rightly recognised Article 8 as integral to both Gateways.[52]

The Strasbourg court and the domestic courts reacted to *Kay* with diametrically opposed views. For the former, *Kay* represented an unacceptably narrow approach to the Convention, as its decision in *McCann* revealed.[53] The case concerned married joint tenants of a council property. The wife moved out owing to domestic violence and was re-housed. The local authority then sought to terminate the couple's joint tenancy with a view to placing the husband in a smaller council property. There were two routes to achieving this. First, the Housing Act 1985 provided that an authority could apply to a court for a termination of the lease and repossession of the property,[54] provided certain statutory grounds were satisfied and the court considered it would be reasonable to make the order. The local authority, however, chose to bypass this first route, preferring instead to rely on the second method, recognised by the common law, which involved procuring one of the joint tenants to sign a notice to quit, thereby terminating the tenancy.[55] In her husband's absence, the authority persuaded the wife to serve a notice without explaining the legal consequences to her. The authority then sought to evict the husband. Having applied – unsuccessfully – for judicial review of the council's conduct,[56] the husband took his case to Strasbourg, where it was held that the council had violated the Convention. The Strasbourg court considered that any person at risk of losing his or her home should be able 'to have the proportionality of the measure determined by an

---

51 *Kay* at [110].   52 *Kay* at [39].   53 (2008) 47 EHRR 40 ('*McCann*').
54 Housing Act 1985, s. 82.   55 See p. 260 above.
56 *McCann* v. *Birmingham City Council* [2004] EWHC 2156 (Admin).

independent tribunal... notwithstanding that, under domestic law, his right of occupation has come to an end'.[57] At no juncture had the husband's Article 8 rights been properly considered. First, the local authority itself, by opting for the common law method of terminating the tenancy, had absolved itself of the need to justify its action within the Housing Act. Second, in summary possession proceedings such as those brought against the husband, the court had had no opportunity to scrutinise the impact of a possession order on his rights. Third, and most significantly, the Strasbourg court found that the judicial review procedure 'did not provide any opportunity for an independent tribunal to examine whether the applicant's loss of his home was proportionate under Art 8(2) to the legitimate aims pursued'.[58] This being so, *McCann* effectively decided that the approach in *Kay*, with its narrow construction of Gateway (b), paid insufficient deference to a citizen's Article 8 rights. The Strasbourg court confirmed this view in *Kay* v. *United Kingdom*, where it decided that in *Kay* itself, the occupiers' Article 8 rights should have been considered by a domestic court and, on the facts, had been violated.[59]

Notwithstanding the decision in *McCann*, domestic courts persisted in keeping Article 8 away from Gateway (b) reviews of local authorities' decisions.[60] Most notably, in *Doherty*,[61] the House of Lords itself, this time sitting as a committee of five, confirmed that Gateway (b) was limited to those grounds of judicial review 'that have nothing to do with the European Convention'.[62] As Toulson LJ subsequently put it, the reviewing court had to apply 'public law principles as they [had] been developed at common law, and not through the lens of the Convention'.[63] On the one hand, this approach carried the distinct practical advantage of allowing possessory actions to be processed efficiently and speedily by County Court judges, unburdened by questions of compatibility with

---

57 *McCann* at [50].   58 *McCann* at [53].   59 (2010) (App. No. 37341/06).

60 *Mullen* v. *Salford City Council* [2010] EWCA Civ. 336 ('*Mullen*'); *R (Coombes)* v. *Secretary of State for Communities and Local Government* [2010] EWHC 666 (Admin), [2010] 2 All ER 940 ('*Coombes*'); *Poplar Housing* v. *Howe* [2010] EWHC 1745; *Wilson* v. *Harrow LBC* [2010] EWHC 1574 (QB) ('*Wilson*'); and *R (Husband)* v. *Solihull MBC* [2009] EWHC 3673 (Admin).

61 [2008] UKHL 57, [2009] 1 AC 367.

62 *Doherty* HL at [109] *per* Lord Walker.

63 *Doran* v. *Liverpool City Council* [2009] EWCA Civ. 146 at [48]–[50] ('*Doran*'). See *Doherty* CA; *Wandsworth LBC* v. *Dixon* [2009] EWHC 27 (Admin); *Defence Estates* v. *JL* [2009] EWHC 1049 (Admin) ('*JL*'); *Stokes* v. *Brent LBC* [2009] EWHC 1426; *Manchester City Council* v. *Pinnock* [2009] EWCA Civ. 852; *Mullen*; and *Coombes*.

Article 8.[64] On the other hand, not only was the Lords' approach incompatible with the Convention, it was legally problematic under domestic law too. Section 6(1) of the HRA provides that it is 'unlawful for a public authority to act in a way which is incompatible with a Convention right'; as such, a reviewing court (in either an application for judicial review or a collateral challenge) should consider whether a public body, in deciding to exercise its property rights, has acted consistently with the Convention. The House of Lords in *Kay* and *Doherty* rendered this sort of review impossible.

Three justifications for the narrowness of Gateway (b) might be gleaned from their Lordships' judgments in *Kay* and *Doherty*; yet none was satisfactory. First, the majority in *Kay* seemed to think that Gateway (a) was sufficient for protecting one's Article 8 rights. According to the majority's analysis, if a local authority's domestic proprietary and procedural rights were compatible with the Convention, the decision to enforce those rights would necessarily also be compliant.[65] While this argument might have some superficial appeal, it is flawed: it is quite possible for a domestic regime itself to be compatible with the Convention, but to be applied in an incompatible way. Indeed, there have been cases, albeit not involving a possessory claim, where this has occurred.[66] Usually, the *law* (be it common law or legislation) is not absolutely prescriptive in its operation, but instead confers a choice or discretion. For example, someone with a domestic law proprietary right is able to choose whether and when to vindicate that right. The *law* itself might be entirely consistent with the Convention in conferring the discretion, but a decision made under that law might not be. Take the *McCann* case as an example. There, the tenancy could have been terminated either via the procedure in the Housing Act, or by procuring the wife's notice to quit. Nowhere in the Strasbourg court's decision was it suggested that either of those processes was itself unlawful; it was the local authority's *decision* to approach the wife, and the

---

64 Of course, it would have been open to an occupier to launch a systemic attack on the applicable *law*, under Gateway (a), but it would be difficult to demonstrate that the whole scheme was incompatible with Art. 8.

65 See further *Treharne* v. *Secretary of State for Work and Pensions* [2008] EWHC 2222 (QB) at [15] and A. Goymour, 'Proprietary Claims and Human Rights – A "Reservoir of Entitlement"', *Cambridge Law Journal*, 65 (2006), 696 at 705.

66 See *Gillow* v. *United Kingdom* (1989) 11 EHRR 335 at [56]–[58]. See, however, *R (Pro-Life Alliance)* v. *BBC* [2003] UKHL 23, [2003] 2 WLR 1403, where the House of Lords adopted the opposite approach. Cf. E. Barendt, 'Free Speech and Abortion', *Public Law* (2003), 580.

manner in which it obtained her signature, which caused the husband's
Article 8 rights to be infringed.[67]

Second, a majority of the House of Lords in *Doherty* justified the
irrelevance of the Convention to Gateway (b) by reference to section 6(2)
of the HRA. That provision states that an act of a public authority will
not be unlawful under section 6(1) if either:

(a) as the result of one or more provisions of primary legislation, the
authority could not have acted differently; or

(b) in the case of one or more provisions of, or made under, primary
legislation which cannot be read or given effect in a way which is
compatible with the Convention rights, the authority was acting so
as to give effect to or enforce those provisions.

Where it applies, section 6(2) renders lawful the conduct of public bodies which infringe the Convention and would otherwise be unlawful
under section 6(1). The majority in *Doherty* considered that section 6(2)
should be given a wide meaning. The subsection would rightly absolve
the public authority where legislation *obliged* it to act in an infringing
manner (section 6(2)(a)). Yet the majority went further and considered
that it should also exempt a public authority from liability where it had
a statutory *power* to act (section 6(2)(b)). That would be so even if the
authority could, within its discretion, have chosen to apply the statute
in a compatible, rather than an incompatible, manner. This was utterly
unconvincing. It is misconceived to interpret section 6(2)(b) as sanction-
ing the incompatible exercise of a statutory power that could have been
exercised compatibly with the Convention. That would result in section
3, which requires legislation to be read in a compatible manner, being
deprived of any real meaning in relation to the actions of public bodies.
The majority justified their reasoning on the basis that were the public
authority compelled to exercise their discretion in a compatible manner,
that would in effect turn the 'power' into a 'duty', which would subvert
Parliament's intentions when enacting that statute.[68] But this argument

67 The case of *Coombes* might also have been decided differently had the court followed
McCann and not *Doherty* HL. A local authority sought to evict the son of its deceased
tenant, who had no right to remain under domestic law, but who had lived in the property
for fifty years. Following *Doherty* HL, the local authority's *decision* to evict could not be
challenged under Art. 8; under *McCann* it could have been and a challenge might have
been successful.

68 See especially Lord Walker at [111]–[124]. Note that his Lordship did not, in principle, agree with his conclusions but deemed himself bound by the decision in *Kay*. See

can be turned on its head: surely, it is more subversive of Parliament's intentions not to give full meaning to section 3 of the HRA, a statute which by its nature sanctions the purposive construction of statutes.

A third possible justification for keeping Article 8 out of Gateway (b) was that the traditional grounds of judicial review provided sufficient protection to Article 8 anyway, thus obviating the need to consider Article 8 separately.[69] The problem with such an approach is that judicial review on the traditional grounds of *Wednesbury* unreasonableness or irrationality is regarded as a lesser form of review than that which is demanded by the proportionality test in Article 8. Admittedly, the gap between the two tests has narrowed: even before the HRA was in force, the courts had started to weave the Convention into domestic law by bringing the *Wednesbury* test closer to proportionality.[70] But in spite of the gap closing, the Strasbourg court has expressly stated that there is still daylight between the tests.[71] The *McCann* case exhibits the gap well. There, the husband had failed to demonstrate that the council had acted unlawfully according to domestic public law, and yet the Strasbourg court decided that his Article 8 rights, for which the proportionality test applied, had been infringed. In a seemingly desperate bid to save Gateway (b) from the Strasbourg court's damning criticism, Lord Hope in *Doherty* purported to widen the grounds of judicial review. He said that, within Gateway (b), review should be wider than the traditional *Wednesbury* grounds, such that the court should ask whether the local authority's 'decision to recover possession' was one which no reasonable person would consider justifiable'.[72] Subsequent cases have treated this as a heightened form of review compared with the normal *Wednesbury* test.[73] Indeed, the Strasbourg court in *Kay* contemplated, without deciding the issue, that Gateway (b) might have expanded sufficiently to satisfy Article 8.[74] With respect, however, that was probably not the case, because the broader Gateway (b) test given

---

further D. Feldman (ed.), *English Public Law* (Oxford University Press, 2009), paras. 7.81–7.86.

69 Lord Hope in *Kay* at [100]. See also *Doherty* HL at [9], [53], [69] and *Mullen* at [61], where Waller LJ suggests that conventional judicial review is being increasingly informed by principles of fundamental rights.

70 *Doran* at [52]. Prior to the HRA, in certain circumstances, courts were prepared to review administrative decisions with 'anxious scrutiny': *R* v. *Secretary of State for the Home Department, ex p. Bugdaycay* [1987] 1 AC 514.

71 See, e.g., *Smith and Grady* v. *United Kingdom* (2000) 29 EHRR 493 at [136]–[137]; *R (Association of British Civilian Internees (Far East Region))* v. *Secretary of State for Defence* [2003] EWCA Civ. 743, [2003] QB 1397 at [33]–[37] and *Doherty* HL at [135].

72 *Doherty* HL at [55].   73 *Doran* at [46] and *Doherty* HL at [116].

74 (2010) (App. No. 37341/06) at [73]. See also *Pinnock* [2009] EWCA Civ 852.

in *Doherty* was formulated in an almost identical fashion to Lord Greene MR's test in *Wednesbury* itself, *viz.* that the court must examine whether a decision was one that 'no reasonable authority could ever have come to'.[75] Therefore, the better view is that a gap continued to exist between traditional review under Gateway (b) and proportionality, the former being an unacceptably substandard guardian of Article 8 rights.[76] Thus, prior to *Pinnock*, the domestic courts clung to their view that the Convention should rarely – and only via Gateway (a) – upset established domestic property law principles. As such, the law of property retained strong – albeit not complete – fortifications against human rights challenges.

(b) The decision in *Pinnock* In terms of the *applicability* of the Convention to property disputes, the Supreme Court's decision in *Manchester City Council* v. *Pinnock* brought property law's fortifications tumbling down.[77] That decision has since been confirmed by the Supreme Court's decision in *Hounslow LBC* v. *Powell*.[78] In *Pinnock* itself, a local authority landlord had sought to evict a secured tenant on the basis of his five children's severe anti-social behaviour. The council had first made a successful application to the court for a 'demotion order', which had removed the tenant's secured status.[79] Thereafter, the tenant having breached the conditions of his demoted tenancy, the authority terminated the agreement and applied to the court for an eviction order. The Supreme Court was invited to review the extent to which such an occupier might raise Article 8 as a defence to domestic possession proceedings.

Sitting as a committee of nine, the judges of the Supreme Court in *Pinnock* were freed from the shackles of the Lords' narrow approach in *Kay*, which had been decided by a committee of seven.[80] Lord Neuberger gave the single and unanimous judgment of the court. His Lordship's reasoning was carefully confined to vertical disputes, leaving it to be

---

75 [1948] 1 KB 223 at 230 *per* Lord Greene MR.

76 See *Doherty* HL at [116] and [135]. See also *JL* at [46], *Mayor of London* v. *Hall* [2010] EWCA Civ. 817; *Wilson* at [36]; and the suggestions of counsel in *McGlynn* v. *Welwyn Hatfield DC* [2009] EWCA Civ. 285.

77 [2010] UKSC 45, [2010] 3 WLR 1441 ('*Pinnock*').

78 [2011] UKSC 8, [2011] 2 WLR 287 ('*Powell*'). Unfortunately, *Powell* was decided too recently for a full discussion in this chapter; only the most important details have been included.

79 See Housing Act 1985, s. 82A and Housing Act 1996, s. 143B–F.

80 In *Doherty* HL, sitting as a committee of five, their Lordships considered themselves bound by the decision of the seven-strong committee in *Kay*. As a matter of constitutional law, this assumption is questionable; however, it is beyond doubt that the Supreme Court, sitting in *Pinnock* as a committee of nine, had the ability to depart from *Kay*.

decided another day how Article 8 might impact on property disputes between private individuals.[81] In terms of the *applicability* of the Convention, his Lordship reached the inevitable conclusion that 'it would be wrong' for the domestic courts to continue fighting against the clear Strasbourg view.[82] This meant that, in principle, when asked to make a possession order in favour of a public authority, a domestic court 'must have the power to measure the proportionality' of making the order in the particular circumstances.[83] This would be implemented in practice by giving the court – normally the County Court – the power to review decisions made by the authority seeking possession, and to decide afresh, according to its own assessment of the facts, whether it would be proportionate to evict the occupier. Accordingly, the judge should be able to choose between declining, postponing or making a possession order as appropriate.[84] Lord Neuberger regarded this as a form of judicial review, expanded – as it should be – by sections 6 and 7 of the HRA to take account of Article 8.[85] His Lordship rightly dismissed the majority's argument in *Doherty* that section 6(2) would immunise a public authority from human rights challenges when exercising statutory powers. Significantly, as a counterbalance to the potential burden this new test would place on County Court judges, the Supreme Court stated that Article 8 should be considered only if raised by the occupier and, even then, only summarily at first.[86] The Supreme Court in *Powell*, sitting as a committee of seven, subsequently confirmed unanimously its approach in *Pinnock*.

These two Supreme Court judgments should be warmly welcomed, for they finally bring domestic law in line with the state's Convention obligations. More significantly from the perspective of property law, they

---

81 *Pinnock* at [4] and [50].   82 *Pinnock* at [48].

83 *Pinnock* at [49]. See also *Powell* at [7] *per* Lord Hope. Although the position was left unclear after *Pinnock*, the Supreme Court confirmed that a court must consider Art. 8, if raised by the occupier, *even if* there is no specific legislative requirement requiring it to assess the 'reasonableness of a public authority's decision': [34].

84 *Pinnock* at [62]–[63], [80]–[81].

85 *Pinnock* at [73], [78]. Unfortunately, however, there is a suggestion in Lord Phillips' speech in *Powell* that a public authority's Art. 8 obligations might differ from their 'English public law' duties: [89]. The preferred view is that Art. 8 forms part and parcel of a public authority's duties under public law.

86 *Pinnock* at [61]. Note that the same point was made in *Paulić v. Croatia* (2009) (App No. 3572/06) ('*Paulić*'). See also *Powell* at [33] *per* Lord Hope, which adds the requirement that the occupier's Art. 8 argument must be 'seriously arguable' in order to be taken further.

render Article 8 widely *applicable* in domestic claims for possession. Gone is the *Kay* distinction between the *law* (Gateway (a)) and its *application* (Gateway (b)): both are now equally susceptible to an Article 8 challenge.[87] In place of the ruined gateways now stands a wide door giving Article 8 full access to property law, at least in a vertical dispute. This level of applicability is entirely appropriate; indeed, it is remarkable that property law had for so long until *Pinnock* remained so strongly insulated from the Convention in vertical cases.

(2) Disputes between private citizens (Box 4)

Dealings with private property most often occur between private parties: for example, a landlord might forfeit a lease, a bank repossess a home or a squatter acquire title to another's land. If the Convention can be applied by domestic courts to these sorts of disputes, its impact on private law is potentially very significant.

This section considers how the Convention rights are enforced in a private domestic dispute, which raises difficult issues concerning the horizontal effect of the Convention in the domestic courts, which have been considered in an earlier chapter.[88] Rather than revisiting the detail of those arguments, this chapter asks, in the specific context of property and housing law, whether the courts have admitted the Convention into private disputes. At the outset, it should be noted that domestic judges have been disappointingly reluctant to commit themselves to a view in the abstract.[89] Instead, they have said that the Convention's horizontal impact in the property law context will be developed on a case-by-case basis.

As a preliminary point, it was clear prior to the decision in *Pinnock* that private parties, in their disputes with one another, had access to Gateway (a) but not (b).[90] Thus, as Lord Scott had explained, 'unless a Gateway (a) attack on the domestic law [could] be sustained' the Convention had no part to play.[91] The Supreme Court in *Pinnock* expressly declined to discuss

---

87 Note that Lord Hope in *Powell* used the language of 'Gateways' ([5]–[6]). These references should not, however, amount to a restoration of the Gateways: it is clear from the remainder of Lord Hope's speech that any distinction between Gateways (a) and (b) can no longer be maintained.

88 See Chapter 2. For an excellent summary, see Phillipson 'Clarity Postponed'; and Allen, *Human Rights*, p. 249.

89 *Wilson* v. *First County Trust Ltd (No. 2)* [2004] 1 AC 816 at [174] (*'First County'*); *Kay* at [61], [64]; *Doherty* HL at [99]; and *Pinnock* at [4], [50].

90 *Kay* at [69].   91 *Kay* at [69].

the horizontal applicability of the Convention. Nonetheless, the court's complete abandonment of the two gateways brings the welcome consequence that there is no longer any distinction, whatever the configuration of the dispute, between the compatibility of the *law* and its *application* to particular facts. Thus, if the Convention applies in a horizontal dispute, there should be scrutiny of both the applicable abstract law (for example, the law of leases) and the way in which the law applies to the particular facts (for example, the impact of forfeiture of a lease on different types of private tenant).[92]

Of course, for the Convention to apply in a horizontal dispute before a domestic court, the aggrieved citizen must channel his or her argument through one or more of the enforcement mechanisms in the HRA.[93] The HRA applies differently according to the type of applicable law.

(a) Legislation   Where the alleged infringement emanates from a statute, the citizen could require that it be manipulated in order to give immediate effect to their Convention rights against the other party. For this, they would invoke the obligation in section 3 of the HRA to read, if possible, any statute associated with the violating claim in a manner compatible with the Convention. If this proves impossible, certain higher courts may make a declaration of incompatibility under section 4. This declaration would not offer a remedy in any real sense to the citizen in the particular dispute, but would facilitate a future change to the law.[94] Together, these two provisions have the potential to impact significantly on the development of statutory property law. Two cases illustrate their operation.

First, the House of Lords was pro-active in applying section 3 in *Ghaidan v. Godin-Mendoza*.[95] The claimant private landlord leased a flat to a tenant, who lived there in a homosexual relationship with his partner. The tenant died, and the landlord sought to evict the partner. Had he been in a heterosexual relationship, the partner would have been entitled by statute to take on the deceased's tenancy. However, the relevant legislation, given its ordinary meaning, did not extend to homosexual couples and thus infringed the defendant's rights under Articles 8 and 14. The House of Lords, empowered by section 3, manipulated the statute to allow the defendant to succeed to the tenancy. This in effect entailed a redistribution of proprietary entitlement.

---

92 See p. 262 above.   93 *Doherty* HL at [45].   94 See Chapter 4.
95 [2004] UKHL 30, [2004] 2 AC 557, discussed further in Chapter 4.

Second, in *Beaulane Properties* v. *Palmer*, a private landowner had lost its registered land to a squatter under the Limitation Act 1980.[96] The owner argued successfully in the High Court that this loss constituted an infringement of its P1–1 rights. Armed with section 3, the judge found in favour of the landowner by redefining the meaning of 'adverse possession' in the Limitation Act to render it impossible for the squatter to meet the criteria.[97] *Beaulane* has since, in substance, been reversed on the *compatibility* issue that is discussed below.[98] Nonetheless, the decision remains an important authority on the *application* of the Convention via section 3.[99]

(b) Courts' discretions Certain property rules require the courts to exercise their discretion in deciding whether a claim should be successful. For example, when one co-owner seeks the sale of a property as against another, the court is required to decide whether the sale is appropriate in the light of several competing factors.[100] It would appear that section 6 of the HRA requires the court, as a public authority, to exercise its discretion in a way that is compatible with the parties' Convention rights. To date, the Convention has been considered in relation to at least three judicial discretionary powers within the law of property: the power to order the sale of co-owned property;[101] the power to order sale pursuant to a charging order;[102] and, in relation to mortgage repossessions,

---

96 [2005] EWHC 817 (Ch), [2006] Ch 79.

97 This entailed adding a requirement that the squatter's possession must be adverse to the owner's intended use of the land. Significantly, such a requirement had been expressly rejected by the House of Lords in *JA Pye (Oxford) Ltd* v. *Graham* [2002] UKHL 30, [2003] 1 AC 419. See A. Cloherty and D. Fox, 'Heresies and Human Rights', *Cambridge Law Journal*, 64 (2005), 558.

98 *Pye* v. *United Kingdom* (2008) 46 EHRR 45 ('*Pye*'); and *Ofulue* v. *Bossert* [2008] EWCA Civ. 7, [2009] Ch 1. Cf. M. Dixon, 'Editor's Notebook', Conv. (2009), 169. Note, however, that the unfortunate squatter in *Beaulane* itself was unable to appeal against the judge's decision: *Beaulane Properties* v. *Palmer* (2008) Ref/2004/0014 (decision of adjudicator).

99 See also *First County; Earl Cadogan* v. *Pitts* [2008] UKHL 71, [2009] 2 WLR 12 (the House of Lords countenanced scrutiny of leasehold enfranchisement legislation); *Pennycook* v. *Shaws (EAL) Ltd* [2004] EWCA Civ. 100, [2004] Ch 296 ('*Pennycook*'); and *Sinclair* v. *Glatt* [2009] EWCA Civ. 176, [2009] 1 WLR 1845.

100 Trusts of Land and Appointment of Trustees Act 1996 (TLATA), ss. 14–15.

101 *Putnam & Sons* v. *Taylor* [2009] EWHC 317 (Ch) ('*Putnam*'). See also the obiter discussion in *Donohoe* v. *Ingram* [2006] EWHC 282 (Ch) ('*Donohoe*') and *Barca* v. *Mears* [2004] EWHC 2170 (Ch) ('*Barca*') concerning Insolvency Act 1986, s. 335A which applies where a co-owner is bankrupt.

102 Civil Procedure Rules, r. 73.10. See *Close Invoice Finance Ltd* v. *Pile* [2008] EWHC 1580 (Ch) ('*Close Invoice*').

the power to adjourn possession proceedings.[103] Each of these examples concerns a statutory discretion; however, in principle there is no reason why the courts' duties under section 6 should not extend to non-statutory powers as well.[104]

(c) **Common law** It has been seen that the HRA easily latches onto property legislation and discretionary powers. However, the bulk of property law lies within neither of these categories and instead involves rules – rather than discretions – created by the common law. Unfortunately, the extent to which the Convention might impact on common law property rules is far from certain. If the Convention is relevant at all, it will be section 6 which makes it so, the argument being that the court's obligation to act compatibly with the Convention encompasses a duty to manipulate the common law to give effect to Convention rights.[105]

The property cases give out mixed signals as to whether the section 6 duty extends this far. Some have indicated that the common law might be scrutinised, but only where one of the parties is a public authority. For example, in *Aston Cantlow Parochial Church Council* v. *Wallbank*,[106] a landowner sought to challenge the presence of a common law liability, binding his land, to repair a church chancel. The challenge failed in the House of Lords, which held that the parochial church council was not a public body and therefore not bound by section 6. However, it is hard to see why this should be a factor bearing on the *court's* – rather than the public body's – own obligation to comply with the Convention.

Since *Aston Cantlow*, the judiciary has been conspicuously non-committal. In particular, Lord Nicholls in *Kay* said 'whether . . . the court's section 6 obligation . . . affects the substantive law to be applied by the court when adjudicating upon disputes between private parties still awaits authoritative decision'.[107] More recently, the Supreme Court in *Pinnock* expressly avoided taking a position on the horizontal applicability of the HRA. Thus, it is still conceivable that the Convention will be set to work

---

103 Administration of Justice Act 1970, s. 36. See *Barclays Bank plc* v. *Alcorn* [2002] EWHC 498, [2002] EWCA Civ. 817 ('*Alcorn*'). Note that in these cases, where the discretion is conferred by statute, the court might have to rely on s. 3 of the HRA to bring the Convention to bear on the discretion. See *Barca* at [41].

104 Examples of a non-statutory judicial discretion would be the equitable power of a court to postpone a mortgagee's possession proceedings; or the court's power to award relief against forfeiture.

105 See Chapter 2.   106 [2004] 1 AC 546 ('*Aston Cantlow*').

107 *Kay* at [61]. See also *First County* at [174].

on the common law. While there is a risk that this would unsettle established property principles, that risk is worth taking. First, it would make for more consistent law in the long term if the Convention were allowed to seep into the whole of property law rather than just its statutory patches. As described above, whether particular facts are governed by statute or the common law is not a matter of design but rather a result of ad hoc legal development. From property law's perspective, the application of the Convention to one type of law and not the other would be incoherent. Second, even if the Convention is extensively *applicable*, it will have a destabilising impact only if significant parts of property law are found to be *incompatible* with the Convention and this is a separate issue. As section 12.3 below reveals, rarely will this be the case.

12.2.3 Conclusions on applicability of Convention rights

The Convention ought to be widely *applicable* in property disputes – whether the disputes are vertical or horizontal, whether they arise in the Strasbourg court or the domestic courts, and whether they concern legislation or the common law. Adopting this strategy avoids having to draw unprincipled distinctions: at all levels property law should be open to scrutiny. This means that attention will rightly shift to the *compatibility* issue to determine the impact of the Convention on property law.

12.3 Compatibility of property law with the Convention

This part considers the compatibility of property law with the Convention according to the jurisprudence of both the domestic and the Strasbourg courts. Property law comprises rules that determine the allocation of scarce and finite resources. Having been developed by judges and Parliament slowly over the centuries with a view to balancing 'conflicting social and economic pressures',[108] one would expect property law to operate broadly in line with the Convention, which itself requires a 'fair balance' to be struck between competing interests. The view advanced here is that, while much of property law indeed complies with the Convention, there are some dark areas where it might be found wanting. This means that the courts must be prepared to view property law through the Convention lens in order to illuminate those areas of incompatibility. To

---

108 *Kay* at [185] *per* Baroness Hale.

date, the judiciary has assumed too readily that property law is inherently Convention-compliant.

12.3.1 Article 1 of the First Protocol (P1–1)

P1–1 is a qualified right: while it asserts that 'every natural or legal person is entitled to the peaceful enjoyment of his possessions', P1–1 is not violated where there is an interference with property which is lawful under domestic law, in the public interest and proportionate with the aim being pursued.

As outlined above, the original function of P1–1 was to provide a check against arbitrary confiscation by the state.[109] Therefore, at its core, P1–1 is relevant to *public* rules of property; its impact on *private* property law must be regarded as peripheral to the core. The analysis here is structured by considering, first, the circumstances in which P1–1 might be engaged by private property law; and, second, when an interference might be justified and proportionate.

(1) Engagement of the right

(a) **Meaning of 'possessions'**   For the right to bite, there must be an interference with one's 'possessions'. The word 'possessions' has an 'autonomous meaning'[110] in the sense that the concept stretches across the signatory states and is not defined by reference to any given state's legal system. This is sensible, for otherwise a particular state could circumvent the spirit of P1–1 by adopting a narrow and technical definition of possessions such that its actions would rarely encroach upon its citizens' rights. The sorts of rights that qualify as 'possessions' are wide-ranging, including rights relating to tangible property (such as estates and other interests over land) as well as rights under contracts.[111] However, P1–1 is not unlimited in its scope: most significantly, P1–1 does not *confer* rights; it merely protects *existing* entitlements.[112]

---

109 *Marckx* v. *Belgium* (1979) 2 EHRR 330 at [20].
110 T. Allen, 'The Autonomous Meaning of "Possessions" under the European Convention on Human Rights', in E. Cooke (ed.), *Modern Studies in Property Law: Vol. 2* (Oxford: Hart, 2003), p. 58. See also B. McFarlane, N. Hopkins and S. Nield, *Land Law: Text, Cases and Materials* (Oxford University Press, 2009), p. 133.
111 See further D. Harris, M. O'Boyle, E. Bates and C. Buckley, *Law of the European Convention on Human Rights*, 2nd edn. (Oxford University Press, 2009), pp. 656–62.
112 Note that 'legitimate expectations' are protected, provided the applicant's claim relates to the existence of a current right, rather than a hope that a discretion might be exercised

(b) Forms of interference   It has been held by the Strasbourg court in *Sporrong and Lonnroth* v. *Sweden* that P1–1 guards against interferences with possessions by way of 'three distinct rules'.[113] First are interferences of a so-called 'general nature'; second are 'deprivations', such as compulsory purchase by the state;[114] and third are measures which 'control the use' of property, such as rent-control or planning restrictions.[115] While the second and third rules target specific types of interference, the first is a residual category which captures interferences which are neither deprivations nor controls of use. For example, there was a 'general' interference in *Loizidou* v. *Turkey* where the state prevented a homeowner from entering his own home.[116] Consistent with the notion that 'possessions' has an autonomous meaning, it should be noted that P1–1 is rightly engaged whether one's possessions are legally or merely factually affected.[117]

The threefold classification is not merely taxonomically elegant; it has important legal consequences, for the three types of interference are justified under the Convention in different ways. This is explained below. Determining which 'rule' a particular interference falls under is, however, far from straightforward. While the three rules make sense in relation to public rules of property, such as planning law (control of use) and compulsory purchase (deprivation), they are an unnatural fit with private property law, which has led to inconsistencies in the cases.

On the one hand, where one private party is deprived of their possessions in favour of another, most cases have classified the interference as a 'deprivation'. For example, in *James* v. *United Kingdom*, the Strasbourg court considered that the Leasehold Reform Act 1967, which permitted tenants to purchase their landlords' freehold at below market value, had operated to 'deprive' landlords of their interests.[118]

On the other hand, more recently the Grand Chamber of the Strasbourg court in *Pye* v. *United Kingdom* reached a different classification in

---

in his favour: *Moskal* v. *Poland* (2010) 50 EHRR 22; *Depalle* v. *France* (2010) (App. No. 34044/03); *Brosset-Triboulet* v. *France* (2010) (App. No. 34078/02); *Adolfsson* v. *Iceland* (2009) 49 EHRR SE4.

113 (1983) 5 EHRR 35 ('*Sporrong*').
114 *Lithgow* v. *United Kingdom* (1986) 8 EHRR 329 ('*Lithgow*').
115 *Hutten-Czapska*.
116 (1997) 23 EHRR 513. See further *Dokic* v. *Bosnia* (2010) (App. No. 6518/04).
117 See, e.g., *Sporrong* and *Papamichalopoulos* v. *Greece* (1993) 16 EHRR 440.
118 *James* v. *United Kingdam* (1986) 8 EHRR 123 ('*James*') at [38], although note that the point was not disputed before the Strasbourg court. Note that ultimately the deprivation was justified, and therefore not a violation of P1–1.

seemingly similar circumstances.[119] By operation of the Limitation Act 1980, a registered corporate landowner had lost the beneficial ownership of its land to a squatter.[120] Technically, after the squatter had been in adverse possession for twelve years, the registered owner held its title on bare trust for the squatter.[121] This was held to be a control of use, rather than a deprivation. The Grand Chamber explained this classification on the basis that limitation periods are a feature of many legal systems, and they generally involve regulating use rather than deprivation. With respect, however, this is an unsatisfactory explanation, for in substance the owner in *Pye* had been deprived of its ownership of the land. It runs counter to the Strasbourg court's usual preference for substance over form to deny that the owner had been deprived of his rights. A possible alternative explanation for *Pye* might be that it stands for a new principle, whereby interferences count as deprivations only where the *state* acquires rights at a private party's expense. This would mean that a re-allocation of property rights between private parties as among themselves, as in *Pye*, amounts to the state *controlling the use* of property by private citizens collectively, and not a *deprivation* for the state's benefit. However, while this explanation might explain *Pye*, it does not account for the classification in *James*, which, by this reckoning, concerned a control of use, not a deprivation. Unfortunately, a clear principle explaining the classification process remains to be discovered.

(c) **The inherent limitation problem**   A final point to consider on the issue of 'engaging' P1–1 is what is termed here the 'inherent limitation problem'. Some property rights might be intrinsically delimited such as to fall outside the protection of P1–1 completely. Take, for example, a situation where X acquires a prescriptive easement over Y's freehold estate. In response to X trying to exercise his easement, Y might argue that the recognition of X's prescriptive right would infringe his rights as freeholder under P1–1. At one stage it was considered that Y's Convention challenge would necessarily fail because his proprietary rights, as owner of the land, were intrinsically burdened by the possibility that someone sometime might acquire a prescriptive easement. Accordingly, by acquiring and enforcing an easement, X would not interfere with the defendant's property rights at all.

---

119 (2008) 46 EHRR 45.   120 Sections 15 and 17.
121 Land Registration Act 1925, s. 75.

However, this argument, while technically compelling, would strip P1–1 of any sensible meaning. Indeed, as discussed above, the type of conduct that P1–1 typically regulates is the arbitrary compulsory acquisition of private property by the state. On the understanding that all property is inherently vulnerable to compulsory acquisition, P1–1 would rarely, if ever, bite.[122] The Convention is supposed to guard against interference with property rights. To say that P1–1 fails to be engaged because property rights are inherently vulnerable to compulsory purchase is logical, but circular. The courts have rightly become aware of the problem and are now developing means to avoid it. A distinction is thus emerging between those circumstances where a property right is indeed inherently limited – and therefore not protected by P1–1 – and those situations which, conversely, involve a genuine interference.

The first category includes *Aston Cantlow Parochial Church Council* v. *Wallbank*, discussed briefly above,[123] where the defendants had acquired land to which chancel repair liability attached under domestic law. The parochial church council sought to enforce the liability by demanding almost £100,000 from the defendant owners of the burdened freehold. In response, the defendants argued that the liability was a disproportionate interference with their P1–1 rights. Although strictly obiter because the case was decided on other grounds,[124] three of their Lordships said that the defendants' rights as freehold owners were inherently limited by the existence of the chancel repair liability; therefore, P1–1 would not have been engaged anyway. This view is spot on: if one acquires already-burdened land, P1–1 cannot be relied upon to rid the land of those burdens; it does not, in other words, 'confer substantive rights to property which do not otherwise exist'.[125]

Pye v. *United Kingdom*, concerning an owner losing title to a squatter, belongs in the second category. It was argued by the United Kingdom that the statutory provisions that deprived the registered owner of its land did not engage P1–1 'because the applicant companies acquired the

---

122 See further *First County* at [40]–[44].   123 [2003] UKHL 37, [2004] 1 AC 546.

124 Because the claimant was not a public authority within s. 6, so its decision to enforce the chancel right could not be impugned in court. This aspect of the decision was criticised above, p. 272.

125 *Aston Cantlow* at [72]. See also *Austin* v. *Southwark LBC* [2008] EWHC 499 (QB) at [11], affd [2009] EWCA Civ. 66, reversed by the Supreme Court on a different point: [2010] UKSC 28. See also *Money Markets International Stockbrokers Ltd (In Liquidation)* v. *London Stock Exchange Ltd* [2002] 1 WLR 1150 at [141]–[143], *Kay* [2004] EWCA Civ 926, [2005] QB 352 at [108]; and *Carson* v. *United Kingdom* (2010) 51 EHRR 13.

disputed land subject to the risk of losing it pursuant to the provisions of the 1925 and 1980 Acts', and 'that risk had to be viewed as an incident of their property'.[126] The argument was, however, rejected by the Strasbourg court, both in the first hearing and by the subsequent decision of the Grand Chamber.[127] In the former, the majority explained that whether P1–1 was engaged 'will depend on whether the law is properly to be seen as qualifying or limiting the property right at the moment of acquisition, or, rather, whether it is to be seen as depriving the owner of an existing right at the point when the events occur and the law takes effect. It is only in the former case that [P1–1] may be held to have no application.'[128]

The Grand Chamber, without much discussion, seemed to agree.[129] On the facts, it was decided in both Strasbourg decisions that the adverse possession rules bit only at the end of twelve years' adverse possession, rather than 'delimiting the [owner's] right at the moment of its acquisition'.[130]

The facts in *Pye* therefore engaged P1–1, and those in *Aston Cantlow* did not. However, formulating a test for determining exactly when a case will fall on one side of the line rather than the other is difficult. The principle emerging from the decisions appears to be that P1–1 bites – whatever the type of interference – only where there is a shift in the beneficial incidents of proprietary entitlement away from the person alleging the P1–1 infringement; it has no part to play where someone's domestic property rights are inherently delimited from the outset. P1–1 protects *existing* entitlements; it does not confer new ones.[131] Accordingly, the facts in *Aston Cantlow* did not engage P1–1 because no shift in entitlement was in issue; instead, only the static existence and the enforcement of the claimant's domestic right were challenged. While the initial creation of the chancel repair liability would have engaged P1–1, that event predated the Convention and – crucially – the freeholders' acquisition of title: by the time the freeholders acquired their title it was already encumbered

---

126 (2008) 46 EHRR 45 at [45].

127 See also *Beaulane Properties* v. *Palmer* [2005] EWHC 817 (Ch), [2006] Ch 79, in which the judge thought that there was a difference between cases where an owner had a right subject to a law which might, and consequently did, strip the owner of a right (which does engage P1–1); and cases where an owner's right was qualified from the start (which does not). An adverse possession case, in his view, was of the former type.

128 (2006) 43 EHRR 3 at [51].   129 (2008) 46 EHRR 45 at [62]–[63].

130 (2006) 43 EHRR 3 at [52], (2008) 46 EHRR 45 at [63]. Contrast O. Jones 'Out with the Owners! The Eurasian Sequels to *JA Pye (Oxford) Ltd* v. *UK*', *Civil Justice Quarterly*, 27 (2008), 260 at 265–6, arguing that the owner's rights in *Pye* should have been regarded as delimited from the outset.

131 See p. 274 above.

by the chancel repair liability. Conversely, P1–1 was engaged in *Pye* because there was a shift in proprietary entitlement from owner to squatter.

Because P1–1 is engaged only by a shift in proprietary entitlement, it becomes necessary to be able to distinguish those situations where there is such a shift from those where there is not. The rule is easier to state than to apply.

It would appear that the ending of a lease in accordance with its terms fails to engage P1–1, because the lessee's rights are circumscribed by the leasehold terms from the outset. For example, Laws LJ has suggested that where a landlord issues a notice to quit in accordance with the terms of the leasehold agreement

> there is no interference with the appellant's property rights. They took the tenancies on terms including the landlord's right to recover possession on service of a good notice to quit. Accordingly, when such a right is activated, the tenant is deprived of nothing which he was entitled to keep.[132]

By contrast, situations where the owner is indeed deprived of some or all of the incidents of his proprietary entitlement will engage P1–1. The shift in proprietary entitlement can occur on varying levels, three of which are identified here. First, outright or partial transfers of existing interests certainly engage P1–1, for example, the conveyance of a freehold estate, or property adjustments made on divorce.[133] Second, shifts in proprietary entitlement might take the form of a new interest being created over an existing right, for example, the creation of a trust (express or implied), or an easement (express, implied[134] or prescriptive[135]) over a freehold estate.

---

132 *Sheffield City Council* v. *Smart* [2002] EWCA Civ. 4 at [46]. See also *Kay* [2004] EWCA Civ. 926, [2005] QB 352 at [107]–[108] and *Lancashire CC* v. *Taylor* [2004] EWHC 776 at [57] (confirmed on appeal [2005] EWCA Civ. 284, [2005] 1 WLR 2668). It is likely that the rule in *Hammersmith* v. *Monk* which allows a lease, held jointly, to be terminated unilaterally by one joint tenant, would be treated in the same way. The other joint tenant's leasehold interest is inherently subject to his co-tenant's continuing agreement to be bound by its terms.

133 *First County* at [42], [106].

134 Note that the creation of easements by implied *grant* would engage P1–1 because the servient landowner loses rights over his land: a shift in entitlement. However, the creation of easements by implied *reservation* would not engage P1–1, because in that case no one is being deprived of any rights they previously had: the purchaser of the servient land simply acquires land which was burdened from the outset.

135 See *R (Whitmey)* v. *Commons Commissioners* [2004] EWCA Civ. 951, [2005] QB 282 at [36]. Accordingly, the example, discussed above, where X acquires a prescriptive easement over Y's land would *engage* P1–1. Of course, whether or not the right is ultimately violated is another matter, which is discussed below.

A third category comprises those situations where one person's interest – the 'possession' – loses priority to another's interest. For example, the Land Registration Act 2002 provides that unprotected interests might be 'postponed' in the event of certain registered dispositions of land: for example, a trust beneficiary will lose their interest to a purchaser of the legal estate unless the beneficiary's interest is 'overriding' by reason of his or her occupation of the land.[136] The postponed right, while technically in existence under the Act, has effectively been stripped of the benefits it would otherwise confer. Hence, P1–1 would be engaged.

Outside these identified categories it is very much more difficult to determine whether facts involve a shift in proprietary entitlement, or merely the enforcement of a pre-existing rights. The difficulties are illustrated by the following four examples.

First is the decision of the House of Lords in *Wilson* v. *First County Trust Ltd (No. 2)*.[137] The claimant pawned her car to the defendant pawnbrokers for six months in return for a loan; however, owing to certain statutory formalities not having been met, the loan agreement was unenforceable.[138] As a result, domestic law allowed the claimant to recover her car without paying back the loan, which she proceeded to do. In response, the defendant pawnbrokers argued, under P1–1, that the stringent formality requirements deprived them of possessions which they would otherwise have: namely, a contractual right against the claimant and a corresponding security right in the car. The claimant counter-argued that the statutory formality requirements constituted an inherent limitation on the defendant's rights, such that P1–1 was not engaged. Ultimately, the defendant's claim failed on another ground,[139] but four of their Lordships commented, obiter, on the issue. While Lords Hope and Scott agreed with the claimants that the defendants' rights were delimited by the statute, Lord Nicholls disagreed, opining that the statute had served to deprive the defendants of rights they would otherwise have. Lord Hobhouse was

---

136 Land Registration Act 2002, ss. 28, 29 and Sch. 3. The Law Commission envisaged that this would engage P1–1: *Land Registration for the Twenty-First Century: A Consultative Document* (Law Com. No. 254, 1998); and *Land Registration for the Twenty-First Century: A Conveyancing Revolution* (Law Com. No. 271, 2001). Note that, conversely, a purchaser whose title is *bound* by a prior interest according to the rules in ss. 28 and 29 of the Land Registration Act 2002 cannot rely on P1–1 because his or her title is flawed from the outset.

137 [2003] UKHL 40, [2004] 1 AC 816, discussed further in Chapter 13.

138 Consumer Credit Act 1974, s. 127(3).

139 The HRA could not be applied retrospectively to the events that occurred prior to the Act coming into force.

equivocal, and suggested that the outcome might depend on the passing of possession. The lack of a clear majority view demonstrates the very real difficulty in establishing exactly when P1–1 might bite.

A second problematic scenario concerns the effect on a trust beneficiary of an overreaching sale of trust property by the trustees to a third-party disponee. An overreaching conveyance results in the disponee taking free of the beneficiary's interest in the original property, and the trustees holding the proceeds of sale on trust for the beneficiary.[140] Significantly, however, overreaching occurs only where the trustees are empowered to make the particular disposition. Where the relevant power is drafted into the terms of the trust instrument, the beneficiary's interest in the original property should be understood as inherently limited from the outset,[141] such that P1–1 is not engaged by the overreaching process. However, assessing the application of P1–1 is trickier where a conveyance has overreaching effect not by virtue of an express provision in the trust instrument, but owing to statute. For example, the Law of Property Act 1925 provides that a conveyance of land by two trustees overreaches beneficial interests under the trust, notwithstanding that the sale might be effected in breach of trust.[142] Two views on the engagement of P1–1 are plausible. On one view, the statutory provisions might limit the beneficiary's interest from the outset, just as if the power to overreach had been drafted into the trust instrument. On another view, the beneficiary's interest is not limited from the trust's creation, but becomes so only if and when the statutory provisions are triggered by an overreaching conveyance. This second interpretation is more consistent with the Strasbourg court's approach in *Pye*: there, the registered owner's estate in land was understood not to be inherently limited by the mere existence of statutory adverse possession provisions; rather, the owner was deprived of his property only upon the actual operation of those provisions.[143] It remains to be seen which view the courts will adopt in the context of statutory overreaching.[144]

---

140 See generally D. Fox, 'Overreaching', in P. Birks and A. Pretto (eds.), *Breach of Trust* (Oxford University Press, 2002), ch. 4.

141 See R. Nolan, 'Understanding the Limits of Equitable Property', *Journal of Equity*, 1 (2006), 18, 23–4.

142 Law of Property Act 1925, ss. 2 and 27; also Trusts of Land and Appointment of Trustees Act 1996, s. 6 and Land Registration Act 2002, s. 26. For an example of this occurring, see *City of London Building Society* v. *Flegg* [1988] 1 AC 54.

143 See p. 278 above.

144 Appropriate facts for consideration of the point arose in *National Westminster Bank Plc* v. *Malhan* [2004] EWHC 847, [2004] 2 P&CR DG9. However, the point was not decided as

Related to this is a third potential source of difficulty, which concerns sales of co-owned property. Section 14 of the Trusts of Land and Appointment of Trustees Act 1996 empowers the court to order a sale of co-owned land following an application from one of the co-owners.[145] Whether this would bite into the other co-owner's P1–1 rights would, once again, turn on the difficult question of whether or not a co-owner's proprietary interest is, from its inception, inherently vulnerable to sale under section 14. In *Putnam & Sons* v. *Taylor*, HHJ Purle QC assumed that P1–1 was engaged.[146] Similarly, the same judge decided in *Close Invoice Ltd* v. *Pile* that a court-ordered sale to enforce a charging order under the Civil Procedure Rules (which contains a power of sale comparable to section 14) would also engage P1–1.[147] However, in neither case was the issue of P1–1's engagement properly argued and so the issue cannot be regarded as fully settled.[148]

A fourth difficult scenario concerns the enforcement of a mortgagee's remedies against a mortgagor. Two cases have countenanced the possibility that repossession by a mortgagee might engage the owner's P1–1 rights.[149] With respect, however, this view seems rather misguided: it is a fundamental characteristic of a mortgage that the mortgagee has a right to repossess the property, normally expressed to be exercisable if and when the mortgagor defaults on the loan. This means that on entering into a mortgage arrangement, the parties agree that the mortgagor's ownership of the property is inherently qualified by the mortgagee's rights from the

---

the facts arose prior to the HRA being in force. Nonetheless, it was considered that there was 'much force' in the argument that the overreaching provisions engaged P1–1, at least when combined with Art. 14. Note that S. Nield, 'Charges, Possession and Human Rights: a Reappraisal of s. 87(1) Law of Property Act 1925', in E. Cooke (ed.), *Modern Studies in Property Law: Vol. 3* (Oxford: Hart, 2005), ch. 8 argues that overreaching, if it engages P1–1, should be classified as 'control of use' rather than 'deprivation' because one's rights are transferred from one form of property to another. In possible support of this view, see *Zehentner*, where a judicial sale of the applicant's co-owned property was classified as 'control of use'.

145 Indeed, any person with an interest in the property subject to the trust may make an application.

146 [2009] EWHC 317 (Ch) at [28]–[29]. See further *Nicholls* v. *Lan* [2006] EWHC 1255. See further p. 271 above, which discusses the applicability of the Convention to courts' discretionary powers.

147 [2008] EWHC 1580 (Ch).

148 See *Hughes* v. *Paxman* [2006] EWCA Civ. 818 at [28], where, in relation to a co-owned patent, it was considered an incident of co-ownership that rights could be altered by application to a comptroller.

149 *Wood* v. *United Kingdom* (1997) 24 EHRR CD69 ('*Wood*'); *Alcorn*.

outset. Accordingly, the mortgagee's act of repossession should not engage P1–1. The same reasoning applies to the exercise of the mortgagee's power of sale, a view which was rightly accepted in *Horsham Properties Group Ltd v. Clark*.[150] A power of sale is usually drafted expressly into the mortgage agreement; where this is not the case, it is implied into the agreement by section 101 of the Law of Property Act 1925. The result is that the power of sale is, from the outset, part and parcel of the mortgage. While the creation of the mortgage itself might engage a landowner's P1–1 rights (since that involves a shift in proprietary entitlement),[151] the exercise of a concomitant power of sale would not.

A slightly trickier issue was raised in obiter dicta in *Horsham Properties*. Briggs J mooted the possibility that a mortgaged estate might be sold pursuant to the implied statutory power of sale, but in circumstances where the statutory preconditions for its exercise, as found in section 103 of the Law of Property Act 1925, had not been satisfied. Generally, these preconditions require that the mortgagor has defaulted on the loan. Section 104 provides that a sale which does not satisfy the preconditions, while unlawful as against the mortgagor, will nonetheless deprive him or her of his or her title in favour of the purchaser, leaving the mortgagor to pursue a remedy in damages against the lender. Briggs J expressed some uncertainty as to whether P1–1 would be engaged by such a sale.[152] The judge's doubt is understandable: it is far from clear whether the mortgagor's title is inherently flawed by the possibility that section 104 might operate to deprive him or her of his or her land. On the one hand, it might be said that sections 103 and 104 are both part and parcel of the power of sale, which itself inherently limits the mortgagor's estate. As such, the operation of section 104 has no effect on the mortgagor's intrinsically limited title and so P1–1 is not engaged. On the other hand, it is arguable that, while the section 103 preconditions are an inherent part of the power of sale, section 104 is not. Because section 104 is aimed at protecting the purchaser, its effects on the mortgagor might be regarded as secondary by-products of the primary purpose. As such, it is plausible that section 104 does not delimit the mortgagor's title from the outset,

---

150 [2008] EWHC 2327 (Ch), [2009] 1 WLR 1255 ('*Horsham*').

151 There is a difference between the creation of a mortgage over an estate in land which one already owns and the creation of a mortgage *on acquisition* of the relevant estate. While the former case involves a shift in proprietary entitlement from the mortgagor to the mortgagee, the latter does not, because the mortgagor's estate is deemed to be charged from the outset: *Abbey National Building Society* v. *Cann* [1991] 1 AC 56.

152 *Horsham* at [41].

but operates to deprive the mortgagor if and when the property is sold. As yet, it is not clear which view will be preferred. The issue is a similar one to that raised above, where trustees are empowered by statute to overreach a beneficiary's interest even where their actions constitute a breach of trust.

In summary, the guiding principle emerging from the cases is that engagement of P1–1 requires a shift in proprietary entitlement. To use the familiar metaphor of proprietary entitlement being a bundle of sticks, P1–1 is engaged by the removal or transfer of any stick from an owner's bundle. While the principle is difficult to apply in certain contexts, it is nonetheless targeted sensibly because it allows those mechanisms that allow proprietary entitlements to move or change hands to be properly scrutinised under the Convention. Of course, whether or not an *engagement* of P1–1 ultimately results in a *violation* of the Convention depends on issues of justification and proportionality, which are discussed in the next section. This being so, in cases where there is doubt as to whether there has been a shift in proprietary entitlement, it would be preferable for the courts to interpret the engagement test broadly, thus shifting to the proportionality test the onus of deciding whether the right is violated.

(2) Justification and the proportionality test

A shift in proprietary entitlement will violate the Convention only where it is not justified. Justification entails, first, that the interference is in the public interest and is sanctioned by domestic law. Second, a justified interference must strike a 'fair balance' between the demands of the public or general interest of the community and the requirements of the protection of the individual's fundamental rights.[153] The test is whether the extent of the interference is proportionate to the legitimate aim pursued. In making this inquiry, the courts allow domestic policy-makers an area of discretion.[154] As the following analysis reveals, interferences with P1–1 in the context of private property law are, in general, easily justified as being proportionate. Three rules of thumb emerge from the cases.

First, consensual shifts in proprietary entitlement do not violate P1–1: for example, a consensual conveyance or the creation of an express

---

153 *R (SRM Global Master Fund LP)* v. *Treasury Commissioners* [2009] EWCA Civ. 788 at [55].

154 This is labelled the 'margin of appreciation' by the Strasbourg court and the 'discretionary area of judgment' by domestic courts.

trust.[155] This is entirely appropriate, for it cannot be disproportionate for the law to respect the wishes of those who consensually dispose of their entitlement.

Second, where there is a strong public interest in the existence of a rule, it is readily justified. The *First County* case provides a good example.[156] It will be remembered that legislation rendered a pawnbroker's rights against his customer unenforceable for failure to observe the requirements of certain formalities. Although their Lordships could not agree whether the facts engaged P1–1, they were unanimous in obiter dicta that, had the right been engaged, the interference with the pawnbroker's rights was proportionate anyway because strict formality requirements were an appropriate means of ensuring consumer protection. Also decided on public interest grounds is the case of *Pennycook v. Shaws (EAL) Ltd.*[157] There, a landlord served on his tenant a notice to quit. The tenant desired to remain in the property, but foolishly wrote back agreeing to leave. Under domestic law, by writing this letter, the tenant lost his right (a 'possession' under P1–1) to issue a counter-notice to his landlord. Arden LJ held that the tenant's loss was justified because there were clear economic advantages in the certainty created by a rule allowing a landlord to rely on a tenant's letter. For similar reasons, in the context of registered land, rules that provide that certain unprotected interests lose their priority in favour of registered purchasers should be understood as justifiable under the Convention: there are clear economic and commercial reasons why a purchaser of land should be able to rely on the Land Register and hence take free from unprotected interests.[158]

Third, the Strasbourg court has frequently stated that an interference that constitutes a 'deprivation' rather than 'control of use' will normally be justified only on payment of compensation to the victim.[159] This guiding principle was applied in *Pye v. United Kingdom*, discussed above, in the

---

155 See *Holy Monasteries v. Greece* (1995) 20 EHRR 1 at [76]–[78] and *Wood*. See also *Horsham*, which decided that, had the sale of mortgaged property by a mortgagee engaged P1–1, the interference would nonetheless be justified as the mortgagor consented to such a sale by agreeing the terms of the mortgage.

156 See p. 280 above.   157 [2004] EWCA Civ. 100, [2004] Ch 296.

158 Law Com. No. 271, (2001); para. 8.89. Overriding interests, exceptionally, bind the purchaser despite not appearing on the Register. In respect of these interests, the Law Commission determined that public policy would favour the interest holder over the purchaser.

159 See *Lithgow*. However, it is not an absolute requirement: see *James*. Controls of use can be proportionate without the payment of compensation: *Friend v. United Kingdom* (2010) 50 EHRR SE6.

context of adverse possession.[160] The Strasbourg court decided in its first decision, by a majority, that the domestic legislation operated in violation of P1–1. Crucially, it classified the interference as a 'deprivation'. This meant that, despite adverse possession serving legitimate policy goals, the interference was inevitably disproportionate in the absence of compensation being payable to the landowner.[161] The Grand Chamber, again by a majority, came to the opposite conclusion on the proportionality issue[162] and held that the interference was justified. Key to its decision was the classification of the interference as a 'control of use', thus side-stepping the requirement of compensation. Further, the majority dismissed concerns that the registered owner would be without procedural protection, reasoning that 'while the limitation period was running, it was open to [the owner] to remedy the position by bringing a court action for repossession of the land'.[163]

As discussed above, the classification of adverse possession as 'control of use' rather than 'deprivation' is artificial.[164] It would appear, from the tenor of the majority's judgment, that the Grand Chamber was satisfied that adverse possession was justified on strong policy grounds despite there being no compensation. To reach what seems to be the court's desired outcome, the majority was compelled by the compensation principle to categorise the interference as a control of use. While the outcome that P1–1 was not violated in *Pye* might be acceptable, the Grand Chamber's reasoning process is not. Rather than shoe-horning the interference into the 'control of use' category, it would have been preferable for the court to revisit the compensation principle itself. That principle has never been stated to be an absolute rule.[165] A departure from the rule would have been appropriate in *Pye*.

Crucially, to date, no area of English private property law has been found to fall foul of P1–1. For example, rules relating to the termination of tenancies,[166] or which allow leasehold enfranchisement by tenants against their landlords[167] have survived P1–1 challenges. Even adverse possession, once considered to be one of the most vulnerable parts of property law,[168] appears to be safe from future attacks. It should be noted that *Pye* concerned a *registered* landowner who lost his beneficial entitlement automatically to the squatter by operation of the Limitation

---

160 See pp. 275–6 and 277–9 above.   161 (2006) 43 EHRR 3 at [73]–[74].
162 *Pye* (2008) 46 EHRR 45.   163 *Pye* at [80].   164 See p. 276 above.
165 *James*.   166 *Pennycook*.   167 *James*.
168 *JA Pye (Oxford) Ltd* v. *Graham* [2000] Ch 676 at 709 and *Beaulane*.

Act 1980.[169] Because the 1980 Act also governs adverse possession of *unregistered land*, there is no doubt since *Pye* that this regime also complies with P1–1. Indeed, the policy arguments in favour of adverse possession are stronger for unregistered land because, in the absence of registration, it provides a useful mechanism for determining title to the land. Today, in relation to *registered land*, the Land Registration Act 2002 has replaced the Limitation Act 1980 with a system whereby the registered landowner receives notification of, and can normally object to, a squatter's claim to the land.[170] By thus providing *better* protection to the registered owner's P1–1 rights than the Limitation Act 1980 which governed *Pye*, the new regime must be immune from challenge under P1–1.

However, while property law has thus far escaped unscathed from P1–1 challenges, it should by no means be regarded as a foregone conclusion that all aspects of property law are compatible, and it is important that courts be willing to act as scrutinisers where appropriate. Indeed, three particular branches of property law stand out as potential violators.

First, as noted above, in *Horsham Properties*, Briggs J considered obiter the situation where a mortgagee sells mortgaged property pursuant to the statutory power of sale but before the power has become exercisable, for example, by the mortgagor defaulting on the loan, where section 104 of the Law of Property Act 1925 provides that the purchaser may take a clean title, thus depriving the mortgagor of his land. It will be recalled that it is unclear whether such a sale actually engages P1–1. If it does, Briggs J was unsure whether or not the interference would be justified. It is easy to see why he was uncertain. On the one hand, the legislation serves the clear public purpose under P1–1 of facilitating sales by mortgagees: section 104 means that prospective purchasers can be sure of acquiring a clean title without having to ascertain that the power of sale is being properly exercised. On the other hand, section 104 operates to strip the mortgagor of his title even though he might not have defaulted on the mortgage. It is at least arguable that the commercial advantages of the rule might be insufficient to outweigh the mortgagor's loss under P1–1.

A second situation where property law might fall foul of P1–1 is in the context of overreaching. In *National Westminster Bank Plc* v. *Malhan*, the claimant asserted a beneficial interest in a property which was legally owned by two brothers who had granted a mortgage over the property in favour of a bank.[171] As a matter of domestic law, the claimant's right, if he

---

169 See p. 276 above.   170 Land Registration Act 2002, Sch. 6.
171 [2004] EWHC 847 (Ch).

had one, would have been overreached by the brothers' transaction with the bank. The claimant argued that the doctrine of overreaching would infringe his beneficial interest under P1–1, especially when combined with the prohibition against discrimination under Article 14. He argued that because overreaching operated when there were two or more trustees, but not when there was only one, this constituted a discriminating deprivation of his possessions. There were problems with his argument on the facts: he was unable to establish a beneficial interest in the first place; furthermore, the HRA was not in force at the time when the facts arose. Nonetheless, the Vice-Chancellor considered, obiter, whether there was any strength in the claimant's Convention-based argument. Without considering properly whether P1–1 was engaged, the difficulties with which are discussed above, the Vice-Chancellor said there was 'much force' in the argument that P1–1 had been violated.[172] Should the issue arise again, the court would have to evaluate whether it is justifiable for the doctrine of overreaching to depend so heavily on the number of trustees making the overreaching conveyance.[173]

A third doctrine of property law that stands out as a possible P1–1 violator is that of impliedly granted easements. Where an owner sells off part of his or her land, he or she might find that the conveyance carries with it an implied easement over the land which he retains. Easements implied under the rule in section 62 of the Law of Property Act 1925 are particularly objectionable. According to the doctrine, a landowner who allows someone to occupy part of his or her land before legally convey-ing it to them[174] might find that personal rights, that is, licences, that the occupants previously enjoyed over the retained land are upgraded into for-mal easements despite not being expressly included in the conveyance.[175] This result was not the intended consequence of the statute, and usually thwarts the conveying landowner's expectations. Much criticised by the judiciary, the Law Commission and academics,[176] the doctrine stands out

---

172 *Malhan* at [53].
173 See Law Commission, 'Transfer of Land – Overreaching: Beneficiaries in Actual Occu-pation' (Law Com. No. 188, 1989).
174 The conveyance could take the form of a freehold disposition or the creation of a legal lease over the dominant tenement.
175 See, e.g., *International Tea Stores Co.* v. *Hobbs* [1903] 2 Ch 165.
176 *Wright* v. *Macadam* [1949] 2 KB 744 at 755 *per* Tucker LJ; Law Commission, 'Easements, Covenants and Profits à Prendre' (CP No. 186, 2008), paras. 4.73–4.74 and L. Tee, 'Metamorphoses and Section 62 of the Law of Property Act 1925', *Conveyancer* (1998), 115.

as one that potentially interferes with the landowner's P1–1 rights in an unjustifiable, disproportionate fashion.

(3) Conclusions

From this brief survey of the case law, it is apparent that rarely will the application of domestic property law violate P1–1. However, it is crucial that courts do not complacently assume property law's compatibility with the Convention. P1–1 performs a valuable stabilising function: it ensures that proprietary entitlements shift away from their owners only under justifiable conditions: the courts must use it as a tool for illuminating those dark areas of property law where this might not be the case.

12.3.2 Article 8

Article 8 provides that 'everyone has the right to respect for his private and family life, his home and his correspondence'. Like P1–1, the right is qualified: Article 8 is not violated by interferences that are legitimate, in the public interest and proportionate.

Because much of property law affects, to some degree, people's enjoyment of their homes, Article 8 has the potential to have a significant impact. In practice, however, until the Supreme Court's decision in *Pinnock*, domestic courts were reluctant to countenance the possibility that Article 8 might be violated by the operation of property law. It is argued here that this reluctance was unwarranted and unacceptable: property law must be subjected to proper scrutiny under Article 8; by no means is it a foregone conclusion that the domestic rules are compliant.

(1) Engagement of the right

Article 8 is engaged by an interference with one's home. The Commission has explained that 'home' 'is an autonomous concept' and that 'whether or not a particular habitation constitutes a "home" . . . will depend on the factual circumstances, namely the existence of sufficient and continuous links'.[177] Significantly, the meaning of 'home' 'is not limited to those which are lawfully occupied or which have been lawfully established':[178]

---

177 *Buckley* v. *United Kingdom* (1995) 19 EHRR CD20 at [63], confirmed in *McCann.*
178 *Buckley* at [63].

even a squatter can enjoy land as his or her home. In this respect, Article 8 differs from P1–1, which only protects lawful entitlements.[179]

The two cases in the conjoined appeal in *Kay; Price*[180] fall on either side of the factual test of a home. In *Kay*, the House of Lords found that a former tenant who was still living in the property enjoyed it as his 'home' despite having no remaining entitlement to remain there under domestic law. By contrast, in *Price*, gypsies had been living on a recreation ground for two days when the local authority landowner sought to evict them. The gypsies were unable to convince the House of Lords that a possession order would engage Article 8: two days' occupation was insufficient for forging the necessary factual links with the land.

Being a factual rather than a legal concept, the 'home' is frequently affected by the operation of property law. For example, rules that sanction the taking of possession from an occupier, or that permit the sale of a co-owned or mortgaged home engage Article 8.[181] Even the recognition of an easement or a freehold covenant might affect the enjoyment of one's home. Hence, Article 8 is frequently *engaged* by the operation of property law. However, until recently it was rare – and unacceptably so – for the domestic courts to recognise that an engagement ultimately amounted to a *violation* of Article 8.

(2) Justification and the proportionality test

(a) **Local authority eviction cases**   Cases where local authorities have evicted occupiers of their land are a fertile ground for analysing the proportionality test because the issue has arisen repeatedly before the House of Lords, the Supreme Court and the Strasbourg court. These cases were discussed in section 12.2 above, in the context of the *applicability* of the Convention; yet they are equally instructive on the *compatibility* issue. As discussed earlier, the cases take a number of different configurations, but essentially boil down to the same fact pattern whereby a private citizen, who is living without permission on local authority land, faces eviction under domestic property or housing law. The trespassing citizen

---

179 *Qazi* at [50]. Note that owing to the different interests they respectively protect, Art. 8 and P1–1 do not stand and fall together; the judge in *Horsham* erroneously thought otherwise; cf., in the context of nuisance law, Chapter 8 above.

180 [2006] UKHL 10; [2006] 2 AC 465.

181 Whether the interference engages Art. 8 depends on the facts. For example, sale of the property might not, in itself, be an interference with the home if the occupier is permitted to remain living there: *Zehentner*. By contrast, it has been held that an eviction order engages Art. 8 even before the order is enforced: *Paulić*.

might, for example, have been unlawfully present from the outset (in the case of a squatter), or he or she might have entered the land lawfully, pursuant to permission which has since expired (in the case of a former tenant or licensee).[182] Could an eviction of such occupiers ever amount to a violation of their Article 8 rights? On the one hand, the eviction will clearly engage Article 8; on the other, the eviction is legitimate, being sanctioned by domestic law. Hence, the crux is whether the interference strikes a proportionate balance between the dweller's interest in the home and the public interest served by the authority being able to exercise its property rights. As a preliminary point, it should be noted that these cases arise in a vertical situation between a public authority and a private party. Nonetheless, discussion of these cases is useful for illuminating the courts' general attitude to the proportionality test.

On the compatibility issue, it was observed in section 12.2 above that, prior to *Pinnock*, the House of Lords and the Strasbourg court adopted diametrically opposed views. The same sequence of cases witnessed a battle of equivalent proportions concerning the proportionality test. The first round in the battle was *Qazi*, where a local authority sought to repossess a flat occupied by a former tenant, whose tenancy had been unilaterally terminated by his wife. A majority of the House of Lords decided that the authority's 'rights to possession' made it a 'foregone conclusion' that the repossession was justified.[183] There was no need to perform the proportionality test because there was 'simply no balance to be struck'.[184] Implicit in the majority's reasoning was the premise that domestic property law, which conferred the right to possession, was inherently compatible with Article 8.[185] With respect, however, this reasoning is fundamentally flawed, for it assumed that one Convention right – the local authority's P1–1 property right – was inherently more important than another – the occupier's Article 8 right. The Convention neither requires nor authorises one right to have automatic priority over another; instead, the proportionality test should be employed to resolve disputes between competing rights.

---

182 The lease might have reached the end of its term or it might have been ended prematurely (e.g., through forfeiture, or by termination by one joint tenant (as occurred in *Qazi* and *McCann*)).

183 *Qazi* at [84], [103].   184 *Qazi* at [103].

185 Note that Lord Hope and possibly Lord Millett, however, seemed to reserve their opinion obiter as to whether an Art. 8 defence might succeed in 'exceptional circumstances'. Unfortunately, neither was clear as to when the exception might apply and what it might entail.

The Strasbourg court fought back in *Connors* v. *United Kingdom*, where it rightly shattered the illusion that proprietary claims are immune from Article 8 challenges.[186] The facts, outlined above, require elaboration here. The case concerned a local authority which was seeking to evict certain anti-social gypsies from one of its sites. Acting consistently with its rights under domestic law, the authority had terminated the gypsies' contractual licence to occupy the site without stating its reasons or giving the gypsies a chance to object. The gypsies argued that Article 8 gave them a right to remain in spite of the authority's domestic law rights. Crucially, the Strasbourg court decided, contrary to the majority view in *Qazi*, that it was necessary in such circumstances to carry out the proportionality test. And, having weighed up the competing interests, it found that Article 8 had indeed been violated. The gypsies were a vulnerable minority whose needs required a high level of protection under Article 8, and to whom the state owed a positive obligation under the Convention.[187] Unfortunately for the local authority, the summary eviction had been attended by insufficient procedural safeguards to satisfy the Convention. *Connors* was a significant decision, for it meant that the bringing of a proprietary claim under domestic law could no longer be regarded as inherently compatible with Article 8.

The House of Lords came back fighting in *Kay*, this time as a committee of seven. Their Lordships were invited to confront the apparent conflict between *Qazi* and *Connors*, and to consider whether the bringing of a claim to recover property would ever violate Article 8 as a disproportionate interference with an occupier's home. All seven Lords conceded that, following *Connors*, domestic property law was not inherently compliant. But the concession made to *Connors* was a very small one. Their Lordships rightly identified that a tension exists between an occupier's right to make an Article 8 challenge and the 'colossal waste of time and money' that would result if for every possession action the judge had to perform the proportionality test.[188] A compromise was reached: domestic courts were told to proceed on the assumption that domestic possession proceedings strike a proportionate balance because land law, over the years, has sought to balance the 'human, social and economic considerations involved'.[189] Only in those rare and 'exceptional' cases where an Article 8 infringement was 'seriously arguable' did the Lords consider it appropriate for courts to perform the proportionality test to see whether

---

186 (2005) 40 EHRR 9.   187 See pp. 255–8 above.
188 *Kay* at [55].   189 *Kay* at [33], [109].

there had been a violation.[190] Their Lordships divided on when it would be 'seriously arguable' to argue an infringement of Article 8. A majority of four decided that the occupier's 'personal circumstances' should be irrelevant; instead, the home occupier would have to show, at a more abstract level, and without pointing to the particular hardship he or she would suffer, that the entire web of applicable rules was incompatible with Article 8,[191] a necessarily difficult task. *Connors* was deemed an exceptional case, which turned on the especially vulnerable position of gypsies and the lack of procedural safeguards available to them. The facts in *Kay* itself – concerning the eviction of a former tenant – did not present a seriously arguably Article 8 case. Thus, the majority in *Kay* accepted the vulnerability of property law to Article 8, yet simultaneously rendered it almost impossible to make a challenge. With respect, the approach in *Kay* was unacceptably restrictive. The plight of individuals in the face of possessory claims should have been of utmost relevance when assessing the legal framework's compliance with Article 8. Personal circumstances should not only be relevant, but crucial, for there is no better test of the law's Article 8 compatibility than its impact on particular people.[192]

After *Kay*, the House of Lords[193] and the Strasbourg court[194] continued on their separate paths. It took the nine-strong Supreme Court in *Pinnock* to bring domestic law into line with the state's Convention obligations. In a remarkably clear judgment, Lord Neuberger, speaking for the whole court, said that consideration of Article 8 should not be confined to 'exceptional cases', exceptionality being an 'outcome and not a guide'.[195] Instead, courts should perform the proportionality test whenever the occupier raises Article 8.[196] When balancing the competing interests, he said that two factors would weigh heavily in the authority's favour: first, the existence of the local authority's 'unencumbered property rights'; and second, the authority's 'right – indeed the obligation . . . to decide who should occupy its residential property'.[197] This means that in virtually

---

190 *Kay* at [39], [56], [110].
191 *Kay* at [110] *per* Lord Hope. The rest of the majority (Lords Scott and Brown and Baroness Hale) concurred.
192 See *McCann*.   193 *Doherty* HL.
194 This is implicit in *McCann* and *Kay*. See also *Zehentner*, which makes the point more expressly.
195 *Pinnock* at [51].
196 It should be noted that the Supreme Court in *Powell*, decided after *Pinnock*, stated that the occupier's reliance on Art. 8 must be 'seriously arguable'. See n. 86 above.
197 *Pinnock* at [54].

every case repossession by the local authority would be proportionate. Crucially, however, and in direct contrast to *Kay*, his Lordship accepted that in some cases the 'personal circumstances' of the occupier would result in a different outcome,[198] for example, where the occupier is especially vulnerable.[199]

This reasoning explains why the eviction in *Connors* was disproportionate: the gypsies were a vulnerable minority. Similarly, the eviction of the occupiers in *McCann* violated the Convention. It will be remembered that the local authority had persuaded an occupier to relinquish her tenancy without fully explaining the consequences, thus seemingly placing her in an unacceptable position of ignorance. By contrast, the eviction in *Pinnock* itself did not violate Article 8. A local authority had evicted a tenant on the basis of the criminal and anti-social behaviour of his five sons. It was clear that the father, who had done nothing to put a stop to his sons' conduct, had no prospect of outweighing the two strong factors counting in the council's favour: its property rights; and its public law duty to manage and allocate its housing stock.[200]

The reasoning in *Pinnock* should be welcomed with open arms. It brings a harmonious balance of principle and pragmatism to the proportionality test. No longer can domestic courts ignore their Convention obligations. And yet, at the same time, by recognising that property rights carry significant weight in the Article 8 proportionality test, Lord Neuberger has managed, in large part, to allay fears that Article 8 might radically destabilise established property rights. Article 8 prevents only the vindication of existing rights where to do so would result in significant personal hardship. In this way, Lord Neuberger seems to strike an eminently sensible balance between the authority's property rights and the occupier's rights under Article 8. It is reassuring to note that the Supreme Court in *Powell* has since reaffirmed the sensible approach taken in *Pinnock*.[201]

(b) Horizontal property disputes   Outside the local authority eviction context, Article 8 has been raised in a handful of horizontal property

198 *Pinnock* at [53].
199 *Pinnock* at [64]. Examples given include occupiers who have mental illness, a physical or learning disability, poor health or frailty.
200 *Pinnock* at [128].
201 See especially *Powell* at [35]. It is of some regret, however, that neither Lord Hope nor Lord Phillips, speaking for the Supreme Court in *Powell*, elaborated on what might count in the occupier's favour as relevant 'personal circumstances' within the proportionality test.

disputes in which it is encouraging to observe that, even prior to *Pinnock*, the domestic courts showed some willingness to engage with the Convention.[202]

Pinnock does not, of course, purport to speak directly to horizontal cases; nonetheless, it offers useful guidance on how the proportionality test might be applied. It will be recalled that in vertical disputes, *Pinnock* decided that two factors weigh in the local authority's favour when evicting an occupier: its property rights; and its public law duties. In the private sector, only the former factor is relevant, which means that the balance should be less heavily weighted in the landowner's favour.

Four key areas of property law have already been considered by the courts in relation to Article 8. First are those cases where the court orders the sale of a co-owned home pursuant to a discretionary power conferred by statute.[203] When making its decision whether to order sale, the court is required by legislation to take account of certain factors, such as the purposes for which the property was bought, the interests of secured creditors and the interests of any children that might be living in the property.[204] In three separate cases, the High Court has indicated that the possible impact of a sale on the occupier's Article 8 home rights should inform the court's decision-making process.[205] This is especially important where the sale is sought by a co-owner's trustee in bankruptcy, for in such circumstances the court is guided by statute to order a sale of the property if the co-owner has been bankrupt for a year or there are 'exceptional circumstances'.[206] Because in such cases there is effectively a presumption in favour of sale, which would deprive a co-owner of their home, the courts have been particularly keen to ensure that Article 8 is borne in mind.[207]

Yet, despite the Convention's relevance, it is unlikely that Article 8 will in practice result in the courts exercising their discretions any differently. This is because domestic case law has built up in such a way that the courts have always been careful to ensure that they only order sale against an occupier where, on balance, it is fair to do so. The factors that would justify

---

202 For more detail, see Goymour, 'Proprietary Claims', pp. 703–8.
203 Section 14, TLATA. See p. 282 above.   204 Section 15, TLATA.
205 *Barca*; *Donohoe* and *Putnam*. It is unclear exactly which mechanism renders the Convention *applicable* in such cases. There are two possibilities: (1) in *Barca*, it was suggested that under HRA, s. 3 that TLATA must be interpreted to require consideration of Art. 8; alternatively, (2) it might be via HRA, s. 6 that the courts must consider Art. 8.
206 Section 335A of the Insolvency Act 1986; this topic is discussed further in Chapter 15.
207 *Barca*.

a court-ordered sale prior to the HRA are exactly the sort of factors that would justify an interference with the home under Article 8. For example, domestic case law suggests that where sale is sought by a creditor whose interest is secured over a share of the co-owned property, sale is usually ordered.[208] There is little doubt that, under Article 8, the public interest in protecting lenders in such circumstances similarly would normally outweigh the adverse impact on the occupying co-owner.[209] Thus, Article 8 is unlikely to have any quantifiable impact on the outcome of section 14 applications for sale. Even so, it is laudable that the courts are alert to their Article 8 responsibilities, and are prepared to adjust their behaviour if required.

A similar analysis pertains for the second area of property law to come under the Article 8 microscope: the repossession and sale of a home by a secured creditor. While there is no doubt that such conduct engages Article 8,[210] here too the cases have found that the law operates in a justifiably proportionate fashion. Domestic courts rightly stress the strong public interest in having efficient mechanisms for the enforcement of a debt: without a power to sell charged property, lenders would inevitably impose higher rates of interest on their loans more generally.[211] Further, before selling mortgaged property, it is usual for the lender to gain possession of the property through the courts, at which point the occupying mortgagor has the opportunity to resist the possession action if he or she can demonstrate that he or she will get back on track with the mortgage repayments within a reasonable period of time.[212] So, it is therefore most unlikely that such sales will result in an Article 8 violation. However, it is conceivable that one exceptional type of case might violate the Convention. The current law contains a loophole allowing mortgagees to sell mortgaged property without first gaining possession, and therefore without using the court process.[213] Where this occurs, the mortgagor has no

---

208 See, e.g., *Bank of Ireland v. Bell* [2001] 2 FLR 809.

209 See *Putnam*, which suggested that s. 15 of the TLATA was itself compatible with Article 8.

210 The judge in *Horsham* who said otherwise seems wrong on this point.

211 *Horsham* (in obiter dicta). See also *Close Invoice*, which employed the same reasoning to justify a sale pursuant to a charging order. See also *Alcorn*, which concerned the taking of possession and the power to adjourn proceedings under s. 36 of the Administration of Justice Act 1970. It was considered justifiable under Art. 8. Note, however, that it is doubtful that the mortgagor's remedy of foreclosure would be Art. 8 compliant.

212 Administration of Justice Act 1970, s. 36.

213 See, e.g., *Ropaigealach v. Barclays Bank Plc* [2000] QB 263, although on the facts the mortgagor was not residing in the property at the time.

opportunity to challenge the mortgagee's conduct before a court, which might serve to violate his or her Article 8 rights. The Ministry of Justice is consulting on the issue and has put forward recommendations to close the loophole such that all sales by mortgagees of residential properties must be conducted either by agreement of the mortgagor or be channelled through the courts.[214] Such a move should be welcomed as one which will bring English law firmly in line with Article 8.

In general, in the mortgage repossession context, the domestic courts are to be commended for taking Article 8 seriously, even though it is unlikely to have much, if any, material impact on the cases.

Third, Article 8 was considered in *Truro Diocesan Board of Finance Ltd v. Foley* in relation to a lease for five years over privately owned property.[215] At the end of the five-year period, the landlord sought to evict the tenant, which he was entitled to do under domestic law. However, the action was opposed by his tenant who argued that Article 8 entitled him to remain in the property. The judge, following *Kay*, decided in favour of the landlord. Since *Pinnock*, however, one would expect such a case to be reasoned differently. At the very least, the court should carry out the proportionality balancing test. The landlord's property rights will, of course, weigh heavily in the balance, for it is in society's interests to protect those with property rights. Nonetheless, the tenant might succeed under Article 8 where he or she can point to personal circumstances that command special protection under the Convention.

The fourth and final area of property law to be scrutinised under Article 8 is overreaching, which was discussed above in relation to P1–1. In the Article 8 context the issue has arisen where trustees have charged the property to a bank, thereby overreaching a beneficiary's interest. This might interfere with the beneficiary's Article 8 rights if he or she was living in the property. The issue has been discussed in two separate cases. In *Birmingham Midshires Mortgage Services Ltd v. Sabherwal*,[216] the judge considered that the overreaching doctrine could be justified as a proportionate interference under Article 8 because it served to protect lenders. That protection was believed to be necessary and in the public interest. The issue was revisited in *National Westminster Bank Plc v. Malhan*,

---

214 Ministry of Justice, 'Mortgages: Power of Sale and Residential Property' (CP No. 55/09, 2009). Note that the Ministry itself believed the current law to be compatible with Art. 8; its recommendations were motivated by more general concerns for occupiers.
215 [2008] EWCA Civ. 1162, [2009] 1 All ER 814.
216 (2000) 80 P&CR 256.

which was discussed above.[217] There, the judge took the opposite view and suggested that overreaching might operate in violation of Article 8.[218] The facts in both cases arose before the HRA was in force, so the comments contained therein are merely obiter. The issue is therefore ripe for further consideration. Arguably, lenders have sufficient alternative means of protecting themselves against prior interest holders – such as asking beneficiaries to waive their rights[219] – that overreaching cannot be regarded as a necessary and proportionate doctrine.

The above analysis has revealed that while property law generally operates compatibly with Article 8,[220] this is not necessarily always the case. The Convention and the HRA require that property law is properly scrutinised to ascertain whether it really does offer proper protection for people's homes. Proper scrutiny will enable those few patches where the law might not be compliant to be discovered and reformed.

12.4 Conclusions

This chapter began by considering the Real Property Commissioners' view in 1829 that the law of real property was a near-perfect human institution. The Convention rights provide a modern benchmark by which the truth of this statement might be assessed today. This chapter has argued that property law should be consistently and thoroughly tested against the Convention rights. To achieve this, it is essential, first, for the Convention to be widely *applicable* in property cases; and, second, that the courts properly reflect on whether particular property rules are *compatible* with the Convention.

The domestic courts' approach to the Convention on both issues was at first disappointingly restrictive. While there is a danger that too much Convention scrutiny might bring unwanted uncertainty to property law, this danger will exist only in those areas where property law falls foul of the Convention. Rarely will this be the case, for domestic property

---

217 See n. 144 above.

218 [2004] EWHC 847 (Ch).

219 See further M. Dixon, 'Equitable Co-ownership: Proprietary Rights in Name Only?', in E. Cooke (ed.), *Modern Studies in Property Law: Vol. 4* (Hart, 2007), ch. 2.

220 Note that some areas of property law are particularly deferential to the needs of occupiers, e.g., the Land Registration Act 2002, Sch. 3, para. 2 (which protects against postponement an interest of someone in 'actual occupation' of the relevant land); and Sch. 4, paras. 3 and 6 (which render it difficult to alter the Register against someone in 'possession' of the land).

law has been developed over the centuries in a manner which is sensitive to the sorts of values protected by the Convention. However, in some dark patches of the law might lurk some rules whose operation infringes the Convention. Therefore, unless judicial minds are alerted to the Convention, those violating property rules will not be noticed and therefore reformed. The Supreme Court's decision in *Pinnock* marks an important step forward in exposing property law to Convention scrutiny in vertical cases. In order to maintain consistency across property law, it is to be hoped that horizontal cases will attract a similar level of human rights surveillance.

It is, of course, unlikely that back in 1829, property law was 'near-perfect' despite what the Real Property Commissioners thought. The same is true today: property law is neither faultless nor inherently compatible with human rights. Thus, English law should not fear the Convention as a destabilising influence; instead the Convention should be embraced. Property and housing law, in the few areas the Convention will affect, will be much the better for its presence.

13

Commercial law

FRANCIS ROSE

Perception of the content of human rights law is nowadays inevitably moulded by the Convention and its adjectival law. However, the Convention does not purport to deal exclusively with every issue that might be thought to be a matter of human rights and freedoms. In particular, it is broadly concerned with personal integrity (protection of life, liberty, personal security, privacy and property; freedom of conscience, expression and assembly, etc.) rather than with interaction between persons, which is the essence of commercial law.

Entitlement to Convention rights has been held to extend beyond human beings, in particular, to non-natural, corporate persons, who constitute the principal group of persons who are engaged – and created to be engaged – in commercial activities. Thus, companies are regarded as having human rights.[1] The same is true of state trading organisations which operate on a commercial basis independently of their government.[2]

However, it is highly unlikely that Convention rights could be held to extend to things that are not treated as persons. In theory, the point could be raised in respect of a ship or other maritime property that is subject to an action *in rem* (independently of a parallel action *in personam* against its owners or other interested parties). However, the point is unlikely to arise. First, it is difficult to envisage why the claimant would have an interest in raising the argument; so, if it were raised, it would be by a defendant legal person, who, by virtue of entering an appearance, would allow an action *in personam* against him- or herself (in which the argument would have more chance of success), thereby rendering the possibility of the argument in the action *in rem* superfluous. Second, despite the English tradition of proceeding against ships independently of persons who are

---

1 *R* v. *Broadcasting Standards Commission, ex p. BBC* [2001] QB 885; pet. diss. [2001] 1 WLR 550. See further D. Kinley, *Human Rights and Corporations* (Farnham: Ashgate, 2009).
2 *Islamic Republic of Iran Shipping Lines* v. *Turkey, The 'Cape Maleas'* [2007] ECHR 1081, [2008] 735 LMLN 1 (*The 'Cape Maleas'*).

interested in them and arguably the more appropriate defendants, rightly or wrongly the House of Lords has recently indicated that actions *in rem* are in reality actions against interested persons,[3] and European Union law has been unsympathetic to the traditional English approach.[4]

On first impression, therefore, the law on human rights has little obvious connection with the concerns of commercial law,[5] which are primarily as follows. First, the law encourages product exchange. Second, there is a connected principle of party autonomy, that is, the law respects freedom of action, most obviously in this context freedom of contract. Third, the law should give effect to the corollary of freedom of action, namely, security of action. Thus, *pacta sunt servanda* (that is, agreements must be upheld), including their consequences, most obviously the effectiveness of transferring interests in commercial products. Fourth, the law must reconcile these principles with competing principles or policies, such as consumer protection and respect for vested rights. Indeed, a tension at the heart of commercial activities is highlighted in the famous dictum of Denning LJ[6] that:

> In the development of our law, two principles have striven for mastery. The first is for the protection of property: no one can give a better title than he himself possesses. The second is for the protection of commercial transactions: the person who takes in good faith and for value without notice should get a better title. The first principle has held sway for a long time, but it has been modified by the common law itself and by statute so as to meet the needs of our times.

Not surprisingly, it is this last context (reconciliation of the specific principles and policies of commercial law with potentially competing principles and policies of other areas of law) that provides the most obvious opportunity for observing the relationship between commercial law and human rights law. At a very generalised level of abstraction, at least some of the principles of commercial law may appear to be reflected in

---

3 See especially *Republic of India* v. *India Steamship Co., The 'Indian Grace' (No. 2)* [1998] AC 878.

4 See *The Deichland* [1990] QB 1; and *The Tatry* [1994] 1 ECR 5439, *sub nom. The Maciej Rataj* [1995] 1 Lloyd's Rep. 302.

5 For an account of the relationship between human rights and *commerce*, see, e.g., J. Harrison, *The Human Rights Impact of the World Trade Organisation* (Oxford: Hart, 2007); C. Harding, U. Kohl and N. Salmon, *Human Rights in the Market Place* (Farnham: Ashgate, 2008). See further S. Bottomley and D. Kinley (eds.), *Commercial Law and Human Rights* (Aldershot: Dartmouth, 2002).

6 *Bishopsgate Motor Finance Corp.* v. *Transport Brakes Ltd* [1949] 1 KB 332 at 336–7.

some of the broad principles underlying Convention-specified human rights. Thus, as far as freedom of contract is a particular example of the general right to freedom of action which English law accepts,[7] it has some affinity with the Convention right of freedom of expression, which, in common with the general principles of commercial law, is expressly subjected to competing interests that are necessary in a democratic society.[8] In particular, on more than one occasion the right to freedom of expression has been held to be displaced by the grant of interim injunctions protecting intellectual property rights. The cases have tended to maintain the balancing approach of English law prior to the implementation of the Convention, though with some ambivalence. In *Imutran Ltd* v. *Uncaged Campaigns Ltd*[9] in 2001, Sir Andrew Morritt V-C held that, though it expressly requires the court to have particular regard to the importance of the Convention right to freedom of expression and places the burden on the applicant for an injunction to satisfy the court that publication should be restrained, section 12 of the HRA (freedom of expression) does not require the court to place greater weight on the importance of freedom of expression than previously and recognises the commercial context. However, six months later, without reference to *Imutran*, the Court of Appeal in *Ashdown* v. *Telegraph Group Ltd*[10] approved a principle of interpretation favouring Convention law upholding freedom of expression, even where it went beyond the public interest defence under the statutory copyright scheme, but upheld an injunction where the defendant's alleged breach of copyright was not for the purpose of free speech, but for journalistic reasons to further its competing commercial interests. More recently, an injunction has been granted where a defendant making unfavourable comments about a product protected by a trade mark had a commercial interest in diverting trade to himself.[11]

However, the scheme of the Convention is to promote not general policies, but particular policies in specified circumstances; and it is inescapable that core commercial law rights and freedoms have not been included in the Convention. Therefore, the impact of Convention-based human rights law on commercial law must be gathered not from generalised

---

7 See, e.g., *Attorney-General* v. *Guardian Newspapers Ltd (No. 2)* [1990] 1 AC 109 at 283 *per* Lord Goff of Chieveley.
8 See Art. 10.
9 [2001] 2 All ER 385. Cf. *Ashdown* v. *Telegraph Group Ltd* [2001] EWCA Civ. 1142, [2002] Ch 149.
10 [2001] EWCA Civ. 1142, [2002] Ch 149.
11 *Boehringer Ingelheim Ltd* v. *VetPlus* [2007] EWCA Civ. 583, [2007] Bus. LR 1456.

abstractions but, if at all, from the particular terms of the Convention and the general principles derived therefrom, and added thereto, as they apply to commercial matters.

There is at present limited treatment of the commercial application of the Convention to commercial matters in case law or literature.[12] However, this does not mean that there is little scope for the application of the Convention in commercial law rather than that there are fertile areas for development awaiting the catalyst of a reported case[13] or academic publication[14] to alert the legal profession to the possibilities. The HRA is still comparatively recent, it is not manifestly applicable to commercial matters, and there may be thought to be limited value in mere speculation as to its effect. Thus, some leading treatises on major areas of commercial law provide little or no guidance on its applicability. For example, no, or almost no, mention of it is made in the leading works on sale of goods, agency, insurance or (perhaps more surprisingly) financial services.[15] Moreover, the impression that Convention-based law has little applicability to commercial matters is perhaps encouraged by the fact that, although it has been seen to have some application in other areas of commercial law, its effect has been at the most limited.

---

12 One exception is P. Duffy, 'The Protection of Commercial Interests under the European Convention on Human Rights', in R. Cranston (ed.), *Making Commercial Law* (Oxford: Clarendon, 1997), ch. 23. This essentially discusses case law of the European Court of Human Rights on matters that may be of interest to those involved in commerce rather than core matters of commercial law. See generally R. Clayton and H. Tomlinson, *The Law of Human Rights* (Oxford: Clarendon Press, 2000), paras. 11.327–11.337.

13 The use of, and a series of reported cases on, retention of title clauses was prompted by the reporting of *Aluminium Industrie Vaassen BV* v. *Romalpa Aluminium Ltd* [1976] 1 WLR 676, a decision which was initially not reported on the ground that it decided no new issue of principle. Similarly, it was the almost unspoken acceptance of the unavailability of pre-trial *Mareva*/freezing injunctions (cf. *Lister* v. *Stubbs* (1890) 45 ChD 1) that provoked Donaldson J's abrupt dismissal of Geoffrey Brice QC's application for one and so in turn prompted Mr Brice's appeal to the Court of Appeal, the reporting of the decisions of which (in *Nippon Yusen Kaisha* v. *Karageorgis* [1975] 1 WLR 1093 and *Mareva CNSA* v. *International Bulkcarriers SA* [1975] 2 Lloyd's Rep. 509) prompted what Lord Denning MR has called the greatest piece of judicial reform in his time (A. Denning, *The Due Process of Law* (Oxford University Press, 1980), p. 134) and a subsequent deluge of applications and reported cases.

14 One of the most active areas of litigation over the last quarter of a century, the law of restitution for unjust enrichment, was largely prompted by an active series of academic publications.

15 E. McKendrick and R. Goode (eds.), *Goode on Commercial Law*, 4th edn. (London: LexisNexis Butterworths, 2009), p. 69 omits discussion with the observation that the implications of the Human Rights Act 1998 for English contract law are still being worked out.

13.1 Arbitration

Commercial disputes may appear to provide more potential than many areas of commercial law for control by the Convention, as they provide the potential for challenge under Article 6 (right to a fair trial). Article 6 generally provides entitlement: to a tribunal that is established by law; that the tribunal is independent and impartial; that the hearing is held within a reasonable time; that the hearing is public; that the hearing is fair; and that judgment shall be pronounced publicly. In practice, it is common for parties to prefer commercial disputes to be settled not by litigation but by submission to arbitration, which has traditionally been assumed to be a speedier, cheaper and more private means of dispute settlement than litigation.[16] Much of the legislation currently governing arbitrations, the Arbitration Act 1996, was specifically designed to uphold the integrity of arbitral proceedings and to safeguard them from circumvention by challenge in the courts. This inevitably raises the possibility of confrontation with the Convention.[17] Moreover, the Court of Appeal has held that, in exercising the supervisory role of the court over arbitrations, which is laid down and defined by the 1996 Act, the court is acting as a branch of the state and in the public interest to facilitate basic fairness in the arbitration process, so the parties' ability to determine their own dispute resolution method outside the courts is continually subject to the ability of either party to exhort the court to exercise its supervisory function in accordance with the Convention,[18] thus invoking the role of the court itself as a public authority subject to the HRA, as well as having to interpret the 1996 Act in accordance with the HRA, as relevant.[19]

Nonetheless, arbitral proceedings challenged on the ground of incompatibility of the Convention have generally been found to be consistent with it. This is essentially for three reasons. First, it has been found possible to reconcile the broad aims of the Convention with the special circumstances of arbitration. Second, English arbitration law, notably the

---

16 Alongside a continuously developing law of arbitration, there has in recent years been a considerable amount of activity in the area of international commercial litigation and this too has raised human rights issues.

17 See generally C. Ambrose, 'Arbitration and the Human Rights Act', *Lloyd's Maritime & Commercial Law Quarterly* (2000), 468; C. Ambrose, K. Maxwell and A. Parry, *London Maritime Arbitration*, 3rd edn. (London: Informa Law, 2009), pp. 12–15.

18 *Department of Economics, Policy and Development of the City of Moscow v. Bankers Trust Co.* [2004] EWCA Civ. 314, [2005] QB 207, [2004] 2 Lloyd's Rep. 179 ('*Bankers Trust*').

19 For further discussion of the role of Art. 6 in the civil procedure generally see Chapter 17.

scheme laid down in the 1996 Act, has been found to be basically compatible with the Convention. And, third, English arbitration practice has generally been found to be compliant with the 1996 Act and likewise with the Convention. In particular, the 1996 Act has both mandatory and non-mandatory provisions.[20] On the one hand, parties are free to make their own decisions about the effect of arbitral proceedings and to take them outside the general requirements of the Convention. This is for two reasons. First is the statute's concession that some of its provisions are non-mandatory. Second, the Strasbourg jurisprudence has recognised that parties may waive Convention requirements[21] – provided they do so unequivocally and voluntarily, without constraint (of illegitimate pressure or mistake),[22] and not contrary to any public interest,[23] and they have validly done so.[24] On the other hand, the mandatory requirements of the 1996 Act authorise the courts to ensure that certain requirements of the Act are always complied with. These mandatory provisions would be subject to challenge if incompatible with the Convention; but in practice they have been found to be both compliant with and to give effect to fundamental Convention policies.

Thus, by choosing arbitration – and appointing the arbitrators – parties are treated as having waived a right to an 'independent and impartial' tribunal,[25] to the safeguards of public court procedure[26] and to a public hearing; and so, it has been held, they have no right to an oral hearing on an appeal from an arbitration award unless there are exceptional circumstances.[27] In general, parties to an arbitration agreement may impose limitations on the right to appeal.[28] Thus, although resort to the courts is deliberately restricted by the governing Arbitration Act 1996, section 69 of the Act provides that a party may appeal to the court on a question of law arising out of such an award; but this is subject to the parties' contrary agreement, for example, by agreeing to dispense with reasons for an arbitral award.[29] Where there is an application for permission

---

20 Arbitration Act 1996, s. 4.
21 *X* v. *Federal Republic of Germany* (App. No. 1197/61) (1962) 5 YB, European Commission 88.
22 The requirement that onerous terms should be brought to the attention of the proferee (*Interfoto Picture Library Ltd* v. *Stiletto Visual Programmes Ltd* [1989] 1 QB 433) must also be satisfied: *Stretford* v. *Football Association Ltd* [2007] EWCA Civ. 238, [2007] Bus. LR 1052, [2007] 2 Lloyd's Rep. 31 at [53] ('*Stretford*'); *Sumukan Ltd* v. *Commonwealth Secretariat* [2007] EWCA Civ. 243, [2007] Bus. LR 1075, [2007] 2 Lloyd's Rep. 87 ('*Sumukan*').
23 *Stretford.*   24 See also *Sumukan.*   25 *Stretford.*
26 *Deweer* v. *Belgium* (1980) 2 EHRR 439; *Bankers Trust*; *Stretford.*
27 *BLCT Ltd* v. *J Sainsbury Plc* [2003] EWCA Civ. 884, [2004] 2 P&CR 32.
28 *Sumukan.*   29 Arbitration Act 1966, s. 69(1).

to appeal, there was initially a practice, albeit not an invariable one, by judges of the Commercial Court not to give reasons for the decision to grant or refuse leave. David Steel J reasoned that the appeal process is intended to be swift and based on principles of privacy and finality, so, if the parties have received a fully reasoned award, there is no unfairness if the court does not give reasons in disposing of an appeal under section 69 of the Arbitration Act 1996; and, although it had been his own practice to give reasons, he concluded that it was desirable for there to be a consistent practice in this respect, which he found to be in favour of not giving reasons.[30] The tendency had been publicly criticised by one of the foremost supporters of the Convention, Lord Bingham of Cornhill,[31] a decade before the United Kingdom's enactment of the Convention and, interestingly, without reference to the Convention. However, his criticism was recalled by the Court of Appeal shortly after the enactment of the HRA, in a judgment that found that *some* reasons were required for compatibility with the Convention.[32] These reasons may be brief. Thus, it might be sufficient simply to identify the grounds for leave (in section 69(3) of the 1996 Act) which had not been satisfied; but, where the arbitral tribunal's award was obviously wrong or open to serious doubt, it might well be necessary to say more.

The Court of Appeal has recognised both a mandatory requirement under the 1996 Act to remove an arbitrator for impartiality (thus complying with the Article 6 requirement of impartiality)[33] and a residual jurisdiction, arising from Article 6 of the Convention, to review on appeal the misconduct or unfairness of a judge's determination concerning the grant or refusal of permission to appeal under section 69(8) of the 1996 Act where there has been such a substantial defect in the fairness of the procedure as to constitute a breach of the Convention right to a fair trial.[34] However, the same court then held that it was insufficient to show that the judge's decision was merely perverse or that he had otherwise erred in law. First, the Strasbourg court is not concerned with the merits of an

---

30 *Mousaka Ltd* v. *Golden Seagull Maritime Inc.* [2002] 1 WLR 395, [2001] 2 Lloyd's Rep. 657.

31 Rt. Hon. Lord Justice Bingham, 'Reasons and Reasons for Reasons: Differences Between a Court Judgment and an Arbitration Award', *Arbitration International*, 4 (1988), 141.

32 *North Range Shipping Ltd* v. *Seatrans Shipping Corp., The 'Western Triumph'* [2002] EWCA Civ. 1, [2002] 2 Lloyd's Rep. 1, pet. diss. [2002] 1 WLR 2970.

33 See *Stretford*.

34 *CGU International Insurance Plc* v. *AstraZeneca Insurance Co. Ltd* [2006] EWCA Civ. 1340, [2007] Bus. LR 162.

impugned decision, but with the fairness of the procedure; and it accords to the national court a margin of appreciation (that is, within the framework of the Convention, national law may provide for local conditions and needs).[35] Second, the Court of Appeal's approach affirms a clear reluctance to allow awards to be undermined by the Convention and a preference for settled commercial legal policy. In the words of the court, 'The courts will not permit the residual jurisdiction, which exists to ensure that injustice is avoided, to become itself an unfair instrument for subverting statute [that is, the 1996 Act] and undermining the process of arbitration'.[36] Indeed, the court has subsequently pronounced that not only may there be no public interest opposing submission to arbitration, but that public interest is inclined to encourage arbitration in commercial cases.[37]

The effect of the arbitration cases has essentially been twofold: in general, to uphold the process of arbitration; and, more particularly, to confirm the compatibility with the Convention of the statutory scheme developed for commercial considerations and embodied in the Arbitration Act 1996 (which *inter alia* empowers the High Court to correct any impartiality or procedural unfairness).

An interesting by-product of the Court of Appeal's recent examination of the compatibility of English arbitration law with the Convention has been its exposure of the relationship between Convention law and important factors within commercial law, namely, information and competition. Dispute resolution services (whether judicial, arbitral or otherwise) are themselves a commercial commodity and capable of constituting a valuable invisible export. The availability of information about commercial products (which has both positive and negative aspects) is an important ingredient in deciding whether to deal with them (and, if so, on what terms). It affects competitiveness, which is a feature that English commercial law generally encourages. In its examination of the compatibility of English arbitration law with the Convention, the Court of Appeal has identified features that enable comparison with similar services in other Convention countries and elsewhere. Thus, it has found that the 1996 Act 'affords greater access to the court by way of appeal than is permitted in

---

35 See *ASM Shipping Ltd of India* v. *Titmi Ltd of England* [2006] EWCA Civ. 1341, [2007] 1 Lloyd's Rep. 136, affg [2005] EWHC 2238 (Comm), [2006] 1 Lloyd's Rep. 375. See further *ASM Shipping Ltd* v. *Harris* [2007] EWHC 1513 (Comm), [2008] 1 Lloyd's Rep. 61.

36 [2006] EWCA Civ. 1341 at [100], [2007] Bus. LR 162 at 187 *per* Rix LJ, with whose reasoned judgment Sir Anthony Clarke MR and Longmore LJ agreed.

37 *Stretford.*

many countries and, indeed, by many standard forms of arbitration such as arbitration under the ICC Rules'.[38] It remains for the market to decide whether this has revealed a feature of the English arbitration system that is likely to attract customers or whether the English market and legislature should endeavour to modify its rules (within the framework sanctioned by the Convention) so as to enhance its attractiveness.

13.2 Ombudsman

Arbitration is perhaps the best known, but it is not the only, other way of settling disputes apart from traditional adjudication. Another common method is under an ombudsman scheme, and this has also come under scrutiny in connection with the Convention. In *R (Heather Moore & Edgecomb Ltd) v. Financial Ombudsman Service*,[39] a complaint that a pension plan had been mis-sold by a firm of independent financial advisers was determined by the defendant (the 'FOS') in accordance with the scheme laid down by the Financial Services and Markets Act 2000. The firm claimed a breach of Article 6 on the ground that the FOS did not determine the claim according to law and with an oral hearing. The Act authorised the FOS to determine complaints by reference to what was in the opinion of the ombudsman 'fair and reasonable in all the circumstances of the case',[40] which required the ombudsman to form a view, not in accordance with the common law, but subjectively in accordance with the law provided by the statutory scheme, failing which his decision would be subject to judicial review. The statutory policy was to create a scheme under which disputes might be resolved quickly and with minimum formality; it allowed parties to provide documentary evidence, upon which it was possible to make a fair decision quickly, at minimum cost and with minimum formality, in which case an oral hearing was unnecessary; and parties could make representations and respond to a provisional assessment by the defendant. Accordingly, Article 6 was not breached. As with cases under the Arbitration Act 1996, the FOS system was treated as subject to review under the Convention and was, again, found to be compliant with it, even though the statutorily authorised system was (*ex hypothesi*) different from the dispute resolution system provided by ordinary adjudication and especially tailored to the market with which it was designed to deal.

---

38 *Stretford* at [65].   39 [2008] EWCA Civ. 642, [2007] Bus. LR 1486.
40 Financial Services and Markets Act 2000, s. 228(2).

13.3 Insolvency

In addition to the effect in the resolution of commercial disputes between private parties, there are, of course, criminal offences that impact particularly on the commercial world, in particular those who police insolvency law, to protect commerce against dishonest exploitation of the insolvency regime. However, here too the HRA has only had a limited impact.[41] For example, in *R* v. *Kearns*,[42] provision by the Insolvency Act 1986 that it is a criminal offence for a bankrupt not to account for the loss of a substantial part of his property in the twelve months prior to a bankruptcy petition[43] was held not to contravene the rights to silence and against self-incrimination under the case law derived from Article 6, since the obligation to disclose was part of an administrative or extra-judicial process rather than to compel information to be used in subsequent criminal proceedings. Likewise, in *R* v. *Muhamad*,[44] the fact that, under the Insolvency Act 1986, it is an offence of strict liability to engage prior to insolvency proceedings in hazardous activities such as gambling[45] was held not to contravene Article 7 of the Convention (no punishment without law). The Court of Appeal held that offences of strict liability were not *per se* objectionable under the Convention; nor did it offend against the principles of legal certainty or of proportionality to find that an offence was one of strict liability. There have, however, been cases where Article 6 has been used to read down burdens of proof placed on the person accused of an insolvency offence so that it is a burden to raise an issue on the evidence, rather than a legal burden to satisfy the court.[46]

13.4 Consumer and commercial law and protection of property

It is noticeable that the areas just considered, where there have appeared slightly more reported decisions than in most other areas of commercial

---

41 Cf. J. Ulph and T. Allen, 'Transactions at an Undervalue', *Journal of Business Law*, (2004), 1–33 for a consideration of the implications for s. 238 of the Insolvency Act 1986 of *Wilson* v. *First County Trust Ltd (No. 2)* [2003] UKHL 40, [2004] 1 AC 816 (*Wilson* is discussed below). For discussion of the interaction between property and insolvency, see Chapter 16.

42 [2002] EWCA Civ. 748, [2002] BPIR 1213.   43 Insolvency Act 1986, s. 354(3).

44 *R* v. *Muhamad* [2002] TLR 350, CA.   45 Insolvency Act 1986, s. 362.

46 For example *Attorney-General's Ref (No. 1 of 2004)* [2004] EWCA Crim. 1025, (2004) 1 WLR 2111, burden in s. 357 to prove transaction not intended to defraud creditors read down; but s. 353 legal burden left in place.

law, though they are of importance to commercial lawyers, do not deal with what may be considered to be core areas of commercial law but rather with collateral issues, which in a wider sense are of concern to all lawyers and citizens, namely, the processes by which rights are determined and remedies or penalties are imposed, particularly in regulatory and disciplinary hearings.[47] Similar issues arose in the current leading case on the effect of human rights law on commercial law, *Wilson* v. *First County Trust Ltd (No. 2)*.[48]

There is a tendency among some lawyers at least to make a distinction between commercial law and consumer law.[49] On that basis, *Wilson* is arguably not a case on commercial law in the stricter sense, since it was concerned with the effect of a section of the Consumer Credit Act 1974. However, on another view, it is at least premature to accept such a distinction, especially since commercial law has traditionally had to take account of supervening legal policy and consumer protection is simply one, though a major, policy impinging on commercial activity. For that reason, it is appropriate to consider *Wilson* here. In any event, there are dicta in *Wilson* with wider significance for commercial law.

The central issue in *Wilson* was that a money-lending contract failed to satisfy the 1974 Act's requirement of a correct statement of the amount of credit and section 127(3) of the Act forbade the court from making an order enforcing such an improperly executed agreement. The question was whether this prohibition was incompatible with the Convention right to a fair trial (Article 6) and/or right to protection of property (Article P1–1). The House of Lords decided: that the effect of section 127(3) was that the substantive right acquired by the creditor under the contract was subject to an initial restriction on enforceability if it was improperly executed; that Article 6 of the Convention did not create substantive rights, but only guaranteed the procedural right to have a claim in respect of existing civil rights and obligations adjudicated by an independent tribunal; and that section 127(3) did not bar access to the court to determine whether or not the agreement was in fact unenforceable, and so was not incompatible with Article 6.

---

47 'In the field of commercial law, the most important area of impact concerns regulatory and disciplinary hearings': Clayton and Tomlinson, *The Law of Human Rights*, para. 11.327.

48 [2003] UKHL 40, [2004] 1 AC 816, reversing [2001] EWCA Civ. 633, [2002] QB 74.

49 Increasingly, consumer rights are derived from EC/EU legislation, thereby forming a body of law that is heavily, if not predominantly, influenced by its European origins and likely to be capable of withstanding challenge under human rights law.

From the perspective of the law generally, *Wilson* decides that, where a statute imposes an initial statutory restriction on a contractual right but the effectiveness of that restriction remains subject to determination in court, the statutory restriction is not incompatible with the Convention right to a fair trial. From a more specifically commercial perspective, their Lordships' speeches raise a number of further points in relation to the Convention's protection of property (by virtue of P1–1).

First, four of their Lordships[50] accepted that this 'property' right, which is to 'peaceful enjoyment of... possessions', includes contractual rights; so, in short, contractual rights are protected by the Convention. However, this protection is limited to existing, valuable assets; it does not extend to the mere opportunity of acquiring such a right or asset. In *R (Malik)* v. *Waltham Forest NHS Primary Care Trust*,[51] a general medical practitioner was unlawfully suspended by the defendant Trust from its list of persons who were entitled to perform medical services.[52] It was held that, if he had clientele or goodwill, that could constitute a possession which would have been protected by P1–1;[53] but that, since regulations forbade him from selling the goodwill in his practice, including that element of goodwill arising from patients coming to him because of his personal reputation or qualities, his goodwill had no economic value, and so did not constitute a possession protected under the Convention.[54] The decision reflects the position in insurance law that a carrier has an insurable interest (entitling him or her to claim an indemnity for loss when he or she is prevented from performing a carriage contract) if he or she has concluded a contract of carriage before the loss occurs, but not if he or she has a mere expectation, however justified, of concluding such a contract.[55] The position is reinforced by the earlier decision in *Re T & N Ltd*,[56] in which it was held that a potential future tort claim (a contingent claim for

---

50 Lords Nicholls, Hope, Hobhouse and Scott.

51 [2007] EWCA Civ. 265, [2007] ICR 1101, [2007] 1 WLR 2092.

52 However, his contract to provide NHS medical services (which could be performed by other practitioners) remained in force during his suspension, during which the Trust paid him under that contract (less expenses not incurred).

53 Cf. *Jain* v. *Trent Strategic Health Authority* [2009] UKHL 4, [2009] 1 AC 853, especially at [17]–[18], [44], [54].

54 The position is succinctly paraphrased in the *Times Law Reports* (2007), 114 as 'The ability to earn a living [is] not a right of possession such as was capable of protection under the European Convention on Human Rights' or 'right to work is not a possession'.

55 See, e.g., F. D. Rose, *Marine Insurance: Law and Practice* (London: Informa Law, 2004), paras. 3.29–3.43.

56 [2005] EWHC 2870 (Ch), [2006] 1 WLR 1728.

personal injuries caused by asbestos but not yet apparent), as a matter of construction, did not constitute the potential claimant a 'creditor' with a debt provable under insolvency legislation,[57] or (with as yet no material damage) entitle him to a cause of action in negligence constituting a 'possession' entitled to protection under the Convention.

Second, since the Consumer Credit Act 1974 was held to have legitimately restricted the right of the creditor acquired by virtue of the contract, *Wilson* indicates that, where a 'property' right is created or transferred subject to an initial qualification, the person acquiring the right cannot rely on the Convention to challenge the qualification, for he or she acquires only a limited right and his or her peaceful enjoyment of that limited right is not impinged on.[58] In this respect, therefore, the Convention is consistent with a traditional common law and commercial law right which the Convention does not address, namely, the right to freedom of contract. This approach is reinforced in the case of defeasible possessions. In *Anheuser-Busch Inc* v. *Portugal*,[59] the Strasbourg court recognised that the American Budweiser company's right to apply for registration of the name Budweiser was a possession, but that its right was subject to (lawful) rejection of its application, whereupon the right ceased.[60] There is a range of commercial situations in which rights are subject to be defeated, for example, where the contract is subject to rescission for a defect in its creation,[61] in cases of termination for repudiatory breach of contract (in particular, and notoriously, for breach of an insurance warranty)[62] and where it may be brought to an end by virtue of a termination clause or forfeiture,[63] where it is assigned or

---

57 The Insolvency Act 1986 and the Insolvency Rules 1986 (SI 1986 No. 1925).

58 By Lords Hope and Scott.   59 (2007) 45 EHRR 491.

60 Moreover, where a right is acknowledged (and therefore treated as a possession), but is legitimately valued at a lower level than it might have been, calculation at the lower level has been held not to be a deprivation of a possession under P1–1: *Head* v. *Social Security Commissioner* [2009] Pens. LR 207 (pension entitlement). See also *SRM* v. *HM Treasury* [2009] EWCA Civ. 788, [2009] UKHRR 1219.

61 For example, for breach of a duty of disclosure, or for misrepresentation (a situation that is discussed further below, pp. 317–20) or if there is a jurisdiction to set aside for mistake (cf. *Solle* v. *Butcher* [1950] 1 KB 671 with *Great Peace Shipping Ltd* v. *Tsavliris Salvage (International) Ltd, The 'Great Peace'* [2002] EWCA Civ. 1407, [2003] QB 679).

62 See *Bank of Nova Scotia* v. *Hellenic Mutual War Risks Assn (Bermuda) Ltd, The 'Good Luck'* [1992] 1 AC 233.

63 See *Mardorf Peach & Co. Ltd* v. *Attica Sea Carriers Corp. of Liberia, The 'Laconia'* [1977] AC 850; *Scandinavian Trading Tanker Co. AB* v. *Flota Petrolera Ecuatoriana, The 'Scaptrade'* [1983] 2 AC 694; *On Demand Information Plc* v. *Michael Gerson Finance Plc* [2002] UKHL 13, [2003] 1 AC 368. Given that the reluctance to relieve from forfeiture in a commercial

transferred,[64] or where goods are rejected and the right to payment is reversed. To challenge the defeat of a contractual right in such cases for non-compliance with the Convention, it will be necessary to prove that: the right was not simply a defeasible right; its termination was not simply an emanation of its limit, but a deprivation of possession; and, further, the deprivation was contrary to the Convention. Arguably, the situation might be more amenable to challenge under the Convention where a contractual right is taken away not by the counter-party's exercise of his or her rights but by the law. This is the position at common law where a contract is frustrated and future rights under the contract are terminated automatically. However, the draconian common law consequences of frustration (that the loss lies where it falls) have been ameliorated now by the possibility of adjustment of the parties' positions under the Law Reform (Frustrated Contracts) Act 1943.

Third, the Convention's protection of 'property' is itself expressly subject to qualification. Thus, it is stated that: 'No one shall be deprived of his possessions except in the public interest and subject to the conditions provided for by law' and 'The preceding provisions shall not . . . in any way impair the right of a State to enforce such laws as it deems necessary to control the use of property in accordance with the general interest . . .'. The Convention therefore accommodates the balance which commercial law has traditionally made between its basic principles and competing policies.[65] Thus, in *Wilson*, it was recognised[66] that Parliament was entitled to decide that the appropriate way of protecting the borrower was to deprive the lender of all rights under the agreement, including the rights to any security, unless the statutory requirements had been strictly complied with.

Moreover, in *Wilson* the legislative provisions were justified as a proportionate means of achieving the legitimate aims of consumer protection.[67] This may be compared with a commercial case in which the detention of a charterer's vessel and cargo, in consequence of a suspicion of smuggling but continued after the suspicion had been dispelled, was held to be an arbitrary control and disproportionate interference with the use of property contrary to P1–1.[68]

---

context is tempered by the fact that relief may be given in appropriate cases, the law on relief from forfeiture is likely to be held Convention-compliant.

64 See, e.g., *Borealis AB* v. *Stargas Ltd, The 'Berge Sisar'* [2001] UKHL 17, [2002] 2 AC 205.

65 See above, p. 301.   66 By Lords Nicholls, Hobhouse and Scott.

67 By Lords Nicholls, Hobhouse and Scott.   68 *The 'Cape Maleas'*.

In *Wilson* the underlying policy (consumer protection) was also held to be a justification for an arguable infringement of another common law right not included within the Convention, that to restitution for unjust enrichment, it being said to vindicate what might otherwise appear to be the unjust enrichment of a borrower who had suffered no prejudice from the non-compliance with the statute, at the expense of a lender who had acted in good faith throughout.[69]

The way in which Convention rights may be balanced with – or obliged to defer to – countervailing considerations was dramatically demonstrated in *SRM v. HM Treasury*.[70] During the recent credit crisis, the government secured the passing of legislation,[71] which it then used to enable it to nationalise the bank Northern Rock Plc. Former shareholders claimed that the assumptions that the valuer was required to make under the Act left them with next to nothing, but enabled the government to acquire the benefit of a valuable company with the potential to collect a handsome profit on resale. In the view of the Court of Appeal, the solution under the Convention depended on the application of three principles: first, the need for a fair balance to be struck between public interest and private right; then, in order to help achieve that goal, the principle of proportionality (that is, expropriation of property must be accompanied by reasonable compensation in relation to the property) and the doctrine of margin of appreciation.[72] In the court's view, in a 'micro-economic' setting, for example, where a single property is expropriated to achieve a specific and limited local objective, the proportionality principle is likely to require payment of the full market price. But, where the objective is in the public interest much broader, for example, protection of the banking system (and thus the general economy), the margin of appreciation may justify a different approach. In this respect the court referred to the practice within the law of maritime salvage, which is based on encouraging maritime commerce and the preservation of property so risked and in danger at sea, in balancing the reward due to salvors against the benefit to salvees from the services provided.[73] However, in *SRM* the general community interest outweighed the claimants' property rights, the expropriation was not in order to secure a profit for the government and was not

---

69 By Lords Nicholls, Hobhouse and Scott; for further discussion of the interaction between the Convention and the law of unjust enrichment see Chapter 14.
70 [2009] EWCA Civ. 788, [2009] BCC 558, [2009] UKHRR 1219.
71 Banking (Special Provisions) Act 2008.   72 See above, p. 307.
73 Citing (at [65]) F. D. Rose and W. R. Kennedy, *Kennedy & Rose on the Law of Salvage*, 6th edn. (London: Sweet & Maxwell, 2000), para. 1457; see now 7th edn. (2010), para. 16.077.

risk-free, and so the compensation paid was reasonable and the claimants' Convention rights were not infringed.

A similar approach is illustrated in *Global Knafaim Leasing Ltd* v. *Civil Aviation Authority*.[74] By statute, route and airport charges are payable to authorities responsible for running airports and for ensuring safety in the air over Europe,[75] and the authorities have a lien authorising them to detain aircraft for unpaid charges. The claimant lessor had leased an aircraft to Zoom, a company that had become insolvent, and was unable to recover its aircraft without satisfying Zoom's entire indebtedness for charges, that is, for those incurred in respect not only of the aeroplane in question but of its whole fleet. The lessor's claim that detention in respect of charges for other aircraft was contrary to the P1–1 failed because of the commercial context. Though the extent of the power of detention under UK legislation was more draconian than elsewhere in Europe, it fell within the margin of appreciation and was not disproportionate. The lessor knew and had to play the game. On the one hand, it was a sophisticated commercial operator that was conscious of the risks in the business in which it operated, and was able to protect its interests when beginning to do business with the lessee by inquiring as to its standing and taking a bond or guarantee, or subsequently by terminating the lease in good time. On the other hand, the scheme of which it complained was in the public interest and on the facts had been applied proportionately and fairly.

In fact, there seems to be some ambivalence in the speeches in *Wilson*. If, as is the main thrust of the speeches, the Act qualifies the creditor's right *ab initio*, so that the right that he or she would acquire in the absence of the Act never comes into being, and if the Convention merely protects already existing property rights, then it is inappropriate even to speak of protecting the borrower by depriving the lender of contractual and security rights, for no rights have arisen of which he or she can be deprived. Similarly, there is no need to justify the apparent unjust enrichment of a borrower in such a case if *ex hypothesi* the enrichment is a consequence of legislation, by virtue of which it is not unjust.

Alternatively, this apparent ambivalence may reveal a sense that a restriction arising from statute on a right which would in the absence of the statute be unrestricted is in reality an infringement of the peaceful

---

74 [2010] EWHC 1348 (Admin).

75 The Civil Aviation Authority (a public corporation) and the British Airports Authority ('a commercial operator . . . also . . . a public authority within the meaning of the Human Rights Act': at [9]).

enjoyment of possessions. No doubt in many cases the policy impinging on the erstwhile property right will be held to be legitimate, so
the outcome will be the same. But the alternative analysis is at least
prone to open more commercial arrangements to challenge under the
Convention.

The Convention's vertical protection of the peaceful enjoyment of possessions mirrors the common law's focus on protecting rights of possession, rather than of ownership, and the horizontal protection of a buyer
conferred by the seller's statutorily implied warranty of quiet possession
under the Sale of Goods Act 1979.[76] Other provisions of the Sale of Goods
Act 1979 may be more problematic. The Act is, in its origins, of a different
nature from legislation such as the Consumer Credit Act 1974, which,
like most legislation, was passed to create a statutory regime to be super-
imposed on the existing law and, for that reason, may be considered an
appropriate piece of lawmaking to be constrained by overriding norms
such as those contained in the Convention. For the preceding legislation,
the Sale of Goods Act 1893, was passed not to make new law but, in common with several pieces of fundamental commercial legislation at the
turn of the nineteenth and twentieth centuries, primarily to codify pre-
existing common law. To that extent, the legislation does not impinge on
the rights and freedoms that parties to a contract of sale would otherwise
have at common law. Nonetheless, it is debatable whether legislation is
any less susceptible to control by the Convention because it is an enacted
codification of a body of common law.

13.5 Transactions

The core concern of commercial law is with transactions, that is, with
transfers of interests in products. The starting point for English law here
is consistent with the Convention's protection of property, in relation to
which the guiding maxim is *nemo dat quod non habet*. In other words, a
person's interest in property may be transferred with his or her consent but
not without it, and it cannot be transferred by a person who is not entitled
to the relevant interest. In similar fashion, the security of receipt of the
person acquiring an interest in normal circumstances is also safeguarded
by, and consistent with, the Convention's protection of his or her acquired
property. However, the principle of security of receipt clashes with the
principle of protection of property where English law allows buyers and

---

76 Sale of Goods Act 1979, s. 12.

their like to acquire a good title without the consent of the original owner, generally through the intervention of an intermediary, by virtue of the so-called exceptions to the *nemo dat* rule.[77] The acquisition of title to products through the medium of a non-owner is generally regarded as one of the most controversial and complex subjects in commercial law.[78] If there is inconsistency with the Convention, it will have to be resolved. For the present, it may be noted that the perhaps most notorious, and therefore vulnerable, of the so-called exceptions to the *nemo dat* rule – whereby buyers could acquire good title in 'market overt' to what in many cases were simply stolen goods – has been abolished.[79] It is possible, however, that a challenge to any of the remaining exceptions as incompatible with the Convention's protection of property may be saved by resort to the Convention's sanction of current commercial law policy as being 'in the public interest and subject to the conditions provided by law'.

Given that the particular rights and freedoms of the Convention are not obviously relevant to core subjects of commercial law, if the Convention is perceived to affect commercial law, it may be more likely to do so by application of adjectival general principles of law that have developed in its jurisprudence, such as proportionality. An obvious candidate for consideration is the remedy of avoidance or rescission. This was recognised at common law for cases of so-called 'actionable' misrepresentation in pre-contractual negotiations and for breach of the duty of disclosure prior to entry into an insurance contract. Interestingly, the duty of disclosure has been codified for contracts of marine insurance, but not for non-marine insurance contracts, in the Marine Insurance Act 1906,[80] though the general principles of the 1906 Act have been treated as applicable to all insurance contracts. The availability of the remedy of avoidance/rescission for a material misrepresentation inducing a contract is also specifically provided for by legislation for (marine) insurance contracts,[81] though not for contracts in general.[82] However, the Misrepresentation Act 1967, section 2(2) created a discretion for a judge or arbitrator, where a

---

77 See generally M. G. Bridge, *Benjamin's Sale of Goods*, 8th edn. (London: Sweet & Maxwell, 2010), ch. 7.

78 It has been considered appropriate to receive the attention of the Law Commission: see Law Commission, *Ninth Programme of Law Reform* (Law Com. No. 293, 2005), para. 1.16 (Project 11: transfer of title to goods by non-owners). However, the controversial nature of the project is such that so far it has not been taken forward: see Law Commission, *Tenth Programme of Law Reform* (Law Com. No. 311, 2008), paras. 4.2–4.4.

79 By the Sale of Goods (Amendment) Act 1994.   80 Marine Insurance Act 1906, s. 18.

81 Marine Insurance Act 1906, s. 20.   82 Though cf. Misrepresentation Act 1967, s. 1.

person induced into any contract by a non-fraudulent misrepresentation was otherwise entitled to rescind, to 'declare the contract subsisting and award damages in lieu of rescission, if of opinion that it would be equitable to do so, having regard to the nature of the misrepresentation and the loss that would be caused by it if the contract were upheld, as well as to the loss that rescission would cause to the other party'. This therefore provides a discretion that may be exercised to provide a more flexible and proportionate remedy than simple avoidance.

The remedy of rescission has traditionally been criticised for its extreme nature (in erasing the contract *ab initio* when invoked), and because in practice it is frequently used not because the complainant believes that he or she was unfairly induced into entering the contract but because he or she can use it as an excuse for escaping obligations in the contract which are unconnected with the information not disclosed or misrepresented. This has become a particularly live issue recently in an active debate over whether the duty of disclosure exists after the contract has been concluded, particularly if in such a case its breach attracts the remedy of avoidance *ab initio*.[83]

There have been recent *dicta* suggesting that the post-contractual applicability of the pre-contractual disclosure rule and associated ideas of good faith depend on whether a remedy is 'appropriate' or 'proportionate'.[84] Moreover, in one case Longmore LJ suggested the remoulding of consequences of non-disclosure 'post-contractually' as follows:[85]

> It seems to me that the solution to the problem must be found in the somewhat broader context of the appropriate remedy . . . [The Marine Insurance Act 1906, section 17] states that the remedy is the remedy of avoidance but does not lay down the situations in which avoidance is appropriate. It

83 See generally F. D. Rose, 'Information Asymmetry and the Myth of Good Faith: Back to Basics', *Lloyd's Maritime & Commercial Law Quarterly* (2007), 152.

84 Thus, in *Manifest Shipping Co. Ltd* v. *Uni-Polaris Ins Co. Ltd, The 'Star Sea'* [2001] UKHL 1, [2003] 1 AC 469 at 470, the views of the Law Lords are synthesised in the headnote in the succinct proposition that 'it would be disproportionate for the insurer to be able to avoid the contract *ab initio* by reason of the post-contract failure of the assured to reveal all facts which the insurer might have an interest in knowing and which might affect his conduct'. See especially [2001] UKHL 1 at [51], [2003] 1 AC 469 at 494 *per* Lord Hobhouse. The same criticism has been made more recently if this were the consequence of holding that an insurer had a duty to warn an insured that he or she had only a limited period of time in which to claim: see *Diab* v. *Regent Insurance Co. Ltd (Belize)* [2006] UKPC 29, [2006] Lloyd's Rep. IR 779, noted BS (2006) 12 JIML 375 at 377.

85 *K/S Merc-Scandia XXXXII* v. *Certain Lloyd's Underwriters, The 'Mercandian Continent'* [2001] EWCA Civ. 1275 at [35]–[36], [2001] 2 Lloyd's Rep. 563 at 575.

is, in my judgement, only appropriate to invoke the remedy of avoidance in a post-contractual context in situations analogous to situations where the insurer has a right to terminate for breach. For this purpose (A) the fraud must be material in the sense that the fraud would have an effect on the underwriters' ultimate liability... and (B) the gravity of the fraud or its consequences must be such as would enable the underwriters... to terminate for breach of contract. Often these considerations will amount to the same thing; a materially fraudulent breach of good faith, once the contract has been made, will usually entitle the insurers to terminate the contract. Conversely, fraudulent conduct entitling the insurers to bring the contract to an end could only be material fraud. It is in this way that the law of post-contract good faith can be aligned with the insurers' contractual remedies. The right to avoid the contract with retrospective effect is, therefore, only exercisable in circumstances where the innocent party would, in any event, be entitled to terminate the contract for breach.

The desirability of aligning the right to avoid with the right to terminate the contract for breach is self-evident... If the right to avoid in a post-contract context is exercisable only when the right to terminate for breach has arisen, the disproportionate effect of the remedy will be considerably less and the extra advantages given to insurers when they exercise a right of avoidance (e.g., non-liability for earlier claims) will be less offensive than they otherwise would be.

Longmore LJ's approach goes beyond the HRA approach, of recognising the incompatibility of a provision of English law with Convention doctrine, to justifying a creative refashioning of the law to avoid perceived undesirable consequences. However, this is an approach from which the Court of Appeal has subsequently recoiled.[86] Moreover, in the leading case in this area, Lord Hobhouse was, with respect, correct to adopt a more restrained approach by suggesting resort to the idea of proportionality simply as a guide to interpretation. He said:

Where the application of the proposed principle would simply serve the interests of one party and do so in a disproportionate fashion, it is right to question whether the principle has been correctly formulated or is being correctly applied and it is right to question whether the codifying statute from which the right contended for is said to be drawn is being correctly construed.[87]

However, in another recent leading case, Rix LJ has demonstrated that the role of proportionality may both contradict a traditional value of

---

86 See especially *Agapitos* v. *Agnew, The 'Aegeon'* [2002] EWCA Civ. 247, [2003] QB 556.
87 *The Star Sea* [2001] UKHL 1 at [61], [2003] 1 AC 469 at 499 *per* Lord Hobhouse.

our commercial law and beneficially support one of the countervailing policies which it has traditionally accommodated. Thus, in *Drake Ins. Plc v. Provident Ins. Plc*,[88] he said:

> On the whole English law has not favoured the process of balancing rights and wrongs under a species of what I suppose would now be called a doctrine of proportionality. Instead it has sought for stricter and simpler tests for certainty... However... the existence of widespread insurance contracts of a consumer nature presents new problems. It may be necessary to give wider effect to the doctrine of good faith and recognise that its impact may demand that ultimately regard must be had to a concept of proportionality implicit in fair dealing.

The reform of insurance contract law is a major part of the Law Commission's current programme of law reform,[89] and for that reason the courts are likely to exercise restraint in judicial reform of the subject. But such restraint is not permissible if there is perceived to be an existing incompatibility with the Convention.

Thus, it is surely arguable that, since a contract which is voidable for non-disclosure or misrepresentation is nonetheless a valid contract until avoided,[90] the remedy of avoidance is not only an interference with the peaceful enjoyment of a contractual right contrary to P1–1 of the Convention, but its draconian nature makes it a disproportionate remedy for the relevant breach of duty. The position is arguably exacerbated by the inconsistency between providing a statutory discretion to relieve from avoidance for an actively negligent misrepresentation and providing no such relief in the case of an innocent non-disclosure.[91]

---

88 [2003] EWCA Civ. 1834 at [88]–[89], [2004] QB 601 at 628–9.

89 See www.lawcom.gov.uk/insurance_contract.htm. The Law Commission has issued a series of publications, of different types, as part of its insurance contract law reform programme, none of which makes any reference to potential human rights issues.

90 Cf. *Proform Sports Management Ltd* v. *Proactive Sports Management Ltd* [2006] EWHC 2812 (Ch), [2007] 1 All ER 356.

91 In 2010, the Law Commission began a project on possible reform of the law on misrepresentation and unfair commercial practices and issued a short paper outlining the current legal framework of some of the difficulties that exist followed by *Unfair Commercial Practices and Private Redress: Feedback from Stakeholders* (2010), neither of which refers to any possible human rights issues.

14

Restitution

DAVID HOFFMAN[*]

The basic principle underlying autonomous causes of action for which the legal response is restitution may be appropriately summarised for the purposes of this chapter as the reversal of unjust enrichment,[1] supplemented by some instances where restitution is a measure of damages rather than a cause of action. In common with many of the rights underlying private law, reversal of unjust enrichment is not one of the Convention rights. Therefore, the European Convention does not, in terms, mandate the reversal of unjust enrichment. Unjust enrichment does require there to be some factor which makes the transaction unjust and therefore liable to be reversed (for example, mistake, duress, failure of consideration, illegality),[2] and there may be some cases where the factor which makes the enrichment unjust does engage or overlap with a Convention Right. For example, one can imagine a case of a payment obtained by duress where the duress involved sufficiently severe physical harm to engage Article 3 (freedom from torture), but to refer to Article 3 there does not necessarily add anything meaningful to the merits of the reversal of the payment.

The Article of the Convention that is most likely to be substantively engaged by an unjust enrichment case is Article 1 of the First Protocol ('P1–1'), which protects rights to property ('the peaceful enjoyment

---

[*] This chapter is based on an article which appeared in the 2004 *Restitution Law Review*, and this revised version appears with the kind permission of the editor, Francis Rose.

[1] This is not an uncontentious statement, but to attempt to justify it here would be a substantial distraction: see especially P. Birks, *Unjust Enrichment* (Oxford University Press, 2003); '*Misnomer*', in W. Cornish *et al.* (eds.), *Restitution, Past Present and Future* (Oxford: Hart, 1998); G. Jones, *Goff & Jones: The Law of Restitution*, 7th edn. (London: Sweet & Maxwell, 2006); A. Burrows, *The Law of Restitution*, 3rd edn. (Oxford University Press, 2010) and elsewhere. The different views about the basis of, and place in the law of, restitution or unjust enrichment do not affect the substance of the law discussed in this chapter.

[2] Again, it would be a substantial distraction to justify the choice of terminology here, which is intended to be summary and not contentious: see the works cited in n. 1.

of . . . possessions'), because it may be engaged by the very act of reversing a transaction, and may therefore require consideration of whether the reversal is a justified and proportionate interference with the property right being reversed. Conversely, if the result of restitution is to undo a transfer of property, P1–1 could apply to support the claim for the return of property unjustly held. In that sense, it does not mandate an answer either way: where it applies depends on the underlying law relating to whether or not the transaction can be reversed.

P1–1 does not specify in terms what a right to property is or how such a right arises. However, the Strasbourg court has taken a broad view of what counts as 'possessions' for the purposes of the interpretation of this Article. Thus, 'possessions' can be real and personal property, including intangible property such as shares or intellectual property, and extends to any chose in action, including a debt, and a claim of any sort, as long as it is sufficiently established as a matter of domestic law.[3] The concept of a legitimate expectation is also relevant here, as it can offset what might otherwise be a 'possession' if there is some arguable right, but no legitimate expectation of its continuing or being enjoyed. For example, the Strasbourg court has held that in a situation where waiters have no property in tips added to a credit card bill, since the property in the tip passes directly to the employer, there is no property right to be protected; as a result, the employee has no legitimate expectation that the tips will count as part of their remuneration for the purposes of minimum wage legislation.[4]

A case which shows the scope of 'possessions' under the Article is *Stretch* v. *United Kingdom*.[5] Here the applicant was deprived of an option to renew a lease on the basis that Dorchester Borough Council, which had granted the lease, had acted outside its powers in granting the option. The Strasbourg court held that this was a breach of P1–1: there was a disproportionate interference with the applicant's property, since the option to renew was an important part of the original obligations into which he had entered and he had a legitimate expectation of being able to renew the lease. In a contractual situation of this sort, if a payment had been made prior to the declaration that the contract was *ultra vires*, such

---

3 *Stan Greek Refineries* v. *Greece* (1994) 19 EHRR 293 (arbitration award); *Pressos Compania Naviera* v. *Belgium* (1996) 21 EHRR 301 (claim in negligence); although it must be a claim that can be brought, not a contingent future claim: *In re T&N Ltd* [2005] EWHC 2870 (Ch) (contingent liability regarding future asbestos claims meant that future victims were contingent creditors but did not have a claim protected by P1–1).

4 *Nerva* v. *United Kingdom* (2002) 13 BHRC 246.   5 *The Times*, 3 July 2003.

a payment could potentially be recovered.[6] However, there does have to be a realistic claim for this to count as a possession: so, for example, where an educational body was required to repay government money to which it was not entitled, its claim that this was in breach of the Convention was declared inadmissible; it had never had the money lawfully in its possession and so had no legitimate claim to retain it.[7]

It should be noted, however, that, as with the earlier Article 3 example, in many cases an argument that a remedy for unjust enrichment is in breach of P1–1 will not add anything of much value to the case, since such an award is likely to comply with the justificatory conditions of P1–1, which states that 'No one shall be deprived of his possessions except in the public interest and subject to the conditions provided for by law and by the general principles of international law.' Indeed, thus far, there appear to be no reported cases where it has done so. For example, in *Shanshal* v. *Al-Kishtani*,[8] it was argued that the unenforceability of a claim on the grounds of illegality was a breach of P1–1. The Court of Appeal rejected that argument, holding that even if there was a deprivation of possessions, the case clearly fell within the public interest exception, in this case the policy against enforcing illegal transactions.[9] The general principles that govern when the law reverses transactions that are unjust are likely to be sufficient justification for the interference, as long as they are sufficiently certain to be 'provided for by law'.

Likewise, in *Wilson* v. *Secretary of State for Trade and Industry*,[10] the House of Lords decided that there was no incompatibility between the Consumer Credit Act 1974 and P1–1. Although their Lordships considered that the HRA did not apply in any event, since it was not in force at the relevant time, their Lordships considered the arguments on P1–1, and also Article 6, and held that the inflexible exclusion of a judicial remedy by section 127(3) of the Consumer Credit Act, which makes certain credit agreements wholly unenforceable, did not infringe the Articles, nor did the lack of a restitutionary remedy in such a case.[11] There was some

---

6 *Westdeutsche Landesbank Girozentrale* v. *Chichester DC* [1996] AC 669.
7 *Stichting Voor Educatie en Berosepsonderwijs Zadkine* v. *Netherlands* (2010) 50 EHRR SE2.
8 [2001] EWCA Civ. 264, (2001) 2 All ER (Comm.) 601.
9 Of course, a breach of the HRA could now in theory cause a transaction to be illegal, perhaps in the form of a transaction by a public authority that infringes the HRA.
10 [2003] UKHL 40, [2003] 3 WLR 568, reversing Court of Appeal sub nom. *Wilson* v. *First County Trust* [2001] EWCA Civ. 633, [2002] QB 74.
11 For the lack of a restitutionary claim in this situation see *Dimond* v. *Lovell* [2002] 1 AC 384.

difference of view between their Lordships about whether the rights of a lender in fact engage P1–1 in a situation where, as in this case, there is a delivery of the car as security but the security is not enforceable.[12] However, their Lordships did not consider that the statute infringed P1–1: it pursued a legitimate purpose, namely, the protection of consumers, and was a reasonably proportionate expression of that aim, bearing in mind also the need for the courts to give due deference to the role of Parliament in choosing the appropriate policy response to this situation.[13] The lack of a restitutionary remedy in this situation was equally justified as a consequence of this statutory policy.

Thus, so far, the HRA has at the most had only a background horizontal effect[14] on the substantive law of restitution, rather than leading directly to changes in the law. There are, however, some areas where the HRA could have a further effect, whether background or more directly requiring the courts to take Convention rights into account. This is perhaps more likely to come into consideration in this area of the law, which has been the subject of recent development and lively academic debate: issues of principle are brought to the fore in a way that is not as common in other areas.[15]

14.1 The *Woolwich* principle

One situation involving unjust enrichment that has resulted in a case being considered by the Strasbourg court is where the payment that is to be reversed was made to the state by way of taxation, which turns out to be unauthorised. This is the principle exemplified by the leading case of *Woolwich Equitable Building Society* v. *Inland Revenue Commissioners*:[16] 'money paid by a citizen to a public authority in the form of taxes or other levies paid pursuant to an *ultra vires* demand by the authority is *prima facie* recoverable by the citizen as of right'.[17]

---

12 [2003] UKHL 40 ('*Wilson*'): e.g., Lord Nicholls considered that this was an interference with a proprietary right (at [39]–[41]), but Lord Scott considered that the HRA prevents the lender having any proprietary rights in the first place (at [168]).

13 *Wilson*, e.g., *per* Lord Nicholls at [68]–[80], *per* Lord Scott at [169]–[170], *per* Lord Hope at [138].

14 Defined in Chapter 2.

15 For example, discussion of underlying principle in House of Lords in *Deutsche Morgan Grenfell Group Plc* v. *Inland Revenue Commissioners* [2007] 1 AC 558, especially *per* Lord Walker at [150]–[158] ('*Deutsche Morgan Grenfell*').

16 *Woolwich Equitable Building Society* v. *Inland Revenue Commissioners (No. 2)* [1993] AC 70 ('*Woolwich*').

17 *Woolwich* at p. 177.

This is a situation on the public–private border. It is vindicated by a civil action – an action that is private in form – but against a public authority as defendant, and so is effectively public law unjust enrichment. This is relevant to the present discussion, though, because of the need for consistency across the law of unjust enrichment, and because it tells us something about the way in which the Strasbourg court approaches such situations.

The principle underlying *Woolwich* is a corollary of the fundamental constitutional principle that taxation requires the authority of Parliament.[18] The basic principle of taxation is recognised by P1–1, which recognises that the state has the right to deprive citizens of their property for the purposes of taxation.[19] However, taxation must be lawful,[20] not arbitrary[21] and proportionate. Thus, where a payment is made in respect of a tax, or a demand for tax, that is unlawful, there is a violation of P1–1. The requirement that taxation must be lawful therefore requires compliance with the Bill of Rights, and a demand for the payment of taxes that is not authorised by Parliament will be an infringement of P1–1. The general principles that apply to Convention rights include the Article 7 freedom from retrospective legislation.[22] As well as applying in its own right to criminal offences, the general principle that the law should be clear and its operation predictable is an implicit requirement in other Articles that contain qualifications allowing an interference with Convention rights that have to be 'according to the law'.[23]

---

18 Bill of Rights 1689, the relevance of which was pointed out by P. Birks, 'Restitution from the Executive: a Tercentenary Footnote to the Bill of Rights', in P. Finn (ed.), *Essays in Restitution* (Melbourne: Law Book Co., 1990), cited in *Woolwich*, e.g., *per* Lord Goff at p. 166.

19 P1–1 expressly provides that: 'The preceding provisions shall not, however, in any way impair the right of a State to enforce such laws as it deems necessary to control the use of property in accordance with the general interest or to secure the payment of taxes or other contributions or penalties.'

20 This refers both to being lawful in the sense of *intra vires* and to complying with the principles of legality (the rule of law), by being certain, clear, etc.

21 This was one point at issue in *Aston Cantlow Parochial Church Council* v. *Wallbank* [2001] 3 WLR 1323, CA, [2003] UKHL 37, (2003) 3 WLR 283, HL: the argument that succeeded in the Court of Appeal was that a liability to repair the chancel of a parish church attaching to a specific piece of land only was an arbitrary tax and therefore in breach of the Convention, but this was reversed by the House of Lords, a majority of whom also did not consider that that Parish Council was acting as a public authority in any event.

22 Article 7(1): 'No one shall be held guilty of any criminal offence on account of any act or omission which did not constitute a criminal offence under national or international law at the time when it was committed . . . '

23 See, e.g., *Halford* v. *United Kingdom* (1997) 24 EHRR 52.

The retrospective aspect was considered in *National and Provincial Building Society* v. *United Kingdom*,[24] which was a sequel before the Strasbourg court to the *Woolwich* case. There, three building societies, the National and Provincial, Leeds and Yorkshire Building societies ('the Building Societies') had all paid tax in the same circumstances as the Woolwich, on the basis of the regulations that were successfully challenged as being *ultra vires* in *Woolwich*.[25] The Building Societies then issued proceedings making the same claim as that which succeeded in *Woolwich*. However, before these reached trial, legislation was passed to retrospectively change the defective regulations,[26] which barred the claims of the Building Societies (the Woolwich itself was excluded from the effect of the legislation), and their attempt to obtain a remedy by judicial review was subsequently also barred.[27] The Building Societies then claimed that the retrospective legislation deprived them of their possessions, namely, their claims to the money that they had paid over pursuant to the *ultra vires* tax demand, in breach of P1–1.

The Strasbourg court was prepared to proceed on the basis that the Building Societies' restitutionary claims were 'possessions' for the purposes of the case. The counter-argument was that the Building Societies did not have a claim that was certain to succeed, and had no legitimate expectation that the situation would not be remedied by legislation. However, the Strasbourg court made the point that the question of whether there was a claim that was sufficiently definite to count as a possession itself turned on the substantive issues about the legislation, since it was that legislation that prevented the Building Societies' claims having any prospects of success in the first place.

It was not disputed that, if the claims were possessions, there was an interference with them by the retrospective legislation. The question then was whether such interference was a proper and proportionate control of the use of property in the public interest to secure the payment of tax. The court's conclusion was that the interference was justifiable. Although the original Regulations had been held to be *ultra vires*, the court considered that this was on the basis of an inadvertent technical defect, and did not affect Parliament's clear original intention, with which the Regulations

---

24 (1995) 25 EHRR 127 ('*NPBS*').
25 Regulations 3 and 11 of the Income Tax (Building Societies) Regulations 1986 (SI 1986 No. 482) held to be *ultra vires* s. 343(1A) of the Income and Corporation Taxes Act 1970 (added by s. 40 of the Finance Act 1985) by the House of Lords in *Woolwich (No. 1)* [1990] 1 WLR 1400; not cured by s. 47 of the Finance Act 1986.
26 Finance Act 1991, s. 53.   27 Finance Act (No. 2) 1992, s. 64.

conformed. The court considered that the Regulations did not result in double taxation: without the later legislation, the Building Societies would effectively receive a windfall in the form of a substantial amount of untaxed interest. In that sense, the retrospective legislation was doing no more than closing a loophole. The balance between the protection of the Building Societies' claims and the public interest in the payment of taxes was not upset, bearing in mind also the wide margin of appreciation allowed to national legislatures by the Strasbourg court on the substantive law of taxation.[28]

The Strasbourg court also rejected an argument that differentiating between the Woolwich and the other Building Societies was discriminatory within the scope of Article 14, taken together with P1–1, since the Woolwich had borne the costs of litigation. The Strasbourg court considered that this was a relevant ground for distinguishing the Woolwich from other building societies in the legislation. The Building Societies' claims that there was an infringement of Article 6 were also dismissed for reasons equivalent to those that applied to P1–1.

This decision does not tell us a great deal about the *Woolwich* principle itself, since it was not suggested that the Building Societies' claims for restitution as such were necessary to vindicate a Convention right. However, since in the future a governmental response to a similar challenge might well be the same,[29] the analysis of the circumstances under which a *Woolwich* claim can now be said to be protected (or not) from legislative reversal is highly relevant in practical terms to such a situation, especially the Strasbourg court's reluctance to countenance retrospective legislation without a clear justification, albeit that it considered that there was such a justification here.

This approach is of more general application. One can imagine situations where the state legislates as to property rights that are disputed, whether pursuant to a claim by the state, such as tax or compulsory purchase, or by that of an individual, such as relating to money in bank accounts where the bank is nationalised, and legislation intervenes. In such a case, the domestic courts would be likely to allow a wide discretion to Parliament before determining that any primary legislation was incompatible with the HRA: the principle that the courts should not be over-keen to interfere with Parliament's solution to a particular situation

---

28 For discussion of the margin of appreciation see, e.g., D. Hoffman and J. Rowe, *Human Rights in the UK*, 3rd edn. (London: Pearson, 2009), pp. 45–7.
29 As, e.g., in addressing cases of mistaken tax payments: see below, p. 330.

has already been judicially recognised.[30] However, although that gives Parliament some leeway, the courts will still be entitled to limit that leeway by interpretation, or find that such leeway has been exceeded and make a declaration of incompatibility.[31] Further, P1–1 will remain relevant to secondary legislation, including that of the devolved legislatures, which may be quashed if it infringes the Convention.[32] In all such cases, the principles developed by the Strasbourg court generally of proportionality, legality and non-discrimination will apply to such legislation, as demonstrated by the analysis in *National Provincial*, notwithstanding the result of the analysis in that case. This is certainly one of those areas where the property rights of individuals ensures that intervention by Parliament, whether to protect a claim by the state, or a claim between individuals, comes under a scrutiny that was not available before the HRA.[33] Further, the duty of restitution cuts both ways: if a private party is overpaid a state benefit or tax credit, then there is typically a duty to repay this, and again, it will be necessary for the state's claim for repayment to be treated in a way that is compliant with the HRA.[34]

14.2 The right to property and mistake of law

Another unjust enrichment situation where a consideration of the Convention jurisprudence may have some relevance is payments made under a mistake of law, and again the question raised is effectively that of

---

30 This was a factor in the discussion in *Wilson* v. *Secretary of State for Trade and Industry* [2003] UKHL 40, above, p. 323, discussed also in cases such as *R (Pro-Life Alliance)* v. *BBC* [2003] UKHL 23, [2004] 1 AC 185 and *R (Countryside Alliance)* v. *Attorney-General* [2007] UKHL 52.

31 Section 4, discussed in Chapter 3.

32 Section 3(2); Scotland Act 1998, ss. 29, 57(2); Government of Wales Act 2006, s. 81; Northern Ireland Act 1998, s. 6(2).

33 In practice many of the situation which would be covered by *Woolwich* are covered by the Taxes Management Act 1970, s.33(2A): *Monro* v. *Revenue & Customs Commissioners* [2008] EWCA Civ. 306: no common law remedy of restitution for recovery of the money paid under a mistake of law (discussed below) where the HRA applies.

34 Assuming, of course, that the Strasbourg court treats this as an interference with property that has passed and not property to which the citizen has no claim, which was the result in *Stichting Voor Educatie* v. *Netherlands* (2010) EHRR SE2 referred to above; and see generally C. Mitchell, 'Recovery of Ultra Vires Payments by Public Bodies', *Public Law* (2010), 747; and *R (Child Poverty Action Group)* v. *Secretary of State for Work and Pensions* [2010] UKSC 54, which limits social security repayments to the statutory scheme with no common law remedy.

retrospectivity, this time not in the context of legislation, but in judicial decision-making.

Reversal of unjust enrichment where a payment is made under a mistaken belief is practically the *locus classicus* of the law of restitution, but until recently English law recognised a remedy only where the belief was one of fact and not one of law. This changed in 1999, when the House of Lords in *Kleinwort Benson Ltd* v. *Lincoln City Council*[35] held that payments made under a mistake of law could also be reversed where it would otherwise lead to an unjust enrichment.

One of the questions raised by this recognition of mistake of law as the basis for a claim is what should happen where what is alleged that there has been a mistake because the law has been changed. The problematic issue is how this ground of restitution ties into decisions by the courts. A statute is presumptively prospective in effect: it has to be explicit to be retrospective, which is unusual. The legislation that followed *Woolwich* was one example, and as with other such examples, is usually intended to deal with a very specific situation. However, a judicial decision is regarded in common law theory as being declaratory of the law, and not as changing the law. It therefore has an arguably retrospective effect in that it will affect the legal interpretation of facts that have already occurred at the date of the decision. The difficulty is whether the law should recognise that where judicial decisions change the law, a payer with a correct understanding of the law at the time of the payment should not be regarded as mistaken just because the law is later changed. Or should the law maintain the formal position that the effect of a judicial decision is to declare the law and not change it – in which case a payer with what was at the time a correct understanding of the law can be held to have been mistaken on the basis of the law as it is now held to be.[36]

In *Kleinwort Benson*, a majority, Lords Goff, Hoffmann and Hope, rejected the argument that a payment should not be reversed where it is made on a settled understanding of the law, which is later held to be incorrect or which is later changed. Lord Goff considered that in that situation there was simply a mistake of law: to hold otherwise would be inconsistent with the declaratory theory of the common law, since judicial decision-making is inevitably retrospective. Lords Hoffmann and Hope

---

35 [1999] 2 AC 349.

36 This problem is, of course, raised by *Kleinwort Benson* itself, since prior to that case the law was clearly understood to be that a payment made under a mistake of law could not be recovered, and the law afterwards is clearly stated to be that it can.

were particularly concerned with the difficulties of determining whether there was in fact a settled general understanding, and the potential inconsistencies which that could create depending on, for example, whether a claimant took legal advice or not.

This view was re-emphasised by Lord Hoffmann in the later case of *Deutsche Morgan Grenfell Group Plc* v. *Inland Revenue Commissioners*,[37] where the House of Lords held that the lifting of the mistake of law bar means that mistake can also apply in cases of tax demands that turn out to be unlawful:

> It may be that this involves extending the concept of a mistake to compensate for the absence of a more general *condictio indebiti* and perhaps it would make objectors feel better if one said that because the law was now deemed to have been different at the relevant date, he was *deemed* to have made a mistake. But the reasoning is based upon practical considerations of fairness and not abstract juridical correctitude.[38]

This view of the result of a later decision receives academic support from John Finnis, who argues that declaring the law is a normative function and not simply a historical question about the party's state of mind; whether or not the law allows that mistake to found a recovery in unjust enrichment is a separate question.[39]

The question raised by this for present purposes is whether a claim for a payment made under a mistake of law, where the law as a historical fact has changed as a result of the later decision, could be a deprivation of property other than 'in accordance with the law'. Could reversing such a payment be unjustifiably retrospective, which, as we have seen above, can make a state decision unlawful and therefore unjustifiable?

Where the law is unclear and is clarified by a decision there is no breach of Article 7, nor is there if the law is reasonably clear but a change in the law is clearly foreseeable.[40] But it could arguably be an infringement of P1–1 to deprive a person[41] of the benefit of a transaction that was understood at the time to be a lawful transfer, but, potentially quite some time later, was liable to be re-opened because the law has changed with retrospective

---

37 ('*Deutsche Morgan Grenfell*').   38 *Deutsche Morgan Grenfell* at [23].

39 J. Finnis, 'The Fairy Tale's Moral', *Law Quarterly Review*, 115 (1999), 170.

40 *Kokkinakis* v. *Greece* (1994) 17 EHRR 397 applied in *SW and CR* v. *United Kingdom* (1996) 21 EHRR 363, the removal of the marital rape exception, which the Strasbourg court considered to be a foreseeable development.

41 As opposed to the state, which cannot be a victim of a breach of a Convention right: see Chapter 3.

effect. If it is accepted that the relevant judicial law-making does indeed have retrospective effect, this is a situation that the Strasbourg court has considered requires a clear public interest justification not to be a breach of P1–1.[42]

Whether sufficient justification exists simply in the recognition of the merits of reversing a mistake of law is not an easy question, since it has to be weighed against the interest of the payee in the security of trans-action, and it may or may not be the case that the defence of change of position provides sufficient flexibility to protect the payee in the event of, for example, a substantial delay before the transaction is held to have been mistaken. From the perspective of the interest in security of prop-erty and of transactions, there is surely some difficulty in distinguishing between the merits of a person who pays a sum of money on demand without demur with a belief in the law that is commonly understood to be correct at the time, who can then re-open the transaction when the law is changed, and a person who pays an equivalent amount, with the same belief as to the law, but who does so pursuant to a compromise or a judgment and thus cannot re-open the transaction when the law is changed.[43]

The same consideration applies in tax cases: Lord Goff in *Kleinwort Benson* considered that, in the *Woolwich* situation, different arguments might apply to the question of repayment of taxes paid under a clear understanding of the law, because of the public interest against the repay-ment of taxes; this would be especially so as all citizens will have been treated alike.[44] In *Deutsche Morgan Grenfell*, the House of Lords con-sidered that this was more properly a matter for Parliament, which had indeed already acted to create something akin to a settled law defence

---

42 In *NPBS* the Strasbourg court considered that the retrospective provision under consider-ation foreseeably closed a specific loophole, which is a very much more limited situation than, say, abolishing the mistake of law bar.

43 The policy in favour of supporting compromises was upheld in *Brennan* v. *Bolt Bur-don* [2004] EWCA Civ. 1017, [2005] QB 303; for further discussion of this point see, e.g., A. S. Burrows, 'The English Law of Restitution: A Ten-Year Review', in J. Neyers, M. McInnes and S. Pitel (eds.), *Understanding Unjust Enrichment* (Oxford: Hart 2004), pp. 14–18; for an argument that in *Deutsche Morgan Grenfell* there was in fact no mistake, see C. Mitchell, 'Mistaken Tax Payments', *Restitution Law Review*, 15 (2007), 123, and M. Bhandari and C. Mitchell, 'Lessons of the Metallgesellschaft Litigation', *Restitution Law Review*, 16 (2008), 1.

44 [1999] 2 AC 349 at 381–2; see also the Northern Ireland case of *Mallusk Cold Storage Ltd* v. *Department of Finance and Personnel* [2003] NIQB 58.

in tax situations,[45] rather than a matter for judicial decision;[46] though notably there is an issue as to whether this can apply in respect of taxes that are held to be unlawful under European Union law, based on precisely the same underlying issue of retrospectively removing a right.[47]

14.3 Restitutionary damages

It is also appropriate to note here that there is another aspect to the law of restitution, as generally defined, which is the reversal of an enrichment obtained by a wrong, or restitutionary damages, whether reversal of a gain or disgorgement of a profit.[48] It is not proposed to discuss that here at length, since issues concerning damages involving breaches of Convention Right are discussed elsewhere.[49] However, it is worth noting that there is no reason why restitutionary damages could not be 'just and appropriate' (HRA, s. 8) to provide 'just satisfaction' (Article 41) in a particular case, whether for a claim directly under the HRA or an indirect claim vindicating a Convention right through some other statutory or common law right of action. A good example of this is breach of confidence,[50] where an account of profits can be granted to deprive the wrongdoer of the benefit received by reason of the wrong, and which can therefore apply where breach of confidence is used as a cause of action to vindicate Article 8 rights. For example in *Douglas* v. *Hello! Ltd*, Lindsay J awarded substantial damages (just over £1 million) based on loss of expected revenue, but considered an award of a sum for a notional licence fee (arguably a restitutionary measure) in the alternative, which he would have made had that sum not been smaller than the loss of revenue claim[51] (the award was reversed by the Court of Appeal and reinstated by the House of Lords).

---

45 Based on 'the practice generally prevailing' Taxes Management Act 1970, s. 33(2A)(a) as amended by Finance Act 1994, s. 19 and Sch. 19, para. 8(2); see *Deutsche Morgan Grenfell per* Lord Walker [145].

46 A view that mirrors the concerns discussed in this book about the judicial role in implementing Convention rights through the common law.

47 *Franked Investment Group Litigation* v. *Inland Revenue Commissioners* [2010] EWCA Civ. 103: the Court of Appeal held that there was a sufficient remedy, as required by EU law, under *Woolwich* and that the statutory limit on repayments in cases of mistakes did not limit the effectiveness of this remedy, at [217]–[229].

48 For discussion of this area see in particular J. Edelman, *Gain-Based Damages* (Oxford: Hart, 2002).

49 Chapter 11.   50 Discussed in more detail in Chapter 7.

51 [2003] EWHC 2629 (Ch): the main award was to *OK!* magazine, the Douglases had to content themselves with the rather more limited award of £14,600; at the trial on liability [2003] EWHC 786 (Ch) Lindsay J had ruled out awarding aggravated or exemplary damages.

The other remedial aspect of the law of restitution is the issue as to when a proprietary remedy in the form of a trust can be claimed to reverse unjust enrichment,[52] and whether this might be required to provide 'just satisfaction'. This would be unusual, especially as civilian systems tend not to have trusts in the same way as common law systems, so a proprietary claim based on a constructive trust or tracing, that is, other than for the return of specific property in which full legal title still vests, is not as obviously part of the legal arsenal available for most Strasbourg court judges.[53] One case thus far where it has been argued that a proprietary remedy is required is the case of *Duggan* v. *Governor of Full Sutton Prison,*[54] where the argument that P1–1 required a trust to be imposed in respect of money held for, or earned by, a prisoner while in prison was (rightly) rejected. Again, however, it is not beyond the bounds of possibility that this could apply in some cases.

---

52 Again, this is not the place to debate whether this is properly understood to be a remedy or an equitable property right (or both).

53 For example, the *Stichting Voor Educatie* case referred to above could well have included a trust analysis had it been heard in England, rather than simply a case where title did not pass.

54 [2004] EWCA Civ. 78, *The Times*, 13 February 2004, on appeal from [2003] EWCH 361 (Ch), [2003] 2 All ER 678.

15

Insolvency

CHRISTOPHER MCNALL

Personal insolvency (bankruptcy) is a widespread and growing phenomenon in England and Wales.[1] In the simplest case, any person who owes more than £750 can, upon payment of a relatively modest fee[2] and completion of two simple forms (available online), petition for his or her own bankruptcy.[3] The hearing of that petition is advertised, often in the 'small ads' of the local press. All that then remains is for the petitioner to persuade a judge at their local County Court, in a private hearing likely to take only a matter of minutes, that they are genuinely unable to pay their debts.[4] In most cases, this is abundantly self-evident from their Statement of Affairs – indeed, it is not challenged – and the petition is granted without demur. An interview at the local office of the Insolvency Service (often, but not invariably) follows, the creditors are contacted, and the Statement of Affairs is approved. Save in cases of misconduct, most bankrupts are automatically discharged within a year.

Although the administrative ease with which bankruptcy can be entered is perhaps a melancholy counterpart to the ease with which the want of solvency was arrived at,[5] the potentially traumatic effect of bankruptcy

---

1 In 2009, 134,142 people were made bankrupt or entered into Individual Voluntary Arrangements in England and Wales. This equates to 1 in every 322 adults (or about 3 per 1,000): see www.insolvency.gov.uk/otherinformation/statistics/201002/index.htm (table III) and www.statistics.gov.uk. This represents an almost 25 per cent increase from 2008, and is likely to be surpassed in 2010. In addition, 11,831 Debt Relief Orders were made. Debt Relief Orders came into effect on 6 April 2009 and are available as an alternative to bankruptcy where the debtor does not own their own home, has no more than £50 a month surplus income and assets (excluding a car) of not more than £300 and debt of less than £15,000.
2 Currently £150 for the Petition; £450 towards the costs of administration of the bankruptcy; and a £7 swearing fee for the Statement of Affairs.
3 Pursuant to Insolvency Act 1986, s. 264(1)(b).
4 Insolvency Act 1986, s. 272(1).
5 'Living beyond their means' was the most common cause of bankruptcy: in almost 70 per cent of cases: see insolvency.gov.uk, 'Causes of Failure in Bankruptcy and Compulsory Liquidation'.

itself is not ameliorated, especially in relation to what is often the principal asset – the family home.

This aspect of bankruptcy has assumed increasing importance given the massive expansion in home ownership over the last three decades, the result of several concurrent causes. One such cause was the liberalisation of the housing market effected by the Housing Act 1980, which, by its introduction of the 'right to buy' scheme, allowed local authority tenants to buy the freehold reversions of their properties, often at a substantial discount (up to 50 per cent), bringing home-ownership and the corresponding ability to raise credit against the equity of property within the reach of many.[6] Another cause was the liberalisation of the mortgage market, leading to increased competition between mortgage lenders, and a huge growth in lending, often secured.[7]

The bankruptcy regime is governed by Part IX of the Insolvency Act 1986, as amended by Part 10 of the Enterprise Act 2002, a liberalising measure that seeks to promote alternatives to bankruptcy, to help lift the stigma of bankruptcy and to encourage prompt and early financial rehabilitation ('a fresh start') for those bankrupts who cooperate with the Insolvency Service. The policy of the 2002 Act was made clear in Parliament: it sought to strike a balance between 'the benefits brought to the creditors and the rehabilitation of the individual bankrupt... the Government supports the principle of "can pay, should pay" for bankrupts'.[8] It was emphasised that 'If we are to build a truly enterprising economy, we must ensure that our insolvency regime is one that... helps reduce the stigma of failure.'[9]

The law of personal insolvency is one in which the private rights under the statutory regime and the fundamental consequences of bankruptcy, in divesting bankrupts of their personal property, including the potential loss of the roof over their heads, raise stark issues as to competing rights. On the one hand, there are the rights of the bankrupt's creditors, which will usually count as property rights for the purposes of

---

6 Between 1980 and 2000, home ownership in England and Wales grew from about 50 per cent to about 66 per cent, the growth being predominantly homes subject to a mortgage. About 1.6 million council houses were sold to their tenants under the 1980 Act: see J. Banks and S. Tanner, 'Home-Ownership and Saving in the UK', *Housing Finance*, 45 (2000), 25, citing Family Expenditure Survey 1978–96.
7 See I. Hussain, 'Macroeconomic Determinants of Personal Bankruptcies', *Managerial Finance*, 28 (2002), 20.
8 M. Johnson, Hansard HC Deb., cols. 88–9, 17 June 2002.
9 Lord Sainsbury, Hansard HL Deb., cols. 142–3, 2 July 2002.

P1–1 of the Convention.[10] On the other hand, there are the rights of the bankrupt to a measure of protection from the potentially overwhelming consequences of excessive debt;[11] and the rights of bankrupts and their families under Article 8 to respect for their home and family life. And, hedging the bankrupt's right to seek bankruptcy as a protection from their own insolvency, are criminal offences to deter the dishonest from exploiting society's compassion for the unfortunate.

As an area defined and regulated by statute (the 1986 Act and other provisions) this area of the law is already subject to the intervention of Parliament. Thus, the issue for the courts for present purposes is whether the statutory scheme is compatible with the HRA, with or without the interpretative assistance of section 3 of the HRA;[12] and, where the statutory scheme provides a judicial discretion, the extent to which the Convention requires that this be exercised in any particular way.

The area that has produced most reported cases is the ability of the trustee in insolvency to sell the bankrupt's family home. In many cases, the equity in that home constitutes the only substantial asset potentially available for distribution to the creditors.[13]

The bankrupt's interest in the family home automatically vests in the trustee in insolvency.[14] Where the legal title to such a home is held jointly, there is a presumption (rebuttable, albeit with difficulty) that the beneficial interest in the property is also held jointly.[15] The bankruptcy of any joint tenant severs any beneficial joint tenancy,[16] leaving the co-owners as beneficial tenants-in-common. Thus, it is often the case (where property is jointly owned, but only one co-owner enters bankruptcy) that the property comes to be co-owned by a non-bankrupt spouse (whose interest is in remaining in the property) and a trustee (whose duty is to pay the creditors).

Any property that is not owned absolutely by one person is subject to a trust of land, and is governed by the Trusts of Land and Appointment of

---

10 As long as it relates to a present claim rather than a contingent claim: *In re T&N Ltd* [2005] EWHC 2870 (Ch).

11 Article 1 of the Fourth Protocol to the Convention prohibits imprisonment for debt, though the United Kingdom is not a party to this Protocol.

12 See Chapter 4.

13 For a brief discussion of Art. 6 and insolvency offences see Chapter 13, p. x.

14 Insolvency Act 1986, s. 306.

15 Which can be said to result from the maxims that equity follows the law and equality is equity: see *Stack* v. *Dowden* [2007] UKHL 17 at [109] *per* Lord Neuberger.

16 See C. Harpum, S. Bridge and M. Dixon, *Megarry and Wade: The Law of Real Property*, 7th edn. (London: Sweet & Maxwell, 2008), para. 13–046.

Trustees Act 1996. In these circumstances, a trustee of a bankrupt's estate is a person who 'has an interest in a property subject to a trust of land' and can apply under section 14 of the 1996 Act for an order that the property be sold.

However, in such a case, the court exercises its powers in accordance with section 335A of the Insolvency Act 1986, rather than section 15 of the 1996 Act, and is entitled to make such order as it thinks just and reasonable, having regard to a number of factors, including the interests of bankrupts' creditors. Where the application is made in respect of land that includes a dwelling house that is, or has been, the home of the bankrupt, their spouse or civil partner, the court shall consider the conduct of any spouse or partner, 'so far as contributing to the bankruptcy', their needs and financial resources, the needs of any children and 'all the circumstances of the case other than the needs of the bankrupt'.

Section 335A(3) goes on to provide that where such an application is made after the expiry of one year from vesting in the trustee, the court shall assume, unless the circumstances of the case are 'exceptional', that the interests of the bankrupt's creditors outweigh all other considerations.

A final half-twist is to be found in the 'use it or lose it' provisions contained within section 283A of the Insolvency Act 1986 (introduced with effect from 1 April 2004).[17] These provisions, prompted by trustees 'sitting' on their rights (often for many years after the bankrupt's discharge), waiting for the tide to turn in the housing market, afford the trustee only an initial three-year period within which to realise the bankrupt's interest in the family home, following which that interest (in the absence of any application for more time by the trustee) automatically revests in the bankrupt.[18]

The leading pre-1998 authority on the statutory precursor to section 335A (which was couched in materially identical terms) was *Re Citro*.[19] In that case, the majority of a strong Court of Appeal (Nourse and Bingham LJJ; Sir George Waller dissenting) reversed the decision of Hoffmann J, who had postponed sale for several years, until the youngest child was sixteen. The Court of Appeal was firm and unsentimental in its view that 'exceptional' circumstances had to be those outside 'the usual melancholy consequences of debt and improvidence',[20] which included homelessness,

---

17 Enterprise Act 2002, s. 261.
18 This led to a slew of applications by trustees in the spring of 2007 to realise their interests.
19 [1991] Ch 142.   20 *Re Citro* at 157 *per* Nourse LJ.

the eviction of non-bankrupt spouses and children and disruption to schooling.

Even in the reported cases – few and far between – where exceptional circumstances were found to exist, the same did not generally operate to prevent sale, but only to postpone it. For instance, in *Re Raval*,[21] Blackburne J afforded a year (doubling the stay awarded by the Registrar) due to illness of the bankrupt's wife. Time was also given on account of illness in *Claughton* v. *Charalambous*.[22]

Against this harsh background, it is perhaps surprising that it took several years before any reported decision appeared wherein section 335A was challenged on the ground of incompatibility with Convention rights.[23] In *Barca* v. *Mears*,[24] Nicholas Strauss QC, sitting as a Deputy Judge of the High Court, was invited to make such a declaration.

Mr Barca had been made bankrupt eight years earlier. He resisted the application for an order for possession and sale on the basis that a forced move would seriously disrupt the education of his son, who had special educational needs and benefited from considerable support and specialist tuition from his father. Were Mr Barca rendered homeless, it was feared that the help that he would be able to give his son would be severely curtailed, halting his son's educational progress. Mr Barca sought an order deferring possession until 'my son completes his education'. He submitted (with some justification) that 'insolvency legislation in this area is particularly brutal and contrary to the average concept of fundamental freedoms and rights'.

Mr Strauss QC did not decide the point, but recognised that 'a shift in emphasis in the interpretation of the statute may be necessary to achieve compatibility with the Convention',[25] and upheld the order for possession. The astringent dicta of *Re Citro* were followed, but qualified by the remark that:

> there is nothing in the wording of section 335A, or the corresponding wording of sections 336 and 337, to require an interpretation which

---

21 [1998] 2 FLR 718, [1998] BPIR 389.

22 [1999] 1 FLR 740, [1998] BPIR 558 *per* Jonathan Parker J.

23 Although in *Jackson* v. *Bell* [2001] EWCA Civ. 387, the Court of Appeal gave permission to appeal against a decision of a Deputy High Court Judge that s. 335A was compatible with Art. 8 so as to enable submissions to be put forward that s. 335A (and, in particular, the reference to exceptional circumstances in s. 335A(3)) should be reconsidered in the light of Art. 8, the appeal did not proceed to a hearing: see *Nicholls* v. *Lan* [2006] EWHC 1255 (Ch) at [42].

24 [2004] EWHC 2170 (Ch), [2005] BPIR 15.   25 At [41].

excludes from the ambit of 'exceptional circumstances' cases in which the consequences of the bankruptcy are of the usual kind, but exceptionally severe. Nor is there anything in the wording to require a court to say that a case may not be exceptional, if it is one of the rare cases in which, on the facts, relatively slight loss which the creditors will suffer as a result of the postponement of the sale would be outweighed by disruption, even if of the usual kind, which will be caused in the lives of the bankrupt and his family.

Three subsequent decisions are also of relevance. In *Holtham* v. *Kelmanson*,[26] Evans-Lombe J dismissed an appeal against an order for sale of property in which Mr Holtham (who had been made bankrupt in 1995, and discharged in 1998) lived alone. Following his discharge, he had continued to pay the mortgage. In 2004, Mr Kelmanson was appointed as trustee in place of the Official Receiver. Given the (then) improving housing market, he sought to take more proactive steps to liberate the equity. The order was challenged using Articles 6[27] and 8. The learned judge held that Article 6 did not apply since 'the administration of a bankrupt's estate is not a process which results in the determination of the civil rights and obligations of the bankrupt'.[28]

As to Article 8, 'Mr Holtham had no right to occupy the property enforceable against the trustee . . . at any time after the commencement of the bankruptcy and the vesting of the property' and so 'in the absence of any persons other than Mr Holtham having any interest in the property no questions arise under Article 8 such as arose in *Barca* v. *Mears*'.[29]

In *Nicholls* v. *Lan (Trustee in Bankruptcy of Nicholls) and Nicholls*,[30] Paul Morgan QC (as he then was), sitting as a Deputy Judge of the High Court, considered an appeal from an order whereby a co-owned property was to be placed upon the market for sale, but not earlier than eighteen months from the date of the order. At first instance, the Deputy District Judge had found, in a finding which was not challenged, the circumstances to be 'exceptional', in the sense of 'out of the ordinary course, or unusual, or special, or uncommon'.[31] It was accepted that the claimant, Mrs Nicholls, who suffered from health problems, including chronic schizophrenia, met that criterion. The judge remarked that he did not see 'that the statutory test, leading to a balancing exercise, is

26 [2006] BPIR 1422, [2006] EWHC 2588 (Ch) ('*Holtham*').
27 'in the determination of his civil rights and obligations or of any criminal charge against him everyone is entitled to a fair and public hearing within a reasonable time'.
28 *Holtham* at [17](i). 29 *Holtham* at [17](iii). 30 [2006] EWHC 1255 (Ch).
31 *Hosking* v. *Michaelides* [2004] All ER (D) 147 *per* Paul Morgan QC.

inconsistent with the qualified nature of the rights enshrined in Article 8 and in Article 1 of the First Protocol. Indeed, it might be contended that section 335A precisely captures what is required [by those Articles].'[32] Respect for the home was not an absolute objective to be guaranteed in every case, 'but as a consideration in a balancing exercise'. As such, the learned judge reached the conclusion that the submissions that he had heard on the 1998 Act did not take the matter any further.

In *Foyle* v. *Turner*,[33] Mr and Mrs Foyle, who had been made bankrupt in 1991 and discharged in 1994, appealed against an order for sale of their home made in 2004 on the ground that the Deputy District Judge at first instance had failed to recognise that their Convention rights were engaged. HHJ Norris QC (as he then was), sitting as a Judge of the High Court, held that section 335A, as far as possible, should be read and given effect in a way compatible with the Foyles' Convention rights.

However, the learned judge rejected the submission that Article 6 was engaged:

> Mr and Mrs Foyle were divested of the property on the occurrence of their bankruptcy . . . No question of the determination of their civil rights arose until such time as the trustee applied for an order for possession and sale (so bringing to an end their permitted occupation). The process of realisation of property that no longer belonged to them . . . and its distribution for the benefit of their creditors did not of itself involve a determination of their civil rights.

Although Article 8 was relevant, it added nothing. The judge referred to the decision of the House of Lords in *Kay* v. *Lambeth LBC*,[34] in which their Lordships considered the scope and application of Article 8 in the context of possession claims by local authorities against authorised occupiers, holding that, where a statutory regime confers on the court a jurisdiction to make an order for possession if the court thinks it reasonable, then the exercise of the jurisdiction will require the court to undertake the very assessment that Article 8 requires. As such, Article 8 'adds nothing to the substance of the protection which the occupier already enjoys'.

In the view of HHJ Norris QC, the same principle applied to section 335A: 'Parliament has struck the balance between the bankrupt and his creditors, and has provided for the court to undertake a consideration of the interests of the bankrupt's spouse and children . . . Provided that the

---

32 *Hosking* at [43].   33 [2007] BPIR 43.
34 [2006] UKHL 10, [2006] 2 AC 465 ('*Kay*').

provisions of section 335A are faithfully followed and applied there is no need to enter into any separate consideration of Article 8.'[35]

While the passage of time (in principle) was capable of amounting to an exceptional circumstance, 'exceptional' was to be given a narrow meaning. Delay would have to be shown to be both 'inordinate' and 'materially and disproportionately to affect some interest to which the court is directed to have regard'. The delay in Foyle was not inordinate, and so did not avail the claimants. It is to be noted that this approach does not accord with that of the Strasbourg court, which, for example, in *Skurčák* v. *Slovakia*[36] considered the applicant creditor's complaint that a period of just over three years taken in relation to execution proceedings under then-prevailing Slovak insolvency law violated Article 6(1) raised serious issues of fact and law.[37]

If the above cases demonstrate an 'English' approach, then this can usefully be contrasted to more recent judicial exploration of the issue in a parallel jurisdiction. In *Official Receiver of Northern Ireland* v. *Rooney and Paulson*[38] Weir J, sitting in the Chancery Court of Northern Ireland, arrived at radically different conclusions.

There, the Official Receiver's applications for orders for sale of two dwelling houses it jointly owned (together with the respondents' wives) was refused following a delay of almost twelve years, during which the bankrupts and their wives had been left undisturbed. Mr Rooney and Mr Paulson had become bankrupt in 1990, but nothing was done to realise their interests because of the limited realisable value of their properties. In 1992, the Official Receiver wrote to Mr Rooney saying that if the debts were not settled the house would have to be sold, but, in fact, nothing was done. Mrs Rooney paid the mortgage and for expensive redecoration. While there was no correspondence with Mrs Paulson, she had spent considerable sums in building and adapting an extension to accommodate the requirements of her disabled daughter.

The trustee had 'waited for a lift in the incoming tide'. Weir J held that dispossession of the co-owning wives, who had in the meanwhile discharged their mortgages and improved the properties, would have been a disproportionate interference with their rights under both Articles 6 and 8.

---

35 *Kay* at [17].   36 [2007] BPIR 440.
37 *Skurčák* at [31]–[36]. And see L. Sealy and D. Milman, *Annotated Guide to the Insolvency Legislation 2011* (London: Sweet & Maxwell, 2011), p. 307.
38 [2008] NICh 22, [2009] BIPR 536.

A delay of almost twelve years was outside the parameters of a reasonable time for deciding whether to take the properties. The judge was fortified in his conclusion by the 'use it or lose it' provisions, which he considered could be regarded as a useful yardstick of what Parliament regarded as a reasonable period within which the trustee should decide whether to sell the property. On that basis, it was held that it must follow that the circumstances of the cases were 'exceptional' within the meaning of the relevant legislation.

Although the decision was apparently founded on the combined effect of Articles 6 and 8, against the background of a compelling impression of unfairness if the trustee in insolvency could wait almost indefinitely to obtain an order for sale, while failing to tell the occupiers that was his intention, it is nonetheless plain that Article 6 held sway.

The reasoning behind the decision, insofar as it is founded on Article 6, is absolutely unimpeachable, and it is arguable that the same outcome could have been arrived at on the basis of Article 6 alone, or even outside the 1998 Act entirely, for instance, by virtue of an estoppel, or arguments of natural justice.

It is noteworthy, and perhaps disappointing, that the judge did not venture to found his decision on Article 8 alone, as a free-standing ground. While Article 6 was used to attack the unfairness of the procedural position (namely, the trustee's delay), the reasoning and outcome are broadly negative or inhibitory in effect. There is an underlying presumption that the trustee's acts are lawful, rebuttable only by evidence of unusual or unreasonable delay. On the other hand, treatment under Article 8 alone would have needed to start from the opposite – affirmative – position; namely, from the presumption that the Convention rights of the family are fully engaged, and protected, subject only to evidence of prompt and reasonable action by the trustee. Not only does this place Article 8, and the rights that it protects, at the forefront, but it imposes the burden of demonstrating that a departure is justified on the trustee. It is submitted that this stance would accord more closely and intelligibly with the meaning and intent of the Convention.

As matters stand, *Rooney* is one of the few cases in which Convention rights have defeated a trustee's application for possession and sale. But its effect, far from presaging widespread change, is perhaps now limited by the 'use it or lose it' provisions.

Although the general tenor of the amendments to the 1986 Act introduced by the 2002 Act, and the Parliamentary statements made in support of those amendments, would lead the casual reader to suppose that

Parliament was at least giving a strong steer towards bringing the bankruptcy regime into greater harmony with Convention rights, the growing body of case law shows that the general treatment of bankrupts in this sphere has in fact changed little, if at all, since 1998. It has been resistant to change, and, despite token nods in its direction, judicial reasoning has yielded little to the Convention. The emergent judicial view that Article 8 adds nothing to existing law, insofar as it simply requires the court to conduct the balancing exercise under section 335A fairly, but without the protected right itself being a substantive factor in that exercise, appears unduly conservative and fails to convince. It cannot simply be assumed that the content of the rights that are protected under Article 8 is identical to the factors to which section 335A directs the court's attention.

Glimmers of a more enlightened view can be seen in the Insolvency Service, which recognises, in its Technical Manual,[39] that Article 8 might be substantively engaged when the court is considering sections 335A–337 of the 1986 Act, and that the 'exceptional circumstances' that would justify the court in declining to make an order for possession or sale in favour of a trustee should perhaps include all instances where the family home and the rights of children are in issue. But, while the pendulum has perhaps swung some distance from the strongly pro-creditor position expressed in *Re Citro*, there is still a long way to go. Despite several good opportunities, the courts continue to direct their focus (which sometimes seems sterile and artificial) towards whether the procedures and timescales laid down by the domestic legislation have been complied with, upholding these save in cases of flagrant breach or manifest unreasonableness on the part of trustees. This approach seems to flow from the understanding that the adoption of sound decision-making procedure is the best guarantee of fairness. However, the Convention rights – and especially those set out in Article 8 – may well demand a more muscular approach, which places the burden on trustees to demonstrate that their proposed actions conform with the Convention. The door is ajar.

---

39 Available online at www.insolvency.gov.uk at paras 33–135 (drafted May 2008).

16

Employment law

HAZEL OLIVER

Employment law deals with relationships between individuals in a place where the majority of adults spend a significant proportion of their time, namely, the workplace. Although this is generally an arena of private law, there is ample scope for human rights arguments to become relevant in regulating the workplace, both during employment and when the relationship begins to break down.

The application of the HRA in this context seems particularly apt because, unlike in many other areas of private law, there is an unequal balance of power between employer and employee, which can be seen as similar to the relationship between the individual and the state. Although the employment relationship is essentially based on contract, this is not a bargain between equals, meaning that an employer is in a unique position to harm the social and welfare rights of its employees. The ability of employers to rely on the private law of contract to regulate the employment relationship is already considerably circumscribed by statute, through a variety of laws that are designed to protect the individual from the employer's power and the inadequacies of collective bargaining.[1] It is simply one step further to regulate the terms of both the contractual bargain and the protective statutes themselves through the use of human rights principles.

The majority of employment law is statutory, meaning that the courts are able to use section 3 of the HRA and exercise their interpretive function to produce indirect horizontal effect, and this has already been done in some cases.[2] There is also the key common law duty of trust and confidence that is implied into all employment contracts, but the interaction of this duty with Convention rights is as yet unexplored. Overall, to date the actual use of the HRA in domestic employment law cases has

---

1 For a full discussion of these issues see P. Davies and M. Freedland, *Labour Legislation and Public Policy: A Contemporary History* (Oxford: Clarendon, 1993).
2 Section 3 is discussed in more detail in Chapter 4.

been limited, whether in relation to statute or common law. There are a number of possible reasons for this, as discussed further below. These include a failure at the stage of the level one analysis as to whether, on the facts of the particular case, any Convention rights require protection at all.[3]

This chapter looks at the theoretical relevance of human rights to the workplace and how these rights could be given horizontal application through various existing employment law provisions, before considering how the courts and tribunals have been applying Convention rights in their decisions, and why these rights have not been as significant in practice as might have been anticipated.

16.1 Relevance of human rights to the workplace

There can be no doubt that the HRA is fully capable of application to employment law. A number of specific rights under the HRA are potentially directly relevant to disputes that may arise during the employment relationship, and there are also many Strasbourg court cases that consider workplace issues.

The right to respect for private and family life, home and correspondence under Article 8 may be engaged by a variety of workplace practices and situations, and to date in the United Kingdom this has been the most fertile area for raising human rights arguments in the context of employment disputes. It is well established in Strasbourg court case law that Article 8 rights can apply in the workplace, perhaps most notably in the case of *Halford* v. *United Kingdom*,[4] which concerned covert telephone surveillance of a senior police officer by her employer. Privacy rights may be infringed by different types of surveillance practices that may be implemented by an employer, including recordings of telephone conversations, electronic monitoring of email and internet use, and video surveillance of employees both inside and outside the workplace. Article 8 rights may also be engaged where an employer's actions are affected by matters relating to an employee's private life outside work. This includes decisions based on an employee's sexual orientation, as illustrated by the Strasbourg court case of *Smith and Grady* v. *United Kingdom*,[5] which concerned the UK's then ban on gay men and lesbians serving in the military.

---

3 This analysis is introduced in Chapter 1.   4 (1997) 24 EHRR 523.
5 (1999) 29 EHRR 493.

It may also include wider aspects of an individual's private life, such as sexual behaviour[6] or even choice of hobbies or relationships.

The right to freedom of expression under Article 10 can also be directly relevant to the employment relationship, and there are a number of Strasbourg court decisions on this subject. These include cases involving political speech and activities, such as *Vogt* v. *Germany*,[7] concerning a teacher who was dismissed for being a member of the German Communist Party, and *Rommelfanger* v. *Federal Republic of Germany*,[8] where a doctor in a Catholic hospital was dismissed for having signed a letter stating that German abortion legislation was too restrictive. Whistleblowing is another area which is clearly relevant to the workplace and may be affected by Article 10 rights.[9] The court has also considered cases dealing with wider forms of expression by employees, such as challenges to dress codes – as illustrated by the case of *Kara* v. *United Kingdom*,[10] which involved a transvestite male employee who wished to wear female clothing to work.

The right to freedom of thought, conscience and religion under Article 9 may also be invoked by employees. This is most obviously relevant to issues of discrimination on grounds of religion or belief, which is considered separately in the chapter on this topic. However, it may also involve wider issues, such as political activities, in an overlap with freedom of expression rights.[11]

Finally, the right under the HRA that is most obviously applicable to the employment relationship is Article 11 – the right to freedom of assembly and association, which includes the right to form and join trade unions. In *Young, James & Webster* v. *United Kingdom*,[12] the Strasbourg court found that the United Kingdom was under an obligation to protect employees from dismissal for refusing to join a union. The later case of *Wilson and*

---

6 For example, see *Pay* v. *Lancashire Probation Service* [2004] IRLR 129, in relation to sado-masochistic activities (discussed further below) ('*Pay*').

7 (1996) 21 EHRR 205.   8 (1989) DR 151.

9 See, e.g., *Morrissens* v. *Belgium* (1988) 56 DR 127, concerning the dismissal of a teacher for making allegations against the provincial authorities and the heads of her school in a television interview.

10 22 October 1998 (App. No. 36528/97).

11 See, e.g., *X* v. *United Kingdom* (1979) 16 DR 101, concerning a teacher who was dismissed for proselytising, which included wearing an anti-abortion sticker. This was brought as an Art. 10 case, but could also be seen as an example of an attempt to manifest religious belief in the workplace.

12 (1982) 4 EHRR 38.

Palmer v. *United Kingdom*,[13] which involved discrimination on grounds of trade union membership in relation to payment of a bonus, led the UK Government to change the law after a ruling that the state's failure to prevent this practice violated Article 11.[14] Both of these cases related to domestic legislation and are clear examples of Strasbourg decisions against the state leading to changes in the law governing private parties in the employment context. However, aside from these two significant cases for the United Kingdom, there have been few Article 11 cases before the Strasbourg court that deal with key union and employment law issues, and none that use the HRA itself. In addition, as the vast majority of private sector workers in the United Kingdom are non-unionised, it is the other rights discussed above that are more likely to apply directly to most workplace relationships. The remainder of this chapter will focus on these other rights.

16.2 How can human rights affect employment law?

In order for the HRA to affect private employment law, the first step is to establish that some of the key rights under the HRA can be directly relevant to issues that are likely to arise in the workplace. As explained above, it is well established that a number of these rights do have ample scope to influence the employment relationship. For employees who work for public sector employers, these rights can simply be enforced by way of a direct claim for breach of the HRA. However, in order for these rights to have indirect horizontal effect between employees and private sector employers, it is also necessary for there to be some pre-existing legal provisions or principles that are capable of being influenced.[15] Although under the strongest form of indirect horizontality the courts would

---

13 *Wilson and the National Union of Journalists; Palmer, Wyeth and the National Union of Rail, Maritime and Transport Workers* v. *United Kingdom* [2002] IRLR 128.

14 These changes clarified that the law on protection for trade union membership included protection for using the services of the union, and brought forward a new provision on protecting workers from inducements to give up trade union membership, activities or services or give up collective bargaining, both brought in by the Employment Relations Act 2005.

15 This potentially includes private bodies that may be treated as 'public authorities' for other purposes under the HRA, as such employers would be performing private acts when dealing with their own employees and so would fall within the exception in s. 6(5) of the HRA. For further discussion see G. Morris, 'The Act and the Public/Private Divide in Employment Law', *Industrial Law Journal*, 27 (1998), 293.

simply be obliged to create a remedy for employees whose rights had been infringed, even if no other type of claim already existed, most forms of indirect horizontality need to work with an existing private law claim.[16]

Private employment law is primarily contained in legislation, and these basic statutory provisions are continually interpreted and developed by courts and tribunals. Such legislation is clearly subject to the interpretative obligation under section 3 of the HRA to ensure its compatibility with Convention rights. In addition, employment contracts are governed by some key common law principles, which are susceptible to the arguments that the courts should give effect to the Convention rights when applying them.

The key statutory right in employment law is the right to claim unfair dismissal under the Employment Rights Act 1996. This provides that dismissal (including a constructive dismissal) of an employee with more than one year's service can be both substantively and procedurally unfair, and the key test is that of whether the employer's conduct and decision was 'reasonable' under section 98 of that Act. The employer must first show that there is a fair reason for dismissal, either of a type falling within the list at section 98(2) or 'some other substantial reason' for dismissal. An Employment Tribunal must then decide whether the dismissal is fair or unfair in accordance with section 98(4), having regard to the reason shown by the employer. This involves consideration of whether in the circumstances the employer acted reasonably in treating it as a sufficient reason for dismissal, and must be determined 'in accordance with equity and the substantial merits of the case'. In deciding whether there is a sufficient reason for dismissal, the court or tribunal must ask itself whether the employer acted within the 'range of reasonable responses' of a reasonable employer, an addition to the statutory test that has been developed through case law.[17] This section 98(4) test has also been interpreted by the courts and tribunals as requiring an employer to follow reasonable procedural steps before making the decision to dismiss, again looking at all the circumstances of the case, and this has also become an accepted part of the overall test of fairness.

---

16 These classifications are introduced in Chapter 2.
17 The applicability of this test has been affirmed by the Court of Appeal in the cases of *Madden* v. *Midland Bank* and *Foley* v. *Post Office* [2000] IRLR 827 ('*Foley*'). It has also been argued that the HRA may actually require a move away from this relatively weak test where a human right is at stake: see M. Ford, *Surveillance and Privacy at Work* (London: Institute of Employment Rights, 1998), p. 47.

Relatively vague and flexible concepts such as 'reasonableness' and 'equity' are clearly open to interpretation by courts and tribunals, so creating an obvious route for horizontal application of the HRA rights or principles. The test of reasonableness applies both to whether any decision to dismiss the employee for the reason in question was fair, and to whether the disciplinary procedure that was used to dismiss was reasonable in the circumstances. This suggests that there is ample scope for the HRA to apply to the unfair dismissal legislation, particularly when one takes into account the fact that the courts have already expanded and developed key parts of the fairness test. The various concerns about the scope of the courts' powers of interpretation, particularly those relating to legal certainty, have less weight in the context of such broad statutory terms which are already subject to judicial interpretation.[18]

The key question here is whether an employer who acts in breach of human rights when dismissing an employee could be found to have acted appropriately. It is relatively easy to think of examples where a dismissal may engage Convention rights issues. In relation to whether a dismissal is for a fair reason, the dismissal of an employee for a reason connected with their private life, such as sexual conduct outside work, could well be seen as an infringement of privacy. Similarly, there is potentially a clear breach of the rights to freedom of thought and expression if an employee is dismissed for political activities. In relation to whether there has been a fair disciplinary procedure, the collection of evidence for disciplinary proceedings through surreptitious surveillance, a relatively common practice, particularly where evidence is being gathered from computers, could well be a breach of the right to privacy. These are some obvious areas where the HRA can influence what is seen as 'reasonable' employer conduct.

In addition to the basic statutory right of unfair dismissal, there are many other legislative provisions that regulate the employment relationship. The law on discrimination in the workplace is also a very significant area (discussed in Chapter 10). However, leaving aside the various provisions relating to union membership that are subject to Article 11, the remainder of this legislation is not so obviously susceptible to Convention rights arguments. One exception to this is the Public Interest Disclosure Act 1998, which deals with whistleblowing and could potentially be affected by the right to freedom of expression under Article 10, although, at the time of writing, there are no reported cases in this area which invoke

18 Chapter 4.

HRA arguments. However, for the majority of employees, the ability to claim unfair dismissal is both a key right and the central provision which regulates workplace disputes, as well as being defined by flexible concepts of 'reasonableness' which are particularly open to interpretation under section 3.

Turning to the common law, there are a few key provisions that regulate the employment contract. The first of these is the common law of wrongful dismissal, which relates to an employee's contractual notice period. The HRA is most likely to be relevant here in relation to whether a dismissal without notice is lawful. If such a dismissal is based on a reason that is potentially incompatible with a right under the HRA, it is strongly arguable that this reason cannot be used to justify a summary dismissal.[19]

Linked into the right to claim wrongful dismissal is the duty of mutual trust and confidence that is implied into all contracts of employment.[20] This concept has been entirely developed by the courts under common law. This was confirmed by the House of Lords to be a requirement that the employer would not, without reasonable and proper cause, conduct itself in a manner calculated and likely to destroy or seriously damage the relationship of confidence and trust between employer and employee (*Malik* v. *BCCI*).[21] As stated by Lord Nicholls in *Eastwood* v. *Magnox*,[22] this effectively imposes an implied contractual requirement on an employer 'to treat his employees fairly. In the conduct of his business, and in his treatment of his employees, an employer must act responsibly and in good faith.'[23] Where this implied duty has been breached by an employer, the employee can claim that there has been a fundamental breach of contract, and this is most often used as a trigger for a resignation and consequent claims for wrongful dismissal and constructive unfair dismissal.

The obvious question here is whether this duty can remain intact if fundamental human rights are infringed by the employer. It is possible to think of situations where an employer's conduct during the employment relationship potentially infringes rights under the HRA, perhaps most often through implementation of a particular policy or practice. For example, privacy rights may be infringed if the employer decides to introduce an invasive electronic monitoring system. Similarly, implementation

---

19 See K. Ewing, 'The Human Rights Act and Labour Law', *Industrial Law Journal*, 27 (1998), 275 at 287.

20 This implied duty was developed at first instance and applied by the Court of Appeal during the 1980s (see *Woods* v. *WM Car Services (Peterborough) Ltd* [1981] IRLR 347 and *Lewis* v. *Motorworld Garages Ltd* [1985] IRLR 465).

21 [1997] IRLR 462.   22 [2004] IRLR 732 ('*Eastwood*').   23 *Eastwood* at [11].

of a restrictive dress code may infringe both privacy and free expression rights, particularly if the employer is not willing to make exceptions for individuals. Freedom of expression may also be engaged if there is a ban on political speech in the workplace, or if an individual is disciplined for whistleblowing. If the duty of trust and confidence imposes a general requirement on an employer to act 'fairly', how can it be fair to act in breach of human rights? Compliance with this duty in such circumstances seems somewhat unlikely. This suggests that courts and tribunals would almost invariably have to find that the contract had been fundamentally breached where there had been an infringement of rights under the HRA.

The opposite side of the employer's duty of trust and confidence is the employee's duty of good faith towards the employer, which is often described as an obligation of loyalty or fidelity. As on the employer's side, a breach of this duty by the employee can be regarded as a fundamental breach of contract, which would entitle the employer to dismiss without notice. Convention rights arguments are less obviously relevant to the employee-side duties than to the employer's obligation to act fairly, as the employer is not generally in a subordinate position requiring protection of its fundamental rights. Although in theory an employer could claim the protection of the HRA, there are no UK examples of this in practice. However, it is possible that an employee's rights under the HRA could limit the scope of the obligation of loyalty. This obligation potentially includes duties not to damage the employer's business reputation or assist the employer's competitors.[24] The right to freedom of expression under Article 10 might well be engaged where an employee is accused of having breached this implied duty by making public statements that are damaging to the employer's reputation. However, it is the employer's duty of trust and confidence that has the clearer potential to be affected by indirect horizontal application of the HRA, and this will be the focus of the following discussion.

16.3 The application of Convention rights

Having established that there are some central employment law legislative provisions and common law concepts that are susceptible to influence by the HRA, what have the courts and tribunals actually been doing in practice? And what theory of horizontality (if any) have they been using?

---

24 See *Hivac Ltd* v. *Park Royal Scientific Instruments Ltd* [1946] Ch 169.

The impact of the HRA on statutory unfair dismissal law has been considered in cases involving both public and private employers. *Pay* v. *Lancashire Probation Service*[25] involved a public sector employee in the probation service, who was dismissed due to his involvement with sexual activities involving bondage, domination and sado-masochism which were advertised on the Internet. Mr Pay's employer took the view that such activities were incompatible with his role as a probation officer working mainly with sex offenders. Mr Pay claimed that his dismissal was unfair, as it breached his right to respect for private life under Article 8 and his right to freedom of expression under Article 10. Although this case involved a public sector employer, it was not a direct claim for breach of the HRA, but rather a statutory unfair dismissal claim that argued for horizontal application of these rights under the section 3 requirement of statutory interpretation.

In analysing the issues, the Employment Appeal Tribunal ('EAT') expressly confined itself to cases involving a public authority, although without giving a view on what the position would be where a private sector employer was involved. It held that Employment Tribunals should interpret the words 'reasonably or unreasonably' in section 98 of the Employment Rights Act 1996 as including 'having regard to the applicant's Convention rights', at least in a case where the employer is a public authority.[26] It went on to state that a public authority employer would not act reasonably under section 98(4) if it violates an employee's rights as guaranteed by the HRA. This clear statement seems to confirm that a dismissal that infringes such rights can never be fair. The EAT also referred expressly to the recent clarification of the 'range of reasonable responses' test in misconduct dismissals by the Court of Appeal,[27] and suggested that this test now needed to include consideration of Convention rights. In addition, it stated that the 'circumstances' considered by the tribunal under section 98(4) should include all matters weighed in the balance in assessing whether there has been an interference with a Convention right.[28]

Although this decision confined itself to public authority employers, it provides a clear example of how the HRA can affect an existing employment law right. The EAT did not perform a detailed theoretical analysis of how this should be applied to the existing right of unfair dismissal. However, the intended result is more obvious – dismissals that infringe

---

25 *Pay.*   26 *Pay* at 134.   27 *Foley.*   28 *Pay* at 134.

Convention rights cannot be fair – and the entire law of unfair dismissal is made subject to an individual's rights under the HRA.

The comments about the need to consider Convention rights as part of the test for misconduct dismissals are somewhat less clear, and could simply be confirming that these rights will be relevant to the rest of the unfair dismissal tests. However, it seems that the EAT intended to go further, suggesting that the established test of what is within the 'range of reasonable responses of a reasonable employer' will not be sufficient where Convention rights are concerned. This test gives employers considerable latitude in making dismissal decisions, meaning that seemingly harsh dismissals can potentially be fair if it can be shown that other reasonable employers might have made the same decision, even if the tribunal would have decided differently. However, the EAT seems to be saying that misconduct dismissals that infringe Convention rights cannot be fair even if some or all other employers would have behaved in the same way. This 'range of reasonable responses' test has already been criticised as bordering on a test of perversity and limiting the effectiveness of protection from unfair dismissal,[29] and this becomes increasingly undesirable where fundamental human rights are involved. The implications of the EAT's comments are that tribunals ought to play a greater role in setting standards for review of dismissals in such cases, and be willing to substitute their own judgment for that of the employer.[30] The 'reasonable employer' can no longer be someone who fails to respect human rights – at least in the public sector.

Although the *Pay* case establishes that the fairness of a dismissal is directly affected by the HRA where a public authority is the employer, this left open the question of whether private sector employers should be subject to the same degree of scrutiny. On the one hand, it seems undesirable that the level of unfair dismissal protection and interpretation of what is 'fair' or 'reasonable' should vary depending on whether an individual's employer is from the public or private sector.[31] However, these employers are in a different position. A direct action for breach of the HRA can be brought against a public sector employer, and so such employers cannot logically 'fairly' dismiss an employee through an act

---

29 See, e.g., H. Collins, 'Finding the Right Direction for the "Industrial Jury"', *Industrial Law Journal*, 29 (2000), 288.

30 See L. Vickers, 'Unfair Dismissal and Human Rights', *Industrial Law Journal*, 33 (2004), 52 at 58.

31 Vickers, 'Unfair Dismissal and Human Rights', p. 57.

that is separately unlawful under the HRA. The private sector employer is in a different position in relation to the direct enforceability of the HRA, and so arguably the HRA's effect could also be different.

This question was considered by the Court of Appeal in the case of *X* v. *Y*,[32] which involved a claim for unfair dismissal against a charity that worked with young people, a purely private employer. The applicant worked with young offenders, and was dismissed after his employers discovered that he had received a caution for gross indecency following a consensual sex act with another man in a public toilet. The applicant argued that his dismissal was unfair as it infringed his right to private life under Article 8, and also engaged the non-discrimination principle in Article 14. In his leading judgment, Mummery LJ spent some time analysing this issue.

The court primarily relied on the requirement to interpret legislation in a way that is compatible with Convention rights under section 3, to establish that Articles 8 and 14 did need to be taken into account when considering the fairness of a dismissal by a private employer. However, Mummery LJ also referred to section 6, which requires the tribunal as a public authority to act compatibly with the HRA, as reinforcing the 'extremely strong' interpretive obligation imposed by section 3.[33] This analysis seems to be inter-relating both the obligation of statutory inter-pretation and some form of indirect horizontality, but it is not clear from the leading judgment which version of horizontality is being used. In answering the question as to exactly what effect section 3 has on the interpretation of section 98 of the Employment Rights Act, Mummery LJ states that he has 'concluded that in some cases it has some effect',[34] which is far from an authoritative explanation of the position. He goes on to say that this effect 'is more accurately described as oblique, rather than as directly or indirectly horizontal', and Article 8 is 'blended' with the law on unfair dismissal 'by a process of interpretation . . . but without creating new private law causes of action against private sector employers'. Although this analysis of the effect of the HRA is somewhat unclear, it is obviously an analysis that stops short of the strongest version of indirect horizontality. The judgment goes on to specify that the tribunal must read and give effect to the unfair dismissal legislation so as to be compatible with Article 8.

In reaching this conclusion, Mummery LJ took the view that, in general, the reasonable expectation is that a decision that a particular dismissal

---

32 [2004] IRLR 625.   33 *X* v. *Y* at [57].   34 *X* v. *Y* at [58].

was fair would not be incompatible with Articles 8 or 14. There would generally be no need to invoke section 3, on the basis that conduct that was in breach of privacy rights would be likely to make the dismissal unfair in any event, if the tribunal was properly applying objective standards of fairness, reasonableness and equity. However, as discussed above, arguably this is not the case in relation to private sector employers, due to the breadth of the 'range of reasonable responses' test. The judgment does go on to recognise that in some cases the HRA could make a difference to the reasoning of the tribunal and the outcome of a claim, although this is seen as exceptional.

Perhaps the most significant aspect of the judgment is the analysis of whether there should be any distinction between public sector and private sector employers in the interpretation of unfair dismissal. Mummery LJ expresses the view that there would normally be no sensible grounds for making such a distinction, particularly against the background of widespread contracting-out by public authorities to private contractors. The judgment notes that otherwise the claim might be determined differently depending on whether the employer was in the private sector, but working closely with the Probation Service (as in this case), or was a public authority, such as the Probation Service itself (such as in the *Pay* case), and 'it is unlikely that the HRA was intended to produce different results'.[35] While this shows no recognition that a public sector employer is under a direct obligation to comply with the HRA, which already produces different results in relation to whether or not an employee can bring a direct claim for breach of the HRA, this conclusion does avoid the undesirable alternative of there being a two-tier regime of unfair dismissal rights, depending on the nature of the employer. As noted in the judgment, the Employment Rights Act draws no distinction between employers in the private and public sectors,[36] and there is much to be said for the courts and tribunals continuing to interpret this legislation consistently. This approach is also consistent with other decisions in which the courts have been willing to apply section 3 in the same way irrespective of whether the parties to the case were public or private bodies.[37]

It seems clear from the outcome of these two cases that the HRA must be taken directly into account when interpreting the law of unfair dismissal, whether the employer is in the public or the private sector. As noted above, concepts such as 'reasonableness' and 'equity' in the relevant legislation can easily be interpreted so as to include human rights considerations, and

---

35 *X* v. *Y* at [56].   36 *X* v. *Y* at [56].   37 Chapter 4 at p. 68.

the conclusion is that a dismissal that unjustifiably breaches Convention rights cannot be fair. Although no clear theory of horizontality emerges from these decisions, the courts are obviously using Convention rights to inform what amounts to fair and reasonable treatment of employees.

Turning next to the common law, this is a considerably shorter discussion because, at present, there are no reported cases on this topic in the field of employment law. In relation to wrongful dismissal, there are no reported cases solely on this point as generally unfair dismissal will provide a more valuable remedy where there is a summary dismissal for a reason which potentially infringes the HRA. This is somewhat more surprising in relation to the implied duty of trust and confidence, which could well be influenced by the HRA. The cases on statutory horizontality do have some relevance to how this area might develop, particularly in relation to whether there is a difference in treatment between public and private sector employers. It could be argued that trust and confidence is more likely to be breached by a public authority that infringes the Convention rights of its employees, because this conduct would also give rise to a direct claim for breach of those rights under the HRA. However, as with unfair dismissal, the duty of trust and confidence is implied into the employment contract in the same way irrespective of the status of the employer. If a similar approach is taken to that of statutory horizontality, the impact of the HRA on the implied common law duty should be the same for all types of employment. In theory at least, this provides considerable scope for human rights arguments to be raised in cases where trust and confidence has been breached, including in actions for wrongful and constructive unfair dismissal. However, to date this theory does not appear to have been translated into actual claims.

16.4 Future scope for human rights to influence employment law

There is considerable theoretical scope for the HRA to influence the development of employment law, and this has begun to happen through statutory horizontality. However, there are still very few cases in this area, and none directly on the common law contractual duties. There may be a number of reasons for this.

As noted by Mummery LJ in *X* v. *Y*, it may not be necessary for dismissed employees to raise HRA arguments expressly, because in general a dismissal that breaches such rights would not be fair in any event. This might well be the case where the infringement of rights is an obvious one that cannot be justified, rather than a more borderline case that is subject to the range of reasonable responses test. It may be that such unfair dismissal cases are relatively common, but do not reach the appeal courts or even a full tribunal hearing. Possibly this is the same for wrongful dismissal and breach of trust and confidence cases – there is no need to argue the HRA point because the contractual breach is already obvious.

However, this is an over-simplistic answer. Of the cases in this area that have been reported, it should be noted that most are ultimately unsuccessful on HRA points. In both of the unfair dismissal cases discussed above, although the courts accepted that the law needed to be interpreted compatibly with the HRA, the employees' arguments were in fact unsuccessful as there was no actual infringement of their rights. In the *Pay* case, the EAT found that Article 8 rights were not engaged at all, as the activities in question were accessible to the public on the Internet and therefore not subject to a reasonable expectation of privacy. The case was then taken to the Strasbourg court, which was prepared to accept that this activity might be covered by privacy rights even though conducted in public, but declined to decide the point on the basis that the employer's conduct was justified in any event.[38] Similarly, in *X* v. *Y* a majority of the Court of Appeal found that the individual's Article 8 rights were not engaged at all, because the conduct had taken place in a public place and was a criminal offence. These decisions were based on jurisprudence from the Strasbourg court on the extent of Convention obligations. In effect, both of these cases failed at the first level, on the basis that no Convention obligations were in play at all. This is despite the fact that, in both cases, the court had already moved to the next question, and determined that in principle the relevant Convention rights could have been given effect through statutory interpretation.

Even where an employee is successful in overcoming the initial hurdle of showing that a right is engaged, the cases so far have tended to favour the employer's justifications in finding that there has not been an unlawful interference with that right. In the *Pay* case, although the individual's Article 10 rights to freedom of expression were engaged, any infringement was found to be justified by the employer's interests in protecting its reputation and maintaining public confidence. This may well be in line with Strasbourg court cases on freedom of expression, which have accepted that some jobs involve more restrictions on freedom of expression than others,[39] but it is nevertheless possible that the EAT could

38 *Pay* v. *United Kingdom* [2009] IRLR 139.
39 See, e.g., *Vogt* v. *Germany* (1996) 21 EHRR 205.

have reached a different conclusion in the light of the fact that there was no actual evidence of damage to either reputation or public confidence.[40] The Strasbourg court also took the same view on this point, finding that the employer's justifications fell within the margin of appreciation. In another unfair dismissal case, *McGowan* v. *Scottish Water,*[41] the EAT accepted that covert video surveillance of an employee's home for the purposes of a disciplinary investigation raised at least a 'strong presumption' that the right to respect for private life was infringed.[42] However, the EAT nevertheless went on to find (by a majority judgment) that any interference with the right to respect for his private life was justified – the employer was carrying out the surveillance to protect its assets, the video evidence went to the heart of the investigation and this was not a case where surveillance was undertaken for 'whimsical reasons'.[43] It is far from clear that the test of proportionality, which requires a balance to be struck between the Convention rights of the individual and the interests of the other party involved, was applied in a sufficiently rigorous manner in this case. Although the employer's reasons for the surveillance in this case were not 'whimsical', there may be cases where the employer has good reasons for its actions, but nevertheless has acted in breach of Article 8 because the impact on the individual's privacy rights is too great. The EAT also appeared to rely on the fact that the surveillance did confirm the employer's suspicions, which suggests a principle of the 'ends justifying the means'.

In addition, except in circumstances where an employee has been dismissed for a potentially unfair reason, human rights arguments may turn out be of little practical use. Although the HRA may also be relevant to issues of procedural fairness, such as where covert surveillance evidence is used as evidence in disciplinary proceedings, the employee's remedy in such circumstances may be quite limited. Compensation for unfair dismissal is almost exclusively based on loss of earnings arising from the dismissal, and is also subject to a reduction for contributory fault on the part of the employee. The employer may be able to show that the employee would have been dismissed in any event, even if the privacy invasive evidence had not been taken into account.[44] Alternatively, the employee may be held largely to blame for his or her own dismissal on the basis of guilt

---

40 Vickers, 'Unfair Dismissal and Human Rights', p. 56.
41 [2005] IRLR 167 ('*McGowan*').   42 *McGowan* at p. 170.
43 *McGowan* at p. 170.   44 *Polkey* v. *A. E. Dayton Services Ltd* [1988] ICR 142.

shown by the evidence in question.[45] In both cases, compensation may be very limited, meaning that it is simply not worth running complex HRA arguments at first instance or on appeal. In relation to breach of trust and confidence, again a high value claim will tend to arise only where the employee chooses to accept the breach and resign from employment, leading to claims for wrongful and unfair dismissal. An individual who wishes to challenge workplace practices in breach of Convention rights while remaining in employment does not have a financially significant claim to which those arguments can be attached.

Finally, there is one obvious area of employment where there is no remedy for an individual even where it is clear that Convention rights have been breached, namely, where an application for employment is refused. Although an individual applying for a job in the public sector would have a direct claim for breach of the HRA, outside discrimination law (which is considered separately) a private sector job applicant has no statutory or common law rights to which the HRA can attach through any type of indirect horizontality.

In conclusion, employment law has considerable scope to accommodate claims based on rights under the HRA through indirect horizontality, as a continuation of existing statutory and common law limitations placed on the contractual bargain between private parties. The courts have begun to analyse how this can be done in the context of the key statutory right of unfair dismissal, in a way that suggests public and private sector employers should be treated in the same way. There is a lack of detailed analysis as to the form of horizontality that is being applied, but there is a clear willingness to apply Convention rights in deciding on the parameters of fair and reasonable treatment in any form of employment relationship. Although this involves the interpretation of broad statutory concepts, rather than specific statutory wording that is clearly inconsistent with a human right, this is still a form of remedial interpretation under section 3 that is giving effect to particular Convention rights rather than values. However, so far this has not developed into a significant body of cases, and it remains to be seen whether this will change over time as the HRA has increasing influence over other areas of private law.

---

45 Under s. 123(6) of the Employment Rights Act 1996, if a tribunal finds that a dismissal was caused or contributed to by any action of the complainant, compensation can be reduced by such amount as is just and equitable in the light of this finding. The reduction can be up to 100 per cent: see *W. Devis & Sons* v. *Atkins* [1977] ICR 662.

17

Civil procedure: Article 6 – a welcome boost to the development of English procedural law?

JOHN SORABJI

In his recent work on civil procedure, Zuckerman suggested that the introduction of the HRA has had, or rather ought to have, a salutary and beneficial effect on civil justice. As he put it:

> The need to examine English procedure in the light of Convention Art. 6 gives a welcome boost to the development of English procedural law.[1]

Is this correct, or has the HRA and through it the introduction of Article 6 of the Convention into English law had little or no effect on the development of procedural law? That is the question examined here. At first glance it might be thought that Article 6 ought to have had a significant impact. Under the terms of section 3(1) of the HRA the courts are required to interpret and give effect to primary and secondary legislation in a way that is compatible with the various Convention rights. Equally, as public authorities, it is unlawful, under the terms of section 6(1) and (3) of the HRA, for courts to act in any way that is incompatible with a right set out in the Convention. This requires that the court itself in its procedure give effect to the Convention rights (procedural horizontality).[2] In the light of these requirements it might be thought that individuals resorting to litigation before the courts might well expect to benefit from a new Article 6-compliant approach to their procedural rights than was discernible before 2 October 2000.

It might be thought that the Civil Procedure Rules (CPR),[3] as secondary legislation, would be applied so as to give greater effect to the right to fair

---

1 A. Zuckerman, *Zuckerman on Civil Procedure: Principles of Practice* (London: Thomson, 2006), p. 56. Also see J. Jacob, *Civil Justice in the Age of Human Rights* (Farnham: Ashgate, 2007).
2 For a general discussion of the effect of this obligation on the courts, see Chapter 2.
3 SI 1998 No. 3132.

trial than had its statutory predecessor, the Rules of the Supreme Court (RSC).[4] Equally, it might be thought to have a wider effect than simply to recast the CPR. It might be thought to have had an impact on all procedural decisions the courts make, whether those decisions fall under a specific rule in the CPR or arise under the court's inherent jurisdiction. Decisions under the court's inherent jurisdiction not only fall under the ambit of section 6(1) and (3) of the HRA, but also fall under the ambit of CPR, rule 1.1, the CPR's overriding objective, and hence must be consistent with Article 6 pursuant to section 3(1) of the HRA, as has been confirmed by the Court of Appeal in *Tombstone Ltd v. Raja*.[5]

In the light of this, Zuckerman's suggestion might appear all the stronger and more justified. In fact, however, there has been little reasoned re-examination of English procedural law since the HRA's enactment: Article 6 has in general, and despite some degree of early promise, had little real impact on civil justice in this, the procedural, sense. Before assessing the reasons why this is the case, it is useful to outline the positive effect it has had.

17.1 Article 6: a limited positive effect

There is some evidence to support the belief that Article 6's introduction would have a positive effect on the development of English procedural law. This evidence is twofold. First, there have been a small number of cases where the courts have revisited certain aspects of the right to fair trial in the light of Article 6. There have, for instance, been developments in respect of the right to an independent and impartial tribunal and the waiver of that right;[6] the limited nature of the right to an impartial prosecutor;[7] and the right to a reasoned judgment.[8] The most significant, sustained development has arisen in respect of restrictions on the right of access. These developments have, however, not formed part of a wider-ranging reappraisal or redevelopment of procedural law.

Second, shortly after the HRA came into force there was a period when the Court of Appeal appeared to begin to give the HRA a positive effect.

---

4 SI 1965 No. 1776.   5 [2008] EWCA Civ. 1444.
6 *Starrs* v. *Ruxton* [2000] UKHRR 78; *Locabail (UK) Ltd* v. *Bayfield* [2000] QB 451 (*'Locabail'*); *Smith* v. *Kvaerner Cementation Foundations Ltd (General Council of the Bar intervening)* [2007] 1 WLR 370.
7 *R (Haase)* v. *Independent Adjudicator* [2008] EWCA Civ. 1089.
8 *English* v. *Emery Reimbold & Strick Ltd & Others* [2002] 1 WLR 2409 (*'English'*).

In two decisions, *Cachia* v. *Faluyi*[9] and *Goode* v. *Martin*,[10] the Court of Appeal used Article 6(1) with the obligation imposed by sections 3 and 6 to interpret legislation consistently with it. In doing so, it could have forged the beginnings of Zuckerman's welcome boost to procedural law. In *Cachia* the issue before the court was the correct interpretation of 'action' as set out in section 2(3) of the Fatal Accidents Act 1976 (the 1976 Act). *Goode* concerned the correct interpretation of section 35(5) of the Limitation Act 1980 and CPR, rule 17.2.[11]

In *Cachia*, the Court of Appeal noted how the HRA required it to adopt a purposive approach to statutory interpretation. It was thus required to consider arguments based on Article 6.[12] It could therefore in principle apply a wider meaning than it could have done prior to the HRA and interpret the 1976 Act in such a way as to permit claims to be brought which would not otherwise be capable of being issued in order to give proper effect to the right to fair trial. The HRA, and through it Article 6, thus enabled, as Brooke LJ put it in his judgment, 'English judges to do justice in a way which was not previously open to [them]'.[13] Neither the traditional canons of statutory interpretation nor the pre-existing common law right to fair trial enabled the court to take this approach.

This positive step forward was built on in *Goode*. That appeal arose out of a personal injury claim, which the claimant wished to amend after the expiry of the primary limitation period. The application to amend was refused initially on the basis that CPR, rule 17.4(2) did not permit claims to be amended out of time on the basis of facts disclosed in a defence, as was the case here, but which had not been previously pleaded in the claimant's statement of case. The claim in this case was relatively unusual in that the claimant had suffered a brain injury and amnesia and was therefore reliant to a greater degree than usual on the defendant's version of events. The defendant had failed to respond to pre-action enquiries, and the first time the claimant was aware of the defendant's version of events was when the defence was served. The claimant argued before the Court of Appeal that the refusal to permit her to amend her claim was contrary to Article 6.

The argument before the Court of Appeal focused on the correct interpretation of the phrase 'out of the same facts or substantially the same

---

9 [2001] 1 WLR 1966 ('*Cachia*').   10 [2002] 1 WLR 1828 ('*Goode*').

11 See I. Scott, 'Convention Compatible Interpretation of Procedural Legislation', *Civil Justice Quarterly*, 21 (2002), 88.

12 *Cachia* at [17], [20].   13 *Cachia* at [21].

facts as a claim' contained in CPR, rule 17.4(2).[14] Brooke LJ, who gave the lead judgment as he did in *Cachia*, first noted that the first instance decision was arrived at before the HRA came into force.[15] As in *Cachia*, absent the HRA that decision was unassailable. Once more the court held that:

> Without the encouragement of section 3(1) of the 1998 Act, I could see no way of interpreting the language of the rule so as to produce a just result.

Without Article 6, what the court acknowledged was an unjust result would have had to stand. Article 6 and the HRA thus enabled the court to go further in its approach to the CPR than it would otherwise have been able to do. Building on its previous decision in *Cachia*, the court held that Article 6 changed the position as it required that the right of access to justice could be limited only for a legitimate purpose.[16] Brooke LJ held that:

> The 1998 Act . . . [alters] the position. [There is] no sound policy reason why the claimant should not add to her claim in the present action the alternative plea which [the appellant] now proposes. No new facts are being introduced: [the appellant] merely wants to say that if the defendant succeeds in establishing his version of the facts, she will still win because those facts, too, show that he was negligent and should pay her compensation.
>
> I do not consider that the rule, as interpreted by the master and the judge, has any legitimate aim when applied to the facts in the present case . . . Even if the rule had a legitimate aim in the circumstances of this case, the means used by the rule-maker (if we have to interpret the rule in the way favoured by the court below) would not be reasonably proportionate to that aim.[17]

In the light of this, Brooke LJ went on to hold that CPR, rule 17.4(2) had to be given a wide interpretation so as to allow the desired amendment and ensure that 'there would be no question of a violation of the claimant's article 6(1) rights'.[18]

In both *Cachia* and *Goode* the Court of Appeal, under Brooke LJ's guidance, relied on the combined effect of section 3(1) and Article 6 to ensure that the CPR, the 1976 Act and the Limitation Act 1980, were read in a way that permitted the court to arrive at the just result, even though a strict,

---

14 A similar argument also arose as to the correct interpretation of the phrase 'out of the same facts as are already in issue on any claim' in s. 35(5) of the Limitation Act 1980.
15 *Goode* at [41].   16 *Goode* at [35]–[36].   17 *Goode* at [42]–[44].
18 *Goode* at [47].

traditional approach to statutory interpretation would have produced the opposite result and so to develop procedural law in a way that would otherwise not have occurred. These two decisions could have been taken as a statement of intent. They could, for instance, have signalled the start of a period of positive judicial activism in procedural law, which would have moulded the CPR in its earlier years in the same way as decisions such as *Clarapede & Co.* v. *Commercial Union Association*[19] and *Cropper* v. *Smith*[20] moulded the earlier development and interpretation of the RSC. It could have signalled the start of the 'welcome boost' to procedural law that Zuckerman believed it would.

Cachia and *Goode* did not, however, signal the start of such a period of application of Article 6. They have been applied in only two decisions: *Hemmingway* v. *Smith Roddam*[21] and *Charles Church Developments Ltd* v. *Stent Foundations Ltd*.[22] The approach to interpretation they took has not been followed more widely or applied to other aspects of the CPR or other procedural statutes or provisions. Given the Court of Appeal's lead in *Cachia* and *Goode*, the question, posed at the outset, arises with greater force: why has Article 6 applied consistently with the requirements of the HRA not provided a boost to the development of English procedural law? Why has its introduction been confined to one limited aspect of procedure, limitation and amendment, and to a handful of cases that have reappraised aspects of the fair trial right?

The answer to this is twofold. First, English procedural law, and the civil justice system, already operated consistently with a well-developed common law constitutional right to fair trial; thus, Article 6's incorporation has added nothing of substance to the prevailing position. The second reason is adverted to by Brooke LJ in *Goode*, where he identified the changes to English civil procedure that had occurred since 1999. He put it this way:

> We now possess more tools for enabling us to do justice than were available before April 1999. Since then, the Civil Procedure Rules and the Human Rights Act 1998 have come into force. By the former we must seek to give effect to the overriding objective of dealing with cases justly when we interpret any rule: see CPR, r. 1.2(b). By the latter we must read and give effect to subordinate legislation, so far as it is possible to do so, in a way which is compatible with the Convention rights set out in Schedule 1 of the 1998 Act: see section 3.[23]

---

19 (1883) 32 WR 262.   20 (1884) 26 ChD 700.   21 [2003] EWCA Civ. 1342.
22 [2006] EWHC 3158, [2007] 1 WLR 1203.   23 *Goode* at [35].

Brooke LJ identified in this passage two novel tools available to the court through which it had to interpret procedural law: Article 6 and CPR, rule 1, the overriding objective. In *Goode* the court relied on the former. It need not have done so, however. It could have relied on CPR, rule 1, as procedural law, whether in the CPR or arising under the court's inherent jurisdiction, must be applied consistently with it. In this lies the second reason why Article 6 has failed to provide have a wider effect on procedural law. Its muted effect is a product of the CPR's introduction generally, and specifically of its overriding objective.

17.2 The common law: a well-developed right

If Article 6 was to have a significant effect on the development of English procedural law two things were necessary. First, it would have to operate purposively. That this is the case, as acknowledged in *Cachia* and *Goode*, is evident due to the enactment of sections 3 and 6. On its own, though, that is not sufficient to provide a welcome boost to the development of procedural law. It would also need to add something substantive to English law. The very right itself and the various elements it encompassed would have to provide something over and above what was already present. If there was already a well-developed and well-established common law right to fair trial that mirrored the Article 6 right it would be reasonable to assume that English procedural law would already be consistent with that right. If it was already consistent with that common law right, what additional work would there be for Article 6 to do? Other than the limited class of case, such as that evident in *Cachia* and *Goode*, there would be little work for Article 6 to do even if applied purposively as the HRA requires.

English law has long incorporated a well-developed common law, con-stitutional right to fair trial. Article 6 has, subject to one caveat which is examined below, added nothing significantly novel to English law. It did not because it simply restated the common law in a statutory provision. It was therefore effectively and generally speaking superfluous. Its super-fluity can be seen most straightforwardly by comparing the Article 6 right to fair trial with the common law right.

The starting point for such a comparison is Article 6 itself. It contains a number of both express and implied rights, each of which could, in principle, have influenced English procedural law and its development. The former are: first, the right to a fair and public hearing; second, the right to receive such a hearing in a reasonable time; third, the right to receive that hearing at the hands of an independent and impartial tribunal; and, fourth, the right to receive a public judgment. These express elements of the right can be limited only for certain prescribed reasons provided for in the Article itself or by other Convention rights.[24] The permissible restrictions set out in Article 6 itself are that:

> the press and public may be excluded from all or part of the trial in the interest of morals, public order or national security in a democratic society, where the interests of juveniles or the protection of the private life of the parties so require, or to the extent strictly necessary in the opinion of the court in special circumstances where publicity would prejudice the interests of justice.

Insofar as the implied elements of the right are concerned these are: first, the right of effective access to justice,[25] which includes the right to proper notice and the right to receive justice at a reasonable cost;[26] second, the right to an adversarial hearing;[27] third, the right to evidentiary disclosure and cross-examination of witnesses;[28] fourth, the right to equality of arms;[29] fifth, the right to legal assistance for the impecunious;[30] and, sixth, the right to a reasoned judgment.[31] Limitations can also be placed on these, implied, elements of the Article 6 right. Such limitations can go wider than those applicable to the express elements of the right. They must not, however, reduce the right to such an extent that its very nature is impaired: any limitation must not undermine the practical nature of the right and render it no more than a mere theoretical construct.[32] They must pursue a legitimate aim and must exhibit a reasonable relationship of proportionality between that aim and the restriction imposed.[33] Common limitations are, for instance, those imposed on the right to legal assistance

---

24 *Brown v. Stott (Procurator Fiscal for Dunfermline)* [2001] 2 WLR 817 ('*Brown*'); *Chahal v. United Kingdom* (1997) EHRR 413 at [131] ('*Chahal*').
25 *Golder v. United Kingdom* (1975) 1 EHRR 524 ('*Golder*'); *Hornsby v. Greece* (1997) 24 EHRR 250.
26 *De Geouffre de la Pradelle v. France* (1992) (App. No. 12964/87), unreported.
27 *Brandstetter v. Austria* (1993) 15 EHRR 378.
28 *Feldbrugge v. Netherlands* (1986) 8 EHRR; *X v. Austria* (1972) 42 CD 145.
29 *Delcourt v. Belgium* (1969) 1 EHRR 355.
30 *Munro v. United Kingdom* [1987] 52 DR 158, *Airey v. Ireland* (1979–80) 2 EHRR 305; *Steel & Morris v. United Kingdom* (2005) 41 EHRR 22 ('*Steel & Morris*').
31 *Ruiz-Mateos v. Spain* [1999] EHRLR 344; *Tolstoy Miloslavsky v. United Kingdom* (1995) 20 EHRR 442 at [6] ('*Tolstoy*').
32 *Ashingdane v. United Kingdom* (1985) 7 EHRR 528 at [57]; *Brown* at p. 840.
33 *Golder, H v. United Kingdom* (1985) 45 DR 281; *Tolstoy.*

whether through restrictions on the right to receive legal aid[34] or the right to receive *pro bono* legal assistance in court by way of court-ordered assistance.[35]

This must be contrasted to the common law constitutional right to fair trial that existed in England prior to 2000.[36] That right contained and continues to contain each of the elements both express and implied contained in Article 6. Insofar as the express rights are concerned the right to a fair and public hearing was recognised at common law in *R v. Sussex Justices, ex p. McCarthy*, although its lineage can be traced back to Magna Carta.[37] All Article 6 has done is reinforce this aspect of the common law right. It has not added something to English procedural law that it previously lacked.[38] The right to receive such a hearing in a reasonable time was also established in Magna Carta, which did no more than recognise the common law position that justice should neither be delayed nor denied.[39] The right to an independent and impartial tribunal is no more than the long-standing principle that no one should be judge in his own cause (*nemo judex in causa sua*).[40] As Lord Clyde noted in *Miller v. Dickson*, this aspect of the Article 6 right was of 'fundamental constitutional importance'. As such its pre-2000 existence was implicitly acknowledged, not least as it was analysed in common law terms.[41] The

---

34 *Steel & Morris.*

35 *Perotti* v. *Collyer-Bristow (A Firm)* [2004] 2 All ER 189 at [32].

36 *Attorney-General* v. *Times Newspapers Ltd* [1974] AC 273 at 307; *Bremer Vulkan Schiffbau und Maschinenfabrik* v. *South India Shipping Corp. Ltd* [1981] AC 909 at 979; see also *Ng Ta Chi* v. *Max Share Ltd (No. 5 of 2004)* [2005] HKCFA 9 at [5].

37 *R* v. *Sussex Justices, ex p. McCarthy* [1924] 1 KB 256 at 259.

38 *Lilly Icos Ltd* v. *Pizer Ltd (No. 2)* [2002] 1 WLR 2253 at [25].

39 Magna Carta (1215), chapters 39 and 40; Magna Carta (1354), chapter 29; Edward Coke, 'Institutes of the Law', in S. Sheppard (ed.), *The Selected Writings of Sir Edward Coke, Vol. II: Liberty Fund* (Indianapolis, IN: Liberty Fund, 2003), pp. 50, 55. For a continuous line of authority as to the need to ensure that justice was done in reasonable time, and for that matter at reasonable cost, see: *First Report of the Common Law Commissioners into the Practice and Proceedings of the Superior Courts of Common Law* (House of Commons, 1829); *First Report of Her Majesty's Commissioners into the Process, Practice and System of Pleading in the Court of Chancery* (HMSO, 1852); *Final Report of the Committee on Supreme Court Practice and Procedure* (Cmd 8878, 1953); *Report of the Review Body on Civil Justice*, Cm 394, 1988).

40 *Dimes* v. *Properties of the Grand Central Canal* (1852) 10 ER 301; *R* v. *Hammond* (1863) 9 LT (NS) 423; *R* v. *Gough* [1993] AC 646; *Re ex p. Pinochet* [2000] 1 AC 119; *Taylor* v. *Lawrence* [2002] 3 WLR 640; *Seray-Wurie* v. *London Borough of Hackney*, 25 June 2002, unreported; J. Sorabji, '*Taylor v Lawrence* revisited: *First Discount Ltd* v. *Guinness* and *Jaffrey* v. *Society of Lloyds*', *Commercial Law Quarterly*, 26 (2007), 413–18.

41 [2002] 1 WLR 1615 at 1645. The appeal specifically examined the right to judicial independence as it arose under Art. 6(1); also see *Locabail*.

right to receive a public judgment fell under the general principle that justice should be administered in public.[42]

Insofar as the implied elements of the Article 6 right are concerned these were equally well established at common law. The right to receive proper notice was not only well established, but it also went further than the Article 6 right, which can be subject to limitation. At common law the right to proper notice was absolute. The clearest common law expression of this element of the right was made by Lord Denning MR in *ex parte Rossi*, in which he stated that it was a fundamental right and one which could not be abridged. He put it this way:

> it is a fundamental principle of our law that no one is to be found guilty or made liable by an order of any tribunal unless he has been given fair notice of the proceedings so as to enable him to appear and defend them. The common law has always been very careful to see that the defendant is fully appraised of the proceedings before it makes any order against him.[43]

Absent proper notice a defendant could have any judgment made against him set aside as of right (*ex debito justitiae*).[44]

It is one thing to require proper notification of an action and a hearing, it is another to lay down guidance as to the nature and form such hearings must take. The common law again provided standards which are reflected in the implied elements of the Article 6 right. The common law, through an application of the *audi alteram partem* principle, gave expression to the right to an adversarial hearing. Lord Diplock in *O'Reilly* v. *Mackman*, in terms which advert to its status as a constitutional right, put it in these terms:

> the requirement that a person ... should be given a fair opportunity of hearing what is alleged against him and of presenting his own case, is ... fundamental to any civilised legal system.[45]

A fair opportunity to hear what is alleged against you and to present your own case encompasses the right to evidentiary disclosure, the right to call your own witnesses, lay or expert, and the right to cross-examine

---

42 *Scott* v. *Scott* [1913] AC 417.
43 *R* v. *London Quarter Sessions Appeal Committee, ex p. Rossi* [1956] 1 QB 682 at 670, 696.
44 *White* v. *Weston* [1968] 2 QB 647 ('*White*').
45 [1983] 2 AC 237 at 276. J. Jacob, *The Fabric of English Civil Justice* (New York: Stevens, 1987), p. 5; M. Damaska, *The Faces of Justice and State Authority* (New Haven, CT: Yale University Press, 1986), *passim*; J. Jolowicz, 'Adversarial and Inquisitorial Models of Civil Procedure', *International & Comparative Law Quarterly*, 52 (2003), 281.

your opponent's witnesses. It encompasses each of these other implied elements of the Article 6 right.[46]

Implicit in the common law right to an adversarial hearing and that which it entails is an acceptance of the right to equality of arms. By ensuring that both parties have equal opportunities to participate in the action, to present and challenge evidence, to make submissions to the court, the common law protects this aspect of the right to fair trial. It can just as clearly be seen to be implicit in the requirement that the tribunal must be independent and impartial. Dependence or partiality are, of course, inimical to equality of arms in that they give rise to one party obtaining an unjust advantage, that is, one not based on an assessment of fact or law, over the other. Through this arises the common law's commitment to assisting the impecunious, in that the courts were willing to allow lay litigants to obtain lay assistance in court and to permit, where it assists the course of justice, such lay assistants to address the court on their behalf.[47] Finally, it was equally well established, although perhaps not clearly enunciated, that the common law right to fair trial incorporated the right to receive a reasoned judgment[48] and that litigation was to be conducted at reasonable cost.[49]

Spread across the case law the common law right to fair trial might not provide as clearly enunciated a general principle as Article 6 does. A lack of clarity or elegance in the development of the common law principle does not, however, undermine the conclusion that the common

---

46 *Kanda* v. *Government of Malaya* [1962] AC 322 at 337 *per* Lord Denning; *Re D (Minors)* [1996] AC 593 at 603; *R* v. *Thames Magistrates' Court, ex p. Polemis* [1974] 1 WLR 1371; *Hadmor Productions Ltd* v. *Hamilton* [1983] 1 AC 191 at 233.

47 *Collier* v. *Hicks* (1831) 2 B&Ad 669; *McKenzie* v. *McKenzie* [1970] 3 All ER 1034; *R* v. *Leicester City Justices, ex p. Barrow* [1991] 3 All ER 935; *Re G (A Minor) (Chambers Hearing: Assistance) (1991)* Note [1999] 1 WLR 1828; *Re H (Minors) (Chambers Proceedings: McKenzie Friend)* [1997] 3 FCR 618; *R* v. *Bow County Court, ex p. Pelling* [1999] 4 All ER 751; *O (Children) (Representation: McKenzie Friend)* [2005] 3 WLR 1191. Also see *Paragon Finance Plc* v. *Noueiri* [2001] 1 WLR 2357 at [62]–[64]: the right to choose a legal representative can be made subject to reasonable restrictions.

48 For a discussion of the common law position and the position under Art. 6(1) as to a reasoned judgment: *English* at [8], [15]. The post-2000 decisions in this area have not developed the law as Zuckerman envisaged, they have simply led to the law in this area being enunciated clearly.

49 *Smith* v. *Buller* (1875) LR 19 Eq. 473 at 475, where it was held by Malins VC that 'Any charges merely for conducting litigation more conveniently may be called luxuries and must be paid by the party incurring them.' The paying party was thus only required to pay that which was necessary to secure justice and anything more than that was unreasonably incurred.

law demonstrated an unequivocal commitment to the right to fair trial. Not only that, but more importantly it developed a commitment to it as a fundamental, constitutional right; a right which arguably forms part of the UK's constitutional framework which Parliament could not limit unless it wished to denude the civil courts of their primary constitutional purpose: to do 'justice between man and man'.[50] When looked at together it becomes clear why, when striking down a statutory instrument that imposed excessive court fees on impecunious litigants, Laws J, giving the judgment of the Divisional Court in *ex parte Witham*, held that Article 6 added nothing to the case. It was superfluous to the argument, not because it had not then been incorporated into English law, but rather because it did no more than cover the same ground as the common law right. It was superfluous because given the common law right it had no work to do.[51] The same point has been reiterated on a number of occasions by the courts post-2000.[52]

Thus, Article 6 did no more than encapsulate in elegant drafting and Strasbourg jurisprudence what was already well established, albeit in an untidy fashion, in English law. Unlike the other Convention rights, which introduce concepts such as the right to a private life that have historically been under-developed in English law, there is little room for Article 6 to work. This is hardly the basis on which to conclude with any confidence that it would give birth to a golden age in the development of procedural law. On the contrary, it suggests why there has been little development based on Article 6 and why *Cachia* and *Goode* present something of a cul-de-sac insofar as civil procedure is concerned. For Article 6 to have a significant impact it would have had to add something novel to English procedure. If this had been the case the courts would not just have been able to, but would have been required to, rely on it to interpret and apply the CPR consistently with its novelty. They would have had to interpret aspects of procedure that were not consistent with its express or implied elements so as to be consistent with them. However, English civil procedure has developed since the RSC's introduction and after it the CPR's introduction, with the common law right to fair trial in the

---

50 *Per* Lord Brougham LC, *Speeches of Henry Brougham* (1838), vol. 2, p. 324, cited in Jacob, *Fabric of English Civil Justice*, p. 1.
51 *R* v. *Lord Chancellor, ex p. Witham* [1998] QB 575 at 575.
52 *The Owners of the Ship Bow Spring* v. *The Owners of the Ship Manzanilli II* (Practice Note) [2005] 1 WLR 144 at [57]: 'The common law principles of natural justice anticipated by many years the concept of a fair trial which has been elaborated by the European Court of Human Rights under article 6.'

background. The rules of court, English civil procedure, have historically been drafted and interpreted in the light of a well-developed right to fair trial, which Article 6 does no more than substantively replicate. Requiring the court to interpret and apply procedural law consistently with Article 6, as the HRA does, in those circumstances is actually to require it to do little of substance.

The clearest example of how the extant common law right has muted Article 6's impact comes through the development of the civil restraint order, which is now set out in CPR, rule 3.11. A limited common law jurisdiction to restrain litigants from issuing and continuing proceedings in abuse of process was recognised in the nineteenth century in *Grepe v. Loam*.[53] This jurisdiction underwent significant development post-2000. It did so primarily due to the growth in abusive litigation following the CPR's introduction and the HRA's enactment.[54] The jurisdiction now enables the court to impose restrictions on the right of access of varying and increasing strength. The weakest form of restriction requires a litigant to obtain permission prior to issuing applications in any single set of proceedings. The strongest form of restriction is akin to a civil proceedings order under section 42 of the Senior Courts Act 1981.

In developing this aspect of its jurisdiction the Court of Appeal made particular reference to Article 6.[55] It did so substantively in *Bhamjee v. Forsdick (No. 2)*.[56] Article 6 could have formed the basis of its development. The court noted, however, that the jurisdiction to protect its process from abuse was consistent with both the common law right of access and the Article 6 right of access. Both bases of the right permitted restrictions to be placed upon it as long as they served a legitimate purpose and were proportionate to the aim.[57] The restrictions that arose from civil restraint orders were aimed at ensuring that vexatious litigants, in the general sense, were not able to fruitlessly waste court time and incur unreasonable court costs. Equally, they were imposed to ensure that those individuals who were the subjects of the abusive litigants' unjustifiable attentions did not suffer the expense and inconvenience of having to

---

53 (1887) 37 ChD 168; the 'right of unimpeded access to a court' acknowledged in *R* v. *Secretary of State for the Home Department, ex p. Leech* [1994] QB 198 at 210 must be read in light of this, i.e., the right of access is not a right of access to abuse the court's process.

54 *Ebert* v. *Venvil* [2000] Ch 484 ('*Ebert*'); *Bhamjee* v. *Forsdick (No. 2)* [2004] 1 WLR 88 ('*Bhamjee*'); *Mahajan* v. *Department of Constitutional Affairs* [2004] EWCA Civ. 946. [2004] 101 EG 26.

55 *Ebert* at p. 497.   56 [2004] 1 WLR 88.   57 *Bhamjee* at [16].

engage in fruitless proceedings. Because the restrictions were time limited to two years, subject to renewal, and permitted those subject to them to apply for permission to bring proceedings they were proportionate to their aim and satisfied the approach to such restrictions set out under Article 6.

While the court made reference in developing the jurisdiction to Strasbourg jurisprudence and Article 6, it did so with an eye to the question as to whether the restrictions were consistent with the right of access as developed by that court.[58] In doing so it did not, however, go beyond the position it would have reached if it had simply applied the common law approach to the right of access. As that too allowed restrictions to be placed on the right, and did so in the same circumstances, reference to Article 6 added nothing to the court's assessment of the issue. This was a point that Lord Woolf MR made in *Ebert*, the first of the decisions which developed this aspect of the jurisdiction. Following Laws J in *Witham*, he stated: 'Article 6 does no more than reflect the approach of the common law.'[59]

This lays bare the reason for Article 6's limited impact.[60] It did little to guide the court in developing the civil restraint order other than to provide confirmation, at best, of the approach necessitated by the common law right of access: providing confirmation of that approach, with an eye to the view that might be taken by the Strasbourg court, does not give a basis for concluding that it has had a significant impact on the development of procedural law. In its replication of the common law lies the first reason why it has had a muted influence since its introduction.

17.3 The overriding objective: a purposive provision

The second reason why Article 6 has had a muted effect is the introduction, in 1999, of the CPR and most specifically its overriding objective: CPR, rule 1.1. This is a purposive provision designed to ensure that a new litigation culture, and one that increased access to justice, rendered litigation more efficient and cost-effective, was introduced into English civil procedure. Its purpose, and role, thus mirrored the Article 6 right.

---

58 *Bhamjee* at [54].   59 *Ebert* at p. 497.
60 Dyson LJ would make essentially the same point in *Estate Acquisition & Development Ltd v. Wiltshire* [2006] EWCA Civ. 533 at [25] where he would hold that both Art. 6 and the overriding objective were mutually consistent guiding principles. Neither added anything that the other did not provide.

It did so in two ways. First, courts are required to give effect to the over-riding objective when they interpret any power given by the rules or any individual rule of procedure, statutory discretion or arising under the inherent jurisdiction.[61] They are therefore required to interpret proce-dural law in accordance with the overriding objective, in just the same way as they are required to interpret it, as a statutory instrument, in accordance with Article 6. On its own this would not tend to undermine Article 6's impact. However, that consequence arises from the second of the two ways in which it mirrors Article 6. The overriding objective is itself substantially a restatement of the various elements of the right to fair trial. It is, in its explicit and implicit elements, a synthesis of what the Strasbourg court and Lord Woolf MR have both described as procedural justice, that is, the various elements long developed under the common law and articulated in Article 6 of the right to fair trial.[62] What formal differences there are between the wording of CPR, rule 1 and Article 6 and between what is implicit to both those differences have, as Lord Hope acknowledged in *Three Rivers District Council* v. *Governor and Company of the Bank of England (No. 3)*, little practical effect[63] because the sub-stantive principles to which they give form are the same. The overriding objective has undermined Article 6's utility because it translates the right to which it gives expression into the rule that governs the application of procedural law. Resort to Article 6 becomes unnecessary because all the work it could do is being done by CPR, rule 1.1. It might be said that it has an indirect effect through the overriding objective, but an indirect effect is not one that Zuckerman spoke of when he expressed the hope that Article 6 would provide a stimulus to procedural law's development.

The limiting effect that the overriding objective has had can be seen through a number of procedural developments that have occurred since the CPR's introduction. Dealing with a question as to the scope of the right to equality of arms, Neuberger J (as he then was), rather than refer to Article 6 and its attendant jurisprudence, dealt with the question purely

---

61 CPR 1.2; *Purdy* v. *Cambran* [2000] CP Rep. 67 at [46]; *Asiansky Television Plc* v. *Bayer-Rosin (A Firm)* [2001] EWCA Civ. 1792, [2002] CPLR 111 at [41]; *Clarkson* v. *Gilbert (Rights of Audience)* [2000] 2 FLR 839 at [17]; *Tombstone Ltd* v. *Raja* [2008] EWCA Civ. 1444 at [85] ('*Tombstone*').

62 *Chahal*; H. Woolf, *Access to Justice: Interim Report to the Lord Chancellor on the Civil Justice System in England and Wales* (London: HMSO, 1995), p. 216; *Less* v. *Benedict* [2005] EWHC 1643.

63 [2003] 2 AC 1 at [92]–[93].

by reference to the express provision in the overriding objective and its role within that rule. A question that provided a golden opportunity for Article 6 to be deployed to shape the development of this aspect of procedural law was resolved with no reference to it whatsoever.[64] That it arose shortly before the HRA entered into force might explain Neuberger J's reticence in this instance. That there was no discussion of it at all, however, suggests that the reasons for the omission went wider and were, in fact, based in its redundancy as a jurisprudential aid. That later opportunities to develop procedural law were also guided by the overriding objective rather than Article 6 bear this out.

The most significant area of procedural law that has undergone development since 2000 and which bears out the overarching importance of the overriding objective at the expense of Article 6 is that which governs service of process, specifically of claim forms. Such service is of importance for two reasons. First, it ensures that a defendant is provided with proper notice of the claim he must answer. Second, it ensures that the procedural timetable commences. English procedure had traditionally taken an absolutist approach to service qua notice. It was long established that a failure to effect actual service of a claim form on a defendant enabled any judgment subsequently obtained to be set aside as of right.[65] A reappraisal of this principle in the light of Article 6 could well have seen the principle weakened consistently with the approach that the right to receive proper notice, as an implicit right, could be subject to restrictions that served a legitimate purpose and were proportionate to it. The right to set aside could, therefore, have been developed in this context to one that permitted the court a discretion to set aside; that discretion could be exercised against a defendant in circumstances where, for instance, the defence had no real prospect of success. That is in fact what happened. It happened, however, without any detailed reliance on Article 6, but rather by relying on the overriding objective.

The first case in this line of authorities was *London Borough of Hackney* v. *Driscoll*.[66] The issue that arose was whether a defendant who had notice of the proceedings, but who did not receive actual notice of the trial date could have the judgment obtained in his absence set aside as of right. The judge had held that he could not and that CPR, rule 39.3(5) governed the court's discretion as to whether the judgment should be set aside. Brooke LJ in his judgment made reference not only to *White* v. *Weston*,

---

64 *Maltez* v. *Lewis* [1999] 4 All ER (D) 425.
65 *White; ex p. Rossi* [1956] 1 QB 682.   66 [2003] 1 WLR 2602.

but equally to Lord Denning MR's dicta in *ex parte Rossi*, neither of which were held to govern the instant factual scenario.[67] While no arguments were advanced based on Article 6 and the court did not need to consider whether the principle set out in *White* v. *Weston* continued to hold good under the CPR,[68] Brooke LJ noted that the requirement for a defendant to show that his claim had a reasonable prospect of success under CPR, rule 39.5 offended neither any 'fundamental principle of justice [n]or any principle of Strasbourg jurisprudence'.[69] In other words, consistently with the position advanced above, neither the common law nor Article 6 required such decisions to be set aside as of right: CPR, rule 39.5 was in this respect consistent with both.

Driscoll was followed shortly after by *Akram* v. *Adam*.[70] In this case the defendant had not received actual notice of the claim form. He had, however, been validly served pursuant to the rules on deemed service. Judgment had been entered following a hearing that took place in his absence. The judgment against him was therefore a regular judgment.[71] The case thus seemed to raise the issue of the continued existence of the principle set out in *White* v. *Weston*. The defendant relied on Article 6(1) and arguments advanced by Zuckerman[72] to support his claim that he should be able to set aside the judgment as of right. The appeal failed for two reasons. First, because the judgment was regularly entered, *White* v. *Weston* did not apply: its principle applied only to judgments irregularly entered.[73] Second, there was no reason to exercise the discretion under CPR, rule 13.3(1) to set aside the judgment against him.[74] Insofar as the argument based on the right to fair trial was concerned, Brooke LJ rejected it on the basis that there was nothing in Article 6 that required a court to set aside a regular judgment, that is, one obtained in conformity with fair

---

67 *Ex p. Rossi*: 'it is a fundamental principle of our law that no one is to be found guilty or made liable by an order of any tribunal unless he has been given fair notice of the proceedings so as to enable him to appear and defend them'; [2003] 1 WLR 2602 at [25] and see *Grimshaw* v. *Dunbar* [1953] 1 QB 647 for an earlier approach which adopts the same position.

68 *Driscoll* at [24].   69 *Driscoll* at [27].

70 [2003] 1 WLR 2762.   71 *Akram* at [34].

72 Zuckerman, *Civil Procedure*; and see [2003] 1 WLR 2762 at [37].

73 *Akram* at [34].

74 No one seems to have pointed out that CPR, r. 13.3 did not apply to this case, as the judgment was obtained in possession proceedings. Default judgments cannot be obtained in such proceedings. The correct provision of the CPR which ought to have governed the court's discretion was CPR, r. 39.3(5): see CPR, rr. 12.2(c) and 55.7(4), *Nelson* v. *Clearsprings (Management) Ltd* [2006] EWCA Civ. 1252, [2007] 1 WLR 962 at [55] ('*Nelson*').

process rules, as of right because the defendant had not received actual notice. It was rejected because the right to proper notice under Article 6 was not an absolute requirement. It was one that could be made subject to legitimate restrictions that ensured that the court only had to adjudicate on arguable claims.[75] Without deciding the issue as to *White* v. *Weston's* continued validity Brooke LJ, in dismissing the Article 6 point, indicated that it was no longer valid. He did so, however, only as an obiter dictum. If this aspect of the decision had later been adopted by the court it could be said to have played a part in providing a boost to procedural law's development. It did not, however, do so.

The issue that was ducked in both *Driscoll* and *Akram* arose directly in *Nelson* v. *Clearsprings (Management) Ltd.*[76] In this case the claimant attempted to serve the claim form on the defendant. Unfortunately, the claim form was incorrectly addressed. The defendant, understandably, failed to acknowledge service as it never received the claim form and judgment was entered in its absence. When the defendant became aware of this an application was made to set the judgment aside. An issue arose as to which was the appropriate test to apply on the set-aside application: was it CPR, rule 13, CPR, rule 39.5(3) or the *White* v. *Weston* test? CPR, rule 13 did not apply as judgment was not a default judgment. CPR, rule 39.5 was held not to encompass situations where a defendant had never been served either actually or by way of deemed service. *White* v. *Weston* remained the answer, although in a substantially modified fashion.[77] It no longer provided the basis to set aside judgments arrived at following non-service as of right. The power to set aside following the CPR's introduction was a discretionary one. It was, as Brooke LJ had indicated in *Driscoll,* one that required the court to assess whether it was appropriate in the circumstances to permit a defendant to defend its claim.[78] In arriving at this conclusion the court did not, however, rely on Article 6. On the contrary, it arrived at its decision solely by reference to the overriding objective. It held that setting aside as of right was contrary to the overriding objective. It was, for instance, contrary to it to permit a defendant to proceed with a defence to no good purpose or where there were other circumstances that justified the court refusing to set aside the judgment, such as inordinate delay in bringing the set-aside application.[79] Restrictions could thus be placed on the right of access and the right of proper notice by reference to the overriding objective. While, as Lord

75 *Akram* at [41]–[43].   76 [2006] EWCA Civ. 1252.   77 *Nelson* at [42].
78 *Nelson* at [49].   79 *Nelson* at [43].

Hope would no doubt have recognised in *Three Rivers*, the same practical result could have been arrived at by relying on Article 6 as Brooke LJ alluded to in *Driscoll* and *Akram*, the court arrived at it by reliance on the overriding objective.[80] The overriding objective did the work that would otherwise have been carried out by Article 6.

17.4 Conclusion

The difficulty which Article 6 has faced since its introduction into English law has been twofold. On the one hand, it substantially replicates the common law right to fair trial. In this it adds little to English law. On the other hand, it is replicated by the overriding objective, which also acts as a purposive provision guiding the court in its interpretation of procedural law. As Lord Phillips MR put it in deciding whether a claim could properly be terminated prior to judgment on procedural grounds, the ultimate issue was not the Article 6 right but 'whether the overriding objective of dealing with this case justly calls for us to bring these proceedings to an end'.[81] It has been limited in its effect by the combined effect of these two features of English law. In the first instance, the long-standing common law right ensured that procedural law had developed consistently with the very provisions that Article 6 articulated. There was thus little scope for it to play the significant role that Zuckerman hoped it would. The overriding objective's introduction reduced its potential application even further as it played the guiding and developmental role that he anticipated Article 6 would.

The one area where Article 6 goes beyond both the common law and the overriding objective and which could ensure it plays the role Zuckerman hoped it would is that provided by sections 3 and 6: its purposive role in respect of statutory interpretation. Unfortunately for Zuckerman, and perhaps for civil procedure, apart from *Cachia* and *Goode* the courts have not utilised this facet of the Article 6 right. *Cachia* and *Goode* present something of a procedural cul-de-sac. If the courts were to apply the approach taken in these cases more widely, and there is no reason, given the effect of the HRA, that they could not, Article 6 might find a much wider role for itself to play. Given the wide-ranging applicability of the overriding objective, this role would, however, be limited to statutory procedural

---

80 Since approved in *Tombstone*.
81 *Flaxman-Binns* v. *Lincolnshire County Council* (Practice Note) [2004] 1 WLR 2232 at [41].

law, such as contained in the Limitation Act 1980,[82] the Senior Courts
Act 1981, the Courts and Legal Services Act 1990 or the Legal Services
Act 2007. This limitation, and the limited range of applicability that it
provides Article 6 right's potential effect, suggests, however, that its wider
role may well prove as etiolated as its effect generally. It may well prove to
be the case that the highpoint of Article 6's influence was *Cachia* and
Goode and that Zuckerman's hope that it would provide a welcome boost
to the development of English civil procedure remains no more than a
hope. Given the significant role played by the overriding objective now,
in the future it is more than likely that that will be the case.

82 Discussed further in the context of adverse possession of land in Chapter 12.

18

Conclusions

DAVID HOFFMAN

The HRA has clearly had an impact on private law, both directly and indirectly. Directly, in that there are now areas of the law that have been changed as a result of its enactment, both through statutory interpretation and through modification of the common law. Indirectly, in cases where the values underlying the Convention have had an impact, or at least had an effect on the way in which cases have been argued and determined, but which has fallen short of specific changes in the law.

Further, as most public authorities (whether defined generally or under the HRA) are sooner or later parties to litigation in respect of their own rights and obligations, this has led to consideration of the interaction between the Convention rights and the common law in a variety of areas. In addition, the courts themselves have had to take the Convention rights into consideration when exercising their own powers as to procedure and remedies.

Perhaps the Convention right that has had the most impact is Article 8. Unlike many of the other Articles, it represents a broad set of interests – private life, family life, home and correspondence[1] – many of which were not directly protected within English law previously, and where they were protected, it was through the protection of property rights, rather than directly. Thus, the law of nuisance protects equivalent interests to rights to the home, but the basis of the tort is a right of property in the home. As such, protection is only extended to home-owners – the right to the home protected indirectly through the tort of nuisance does not protect a non-homeowner. The law of landlord and tenant, and especially public housing, is a balance of property rights with no weight traditionally given

---

1 For discussion of the breadth of Art. 8 see C. Warbrick, 'The Structure of Article 8', *European Human Rights Law Review* (1998), 32; N. Moreham, 'The Right to Respect for Private Life in the European Convention on Human Rights: A Re-examination', *European Human Rights Law Review* (2008), 44.

to the tenant's right to a home as such, but rather an issue about rights to property, as defined in the legal contract between the parties, and any relevant statutory regulation. The law of breach of confidence developed as a quasi-intellectual property right to confidential information born out of a relationship between the parties, rather than the protection of privacy as such.

All of these areas of the law have generated a plethora of case law where the courts have been required to confront the Convention rights and values found in Article 8 head on and amend the law accordingly. The impact in the law of nuisance has been less marked, given that the tort did, to a large extent, protect the home. Housing law, an area governed by statute, has seen the courts struggle to integrate the requirements of protection of the home with the statutory schemes in a series of cases remarkable for the judicial dialogue between the United Kingdom and the Strasbourg courts. The interest in the home has also come to the fore in the balance between a bankrupt and their family and the bankrupt's creditors where this home interest has now had to be taken into account.

Breach of confidence, above all, has been radically remodelled. As discussed in Chapter 7, three main reasons can be proffered for this. First, there was already seen to be a serious gap in the protection of privacy by English law – even without taking into account the likely Strasbourg stance – which was becoming embarrassing to the judiciary. Second, it had become clear that this lacuna was not going to be filled by legislation, since Parliament was unwilling to act, probably for political reasons. Third, breach of confidence was primarily an equitable cause of action, which is inherently flexible, and it had already been subject to quite extensive development even before the coming into force of the HRA, which had brought it into a fairly inchoate state, ripe for further judicial reform.

In the case of other Articles, the effect has been less marked. Perhaps unsurprisingly, the protection of property under P1–1 has had less impact on the private law of property than has Article 8, since rights to property have long been a primary feature of English law (both in the law governing property rights and torts protecting property right, such as nuisance, trespass and conversion). The Article 6 rights to a fair trial had in effect already been implemented domestically by the Civil Procedure Rules. A number of other torts such as trespass, assault, false imprisonment, malicious prosecution, and in some contexts negligence, already protected rights to personal integrity and liberty,[2] the subject of Articles 2, 3, 4 and 5, so there has been no need for these torts to expand to any great extent, although the potential for parallel remedies is most marked here in the divergent law on damages as compared with remedies under the HRA itself. Articles protecting various forms of self-expression, Articles 9, 10 and 11, have had only a limited impact, with some bearing where behaviour is governed by contract, especially during the course of employment, though Article 10 has also acted as a counterweight to Article 8 in some areas. In particular, Article 10 had already been a point of reference for the law of defamation. The discrimination provisions of Article 14 have been largely surpassed by anti-discrimination legislation.

The courts have certainly been alert to the need to restrain their use of the HRA and the Convention rights: both to avoid uncertainty, as is shown in the way the courts have addressed the issues of how to integrate Strasbourg law into the doctrine of precedent; and to avoid too eager an embrace of the Convention as requiring the development of new law, which is sensible as this may or may not be the best way of protecting Convention rights, as discussed in Chapter 6 and elsewhere.

But it is also clear that there is no overall theory of how the HRA works horizontally which has received judicial approval, or even been adopted generally – indeed, sometimes the Convention rights are simply applied without any consideration of whether or not there is an obligation to do so, and whether or not they apply as between individuals. It is not surprising that different courts in different areas have taken different views about what the HRA requires of them, depending on factors such as the level of regulation, the interaction between common law and statute, or the interests at stake. Nonetheless, clearer reasoning in the use of the HRA can only assist in the legal virtues of clarity and consistency, even if the results differ: considering how different responses to the HRA can be brought into line for consistency; ensuring that the courts are aware of what is and is not required of them; and bringing to the fore what the Convention does, and does not, require, so that there is clarity of reasoning. It is hoped that the discussion here can assist in that process.

---

2 Some of the underlying law on police powers of arrest has been affected by Art. 5: see *R (Laporte)* v. *Chief Constable of Gloucestershire* [2006] UKHL 55, [2007] 2 AC 105; *Austin* v. *Metropolitan Police Commissioner* [2009] UKHL 5.

INDEX

absolute privilege, protection of
    complainant by 197–8
adverse possession 14, 69, 275–6,
    277–8, 281, 285–6
amends *see* offer of amends
arbitration *see* commercial law
arbitrators, mandatory removal for
    lack of impartiality 306–7
assault 235, 241–2, 380–1
avoidance as remedy for
    misrepresentation 317–20

background horizontality, source of
    21–2
bankruptcy *see* insolvency
bare trust 276
battery 234, 235, 241–2
breach of confidence
    chapter summary 12, 137–8
    Convention rights applied to
        139–42
    Convention's effect on, conditions
        for 162
    development of
        in recent cases 138–9
        state of 160–1
    duty to act in way compatible with
        Convention
        content of 141–2
        courts' approach to, problems
            with 140–1
    general issues 136–9
    horizontal effect in case law
        earlier cases 146–50
        later cases 150–8
    HRA's impact on, defamation
        contrasted 161

impact of horizontal effect
    136–7
incremental development of 160
lack of remedy for 158
legislative action, expectation of
    158–60
misuse of private information,
    creation of tort of 147
privacy as fundamental value 41
reasons for 158–63
reform of, need for further
    160
right to privacy, creation of general
    137
Strasbourg case law, reluctance to
    apply fully 142
summary of issues 163–4
and *Von Hannover* case 142–6
breach of trust 284, 357, 359

case law, mirror principle as to *see*
    precedent
causes of action
    basis in legislation 57–8
    breach of Convention 2
    creation of new causes 43–4, 146–50
        see also tort duties, design of
        chameleonic horizontality
    effectiveness of 49, 60–4
    occurrence of
    use of 57–60
civil procedure *see* right to fair trial
Civil Procedure Rules (CPR),
    overriding objective and right
    to fair trial 372–7
commercial law
    arbitration

382